THAT THE WORLD MAY KNOW™

THAT THE WORLD MAY KNOW™

FAITH LESSONS 19-27

Raynard Vander Laan

PUBLISHING

Colorado Springs, Colorado

THAT THE WORLD MAY KNOW™: Leader's Guide for Faith Lessons 19–27

Copyright © 1997 by Raynard Vander Laan
All rights reserved. International copyright secured.

ISBN: 1-56179-420-1

Published by Focus on the Family, Colorado Springs, CO 80995.

Focus on the Family books are available at special quantity discounts when purchased in bulk by corporations, organizations, churches, or groups. Special imprints, messages, and excerpts can be produced to meet your needs. For more information, contact: Sales Dept., Focus on the Family Publishing, 8605 Explorer Dr., Colorado Springs, CO 80920; or phone (719) 531-3400.

All Scripture quotations, unless otherwise indicated, are from the HOLY BIBLE, NEW INTERNATIONAL VERSION ®. NIV ®. Copyright © 1973, 1978, 1984 by International Bible Society. Used by permission of Zondervan Publishing House. All rights reserved.

Editors: Amy Simpson and Michele A. Kendall
Black-and-White Maps and Overhead Transparency 6: BC Studios
Overhead Transparencies 4, 5, 7–12, 14, and 16: Charles Shaw
Overhead Transparency 13: Leen Ritmeyer
Overhead Transparency 15: Ray Vander Laan
Cover Design: Marvin Harrell
Photograph of Author on Back Cover: Patrick Brock

Printed in the United States of America

97 98 99 00 01 02 03/10 9 8 7 6 5 4 3

CONTENTS

Overhead-Transparency Masters:
1. The Roman World
2. The Topography of Israel: New Testament
3. Galilee
4. Land of Jesus' Ministry
5. Galilee of Jesus' Ministry
6. New Testament Chronology
7. Topography of Jerusalem
8. Jerusalem's Districts
9. Jerusalem of David and Solomon
10. Jerusalem of Jesus' Time
11. Temple Courts
12. The Temple Mount: A.D. 70
13. Development of the Temple Mount
14. Herod's Temple
15. The Olive Press
16. Caesarea

OPTIONAL FULL-COLOR OVERHEAD-TRANSPARENCY PACKET

(see page 307 for ordering information)

1. The Roman World
2. The Topography of Israel: New Testament
3. Galilee
4. Land of Jesus' Ministry
5. Galilee of Jesus' Ministry
6. New Testament Chronology
7. Topography of Jerusalem
8. Jerusalem's Districts
9. Jerusalem of David and Solomon
10. Jerusalem of Jesus' Time
11. Temple Courts
12. The Temple Mount: A.D. 70
13. Development of the Temple Mount
14. Herod's Temple
15. The Olive Press
16. Caesarea
17. The Sea
18. The Plain of Gennesaret
19. Scenes from the Lake
20. Ancient Fishing
21. Susita
22. The Remains of Susita
23. Hammat Gader
24. Scenes from Hammat Gader
25. Mount Hermon
26. The Grotto of Pan
27. Scenes from Caesarea Philippi
28. Modern-day Jerusalem from the South
29. The Mount of Olives
30. The Western Hill
31. The Western Wall
32. Scenes of the Temple Mount
33. The Southern Stairs
34. Scenes from the Southern Stairs
35. Mansions on the Western Hill
36. Ancient Jerusalem from the South
37. The Upper City
38. The New City
39. Ancient Jerusalem from the North
40. The Temple Mount
41. The Temple
42. Scenes from the City of Jesus' Day
43. The Road to Jerusalem

44. Jerusalem from the Traditional Garden of Gethsemane
45. Olive Presses
46. Olive Farming
47. The Garden Tomb
48. Burial Customs
49. Ruins of the Harbor
50. Scenes from Caesarea
51. Herod's Palace
52. The Ruins of Herod's Dream

Overhead Transparencies 1, 2, 3, 6:..*BC Studios*

Overhead Transparencies 4, 5, 7–12, 14, 16:...*Charles Shaw*

Overhead Transparency 13:...*Leen Ritmeyer*

Overhead Transparencies 15, 17, 19 (lower left), 20 (upper right, lower left),
21, 22 (bottom), 25, 26, 27 (upper left, lower left), 28, 29, 31, 32 (upper left, lower left),
33, 34 (upper right), 35 (upper left), 36, 37, 38, 41, 42 (lower right),
43, 45 (upper right, lower right), 47, 48 (upper right, lower right):.....................................*Ray Vander Laan*

Overhead Transparencies 18, 19 (upper left, upper right, lower right),
20 (upper left, lower right), 22 (top), 23, 24, 27 (upper right, lower right),
30, 32 (upper right, lower right), 34 (lower left, lower right),
35 (upper right, lower left, lower right), 39, 40, 42 (upper left, upper right, lower left),
45 (upper left, lower left), 46, 48 (upper left, lower left),
49, 50, 51, 52 (upper left, lower left):..*Eyal Bartov*

Overhead Transparencies 34 (upper left), 52 (upper right):..*JoLee Wennersten*

Overhead Transparency 44:..*Greg Holcombe*

Overhead Transparency 52 (lower right): ....*The Israel Museum, Jerusalem*

"THAT THE WORLD MAY KNOW . . ."

More than 3,800 years ago, God spoke to His servant Abraham: "Go, walk through the length and breadth of the land, for I am giving it to you" (Genesis 13:17). From the outset, God's choice of a Hebrew nomad to begin His plan of salvation (which is still unfolding) was linked to the selection of a specific land where His redemptive work would take place. The nature of God's covenant relationship with His people demanded a place where their faith could be exercised and displayed to all nations so that the world would know of Yahweh, the true and faithful God. God showed the same care in preparing a land for His chosen people as He did in preparing a people to live in that land. For us to fully understand God's plan and purpose for His people, we must first understand the nature of the place He selected for them.

In the Old Testament, God promised to protect and provide for the Hebrews. He began by giving them Canaan—a beautiful, fertile land where God would shower His blessings upon them. To possess this land, however, the Israelites had to live obediently before God. The Hebrew Scriptures repeatedly link Israel's obedience to God to the nation's continued possession of Canaan, just as they link its disobedience to the punishment of exile (Leviticus 18:24–28). When the Israelites were exiled from the Promised Land (2 Kings 18:11), they did not experience God's blessings. Only when they possessed the land did they know the fullness of God's promises.

By New Testament times, the Jewish people had been removed from their Promised Land by the Babylonians due to Israel's failure to live obediently before God (Jeremiah 25:4–11). The exile lasted 70 years, but its impact upon God's people was astounding. New patterns of worship developed, and scribes and experts in God's law shaped the new commitment to be faithful to Him. The prophets predicted the appearance of a Messiah like King David who would revive the kingdom of the Hebrew people. But the Promised Land was now home to many other groups of people whose religious practices, moral values, and lifestyles conflicted with those of the Jews. Living as God's witnesses took on added difficulty as Greek, Roman, and Samaritan worldviews mingled with that of the Israelites. The Promised Land was divided between kings and governors usually under the authority of one foreign empire or another. But the mission of God's people did not change. They were still to live *so that the world may know that our God is the true God*. And the land continued to provide them opportunity to encounter the world that desperately needed to know this reality.

The land God chose for His people was on the crossroads of the world. A major trade route, the Via Maris, ran through it. God intended for the Israelites to take control of the cities along this route and thereby exert influence on the nations around them. The Promised Land was the arena within which God's people would serve Him faithfully as the world watched. Through their righteous living, the Hebrews would reveal the one true God, Yahweh, to the world. (They failed to accomplish this mission, however, because of their unfaithfulness.)

Western Christianity tends to spiritualize the concept of the Promised Land as it is presented in the Bible. Instead of seeing it as a crossroads from which to influence the world, modern Christians view it as a distant, heavenly city, a glorious "Canaan" toward which we are traveling as we ignore the world around us. We are focused on the destination, not the journey. We have unconsciously separated our walk with God from our responsibility toward the world in which He has placed us. In one sense, our earthly experience is simply preparation for an eternity in the "promised land." Preoccupation with this idea, however, distorts the mission God has set for us. That mission is the same one He gave to the Israelites. We are to live obediently *within* the world so that through us, *it may know that our God is the one true God.*

Living by faith is not a vague, other-worldly experience; rather, it is being faithful to God right now, in the place and time He has put us. This truth is emphasized by God's choice of Canaan, a crossroads of the ancient world, as the Promised Land for the Israelites. God wants His people in the game, not on the bench.

The geography of Canaan shaped the culture of the people living there. Their settlements began near sources of water and food. Climate and raw materials shaped their choice of occupation, dress, weapons, diet, and even artistic expression. As their cities grew, they interacted politically. Trade developed, and trade routes were established.

Biblical writers assumed that their readers were familiar with Near Eastern geography. Today, unfortunately, many Christians do not have even a basic geographical knowledge of the region. This series is designed to help solve that problem. We will be studying the people and events of the Bible in their geographical and historical contexts. Once your students know the *who, what,* and *where* of a Bible story, they will be able to understand the *why.* In deepening their understanding of God's Word, they will be able to strengthen their relationships with Him.

Terminology

The language of the Bible is bound by culture and time. Therefore, understanding the Scriptures involves more than knowing what the words mean. We need to understand those words from the perspective of the people who used them. The people God chose as His instruments—the people to whom He revealed Himself—were Hebrews living in the Near East. These people described their world and themselves in concrete terms. Their language was one of pictures, metaphors, and examples rather than ideas, definitions, and abstractions. Where we might describe God as omniscient or omnipresent (knowing everything and present everywhere), a Hebrew preferred: "The Lord is my Shepherd." Thus, the Bible is filled with concrete images from Hebrew culture: God is our Father and we are His children. God is the Potter and we are the clay. Jesus is the Lamb killed on Passover. Heaven is an oasis in the desert, and hell is the city sewage dump. The Last Judgment will be in the Eastern Gate of the heavenly Jerusalem and will include sheep and goats.

Several terms are used to identify the land God promised to Abraham. The Old Testament refers to it as Canaan or Israel. The New Testament calls it Judea. After the Second Jewish Revolt (A.D. 132–135), it was known as Palestine. Each of these names resulted from historical events taking place in the land at the time they were coined.

Canaan is one of the earliest designations of the Promised Land. The word probably meant "purple red," referring to the dye produced from the shells of murex shellfish along the coast of Phoenicia. In the ancient world, this famous dye was used to color garments worn by royalty. The word for the color eventually was used to refer to the people who produced the dye and purple cloth for trade. Hence, in the Bible, *Canaanite* refers to a "trader" or "merchant" (Zechariah 14:21), as well as to a person from the "land of purple," or Canaan. Originally, the word applied only to the coast of Phoenicia; later, however, it applied to the whole region of Canaan. Theologically, Canaanites were the antithesis of God's people; therefore, the opposition between the Israelite and the Canaanite was total.

The Old Testament designation for the Promised Land derives from the patriarch Jacob, whom God renamed Israel (Genesis 32:28). His descendants were known as the children of Israel. After the Israelites conquered Canaan in the time of Joshua, the name of the people became the designation for the land itself (in the same way it had with the Canaanites). When the nation split following the death of Solomon, the name *Israel* was applied to the northern kingdom and its territory, while the southern land was called Judah. After the fall of the northern kingdom to the Assyrians in 722 B.C., the entire land was again called Israel.

The word *Palestine* comes from the people of the coastal plain, the Philistines. Though *Palestine* was used by the Egyptians long before the Roman period to refer to the land where the Philistines lived—Philistia—it was the Roman emperor Hadrian who popularized the term as part of his campaign to eliminate Jewish influence in the area.

During New Testament times, the Promised Land was called Palestine or Judea. *Judea* (which means "Jewish") technically referred to the land that had been the nation of Judah. Because of the influence the people of Judea had over the rest of the land, the land itself was called Judea. The Romans divided the land into several provinces, including Judea, Samaria, and Galilee (the three main divisions during Jesus' time); Gaulanitis, the Decapolis, and Perea (east of the Jordan River); and Idumaea (Edom) and Nabatea (in the south). These further divisions of Israel only add to the rich historical and cultural background God prepared for the coming of Jesus and the beginning of His church.

Today the names *Israel* and *Palestine* are often used to designate the land God gave to Abraham. Both terms are politically charged. *Palestine* is used by the Arabs living in the central part of the country, while *Israel* is used by the Jews to indicate the State of Israel. In this study, *Israel* is used in the biblical sense. This choice does not indicate a political statement regarding the current struggle in the Middle East but instead is chosen to best reflect the biblical designation for the land.

Josephus, the Jewish Historian

The most important source of information about life at the time of Jesus comes from a Jewish historian who is known to history as Josephus Flavius. His extensive writings on first-century Israel's history, politics, culture, and religion are invaluable in helping us understand the setting in which God placed His people. Though Josephus's supposedly firsthand accounts, complete with commentary, are written by a man and therefore are subject to the bias any individual would have, archaeology and historical research have shown Josephus to be remarkably accurate in his descriptions of life during New Testament times.

Josephus was born into a wealthy family of priests about A.D. 38, shortly after Jesus was crucified. Josephus's Hebrew name was Joseph Ben Mattathias. A brilliant young man, he studied under the leaders of several Jewish movements of his day, including the Pharisees, Sadducees, and Essenes. He was familiar with the Roman world, having spent time in Rome, and was impressed with the glory and might of the empire. He was fluent in Aramaic, Greek, and Hebrew, the major languages of his day.

As the First Jewish Revolt began (A.D. 66), Josephus was placed in charge of the Jewish resistance in Galilee. He surrendered to Vespasian, the Roman general, and boldly predicted that Vespasian would become the next emperor based on Josephus's interpretation of the prophecies of the Old Testament. Since Vespasian was superstitious and Josephus was a priest, Josephus's life was spared. When Vespasian became emperor, Josephus became a personal scribe to the family, even taking their name, Flavius, and receiving Roman citizenship. Josephus spent the rest of his life writing the history of the Jewish people, focusing on the crucial years from 168 B.C. to A.D. 100, the period of the New Testament. Because he was hated by the patriotic Jews for being a traitor, and was suspected by the Romans because of his role in the Jewish revolt, Josephus wrote to justify himself and to present the Jewish people in the best possible light. Given those biases, his major works, *The Jewish War* and *Antiquities of the Jews,* are vital sources for any student of the New Testament.

Josephus did not mention Jesus or the early church (the one passage about Jesus was probably added by Christian writers long after Josephus's death). He did write extensively about the Herod family, including descriptions of John the Baptist's execution, the death of Herod Agrippa, and other characters mentioned in the Bible. Ironically, because they offer extensive background information,

Josephus's writings are a key element in understanding Jesus, His message, and His ministry in first-century Israel. Josephus was another part of God's plan that everything should be complete for the coming of His Son.

Introduction to the Study

Because God speaks to us through the Scriptures, studying them is a rewarding experience. The inspired human authors of the Bible, as well as those to whom the words were originally given, were primarily Jews living in the Near East. God's words and actions spoke to them with such power, clarity, and purpose that they wrote them down and carefully preserved them as an authoritative body of literature.

God's use of human servants in revealing Himself resulted in writings that clearly bear the stamp of time and place. The message of the Scriptures is, of course, eternal and unchanging—but the circumstances and conditions of the people of the Bible are unique to their times. Consequently, we most clearly understand God's truth when we know the cultural context within which He spoke and acted and the perception of the people with whom He communicated. This does not mean that God's revelation is unclear if we don't know the cultural context. Rather, by learning how to think and approach life as Abraham, Moses, Ruth, Esther, and Paul did, modern Christians will deepen their appreciation of God's Word. To fully apply the message of the Bible to our lives, we must enter the world of the Hebrews and familiarize ourselves with their culture.

That is the purpose of this curriculum. The events and characters of the Bible will be presented in their original settings. Although the videos offer the latest archaeological research, this series is not intended to be a definitive cultural and geographical study of the lands of the Bible. No original scientific discoveries are revealed here. The purpose of this series is to help students better understand God's revealed mission for their lives by allowing them to hear and see His words in their original context.

This curriculum provides additional cultural background and biblical material for study. Encourage your students to read the appropriate Bible passages and to think through God's challenge for their lives today.

Guidelines for Leading the Sessions

1. Be sure to read through the curriculum and view all the videos before you begin teaching the sessions. To lead this study effectively, you will need to spend several hours preparing for the course. In addition, you will need time to set up your class materials and to decide which activities you will use in each session, depending on the time you have allotted for the course.

2. Develop the answer you want your students to reach for each question, but during class allow them to arrive at their own conclusions before you present yours. This is the essence of the "guided discussion" method. The most effective way to discover the Bible in its setting is for the teacher to be a fellow learner with the class. Cultivate discussion, and guide students in their conclusions by becoming adept at asking the kinds of questions that will help them explore different answers. Most important, encourage your students to respect the responses of others.

3. At the beginning of each session, review the key materials. Students need time to absorb and integrate the new information into their understanding of the Scriptures. If you occasionally review important locations on maps, refer to people and events in the biblical chronology, and repeat the main points in previous lessons, students will develop the ability to read the Bible in context. It is also important for you as the teacher to be well versed in the basic cultural background of the Bible. Consider memorizing key details on the maps and in the chronology.

4. To learn more on the cultural and geographical background of the Bible, consult the following resources:

History

Connolly, Peter. *Living in the Time of Jesus of Nazareth*. Tel Aviv: Steimatzky, 1983.

Ward, Kaari. *Jesus and His Times*. New York: Reader's Digest, 1987.

Whiston, William, trans. *The Works of Josephus: Complete and Unabridged*. Peabody, Mass.: Hendrikson Publishers, 1987.

Wood, Leon. Revised by David O'Brien. *A Survey of Israel's History*. Grand Rapids: Zondervan, 1986.

Jewish Roots of Christianity

Stern, David H. *Jewish New Testament Commentary*. Clarksville, Md.: Jewish New Testament Publications, 1992.

Wilson, Marvin R. *Our Father Abraham: Jewish Roots of the Christian Faith*. Grand Rapids: Eerdmans, 1986.

Young, Brad H. *Jesus the Jewish Theologian*. Peabody, Mass.: Hendrickson Publishers, 1995.

Geography

Beitzel, Barry J. *The Moody Atlas of Bible Lands*. Chicago: Moody Press, 1993.

Gardner, Joseph L. *Reader's Digest Atlas of the Bible*. New York: Reader's Digest, 1993.

General Background

Alexander, David, and Pat Alexander, eds. *Eerdmans' Handbook to the Bible*. Grand Rapids: Eerdmans, 1983.

Butler, Trent C., ed. *Holman Bible Dictionary*. Nashville: Holman Bible Publishers, 1991.

Edersheim, Alfred. *The Life and Times of Jesus the Messiah*. Peabody, Mass.: Hendrickson Publishers, 1994.

Archaeological Background

Charlesworth, James H. *Jesus Within Judaism: New Light from Exciting Archaeological Discoveries*. New York: Doubleday, 1988.

Finegan, Jack. *The Archeology of the New Testament: The Life of Jesus and the Beginning of the Early Church*. Princeton: Princeton University Press, 1978.

Mazar, Amihai. *Archaeology of the Land of the Bible: 10,000–586 B.C.E.* New York: Doubleday, 1990.

5. To learn more about the specific backgrounds of the fourth set of videos, consult the following resources:

Avigad, Nahman. "Jerusalem in Flames—The Burnt House Captures a Moment in Time." *Biblical Archaeology Review* (November-December 1983).

Barkey, Gabriel. "The Garden Tomb—Was Jesus Buried Here?" *Biblical Archaeology Review* (March-April 1986).

Ben Dov, Meir. "Herod's Mighty Temple Mount." *Biblical Archaeology Review* (November-December 1986).

Bivin, David. "The Miraculous Catch." *Jerusalem Perspective* (March-April 1992).

Burrell, Barbara, Kathryn Gleason, and Ehud Netzer. "Uncovering Herod's Seaside Palace." *Biblical Archaeology Review* (May-June 1993).

Edersheim, Alfred. *The Temple*. London: James Clarke & Co., 1959.

Edwards, William D., Wesley J. Gabel, and Floyd E. Hosmer. "On the Physical Death of Jesus Christ." *Journal of American Medical Association (JAMA)* (March 21, 1986).

Flusser, David. "To Bury Caiaphas, Not to Praise Him." *Jerusalem Perspective* (July-October 1991).

Greenhut, Zvi. "Burial Cave of the Caiaphas Family." *Biblical Archaeology Review* (September-October 1992).

Hareuveni, Nogah. *Nature in Our Biblical Heritage*. Kiryat Ono, Israel: Neot Kedumim, Ltd., 1980.

Hepper, F. Nigel. *Baker Encyclopedia of Bible Plants: Flowers and Trees, Fruits and Vegetables, Ecology*. Ed. by J. Gordon Melton. Grand Rapids: Baker Book House, 1993.

"The 'High Priest' of the Jewish Quarter." *Biblical Archaeology Review* (May-June 1992).

Hirschfeld, Yizhar, and Giora Solar. "Sumptuous Roman Baths Uncovered Near Sea of Galilee." *Biblical Archaeology Review* (November-December 1984).

Hohlfelder, Robert L. "Caesarea Maritima: Herod the Great's City on the Sea." *National Geographic* (February 1987).

Holum, Kenneth G. *King Herod's Dream: Caesarea on the Sea*. New York: W. W. Norton, 1988.

Mazar, Benjamin. "Excavations Near Temple Mount Reveal Splendors of Herodian Jerusalem." *Biblical Archaeology Review* (July-August 1980).

Nun, Mendel. *Ancient Stone Anchors and Net Sinkers from the Sea of Galilee*. Israel: Kibbutz Ein Gev, 1993. (Also available from *Jerusalem Perspective*.)

———. "Fish, Storms, and a Boat." *Jerusalem Perspective* (March-April 1990).

———. "The Kingdom of Heaven Is Like a Seine." *Jerusalem Perspective* (November-December 1989).

———. "Net Upon the Waters: Fish and Fishermen in Jesus' Time." *Biblical Archaeology Review* (November-December 1993).

———. *The Sea of Galilee and Its Fishermen in the New Testament*. Israel: Kibbutz Ein Gev, 1993. (Also available from *Jerusalem Perspective*.)

Pileggi, David. "A Life on the Kinneret." *Jerusalem Perspective* (November-December 1989).

Pixner, Bargil. *With Jesus Through Galilee According to the Fifth Gospel*. Rosh Pina, Israel: Corazin Publishing, 1992.

Pope, Marvin, H. "Hosanna: What It Really Means." *Bible Review* (April 1988).

Reich, Ronny. "Ossuary Inscriptions from the Caiaphas Tomb." *Jerusalem Perspective* (July-October 1991).

———. "Six Stone Water Jars." *Jerusalem Perspective* (July-September 1995).

Ritmeyer, Kathleen. "A Pilgrim's Journey." *Biblical Archaeology Review* (November-December 1989).

Ritmeyer, Kathleen, and Leen Ritmeyer. "Reconstructing Herod's Temple Mount in Jerusalem." *Biblical Archaeology Review* (November-December 1989).

———. "Reconstructing the Triple Gate." *Biblical Archaeology Review* (November-December 1989).

Ritmeyer, Leen. "The Ark of the Covenant: Where It Stood in Solomon's Temple." *Biblical Archaeology Review* (January-February 1996).

———. "Quarrying and Transporting Stones for Herod's Temple Mount." *Biblical Archaeology Review* (November-December 1989).

Ritmeyer, Leen, and Kathleen Ritmeyer. "Akeldama: Potter's Field of High Priest's Tomb." *Biblical Archaeology Review* (November-December 1994).

Sarna, Nahum M. *The JPS Torah Commentary: Exodus.* New York: Jewish Publication Society, 1991.

"Sea of Galilee Museum Opens Its Doors." *Jerusalem Perspective* (July-September 1995).

Shanks, Hershel. "Excavating in the Shadow of the Temple Mount." *Biblical Archaeology Review* (November-December 1986).

"Shavuot." *Encyclopedia Judaica*, Volume 14. Jerusalem: Keter Publishing House, 1980.

Stern, David. *Jewish New Testament Commentary.* Clarksville, Md.: Jewish New Testament Publications, 1992.

Taylor, Joan E. "The Garden of Gethsemane." *Biblical Archaeology Review* (July-August 1995).

Tzaferis, Vassilios. "Crucifixion—The Archaeological Evidence." *Biblical Archaeology Review* (January-February 1985).

———. "A Pilgrimage to the Site of the Swine Miracle." *Biblical Archaeology Review* (March-April 1989).

———. "Susita." *Biblical Archaeology Review* (September-October 1990).

Vann, Lindley. "Herod's Harbor Construction Recovered Underwater." *Biblical Archaeology Review* (May-June 1983).

Ritmeyer Archaeological Design publishes two slide-study booklet sets that provide greater detail on the topics of the visual studies provided here. They are:

Alec Garrard's Model of the Second Temple

Jerusalem in 30 A.D.

They are available from Ritmeyer Archaeological Design, 50 Twit Well Road, Harrogate HG2 8JJ England.

6. This curriculum is designed to offer you, the teacher, maximum flexibility in scheduling and pacing the sessions. Depending on how much material you choose to use, each lesson can cover anywhere from one 50-minute session to a series of four, five, or even six 60- or 75-minute sessions. For your convenience, each lesson has been divided into two units. Unit One is an overview to be used if the leader wants to complete a faith lesson in one class period—whether 50 minutes or two hours. It contains key review questions from each element contained in the video without going into a great deal of background or detail. Unit Two is divided into several steps that take the elements in Unit One to greater depth. An example of a lesson layout follows:

A. Unit One: Video Review

   1. Digging Deeper I

B. Unit Two

   1. Step One

      a. Digging Deeper II

      b. Digging Deeper III

   2. Step Two

3. Step Three

    a. Digging Deeper IV

In preparing your class sessions, be sure to look over the **Digging Deeper** optional sections, as you may find information there that you'll want to present, either as a supplement to the core material or—if time is limited—even in place of some core material. The time needed for the **Digging Deeper** sections will vary greatly depending on the number of students in the class and the amount of detail you wish to discuss. The suggested time allotments range from a minimum to a maximum.

NOTE TO THE TEACHER: *Some discussion sections and topics in Set 4 are repeated from Sets 1, 2, and 3. Although they are relatively few, they do provide important information for the lessons of Set 4. If you have already covered them in the first three sets, a simple review is probably sufficient. If you have not completed Sets 1, 2, and 3, the sections and topics repeated here are essential background to understanding the material in this set.*

WHEN STORMS COME

For the Teacher

Most people in modern times enjoy the beauty and recreational benefits of lakes and oceans and other bodies of water. When modern-day people read about Jesus and His ministry around the Sea of Galilee, they often assume that the disciples and other ancient Palestinians had the same sense of the sea that we have. But the significance of the sea was actually quite different for ancient peoples from what it is for us today. To some, the sea could be a source of fear, chaos, and evil.

This study will help students understand the significance of the sea in Jesus' culture and appreciate the lessons the Bible teaches us through accounts of Jesus' ministry around (and on) the sea. This understanding will make it clear to them that Jesus intentionally chose the location for His ministry so He could illustrate important lessons to His disciples and others.

Before you begin this lesson, ask your students what they think the sea meant to ancient Jews. Your students may point to the sea as a picture of God's creative ability or a symbol of life. If your students don't think of it on their own, point out to them the negative images the sea also portrayed to God's people. For example, the sea was a frightening reminder of storms. For individuals who understand those negative images, Jesus' ministry takes on a deeper and richer meaning. Seeing Jesus' power over the wind and the waves will help prepare your students to depend on Christ in dealing with the storms in their own lives.

Your Objectives for This Lesson

At the completion of this section, you will want your students:

To Know/Understand

1. The geography of the area around the Sea of Galilee.
2. The various types and groups of people who lived around the Sea of Galilee.
3. The aspects of Jesus' ministry involving the Sea of Galilee.
4. The nature of the fishing industry on the Sea of Galilee.
5. The religious imagery of the sea to the Israelites.

To Do

1. Seek God's help in confronting evil, even in their own lives.
2. Commit to being more devoted in persevering through the struggles in their lives.
3. Learn to ask for God's help when times are difficult.
4. Practice seeing interruptions as opportunities for ministry.
5. Develop plans for sharing God's truth with others.

How to Plan for This Lesson

Because of the volume of material in this lesson, you may need to divide it into several class sessions. To help you determine how to do that, the lesson has been broken into segments. Note that the time needed may vary significantly, depending on elements such as the leader, the size of the class, and the interest level of the class.

If you wish to cover the entire lesson in one session, you should complete Unit One. This unit provides a guided discussion covering the major points in the video. It does not go into great depth. If you wish to go into greater depth on any of the points in Unit One, they are covered more thoroughly in the remainder of the material.

How to Prepare for This Lesson

Materials Needed

Student copies of the maps:	"The Roman World" "The Topography of Israel: New Testament" "Galilee"
Overhead transparencies:	"The Roman World" "The Topography of Israel: New Testament" "Galilee"
Student copies of the handouts:	"The Sea Is His Delight" "They Left Their Nets"

Video: **When Storms Come**

Overhead projector, screen, TV, VCR

1. Make copies of the maps listed above for your students.

2. Prepare the overhead transparencies listed above. (You'll find them at the back of the book.)

3. Make copies of the handouts listed above for your students. (If possible, students should receive and read these handouts before the lesson.)

4. Review the geography of the lands of the Bible from the "Introduction."

5. Determine which **unit** and which **Digging Deeper** sections, if any, you want to use in your class session(s). NOTE: You can use these sections in any order you wish (e.g., you might want to use **Digging Deeper III,** but not **Digging Deeper I** or **Digging Deeper II).**

6. Prepare your classroom ahead of time, setting up and testing an overhead projector and screen (for the overhead transparencies) and a TV and VCR. If you plan to hand out biblical references for your students to look up and read aloud, prepare 3x5 cards (one reference per card) to distribute before class.

Lesson Plan

UNIT ONE: Video Review

1. Introductory Comments

When God came to earth as Messiah, He chose a specific culture, location, and time period in which to unfold His plan. Understanding the context in which Jesus chose to minister helps us to better understand His ministry itself and how it applies to us today, in a different geographical and cultural context.

In this lesson, we will explore what we can learn about Jesus, His disciples, and His promises and call to us by studying His ministry on and around the Sea of Galilee. It is important to remember that because Jesus deliberately chose the Sea of Galilee as a location for His ministry, the significance of the sea must have been important to Him. He called fishermen to be His first disciples, and He performed miracles on the water. We seek to understand His ministry better by understanding this location and the cultural significance it held for the ancient Israelites.

2. Show the Video *When Storms Come* (*19 minutes*)

3. Map Study: The Sea of Galilee

HINT: *Begin this map study session by reviewing the geography of the overall region and working down to the area the lesson is dealing with—the Sea of Galilee.*

Using the overhead transparency "The Roman World," point out the following areas, and have your students locate them on their maps.

> Rome
> Mediterranean Sea
> Egypt
> Judea
> Caesarea

Using the overhead transparency "The Topography of Israel: New Testament," point out the following areas, and have your students locate them on their maps.

> Bethlehem
> Jerusalem
> Nazareth
> Capernaum
> Galilee
> Sea of Galilee

Using the overhead transparency "Galilee," point out the following areas, and have your students locate them on their maps.

> Sea of Galilee
> Decapolis
> plain of Gennesaret
> Capernaum
> Chorazin

Bethsaida
"Way of the Sea" (Via Maris)

4. Guided Discussion: The Place Where Jesus Ministered

This curriculum series has stressed God's careful plan for the people, the times, and especially the places to which He revealed His marvelous acts of salvation. Jesus came, a Jewish rabbi, in the first century during the Roman peace, and He chose Galilee as the base of His teaching ministry. More specifically, He chose the northern shore of the Sea of Galilee. In previous studies, we have examined the backgrounds of the Zealots (Lesson 15), the religious Jews (Lesson 14), and the Herodians and the Pharisees (Lesson 16). This lesson spotlights the setting of Jesus' ministry by the sea.

a. Jesus Around the Lake

Ask students to look up the following passage:

- Matthew 4:12–17

Have your students respond (individually or in small groups) to the following questions:

1. What place or area did Jesus call home?

2. What was the "Way of the Sea"?

3. Did Jesus minister in a public place? Does this help you understand your calling as His disciple? If so, how? (See Isaiah 43:10.)

4. Is there something comparable to the "Way of the Sea" in our culture? If so, what is it? Does the Christian community isolate itself from this element of culture or use it to share Jesus with the world?

(NOTE: Lesson 1 and Lesson 6 of this curriculum series both deal with living on the crossroads, where culture was shaped. If you wish to cover this information in greater detail, see Set 1, Lesson 1, Guided Discussion 4 [page 10], **Digging Deeper III** [page 11], and **Digging Deeper IV** [page 12]; and Set 2, Lesson 6, Map Study [page 7] and Guided Discussion b [page 8].)

b. Jesus Calls Fishermen

Ask students to look up the following passage:

- Matthew 4:18–22

Have your students respond (individually or in small groups) to the following questions:

1. What mission did Jesus give to the fishermen? How would their occupation have prepared them for that mission?

2. What did they do immediately? What does this tell you about their commitment and their faith in Jesus?

5. Prayer

Ask God to encourage you with the assurance of Jesus' power over life's storms. Share with Him the things that frighten you, such as disease, disasters, accidents, and disabilities, and ask Him to show you His power over them. Talk to God about your personal struggles with Satan over a temptation in your life. Ask Him to defeat the power of evil and to make you a more devoted "fisher of men." Ask Him to guide you to a more total commitment to Him. Now ask the Holy Spirit whom He would have you seek out to "catch" for Jesus.

UNIT TWO
"He Lived by the Lake"

1. Introductory Comments

This curriculum series has stressed God's careful plan for the people, the times, and especially the places to which He revealed His marvelous acts of salvation. Jesus came, a Jewish rabbi, in the first century during the Roman peace, and He chose Galilee as the base of His teaching ministry. More specifically, He chose the northern shore of the Sea of Galilee. In previous studies, we have examined the backgrounds of the Zealots (Lesson 15), the religious Jews (Lesson 14), and the Herodians and the Pharisees (Lesson 16). This lesson spotlights the setting of Jesus' ministry by the sea.

2. Show the Video *When Storms Come* (19 *minutes*)

3. Map Study: The Sea of Galilee

HINT: *Begin this map study session by reviewing the geography of the overall region and working down to the area the lesson is dealing with—the Sea of Galilee.*

Using the overhead transparency "The Roman World," point out the following areas, and have your students find them on their maps.

> Rome
> Mediterranean Sea
> Egypt
> Judea
> Caesarea
> "Way of the Sea" (Via Maris)

Using the overhead transparency "The Topography of Israel: New Testament," point out the following areas, and have your students find them on their maps.

> Bethlehem
> Jerusalem
> Nazareth
> Capernaum
> Galilee
> Sea of Galilee
> "Way of the Sea" (Via Maris)

Using the overhead transparency "Galilee," point out the following areas, and have your students find them on their maps.

> Sea of Galilee
> Decapolis
> Gamla
> Tiberias
> Magdala
> plain of Gennesaret
> Kursi
> Hippos (Susita)

Mount Arbel
Capernaum
Chorazin
Bethsaida
Mount of Beatitudes (traditional)
"Way of the Sea" (Via Maris)

4. Guided Discussion: The Sea of Galilee

Your students should read the handout "The Sea Is His Delight" and look up the passages found in it.

a. The People Around the Lake

Use the following passages to help your students understand the several types of people Jesus interacted with during His ministry. Ask students to look the passages up and think about the following questions: What type of person was Jesus speaking to? How would this person have reacted? Does understanding the different types of people help you to understand Jesus' message?

- Mark 5:1–20

- Matthew 22:15–22

- Matthew 10:4 (point out Simon the Zealot); Matthew 5:38–42 (assume that Simon was part of Jesus' audience in Matthew 5)

- Matthew 11:28–30 (NOTE: Jesus was speaking to religious Jews on the northeastern corner of the sea. They were constantly urged by the Pharisees to take the "yoke of Torah.")

b. Jesus and the Storms

Clearly, storms were forces of nature that threatened the disciples. As fishermen, their vocation and livelihood, even their very lives, were in jeopardy when bad weather struck. But they weren't alone in their fear of storms. Many people in Jesus' day thought that storms were caused by evil forces. (For passages about the sea as evil, see Psalm 30:1 and Psalm 69:1–3.) The sea was even thought to contain monsters (Psalm 74:13–14; Daniel 7:2–7). The Scriptures imply that it was the Abyss (Luke 8:30–33; Revelation 13:1–4). Jesus' power over storms was startling to His disciples because He could control the forces of nature and because, in the Old Testament, the sea represented the power of evil. To the disciples and other people of Jesus' day, only God could calm the chaos of stormy water because only God could control evil. This exercise explores the lessons we can learn from Jesus' ministry *on* the Sea of Galilee.

Ask students to look up the following passages:

- Mark 4:35–41
- Matthew 8:18,23–27

Have your students respond (individually or in small groups) to the following questions:

1. Where were the disciples when the story began? What did Jesus tell the disciples to do? What was on the other side? Do you think the disciples wanted to go to the other side? What happened when they reached the other side? (See Matthew 8:28–34.) Does this fit the disciples' conception of the sea as the Abyss?

2. What time of day was it? Would the sea have been more frightening to the disciples at that time? Why or why not?

3. What did Jesus do? Why do you think He did this?

4. How did Jesus display His power? Why did the disciples react the way they did?

5. What significance do Jesus' actions in this passage have for your life? What encouragement do they give you?

Ask students to look up the following passages:
- Matthew 14:22–34
- Mark 6:45–53

Have your students respond (individually or in small groups) to the following questions:

1. To what town were the disciples headed on the sea? Where did Jesus go? What was He doing? What did Jesus tell the disciples to do?

2. What did Jesus do? Why?

3. What happened to the disciples?

4. When He walked out to them, what was Jesus going to do? Does this surprise you? Why or why not? What happened to change His plans? (NOTE: Jesus could probably see the disciples.) What did He do? What was the disciples' response? Why might they think He was a ghost?

5. How long did the disciples row before Jesus took action? Why do you think He let them row so long before He helped them? (NOTE: The fourth watch began at 3:00 A.M. and ended at 6:00 A.M. Jesus had prayed for a while, and then evening came; so the disciples must have started before sundown.)

6. What was Peter requesting when He asked to come to Jesus? Power over nature? Power over the Abyss? Would the fact that he sank because of lack of faith indicate he wanted to overcome the Abyss? When did Jesus help him? Why is it important for you to cry out to God? Have you ever done that? What happened?

7. When Jesus quieted the wind and sea, why did the disciples think Jesus was the Son of God and not just filled with God's power? (NOTE: Point out to your students that people in the Old Testament were given God's power to control nature [e.g., Elijah—1 Kings 17; Moses—Exodus 14; Joshua—Joshua 3], but only God could control the evil of the sea because it was linked to the devil himself [Jonah 2:5–6].)

8. Why do you think there is no sea in heaven (Revelation 21:1)? (Possible answer: The sea is the home of evil, and there is no evil in heaven.)

9. Why do you think Satan will be put into a lake of fire (Revelation 20:10)? (Possible answer: The sea is the domain of evil, so Satan belongs in the sea.)

Spend some time reflecting with your students on the lessons they can gain from this story. Here are some of the key points (ask your students if they can think of any others):
- God is always watching.
- Storms in life are part of His plan.
- We must persevere no matter how powerful a storm we find ourselves in.
- Jesus can provide, even in the most difficult circumstances.
- We must call out to Him.

1. Life is full of storms. What are some of the storms you have been through? In the storms of your life, have you ever felt as if you have rowed until you couldn't struggle anymore? Did Jesus come? How does this encourage you to persevere?

2. Jesus has total power over creation and over evil. How does it encourage you to know that Jesus is the Son of God? That He can defeat the power of Satan himself? Have you ever experienced

Jesus' power in that way? When? What kinds of evil do you face? How can that evil be overcome? What are the greatest evils of our culture? Are they beyond Jesus' power? Does it seem hopeless at times? Did it seem hopeless to the disciples? What did the disciples do to receive Jesus' delivering power against the storm? What can we learn from the disciples' experience?

3. In the story, the disciples started to row toward Bethsaida to the east. But after rowing all night and into the morning, they ended up at Gennesaret, on the western side of the lake. Have you ever followed Jesus, struggling for a long time toward one destination, and ended up somewhere else because of His intervention? Why is it important to keep rowing in these situations?

4. Prayer: If it seems appropriate, spend time in prayer over examples of personal storms shared by class members.

c. **Fish and Fishermen**
Students should read the handout "They Left Their Nets" before beginning this section.
Jesus chose four fishermen to be among His 12 disciples: Peter, Andrew, James, and John. This means that one-third of His inner circle of students, the foundation of the church, consisted of fishermen. Understanding fishermen and fishing can enhance your understanding of Jesus' call to you.
Ask students to look up the following passage:

- Luke 5:1–7

Have your students respond (individually or in small groups) to the following questions:

1. What does this passage teach you about the types of people Jesus chose to be His disciples? Did they give up when things got tough? How willing were they to follow Jesus' advice?

2. What other ideas can you learn from this Scripture passage?

Ask students to look up the following passage:

- Matthew 13:47–50

Have your students respond (individually or in small groups) to the following questions:

1. What is the point of Jesus' parable for those who are His "fishermen"?

2. What does the parable mean for those who are "caught" (who become interested in Jesus)? How did being fishermen help the disciples understand this parable?

3. What can you learn about your Christian life from this parable?

Ask students to look up the following passages:

- Matthew 4:18–22
- Mark 1:16–20
- Luke 5:2–11
- John 1:35–42

Have your students respond (individually or in small groups) to the following questions:

1. What did Jesus say to the fishermen whom He wanted to be His disciples?

2. How would the disciples' occupation help them understand their mission?

3. What was the disciples' reaction to Jesus' call? What does this tell you about their commitment to and attitude toward Jesus? About their priorities?

4. What can you, as Jesus' disciple, learn from Jesus' call to the disciples and the disciples' response?

Ask students to look up the following passages:

- John 21:1–6
- Luke 5:4–7
- Mark 1:16–18
- Matthew 17:24–27

Have your students respond (individually or in small groups) to the following questions:

1. How many methods did fishermen use to catch fish? (Possible answers: seine net, cast net, hook.) Why? (Possible answer: They used different methods to catch different kinds of fish.)

2. At what time of day did each of these fishing expeditions occur? Why did they happen at different times? (Possible answer: They fished at different times to catch different fish.)

3. What do these details tell you about their skill as fishermen?

4. As a "fisher of men," what lessons can you learn from these examples?

5. How does understanding the fishermen Jesus called help you be a better disciple?

d. Conclusion

There is no evil—including the Abyss and the devil for whom it is being prepared—that is greater than the power of Jesus (1 John 4:4). During difficult times, don't be afraid to ask God for help. Doing what Jesus wants is always worth the struggle. Keep rowing, because Jesus is watching! And when we ask Him to save us, we should be prepared for miracles. Don't be surprised, however, when His plans are different from your own. Be prepared to accept His results.

OPTIONAL — Digging Deeper I: The Abyss (30–45 minutes)

A. Lecture

The sea as a symbol of evil and chaos is not usually considered in studies of Jesus' miracles on the Sea of Galilee. Jesus had power over creation, and He performed miracles as a witness to His divinity. But He also came to demonstrate His power over evil and the source of evil—the devil himself. This power was apparent when Jesus stilled the storms. In this section, we will explore further the biblical theme of God's power over everything, even evil.

It is important to remember that the sea is not evil, the devil does not live there, and hell is not beneath it. The sea was used symbolically to represent evil, much as a shepherd, a rock, and living water were used to represent God. The term *depths* in the Old Testament is represented in the Greek translation by the same word translated as *abyss* in the New Testament. It would not be inaccurate to use the word *abyss* in place of the word *depths* or *deep* in the Old Testament (see, e.g., Genesis 1:2). Jewish tradition held that evil spirits were confined there.

B. Guided Discussion

Read each of the following points. Then have your students look up the Scripture passages and discuss how those passages support the points.

1. As God began creation, everything (He had previously created) was chaotic—the opposite of the nature of God, which is order. This chaos provided imagery of the destructive forces in the world.

- Genesis 1:2
- Psalm 74:13–17

2. Out of and on this chaos, God created the earth. The chaos did not stop Him. God used and shaped the chaotic water "below." It could be both an instrument of God's judgment against evil and a blessing to His people.

- Psalm 24:1–2
- Psalm 105:4–9
- Genesis 7
- Exodus 14:26–28

3. Yet the water remained dangerous to God's people. Only God could deliver them from its threat. The Lord brought miraculous deliverance to those who called on Him for help from the forces of the "deep" (the Abyss).

- Psalm 30:1
- Psalm 69:1–3
- Jonah 2:5–6 (What would it have meant to throw Jonah into the raging sea?)
- Psalm 65:5–7
- Psalm 77:16–19
- Psalm 89:9
- Psalm 93:3–4
- Isaiah 51:10

4. Sometimes the chaos of the sea was personified as a dragon or monster that lived in the depths. Again, only God could defeat this evil creature.

- Psalm 74:13–14
- Isaiah 27:1
- Isaiah 51:9–10 (God used the sea to defeat Egypt.)
- Daniel 7:2–7 (The evil beasts of the sea are described in frightening detail.)
- The book of Revelation applied this significant Old Testament imagery to Satan himself. To the people of the New Testament, the depths of the sea symbolized Satan's dwelling place. Therefore, the "depths" or "Abyss" represented great evil, which *only God* could defeat.

The Abyss:

- Revelation 9:1,11
- Revelation 11:7
- Revelation 17:8

The dragon lives in the Abyss or the sea:

- Revelation 13:1–4 (See also 11:7.)
- Revelation 20:1–6 (God's angel holds the key to the Abyss.)
- Revelation 20:10 (A new dwelling place is prepared for the devil, but it is still a body of water—a lake.)

Heaven, where there is no evil, will be without a sea:

- Revelation 21:1

5. The imagery of the sea as evil and as the home of the devil himself was part of the mind-set of the people of Jesus' day. Though they lived near and even worked on the Sea of Galilee, the sea remained a symbol to them of the evil forces present in the world and opposed to God. Only God Himself could rescue His people from the evil symbolized by the sea.

   Have your students look up the following passages in which the sea symbolized evil.

   - Matthew 11:20–24 (Jesus condemned Chorazin, Bethsaida, and Capernaum to God's judgment because of their unbelief. Capernaum, which was on the shore of the sea, was condemned to a specific judgment: "You will go down to the depths.")

   - Luke 8:30–33 (Jesus sent the demons into a herd of pigs, which promptly ran off a cliff into the sea. Given the context, the sea appears to be the Abyss.)

   - Matthew 14:32–33 (Jesus "defeated" the storm. The disciples were amazed and afraid. They immediately identified Jesus as God because only God could defeat the power of evil manifested by the sea.)

   - Mark 4:39–5:19 (Immediately after He calmed the storm and the sea, Jesus encountered a demoniac possessed by a "legion" of evil spirits. It is possible that these incidents were linked. Jesus defeated the power of the sea, showing His authority over evil itself. Threatened, the demons confronted Him through a dangerous man. See also Matthew 8:28 and Luke 8:29.)

6. Those who belong to Jesus and who cry out for His deliverance will be delivered from the devil and the Abyss.

   Have your students look up the passage below to see the deliverance Jesus promised.

   - Matthew 14:28–31

   Spend a few minutes discussing the following questions as a class:

   a. Where in our culture does Satan seem the strongest? Where does He seem strongest in your life? If those areas could be considered the "Abyss" of today, what should be our strategy for resisting the evil?

   b. If life's storms represent the times when the devil becomes most threatening to us and to our culture, where are the storms in our society? Where are the storms in your life? Ask God to deliver all of us from the "storms" of the evil one.

OPTIONAL — Digging Deeper II: A Solitary Place *(20–35 minutes)*

In studying Jesus and His life, we tend to place a lot of emphasis on His nature as the divine Son of God. Although He truly was "God with us"—an incredible fact we cannot overemphasize—sometimes we overlook the fact of His (sinless) human nature as well. Somehow His divinity makes it difficult for us to imagine Him becoming tired, dealing with pain, or suffering in any other way. Yet because He was fully human, He experienced the same things we experience, yet without sin. While He was on earth, Jesus regularly went to a quiet place to be with His Father. Sometimes He went alone; at other times He brought His disciples with Him. This practice of Jesus the Man illuminates our own needs as people.

Ask your students to read the Scripture passages below and then, for each passage, answer the questions:

- Matthew 3:13–4:12
- Matthew 14:6–14,19–32
- Mark 1:32–38
- Mark 1:40–2:5
- Luke 6:6–16
- Luke 22:19–30,39–53

1. Why was it so important for Jesus to spend time alone?

2. What drove Him to these lonely places?

3. What types of ministry usually followed His time alone with God? (Students should be encouraged to see that He would usually immediately minister to others after spending time alone with God. Apparently, the strength to minister to others came from the time He spent alone with His Father.)

4. Do you ever feel as if you have nothing left to offer to those who need you? Relate an example to the group. What would Jesus do in that situation?

5. Do you have a solitary or "lonely" place you go to be with God?

6. What should you do to find these opportunities to be alone with God? What would be the effect on your life if you spent more time alone with God?

Take a few moments to pray. Ask God to provide opportunities and motivation for you to find a "lonely" place to meet with Him. Ask Him to work through you and provide the strength you need to be able to minister to those who need God.

OPTIONAL — Digging Deeper III: Ministry of Interruption *(10–20 minutes)*

A. Lecture

Jesus had common, frustrating experiences that are all too familiar to those who seek to be sensitive to the people God has placed in their lives: People often interrupt our important activities with their needs. Children, students, coworkers, friends, neighbors, and even strangers place demands on people whom God has blessed with the gifts of compassion and wisdom. Certainly, there are times when our activities cannot and should not be interrupted, but sometimes the greatest opportunities for ministry begin with interruptions.

B. Guided Discussion

Ask your students to read each of the Scripture passages below and then, for each passage, answer the questions that follow:

- Matthew 8:18–22, 9:18–26, 12:46–50, 14:13–14, 19:13–15
- Luke 8:40–48, 18:35–43

1. What was Jesus doing when He was interrupted? Was it important?

2. Who interrupted Him? Why? Was it important?

3. What did Jesus do? What was the result?

Have your students respond (individually or in small groups) to the following questions:

1. What are some common interruptions in your life?

2. Are they usually important? How do you decide what is and is not important?

3. Do you reject interruptions? What are some examples of interruptions you reject? (Possible answer: I often reject my children's interruptions by telling them, "Not now—later!")

4. Describe an interruption you accepted that produced significant results.

5. How can you become more sensitive to the needs of those around you? How can you become more aware of the things God has given you that would benefit others?

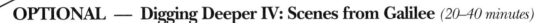

OPTIONAL — Digging Deeper IV: Scenes from Galilee *(20–40 minutes)*

(This section requires the use of the optional full-color overhead-transparency packet. For information on ordering it, see page 307.)

Have your students read the handout "The Sea Is His Delight."

The following overhead transparencies should give you a good picture of the Sea of Galilee and the area around it. These transparencies show various seasons and vantage points. It would be wise to refer to the map "Galilee" to find the location of each slide. These photographs will help you see what Jesus' world looked like and make it a bit more real to you.

Overhead Transparency 17. The Sea. This photograph is taken from the hills north of the Sea of Galilee, looking south. Almost all of the sea is visible here. The sea is nearly 13 miles long and more than seven miles wide. The area in the foreground is the northwestern corner of the sea, where most of Jesus' miracles were performed (see Matthew 11:20–24). Hidden below the hill are the remains of the ancient cities of Chorazin and Capernaum. On the left side of the photo, one can see the high hills where the pagan Decapolis of Jesus' time was located. Jesus sailed across the sea from the area in front of the Decapolis. On His way across the lake, He stilled the storm. When He arrived at the other side, He met the man from whom He cast out a legion of demons; the demons entered a herd of pigs that promptly ran off a cliff into the sea (see Mark 4:35–5:20). On the far right side of the photo are the cliffs of Mount Arbel. Hidden from sight at the foot of these cliffs is the plain of Gennesaret and the city of Magdala, the home of Mary Magdalene. Beyond Mount Arbel, on the side of the hill, is modern-day Tiberias, once the ancient capital of Herod Antipas, murderer of John the Baptist. Notice how visible it is from everywhere else.

Overhead Transparency 18. The Plain of Gennesaret. This photograph was taken from Mount Arbel, looking north. In the center of the photo is the fertile plain of Gennesaret. The road follows the route of the biblical Way of the Sea (Matthew 4:12–17). The modern-day Kibbutz Ginnosar is not far from what was Gennesaret in Jesus' time. In the distance along the northern shore, the remains of Capernaum are barely visible as small white buildings. Somewhere on the tree-lined slopes of the hills at that end of the lake is the location where the Sermon on the Mount (Matthew 5–7) and the feeding of the five thousand (Matthew 14:13–21) took place. Across the sea on the far right are the hills of the Decapolis—today's Golan Heights. The hump-shaped hill on the edge of this photo was the Decapolis city of Susita, not far from where the herd of pigs ran into the lake.

Overhead Transparency 19. Scenes from the Lake. *Upper Left:* ***Tiberias.*** Looking southeast from Mount Arbel, we can see the city of Tiberias descending the hill to the sea. Herod Antipas named his capital city after the emperor Tiberius. On the left, to the east of the sea, are the hills of the Decapolis. The Jordan River ran out of the southern end of the sea.

Upper Right: ***The Decapolis.*** The Decapolis was founded by Alexander the Great and was strengthened by the Roman emperor Pompey in 63 B.C. Comprising 10 (or more at times) city-states, the Decapolis was largely Gentile, Hellenistic, and pagan. Religious Jews would have resented its theaters, stadiums, statues, and temples. Directly across the sea is the hump-shaped hill where the Decapolis city of Susita was located. It is likely that the man from whom Jesus drove out the legion of demons returned to this city (or at least to this area) to tell others of the miracle (Mark 5:18–20). Some believe that the strong Christian community in Susita during ancient times was due to his witness.

Lower Left: ***Mount of Beatitudes.*** Tradition holds that this is the place where Jesus preached the Sermon on the Mount (Matthew 5–7 and Luke 6). There is no concrete evidence to support this belief because the exact location is not specified in the Scriptures. However, this slope is in the right geographical *area*, and its appearance is certainly similar to what we might expect. One can imagine crowds seated on the rocks and the dirt of the hillside, listening to the Rabbi speak the message of the kingdom of God. Notice the difference in season from the previous transparencies.

Lower Right: ***Modern-day Fishing.*** This small modern fishing craft returns to Tiberias after a night of fishing. Today fishermen catch the same fish and use the same nets as the disciples did. The hills of today's Golan Heights, the Decapolis of Jesus' day, are in the background. The cool wind blowing off these hills sinks rapidly onto the sea, displacing the warmer air and causing sudden storms to strike. The size of this boat helps us understand the terror the disciples felt after being caught in the storm at sea. The beauty of this sea helps us understand what the rabbis meant when they said, "God created seven seas, but the Sea of Galilee is His delight."

Overhead Transparency 20. Ancient Fishing. *Upper Left:* ***Net Weight.*** In Jesus' day, fishing nets were made of fibers, sometimes linen. They had wood floats along one edge and sinkers attached to rope at the bottom. These net sinkers were often made of small stones of basalt, flint, or limestone. A small hole was drilled into each sinker so it could be fastened to the net. The weights shown here were found in ancient Galilean harbors by Mendel Nun, the leading scholar on the Sea of Galilee. The disciples spent a lot of time making these weights and attaching them to their nets.

Upper Right: ***Ancient Anchor.*** This stone anchor was found in one of the ancient harbors in the Sea of Galilee. It is a large piece of basalt in which a hole has been made and to which a rope has been attached. This anchor would have been thrown into the sea to hold the boat in position while the fishermen worked. Jesus' disciples would have been quite familiar with such an anchor (see Mark 6:53). Many of these anchors have been found in the Sea of Galilee. They have become symbols of hope for Christians (Hebrews 6:19).

Lower Left: ***Galilean Boat.*** This replica has been constructed based on the remains of a first-century boat found recently in the mud of the Sea of Galilee. It is considered to represent the type of boat the disciples used for fishing and in their travels across the sea. It is 26 feet long and seven and one-half feet wide. It is made of wood, and the planks are joined with mortise-and-tenon construction. The boat would have had a small sail and a crew of five. Four crew members would have used the two pairs of oars while the other person steered. The sail would also have been used. The boat is large enough to have held several people besides the crew members. A cushion could be placed on the small deck at either end of the boat so someone could sleep (see Mark 4:38). The sides of the boat are low to make it easier for the fishermen to cast their nets over the edge and then pull them back. Waves did not have to be high to threaten the boat.

*Lower Right: **Casting the Net**.* This modern-day fisherman demonstrates how to use a cast net, one type of net used in New Testament times (see Mark 1:16–18). The net is 18 to 25 feet in diameter. The fisherman arranges it on one arm, stands in the boat, and throws it like a parachute into the water. The weights along the edge, which were made of stone in Jesus' day, carry it to the bottom of the sea. The fisherman can either pull out the fish caught in the net or pull the bottom of the net together, trapping the fish inside. Either way, he must jump into the water. In John's account of the miraculous catch, Peter apparently was the "man in the water" (John 21:7). The rugged appearance of the fisherman helps us appreciate the long hours, under difficult conditions, that Jesus' disciples worked. This conditioning certainly prepared them for the demanding mission to which Jesus called them.

Conclusion

Jesus deliberately chose the Sea of Galilee as the setting for His ministry. Its beauty, its people, and even its storms were the things He experienced during His time on earth. It can be inspiring for us to become familiar with His world, but we must also learn what He taught through the sea. We can be encouraged, knowing that He is more powerful than everything, including nature and the power of Satan himself. He watches us in our struggles, knowing when to respond to our calls for help. He guides our direction, even when we end up somewhere other than where we thought we were going. He always carries out His purposes.

As Jesus' disciples, we need to develop the relational and practical skills necessary for achieving our mission of bringing others to Christ. We also must be willing to work hard. Only then will we truly be "fishers of men." Rather than focusing on ourselves and our own needs, we must be willing to "leave our nets" to follow Jesus.

THE SEA IS HIS DELIGHT

The rabbis of ancient times said, "The Lord has created seven seas, but the Sea of Galilee is His delight." Anyone who has seen the beauty of the blue water against the green and brown background of the mountains around the Sea of Galilee would understand that statement. This freshwater lake is the largest in Israel and among the world's most beautiful. The Bible does not tell us specifically why God chose this place as the location for Jesus' ministry, but certainly He (and His Son), having created it, appreciated its beauty. Since Jesus spent most of His short time of ministry near or on the Sea of Galilee, we will be able to enhance our understanding of His message and ministry by learning as much as we can about it.

THE SEA

This sea has many names, but most New Testament readers recognize "the Sea of Galilee" as its most common designation. It is also called the Sea of Kinnereth (Numbers 34:11; Joshua 12:3), the Lake of Gennesaret (Luke 5:1), the Sea of Tiberias (John 6:1, 21:1), and sometimes simply "the lake" (John 6:16). Set in the hills of northern Israel, the sea is nearly 700 feet below sea level. It is nearly eight miles wide at its widest point, and more than 12 miles long from north to south. Its depth is more than 150 feet in some places.

Surprising to many first-time visitors is the fact that from any point on the rocky shore, all other locations along the shoreline are visible. Around the sea, the hills of Galilee reach nearly 1,400 feet above sea level, and the mountains of the Golan Heights (the Decapolis in Jesus' time) reach more than 2,500 feet above sea level.

Much of the sea's beauty comes from its being nestled among the hills, which are green in the spring, brown during the dry season, and always in contrast with the deep blue of the sea. The slopes of the Golan Heights on the east and Mount Arbel on the west drop sharply down to the sea.

The sea's location below the mountains to the east makes it subject to sudden and violent storms as the wind comes over these mountains and drops suddenly onto the sea. This happens especially when an east wind brings cool air over the warmer blanket of air that covers the sea itself. The cold air, which is heavier, drops as the warm air rises. This sudden change can produce surprisingly furious storms in a short time, as it did in Jesus' day (Matthew 8:24).

There are several hot mineral springs surrounding the lake. The largest of these is in the capital city of Tiberias, where Herod Antipas included it in his hot baths. Ten of Jesus' 33 miracles—including a majority of His healing miracles—happened near the lake. The number of sick people mentioned in the vicinity of the Sea of Galilee (see Matthew 14:35–36) may be due in part to the hot mineral springs and public baths in the area. When these springs and baths did not provide cures, people sought the Rabbi from Capernaum, who had a reputation of being able to heal.

The Sea of Galilee contains fresh water. It is fed primarily by the Jordan River in the north and several wadis on the east that carry rainfall and melted snow from the Golan Heights.

As it is today, the Sea of Galilee was teeming with fish in Jesus' time. This made for a prosperous commercial fishing industry in the many small villages and larger towns along its shore. Among these was Bethsaida, which means "house of fishermen." Jesus' choice of this location for His ministry, along with His selection of several fishermen as His disciples, made it natural that He would illustrate much of His teaching with fishing imagery (Matthew 4:19).

The climate of Galilee is quite tropical, and the soil is fertile. The most productive area is around the sea. In Jesus' time, wheat, barley, figs, grapes, and olives were produced in large quantities. The fertile fields often gave Jesus opportunities to illustrate His teaching (Matthew 12:1, 13:1–43; John 12:24). Jesus' messages about wealth and earthly treasures were also easily understood by the inhabitants of the prosperous communities around the lake (Matthew 6:19–21, 16:26; Luke 12:16–21).

THE PEOPLE AROUND THE SEA

Galilee was heavily populated in the first century, especially around the sea. The remains of the area indicate that several villages and towns had populations of more than 5,000 people. Perhaps that is one of the reasons Jesus chose this location. Although the people living around the sea mixed to some degree, they tended to congregate in groups. This fact helps us understand the relationship between Jesus' actions and teachings and the area He was in. The following identifications of groups of people are those of the author and are based on a variety of sources.

The Northwestern Side of the Sea: Land of the Religious Jews

Certainly not all the people who lived on this fertile side of the sea were religious or even Jewish. But it is clear that most of the inhabitants were very religious—a fact supported by the many synagogues discovered in the towns. It was here that Jesus conducted His ministry. In fact, the Bible indicates that most of His miracles were performed in three towns of this area: Capernaum, Chorazin, and Bethsaida. These three cities are sometimes called the "gospel triangle" because they form a triangle, with the points about three to four miles apart.

The international trade route sometimes called the Via Maris (the Way of the Sea) ran through this area near the city of Capernaum. Matthew records that Jesus chose that town as His home to fulfill the prophecy that the Messiah would live in Galilee by "the way to the sea" (Matthew 4:12–17). God's people, Israel, had always lived in the land that connected the great empires of the ancient world. The whole world knew of them because the trade routes passed through their country. As the nations of the world passed by, Israel could obey God's command to be His witnesses (Isaiah 43:10–12). Jesus, bringing the next chapter of God's message to the world, made His home a few yards from the great trade route. Galilee was not a backwoods region; it was on the crossroads of the world. Jesus' message was heard by many people from around the world.

Here are the main towns of this area:

Capernaum—Located on the shore of the Sea of Galilee, this major town was home to fishermen, farmers, a Roman garrison, and a customs house (where tax collectors lived). Capernaum had a large synagogue, the remains of which are beneath the ruins of a later synagogue. Many of the New Testament stories about Jesus took place here. Jesus' disciple Matthew, a tax collector, came from this town (Matthew 8:5–17, 9:1–34, 17:24–27, 18; Mark 1:21–34, 2:1–12; Luke 7:1–10; John 6:16–71).

Chorazin—Chorazin was a village located three miles north of Capernaum. Although this was one of the towns where most of Jesus' miracles took place, the Bible records no specific visit of Jesus to this town. It was large and prosperous and had a synagogue. Its economic pursuits included the processing of olives.

Bethsaida—Peter, Andrew, and Philip were successful fishermen from Bethsaida (John 1:44, 12:21). This town was located on the northern end of the sea near where the Jordan River enters. Jesus fed the five thousand (Luke 9:10–17) and healed a blind man (Mark 8:22–26) here. The ruins of this village are being uncovered for the first time, revealing a prosperous town constructed of basalt, a black rock common to the area.

Magdala—Magdala was a small village on the northwestern shore of the sea. Its name means "tower." As her name suggests, Mary Magdalene came from here (Mark 16:1; Luke 8:2). It stands at a junction of the Way of the Sea, where one branch turns west toward the Jezreel (the route Jesus took to Nazareth) and the other continues south. Apparently, Magdala was also called Magadan (Matthew 15:39) and Tarichaeae (a Greek word meaning "the place where fish are salted"). It was famous for the fish caught locally, salted, dried, and sent throughout the Roman world. This town was also a Zealot base during the First Jewish Revolt.

Gennesaret—A small plain on the northwestern corner of the Sea of Galilee, Gennesaret was the garden spot of the region. Its rich soil and abundance of water produced grapes, figs, olives, wheat, vegetables, and melons. The rabbis called this area "the Garden of God." Gennesaret may have also been the name of a village near the sea at the foot of the Old Testament city of Kinnereth (Joshua 19:35). A large harbor from this town has recently been found under the water in the Sea of Galilee (Matthew 14:22–35; Mark 6:45–56).

The Northeastern Corner of the Sea: Land of Gamla and the Zealots

The Zealots were part of a movement (the term was later applied to a specific group) totally devoted to serving God. They believed it was not possible to both serve the pagan Romans and be faithful to the law of God. They resisted Rome and anyone who sided with the Roman rulers—often with violence. The movement was started by a man named Judah from Gamla who revolted over taxes (Acts 5:37). Although one of Jesus' disciples was a Zealot (Matthew 10:4), there is no specific record that Jesus was ever in this area, although Matthew's Gospel records that He went "through all the towns and villages, teaching in their synagogues" (Matthew 9:35). He probably did visit the synagogue at Gamla, the remains of which attract visitors today.

The Western Side of the Sea: Land of Tiberias and the Herodians

Easily visible from Jesus' hometown of Capernaum was Tiberias, the regional capital built by Herod Antipas. It was shunned by religious Jews (we have no record that Jesus ever visited it) because it was supposedly built over a cemetery, which made it ritually impure. The city was named after the emperor Tiberius and was built on a hill overlooking the sea. The hot mineral springs in the area were used as a health spa by Herod and the people of the city. Little is known of its inhabitants, who are assumed to be the "Herodians" who opposed Jesus' ministry (Matthew 22:15–22; Mark 3:6, 12:13–17). Apparently, they were an aristocratic group who supported the Herod dynasty and the Romans who kept it in power. The Herodians plotted Jesus' execution, probably because any of the many "messianic" movements of the time threatened those who were used by Rome to keep the peace. It is ironic that Jesus' ministry took place so close to those who bitterly opposed Him.

The Heights of the Eastern Side of the Sea: The Decapolis

The name *Decapolis* means "10 cities." Though the number of cities changed from time to time, the Decapolis was a group of independent city-states, thoroughly pagan and Hellenistic in makeup. Several of them were founded by veterans of Alexander the Great's army in the fourth century B.C. When Pompey and his Roman legions took control of the area in 63 B.C., he kept the Decapolis independent from the Jewish territory to the west. Several of these city-states are mentioned in the Bible, including Philadelphia (modern Amman—Revelation 1:11), Gerasa (Mark 5:1; Luke 8:26), Beth Shean (then called Scythopolis—1 Samuel 31:10), and Gadara (Matthew 8:28). These towns had typically Hellenistic designs, with theaters where lewd plays were performed, temples where sacrifices were offered to pagan gods, and coliseums where nude athletic games and gladiatorial contests took place. Each city controlled the areas surround it, spreading Hellenistic philosophy and religion.

In full view of the religious Jews of Jesus' town of Capernaum, the steep cliffs of the eastern shore must have seemed evil and menacing. The farmers of Galilee could see the sophisticated Gentile world barely eight miles away. Its culture must have been alluring to many of the conservative followers of the Torah. Some scholars believe the "far country" of Jesus' parable of the prodigal son could refer to the Decapolis. It was barely a day's walk from Galilee. Certainly, the riotous lifestyle and the pigs were there. The Talmud and one of the church fathers tell us that many people in New Testament times believed that the inhabitants of this area were those whom Joshua had driven from the Promised Land—the seven pagan nations (Joshua 3:10; Acts 13:19)—making this the land of the "expelled ones," the worshipers of Baal.

In this context, Jesus' ministry here is remarkable. His disciples probably hesitated when He suggested they row to the Decapolis ("the other side"—Mark 4:35). Once they arrived there, it was probably no surprise that they were greeted by a man possessed by a legion of demons—there was a Roman legion stationed nearby (Mark 5:1–20). Uncharacteristically, Jesus, having healed the man, sent him to share the Good News with the people of his town (possibly Susita, which was close by). Apparently, the man's message was blessed before the next time Jesus visited (Mark 7:31–37).

THE SEA AND THE ABYSS

The Sea of Galilee is beautiful. Its calm, peaceful setting, though, does not present a complete picture of the people's perspective in Jesus' day. Many of the biblical images related to the sea reflect a very different cultural understanding.

The Jews were not seafarers; they were desert nomads. Their father, Abraham, was a shepherd in the Negev. At one point, the Israelites wandered in the desert for 40 years before settling in the Promised Land. They rarely controlled the seacoast. Even David spent his childhood caring for sheep in the wilderness pasture around Bethlehem and wandered in the wilderness of Judea for some time before becoming king. The Israelites were not at home on the sea.

The sea in general has a negative connotation throughout the Bible. This may be due in part to the desert background of the Israelites. To them, the sea probably appeared alien and threatening, a reminder of cultural stories depicting the sea as a monstrous beast and as the place Baal went to do battle with Yam, the sea god. Whatever the reasons, the Bible uses sea imagery in a less-than-positive way. For example, in Genesis 1:2, the beginning of the world is described as watery chaos, a primeval sea, from which God brought order. The earth, God's masterly creation, rested *on* the sea (Psalm 24:1–2), and His great power controlled it (Psalm 104:5–9).

In the Bible, the flooding waters of the sea could become a tool of God's judgment (Genesis 6, 7; Exodus 14)—either for the whole earth or for those who opposed God's people. But always the sea remained a dangerous place (Psalm 30:1, 69:1–3). Jonah was thrown into the depths because he turned his back on God (Jonah 2:3–6), but when he remembered God, he was rescued (Jonah 2:6–7). Only God could control the sea and the evil it symbolized (Psalm 65:5–7, 77:19, 89:9, 93:3–4; Exodus 14–15; Isaiah 51:10).

The sea was the home of that terrible dragon, Leviathan, which came to symbolize the pagan nations opposing Israel (Isaiah 27:1, 51:9–10). Daniel's description of the great beasts of the sea and the terror they spread is based on the image of the sea as the home of evil, the chaos that only God can control (Daniel 7:2–7). The evil nations that oppose God are like the roaring of the sea (Isaiah 17:12). In the New Testament, the sea symbolizes chaos, evil, and evil beings. The depths of the sea are seen as the home of demons—a place called the Abyss, the home of evil spirits, according to Jewish tradition. The demons begged Jesus not to send them into the Abyss (Luke 8:31), but He did anyway: The herd of pigs ran into the sea.[1]

John referred to the Abyss often in his Revelation (9:1,11, 11:7, 17:8). It is clearly the abode of the one who is the epitome of evil—Satan (Revelation 20:1–3). Someday the devil himself will rise from the sea (Revelation 13:1–11). Jesus' condemnation of Chorazin, Bethsaida, and Capernaum compares their fate to that of Sodom and Gomorrah. Capernaum will go down to the "depths." It is likely that the biblical use of the sea as the home of the chaotic evil that God alone controlled, along with Capernaum's location at the edge of the Sea of Galilee, meant that the people understood this as a reference to hell itself. To them, Jesus' miracles on the sea meant more than simply that he had power over the forces of nature.

JESUS' AUTHORITY OVER THE SEA

Jesus acted to demonstrate His authority over the sea and its destructive power. He walked on the stormy water (Mark 6:47–50; Matthew 14:22–33; John 6:16–20).[2] He calmed the storms on the sea (Mark 4:35–41; Matthew 8:23–27; Luke 8:22–25).[3] He even empowered His disciple to walk on the water (Matthew 14:28–32). Peter's cry of "Lord, save me!" as his lack of faith caused him to sink into the deep takes on intense meaning in light of the symbolism of the sea (Matthew 14:30). The reaction of the disciples was profound. They were amazed (Matthew 14:33; Mark 6:51) and terrified (Mark 4:41) at Jesus' power. They recognized that His power was more than just authority over the elements of nature. Some Old Testament heroes had controlled nature; for example, at Elijah's word, it did not rain for years (1 Kings 17:1). This is a feat James suggests might be possible for all righteous people (James 5:15–18). But only God can control the Abyss. The stilling of the storm produced not only awe at the power of God within Jesus, but also the realization that He was God. "Then those who were in the boat worshiped him, saying, 'Truly you are the Son of God'" (Matthew 14:33).

CONCLUSION

The Sea of Galilee is one of the most significant locations in the world. Here God sent His Son to continue the work of salvation with the message that the kingdom of God was at hand. The sea and its fishermen provided images He used to explain His kingdom and His followers' role in it. And the sea and what it represented gave Him opportunities to demonstrate that He was truly God.

NOTES

1. The term *Abyss* is a Greek word meaning "depths." In the Old Testament the Hebrew word is translated "depth" or "deep" (Genesis 1:2, 7:11; Proverbs 8:28, Job 7:12 [where the monster lives]; Psalm 42:7. Clearly, it is (symbolically) the abode of the demonic beings who oppose God. But He can control the deep and its forces.

2. The disciples thought Jesus was a ghost (Mark 6:49), consistent with the view that the sea harbored demonic forces.

3. Jesus calmed the storm and immediately met a demon-possessed man (Mark 4:35–5:2), again consistent with the cultural view that storms were somehow caused by evil powers. He defeated them in the storm, then they confronted Him in a dangerous man.

THEY LEFT THEIR NETS

Lesson Nineteen
Handout #2

Before Jesus' time, few Israelites were fishermen. There was only one Hebrew word for *fish*, and it covered everything from minnows to whales. In Jesus' time, a small, flourishing fishing industry developed around the Sea of Galilee. The town of Magdala (in Greek, Tarichaeae, "the place where fish are salted") was a sardine-pickling center. Many of the images Jesus used indicated that He was familiar with fishing and the sea.

The job of a fisherman in Jesus' day was difficult. Fishermen worked year-round in the heat of summer and the cold of winter, often at night. Certainly, Jesus' choice of Capernaum, on the Sea of Galilee, as His home brought Him into contact with many fishermen. Several of His disciples—Andrew, Peter, James, and John—knew the trade well. It's possible that Jesus selected fishermen as His disciples not only because the imagery of their occupation fit well with the mission that He had called them to, but also because they were a hardy group of people, accustomed to difficult work and long hours. Jesus even asked them to return to the lake and fish again after a night of fishing without a catch (Luke 5:1–7).

THE SKILLS OF THE FISHERMAN

One of the most important skills of fishermen was making and mending nets. Made of linen, a common fabric used in the ancient Near East, these nets had to be carefully cleaned and dried each day or they would quickly rot and wear out. The majority of a fisherman's life probably was spent mending nets (Luke 5:2). Net weights, small pieces of stone with holes drilled in them, were fastened to the bottom of the nets. This too took time. Fishermen also had to be skilled, of course, in the use of the nets in fishing for various types of fish.

THE NETS

The Old Testament refers to catching fish with hooks, spears, and several types of nets (Job 18:8; Ecclesiastes 9:12; Isaiah 19:8). Several types of nets were used in Jesus' time. The seine net was probably the oldest. Several hundred feet long and as much as 20 feet high, this net was dropped by fishermen from boats several hundred yards from shore, and parallel to it. Cork or wood floats kept one edge of the net on the water's surface, while stone sinkers fastened to the other edge pulled it to the bottom. As the fishermen pulled the net ashore, the net trapped any fish in its path. When the fishermen had dragged the net ashore, they sorted the catch, throwing out animals without fins and scales. They cleaned and sold the fish, remembering to give Rome's share to the tax collector. Jesus used the seine net as an illustration in His description of the kingdom of heaven (Matthew 13:47–48). James and John were probably mending (preparing) seine nets when Jesus called them (Matthew 4:21).

The circular cast net measured up to 25 feet in diameter and was thrown into the water from the shore or a boat. Simon and Andrew were using this type of net when Jesus called them (Mark 1:16–18).

The trammel net was composed of three walls, reinforcing each other with increasingly smaller mesh. Fish passed through the layers until they found themselves caught against the inner wall and eventually became entangled. The net was retrieved and the fish extracted. This net was washed in the morning, as it traditionally was used at night. Sometimes fishermen encircled a shoal of fish with a trammel net and threw a cast net into the center. Fishermen may have jumped into the water to retrieve the cast net and catch the fish trapped in the circle of the larger net. Often more than one boat was used with the trammel net (Luke 5:1–7). The New Testament reference to Peter putting on his clothes before meeting Jesus probably indicated that he had been fishing in this way (John 21:7).

Besides the nets, fishermen of Jesus' day also used a hook and line. Jesus told Peter to cast a hook, catch a fish, and get a shekel from its mouth (Matthew 17:24–27). Archaeologists have found hooks from Jesus' time in the small fishing villages along the shore of the Sea of Galilee.

The character of the disciples is seen clearly in their willingness to leave their nets and their boats to follow Jesus (Matthew 4:20,22). They were apparently prosperous, even having hired help (Mark 1:20), but they left it all to follow the Rabbi and become like Him. Their commitment and sacrifice were (and would be) enormous.

THE FISH THEY CAUGHT

Various species of freshwater fish in the Sea of Galilee were caught with the different types of nets. Renowned Galilee scholar Mendel Nun has described the three types of fish.[1] Musht, called St. Peter's fish, was, according to tradition, the type of fish caught by Peter. This fish is found on the northern end of the sea, near the area of Jesus' ministry and Peter's fishing. It grows up to 15 inches long and three pounds in weight. It has relatively few bones and is very tasty. (Take my word for it!) It is likely that this is the kind of fish Jesus used to feed 5,000 people (Matthew 14:13–21). Biny, a member of the carp family, was used in Bible lands for feasts and banquets. Sardines are small fish that were caught in enormous numbers. Drying and pickling sardines was the main industry of Magdala, home of Mary Magdalene. These are probably the "small fish" referred to in the Bible (Matthew 15:34; Mark 8:7).

When Jesus asked the disciples to put the net on the other side of the boat near Capernaum and Bethsaida and they caught a large number of fish, they probably caught musht. Their skill in catching, processing, and selling fish provided a ready teaching tool for Jesus. He used imagery from their occupation to explain that they must use the same care and devotion in bringing His message to the world.

THE LESSONS HE TAUGHT

The fishing industry in the area where Jesus ministered, and the fishermen among His disciples, provided effective images for the lessons Jesus taught His audiences. The disciples' task was to become "fishermen" for the kingdom. The long hours, the carefully practiced skills, and the various techniques and nets used in catching specific kinds of fish all must have passed through their minds. Seeking people to follow Jesus would take the same care, dedication, and skill used in fishing (Matthew 4:18–19). The disciples learned that they must seek all kinds of people to follow Jesus, though some would eventually turn away.

The fishing motif apparent in Jesus' teaching about the kingdom was so strong that the Greek word for *fish* (*ichthus*) came to represent Jesus' name. The first letters of the Greek words meaning "Jesus Christ, God's Son, Savior" spell *ichthus*. The fish itself appropriately became a symbol for Jesus. As His disciples, we must learn the lessons He taught, becoming His new fishers of men and women and finding ways to bring all kinds of people to Him.

NOTES

1. Mendel Nun's excellent work can be found in a booklet entitled "The Sea of Galilee and Its Fishermen," published in Israel by Kibbutz Ein Gev. It is available from the museum Nun founded on the kibbutz called Beit Ha-Oganim ("House of Anchors"). Visitors to the Sea of Galilee are urged to see this small museum totally dedicated to the history of fishing around the sea where Jesus lived. Nun's writings have also been published in the *Jerusalem Perspective*.

PIERCING THE DARKNESS

For the Teacher

At times, Satan's evil power seems strong in our world. Christians struggle to respond appropriately to both personal evil, such as immorality, injustice, and hatred, and natural evil, such as death, disease, grief, and loneliness. Sometimes we find it easiest to just ignore the evil around us—especially immorality—and hide in safe communities and churches. At other times, it is easy for us just to compromise with sin since so many other people seem to be comfortable with it. But Jesus, our example, chose not to hide from evil or compromise the truth.

Begin your discussion of this topic by asking your students for examples of Satan's power at work in the world. Tell students you will be examining the example Jesus set for us in confronting evil. This lesson explores Jesus' actions as He challenged the power of the devil himself in the Decapolis, the pagan area under the darkness of sin, across the sea from Jesus' main area of ministry. Jesus, the Light of the World, pierced the darkness with spectacular results. The same opportunity is available for you and your students.

Your Objectives for This Lesson

At the completion of this section, you will want your students:

To Know/Understand

1. The history and character of the Decapolis.
2. The nature of Hellenism and its relationship to our times.
3. The ministry of Jesus in the Decapolis.
4. The specific responsibility Jesus gave to those He delivered from the power of evil.
5. The relationship of the storm on the Sea of Galilee to the legion of demons on the other side of the water.
6. The battle between good and evil that has raged since the beginning and continues today.

To Do

1. Be committed to identifying evil and those under its dominion.
2. Develop the habit of challenging evil with the loving methods used by Jesus.
3. Become combatants in the battle between good and evil—God and Satan—which will continue until the end of time.
4. Practice sharing with others what God has done for them.
5. Be able to recognize similarities to the "Decapolis" in our time and know how to respond to it.

How to Plan for This Lesson

Because of the volume of material in this lesson, you may need to divide it into several class sessions. To help you determine how to do that, the lesson has been broken into segments. Note that the time needed may vary significantly, depending on elements such as the leader, the size of the class, and the interest level of the class.

If you wish to cover the entire lesson in one session, you should complete Unit One. This unit provides a guided discussion covering the major points in the video. It does not go into great depth. If you wish to go into greater depth on any of the points in Unit One, they are covered more thoroughly in the remainder of the material.

How to Prepare for This Lesson

Materials Needed

Student copies of the maps: "Land of Jesus' Ministry"
"Galilee of Jesus' Ministry"
"The Roman World"

Overhead transparencies: "Land of Jesus' Ministry"
"Galilee of Jesus' Ministry"
"The Roman World"
"New Testament Chronology"

Student copies of the handouts: "A Far Country"
"The Sea Is His Delight" (Lesson 19)

Video: **Piercing the Darkness**

Overhead projector, screen, TV, VCR

1. Make copies of the maps listed above for your students.

2. Prepare the overhead transparencies listed above. (You'll find them at the back of the book.)

3. Make copies of the handouts listed above for your students. (If possible, students should receive and read these handouts before the lesson.)

4. Review the geography of the lands of the Bible from the "Introduction."

5. Determine which **unit** and which **Digging Deeper** sections, if any, you want to use in your class session(s). NOTE: You can use these sections in any order you wish (e.g., you might want to use **Digging Deeper III**, but not **Digging Deeper I** or **Digging Deeper II**).

6. Prepare your classroom ahead of time, setting up and testing an overhead projector and screen (for the overhead transparencies) and a TV and VCR. If you plan to hand out biblical references for your students to look up and read aloud, prepare 3x5 cards (one reference per card) to distribute before class.

Lesson Plan

UNIT ONE: Video Review

1. Introductory Comments

When Jesus was on earth, He actively challenged the evil of His day. He confronted the power of the devil, both in the demons who controlled people and in the influence of Satan in the culture surrounding Him. This lesson highlights Jesus' reactions to both manifestations of evil. In reacting to the culture, Jesus chose to sail across the Sea of Galilee to the modern and pagan Decapolis. He didn't hesitate to bring His message to the people of His day who did not honor God. When He arrived at the Decapolis, Jesus came face to face with people who were possessed by demons. He confronted the demons with the power of God and expelled them from the men they controlled.

The darkness in which Satan had held these people was pierced by Jesus—the Light of the World.

2. Show the Video *Piercing the Darkness* *(17 minutes)*

3. Map Study: The Decapolis

HINT: *Begin this map study session by reviewing the geography of the overall region and working down to the area the lesson is dealing with—the Decapolis.*

Using the overhead transparency "Land of Jesus' Ministry," point out the following areas, and have your students locate them on their maps.

> Jerusalem
> Nazareth
> Capernaum
> Galilee
> Sea of Galilee
> Kursi
> Susita
> Decapolis

Using the overhead transparency "Galilee of Jesus' Ministry," point out the following areas, and have your students locate them on their maps.

> Sea of Galilee
> Decapolis
> plain of Gennesaret
> Capernaum
> Chorazin
> Bethsaida
> Tiberias
> Susita (Hippos)
> Kursi

4. Guided Discussion: Jesus Went to the Decapolis

Introduce the discussion by briefly explaining to students that the Decapolis was Hellenistic. Hellenism was similar to humanism. Like humanism, Hellenism emphasized the human mind as the ultimate source of truth. The Decapolis itself was very modern, with pagan temples, a theater, an arena, and a society devoted to human pleasure.

Ask students to look up the following passages:

- Matthew 4:23–25
- Mark 5:20
- Mark 7:31

Have your students respond (individually or in small groups) to the following questions:

1. In these passages, where did Jesus go to minister to people?

2. Why do you think Jesus wanted to go to the pagan Decapolis? What can we learn from Jesus' desire to go to the most modern and the most pagan areas of His world?

Ask students to look up the following passage:

- Mark 5:1–20

Have your students respond (individually or in small groups) to the following questions:

1. What was the condition of the man who was demon-possessed? Did he pose a threat to Jesus and His disciples? How do you know?

2. What was the reaction of the man to Jesus? Why did he react that way?

3. Why did this man seem to recognize Jesus when so many other people did not?

4. What was the name of the demons? What do you think it meant? (NOTE: Point out that "legion" may have a double meaning. A legion was a division of the Roman army, consisting of about 6,000 men. It is probable that the demons were called "legion" as a measure of their number. In addition, though, the Decapolis had been founded by the legions of Pompey, and there was a legion stationed there. Rome and the Romans were sometimes used in the Bible to symbolize evil and even the devil himself. [See Revelation 17:1–17. Many scholars believe the woman on seven hills (verse 9) symbolizes both Rome and future events.] Thus the identification of the demons with the pagan Romans of the area would make sense to the disciples.)

5. What was the place the demons said they didn't want to go? Where did Jesus send them? Do you think there is a connection? (NOTE: Point out that the one place where a steep bank goes down to the sea is just a short distance from Kursi, where *Piercing the Darkness* was filmed. The nearest Decapolis city was Hippos. See **Digging Deeper IV**.)

6. How did the possessed man change after Jesus sent the demons away? How did the towns-people react? Why? What does this indicate about their acceptance of Jesus' message at this time?

Ask students to look up the following passages:

- Matthew 15:29–31
- Mark 7:31–37

Have your students respond (individually or in small groups) to the following questions:

1. What happened when Jesus revisited the area of the Decapolis?

2. Why do you think the towns that had asked Jesus to leave before now had large crowds of His followers? (NOTE: We don't know the exact reason this change took place. It is possible that the ministry of the cured man had an effect. It is clear, though, that the message of Jesus, however it was communicated, had opened minds and hearts.)

Prayer: Ask God to give you an awareness of what He has done for you and the courage you need to tell others. Ask Him to make you willing to confront the power of darkness in the "Decapolis" of our time. Tell Him you're willing to be an instrument through which he can work in changing the lives of people and even our world.

UNIT TWO
"Jesus Confronts the Evil Powers"

1. Introductory Comments

Jesus displayed uncommon love and concern for the outcasts, the unloved, and the despised of His day. He ministered to tax collectors, lepers, and even Gentiles with a gentle, caring attitude that became the model for His disciples and for us. He called on sinners to leave their sinful habits, but He did so in an affirming, encouraging manner.

His reaction to Satan and the power of evil is quite a different story. The compassionate, caring Messiah became righteously confrontational. He deliberately left the familiarity of Capernaum and the area of the religious Jews and sailed with His disciples across the Sea of Galilee to the pagan Decapolis. Here Jesus challenged the power of the devil himself.

Jesus' display of power and authority over Satan can encourage and strengthen us. His deliberate challenge to Satan and Satan's power must become our model. We too should step out of our secure environments to challenge the devil's power wherever we find it. But we must confront these forces of darkness in the power and name of Jesus.

2. Show the Video *Piercing the Darkness* (*17 minutes*)

3. Map Study: The Decapolis

HINT: *Begin this map study session by reviewing the geography of the overall region and working down to the area the lesson is dealing with—the Decapolis.*

Using the overhead transparency "The Roman World," point out the following areas, and have your students find them on their maps.

> Rome
> Mediterranean Sea
> Egypt
> Judea
> Caesarea

Using the overhead transparency "Land of Jesus' Ministry," point out the following areas, and have your students find them on their maps.

> Bethlehem
> Jerusalem
> Nazareth
> Capernaum
> Galilee
> Sea of Galilee
> Kursi
> Susita
> Decapolis

Using the overhead transparency "Galilee of Jesus' Ministry," point out the following areas, and have your students find them on their maps.

> Sea of Galilee
> Decapolis
> plain of Gennesaret
> Capernaum
> Chorazin
> Bethsaida
> Gamla
> Tiberias
> Susita (Hippos)
> Kursi
> Beth Shean

4. Review the Overhead Transparency "New Testament Chronology"

Using the overhead transparency "New Testament Chronology," highlight the following dates for your students.

586 B.C.	Babylonian Captivity of Judah
ca. 500 B.C.	Return to Israel
63 B.C.	Roman conquest of Judea (Pompey)
ca. A.D. 27–30	Jesus' ministry
A.D. 66–73	First Jewish Revolt against Rome
A.D. 70	Jerusalem is destroyed

5. Guided Discussion: The Other Side

Your students should read the handout "A Far Country" before beginning this lesson. If they have not done so, they should read the handout "The Sea Is His Delight" from Lesson 19.

Introduce the discussion by briefly explaining to students that the Decapolis was Hellenistic. Hellenism was similar to humanism. Like humanism, Hellenism emphasized the human mind as the ultimate source of truth. The Decapolis itself was very modern, with pagan temples, a theater, an arena, and a society devoted to human pleasure.

a. Jesus and the Decapolis

Ask students to look up the following passages:

- Matthew 8:28
- Mark 4:35
- Mark 5:1
- Luke 8:22,26,37

Have your students respond (individually or in small groups) to the following questions:

1. Where were Gadara and Gerasa located? (NOTE: Gerasa is believed by some to refer to Kursi, where *Piercing the Darkness* was filmed. There is a problem with the exact meaning of the word in Greek. One scholar says the word referred not to a place but to the pagan people who lived in the Decapolis. Whatever the specific name, the area was located on the eastern shore of the Sea of Galilee, near Kursi.)

2. Why do you think Jesus wanted to go to the pagan Decapolis? What can we learn from the fact that Jesus told His disciples to sail across to the Decapolis? What do you think the disciples thought?

3. Do you think the disciples were surprised to find a demon-possessed man on the other side of the sea? Why or why not?

4. Can you think of an example of a situation in which you might deliberately confront evil in your own culture or community? What do you think would happen? Why might Christians avoid doing this?

5. What are some current places, practices, or ideas in our culture that might be compared to the Decapolis—that seem to be under the power of the devil? (Possible answers: media, arts, education, movies, etc.) How has the Christian community responded to these modern-day examples of the Decapolis?

6. Think of one example of a modern-day Decapolis. What could Christians do to confront this evil in Jesus' name? Discuss your answers.

b. Jesus Quiets the Storm

Understanding the image that the sea portrayed to the people of Jesus' day provides insight into His message.

If you did not do the exercise "Jesus and the Storms," in Lesson 19, Unit Two, Guided Discussion 4, and **Digging Deeper I**, also in Lesson 19, this would be an appropriate place to do them. If you prefer to do a short review of the information covered in those sections, have your students look up the Scripture passages listed below and discuss the questions that follow. (If you covered "Jesus and the Storms" and **Digging Deeper I**, you may want to skip this section.)

- Psalm 74:13–14
- Isaiah 27:1
- Isaiah 51:10
- Daniel 7:2–7

1. To the people of the Old Testament, what did the depths of the sea symbolize?

2. Who or what lived there?

- Luke 8:31
- Revelation 9:1,11
- Revelation 11:7
- Revelation 13:1–4
- Revelation 20:1–6

1. In the New Testament, what did the sea symbolize? (NOTE: The Greek *Abyss* means "depths.")

2. Who or what lived there?

- Matthew 14:22–33

1. What did Jesus' power over the storm show the disciples?

2. Considering the symbolism of the sea in the Scriptures, why do you think the disciples decided that Jesus was the Son of God? Think of Old Testament people who were given power over nature. What made Jesus' display of power different?

- Mark 4:35–5:2

1. Do you think it surprised the disciples that the storm arose when they set out for the Decapolis? Why or why not?

2. Do you think it surprised the disciples that the demon-possessed man met them almost immediately after Jesus calmed the storm? Why or why not?

3. Considering the disciples' understanding of the sea as symbolic of evil and the Decapolis as a pagan area, what can we learn about Jesus' attitude toward confronting evil from His order to sail across the sea? How might you apply that lesson in your culture?

c. Jesus Confronts the Demons

The religious Jews considered the Decapolis pagan country. The people of that area participated in many evil practices, including the worship of foreign gods. Pigs—which, according to Jews, were unclean—were raised there. Bargil Pixner, noted scholar on Galilee, points out that there was even a traditional belief that the people of the Decapolis were the descendants of the seven Baal-worshiping Canaanite nations Joshua and the Israelites had driven from the land (Joshua 3:10; Acts 13:19).[1] It is fascinating that Jesus chose to go to this very pagan area (which Jews considered unclean at the very least), where He confronted the power of the devil (or Beelzebub, as Jesus called him on a number of occasions). That willingness to confront evil directly and defeat Satan is the subject we will explore in this study.

Ask students to look up the following passages:

*   Matthew 8:28–34
*   Mark 5:1–20
*   Luke 8:26–39

(NOTE: Point out that Matthew mentioned two men, while Mark and Luke mentioned only one; otherwise the stories are the same.)

Have your students respond (individually or in small groups) to the following questions:

1. Why do you think the demons recognized Jesus when many other people didn't?

2. Where did the demons beg Jesus not to send them? What did Jesus do?

3. What did the people ask Jesus to do? Why? Did they believe in Him?

4. How were the men changed? What request did the one healed man make of Jesus? What was Jesus' answer? Does Jesus' answer surprise you? Why?

5. What was the man's message to others supposed to be? How long did he have to study to prepare to be a witness for Jesus? What can you learn from this? (Possible answers: Everyone can be a witness; theology and Bible study are important, but the basis for witness is to tell what God has done for you; witnessing is sharing Jesus with those whom you meet in everyday life.) What message do we have as witnesses for Jesus?

6. Whom did Jesus instruct the man to tell? To whom must our message go? Whom did he actually tell?

7. Why is it often difficult for us to tell other people about Jesus? Do you think we make the message too complicated sometimes? If so, how?

Ask students to look up the following passages:

*   Matthew 8:4
*   Matthew 9:30
*   Matthew 12:15–16
*   Mark 1:44

- Mark 5:43
- Mark 7:36

Have your students respond (individually or in small groups) to the following question:

1. When Jesus healed Jews, what did He command them to do? Why? (NOTE: Though there may be more reasons, one is the tendency among His Jewish audience to want to make Him king— see John 6:15. This would be especially true of the Zealots.)

OPTIONAL — Digging Deeper I: The Power of Jesus Today *(20–30 minutes)*

Have students write down their stories of what Jesus has done for them. Tell students their stories should answer the question "What has God done for you?" Have each student relate his or her story to the rest of the class.

Ask students to look up the following passages in which Jesus performed a miracle in someone's life.

- Mark 5:1–20
- Luke 8:26–39

Have your students respond (individually or in small groups) to the following questions:

1. Whom did the man tell about what Jesus had done for him? What was their response?

2. Why is it so hard for us to tell others what Jesus has done for us? Discuss your answers with the class.

3. Have you ever told your story to others? What was their response?

4. Have you ever heard another person tell his or her faith story in an everyday setting? What kind of response did that person receive?

5. Do you know anyone whose story had a great impact on many people? If so, explain.

6. Do you know anyone who was very evil whose story about what Jesus has done for him or her has had a huge impact on many people? If so, explain.

7. What can you learn about Jesus' power over Satan that helps you today?

God can use the simple witness of what He has done for us to impact many people for years. After Jesus' ministry in the Decapolis, there were strong Christian communities in this formerly pagan area. Certainly, this impact was due to Jesus and His power. And although Jesus' power is what changes lives, He chooses to work through human instruments like the men from whom He cast out demons and like us.

Spend a few moments in prayer. Ask God to provide you with a story to tell others. Invite Him to forgive you and to heal you of your own struggles with temptations, hurt, loss, loneliness, and sinful habits. Then ask God for the courage to find others who are captives to evil and to share with them your story so they too may be freed from captivity. Thank Him for the victory you have through Jesus' power.

Conclusion: It is important for students to recognize that Jesus often *confronted* evil, demons, and the devil himself. He did not avoid evil people or places where darkness reigned. He deliberately sailed to the other side of the sea to face the darkness and to let His light pierce through, changing people and sending demons to the Abyss. We must follow Christ's example.

OPTIONAL — Digging Deeper II: Beelzebub *(40–60 minutes)*

Satan has been devoted to the destruction of God's plan of salvation since the original temptation of Adam and Eve in the Garden of Eden (Genesis 3). When Jesus came to earth to complete God's ultimate act of salvation, Satan tried to do whatever he could to prevent Him from completing His work. Even at Jesus' birth, Satan used Herod to try to destroy the baby before He could begin His work (Matthew 2:13–18). Later, at the beginning of Jesus' ministry, Satan tempted Him, hoping Jesus would compromise His mission before it could be completed (Matthew 4:1–11). It is significant to note how often Jesus challenged the power of Satan during His ministry. It is also instructive to see how Jesus linked the demonic forces He faced with those that had tormented ancient Israel.

Just as Satan has been at his insidious work since the beginning, He continues to try to undermine the work of God in our world today. It is important for us to learn from Jesus' ministry how to confront the power of evil around us.

Satan in the Old Testament and the New Testament

Read 2 Kings 1:2–4 and point out to your students that Baal-Zebul was the god of the Philistines. The name *Baal-Zebub* means "Exalted Baal" or "Prince Baal." (*Baal* means "lord.") The Jewish writers changed his name to *Baal-Zebub,* which means "Lord of the Flies."

The Continuing Struggle

Read Matthew 10:25, 12:24–27; Mark 3:22; and Luke 11:14–26. Point out that Jesus used the name *Baal-Zebul* for the prince of demons—Satan. (In the Greek language of the New Testament, *Baal-Zebul* becomes *Beelzebub.*) This usage seems to indicate that Old Testament Baal worship was satanic, a tool the devil used to draw people away from God. Jesus continued the struggle against Satan that had gone on throughout the Old Testament as the Israelites were continually tempted to join the Baal cult.

Have your students look up the Scripture passages listed below and discuss the questions that follow.

- Mark 1:23–28
- Mark 5:1–20
- Mark 9:14–29

1. How did the demons react to Jesus?

2. What did Jesus do to the demons?

3. How did the crowds react to Jesus' actions?

4. Why couldn't the disciples drive out the demons?

5. Why do you think Jesus confronted demonic powers so often?

Lessons

Have your students discuss the following questions:

1. What does the Bible teach us about Satan's opposition to God's plan and His people throughout history?

2. Where is Satan active today? What are some of the forms he takes today? Where do you come into contact with Satan's power? Do you confront that power? Should you?

3. Read James 4:7. How will you keep the command given here concerning the devil?

4. Read James 4:7 again. What will happen to the devil if you follow the Bible's command?

5. Read James 4:7 again. What must precede your resistance to the devil? How can we submit to God?

The struggle between God and Satan has gone on throughout history. In Jesus' ministry, He aggressively continued that battle. We must follow Christ's example and continue to struggle against the devil where he is active in our society. Jesus' victory over Satan can become our victory.

OPTIONAL — Digging Deeper III: Confrontation with Evil in the Bible
(15–30 minutes)

Jesus wasn't the only Bible character who went out of his way to confront evil. In both the Old Testament and the New Testament, God's people boldly faced the forces of darkness, displaying the power of God. Begin this discussion by asking your students for examples of Bible characters who deliberately confronted evil. As students give examples, briefly read or review the stories of the people mentioned. As you review these stories, have students try to answer these questions:

1. What forms of evil did these people face?

2. Could they have avoided facing evil? How?

3. If they could have avoided it, why didn't they? Where did they get their courage?

4. What was the result of these confrontations with evil? When these Bible characters were able to defeat evil, was it clear whose power was at work? How was this made clear?

5. What would have happened if these people had chosen to not act against the evil they faced?

6. What can you learn from their example? Do you tend to avoid or to lovingly confront evil when you encounter it? What are some examples of times when you have faced evil?

7. What do you think would happen to the impact of Christianity on our culture if *all* Christians challenged evil whenever they encountered it?

8. What do you think will happen if Christians don't confront evil?

NOTE: If your students do not come up with examples of Bible characters who confronted evil, or if you want to give some examples of your own, you may point out the following people:

- Elijah (1 Kings 18)
- David (1 Samuel 17)
- Phinehas (Numbers 25:1–13)
- Deborah (Judges 4)
- Josiah (2 Chronicles 34:1–11,29–33)
- Esther (Esther 3:8–11, 4, 5:1–8, 7:1–10)

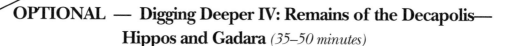

OPTIONAL — Digging Deeper IV: Remains of the Decapolis—
Hippos and Gadara *(35–50 minutes)*

(This section requires the use of the optional full-color overhead-transparency packet. For information on ordering it, see page 307.)

HINT: *If you have the optional full-color overhead-transparency packet for Set 3, you might want to review Overhead Transparencies 43 ("The Theater at Beth Shean") and 44 ("Scenes from the Theater") from Lesson 16. It would also be helpful to review briefly* **Digging Deeper IV** *in Lesson 19 to clarify the location of the Decapolis in relation to the Sea of Galilee.*

Overhead Transparency 21. Susita. This photograph is taken from Mount Arbel on the western shore of the Sea of Galilee near Tiberias. The hilltop where Susita (Hippos) was located is clearly visible on the eastern shore. Towering over the Sea of Galilee, Susita is connected to the other hills by a thin ridge. The city was built on a 35-acre plateau. On both sides of the ridge are deep wadi beds, and the western edge drops steeply to the sea. Today the area around Susita is called the Golan Heights. In the first century, this was the region called the Decapolis.

Susita had no running water, so an aqueduct more than 15 miles long was constructed to bring water into the city for its cisterns and fountains. The aqueduct, a significant achievement, was made of square stones with round openings inside, each fitting perfectly against the next one. Viewed from above, this peak and its connecting ridge look like a horse's head and neck. The Greek word for "horse" is *hippos,* and the Aramaic word is *susita* (mare)—hence the name of the city. In the time of Christ, this city was one of the modern Hellenistic cities of the Decapolis. Perched on its hill, Susita could be seen from other areas all around the sea, including Capernaum, where Jesus made His home. Susita's pagan temples and theater, magnificent Greek buildings, paved, colonnaded streets, and fountains probably made it inviting and forbidding at the same time. Jesus' deliberate choice to sail across the sea to visit Susita illustrates His desire to bring the good news of the kingdom to all people, including the pagans.

Somewhere in this area, Jesus met two demon-possessed men (Matthew 8:28–34; Mark 5:1–20; Luke 8:26–39). After He drove out the demons, Jesus sent these men home to tell others "how much God has done for you" (Luke 8:39). They told about their miraculous healing "all over town." No one knows for certain what town this refers to, but Susita is a probable choice because it was the nearest large city of the Decapolis. But whether Susita was the exact town or not, certainly it was one of the Decapolis cities where people heard the story of what Jesus had done (Mark 5:20). Some of Susita's citizens, who worshiped Zeus, Hera, and Tyche, among other deities, were attracted to the Jewish Rabbi from across the lake and followed Him. This city became a center of early Christianity. Susita itself had several large churches (at least five), which constitute the majority of the archaeological remains of the city.

Overhead Transparency 22. The Remains of Susita. Top: A Christian Church. This neatly arranged row of marble and basalt columns was part of a basilica church during the period after Jesus' time. The floor of the church was made of colored marble tiles arranged in geometric designs. This was one of several churches in Susita. In A.D. 747, an earthquake toppled these columns, and they still remain where they fell. Though this church was built after Jesus' time on earth, the beauty of these columns and their white marble bases and capitals testify to both the glory of the pagan Decapolis and the impact Jesus' ministry had in this region. It is possible that seeing the demon-possessed men become healed may have contributed to the conversion of these formerly pagan people (Matthew 8:28–34).

*Bottom: **The Sea from Susita.*** Susita was perched high above the Sea of Galilee and was clearly visible in areas all around the sea. Across the sea, the city of Tiberias—Herod Antipas's capital—sprawled down the hillside. The port of Susita was located below the city, on the shore of the sea. The economy of Susita was based on agriculture, especially grain production in the fertile heights above the sea. Tiberias was dependent on this grain, shipped across the sea from Susita. To the right, across the sea, is the plain of Gennesaret and the area of Jesus' ministry. (The steep cliff of Mount Arbel is between the plain and Tiberias.) The religious Jews of the region could clearly see the glory of this Decapolis city, a constant reminder of the Hellenistic values of the pagan world.

In the foreground are the remains of the basilica shown in the previous photo. We can clearly see the fallen columns and the marble floor. Beyond the ruins of the basilica are the fallen stones of a *nymphaeum*, or fountain building. These structures, often including statues of gods, were found in most Hellenistic cities. As these ruins illustrate, Jesus' determination to bring His message to the pagan people of His world as well as the religious people is a lesson for our own walk as His disciples: The gospel overcame the power of pagan values just as it overcame the demons in the man who lived near here (Mark 5:1–20).

Overhead Transparency 23. Hammat Gader. One ancient writer called the bath complex at Hammat Gader the second most beautiful in the world. This bath complex, which was probably connected to the Decapolis city of Gadara (Matthew 8:28), made use of the hot mineral springs that run from the foot of the nearby Gilead Mountains. The remains are from a century after Jesus was on earth, but they probably represent similar baths from earlier times, so they can help us understand the opulence of the Decapolis. Hammat (which means "hot springs") Gader (probably the same as "Gadara") is just five miles from the Sea of Galilee and not more than 15 miles from Capernaum, Jesus' hometown. The free-standing colonnade was part of the entrance to the bathing complex. Beyond the entrance is the first of at least eight pools in what was called the hall of pillars. According to the archaeologists who discovered it, this first pool probably contained warm mineral water as the first step in the therapy of the hot baths. On the upper part of the far wall are openings that probably held images of the gods believed to have the power to heal. People from around the world came to spas like this one (there was another in Tiberias, even closer to Jesus' home), not only for enjoyment but also for the cures its mineral waters were said to provide. The fact that many sick people thronged to Jesus for healing may be due in part to the presence of baths like this one in the area. When people found no cure in the baths, they sought the Rabbi whose healing powers were known in the Decapolis (Mark 7:31–37). The bath complex also included a theater and other buildings. There was a synagogue nearby, and although it was built after Jesus' time, it indicates the presence of a small Jewish community in the area.

Even though these pictures were taken long after New Testament times, the beauty of this place highlights the glory of the Hellenistic Decapolis, to which Jesus deliberately came to bring His message of spiritual and physical healing. Jesus brought the gospel to the people in this area because they needed the "therapy" that He alone could provide. Their pagan gods were empty hope. Jesus' example must become the model for His disciples today. Jesus' message is for the culture around us. No matter how sophisticated people become, we all need His healing power in spite of all the "cures" our culture proposes.

Overhead Transparency 24. Scenes from Hammat Gader. *Upper Left: **The Spring.*** The mineral-rich hot springs of Hammat Gader (part of the Gadara of the New Testament—see Matthew 8:28) still bubble up due to volcanic activity below the surface of the ground. The water is extremely hot, sometimes over 120 degrees Fahrenheit. In ancient times, it was mixed with colder water to make it comfortable. This process allowed for varied temperatures in the several pools of the complex. The water has an unusually high mineral content, which may have made it medicinal for some ailments.

*Upper Right: **Lepers' Pool.*** This small pool, isolated from the rest of the complex, is believed by archaeologists to be for people suffering from assorted skin diseases called "leprosy" in the Bible. Based on ancient descriptions of such a pool and the isolation of the pool itself, this identification seems sound. While people came to the pools to be cured of a variety of illnesses (either through the mineral baths or by the gods of healing who were worshiped here), leprosy was particularly dreaded because it rendered the sufferer unclean, at least in the Jewish community. Although there is no record that Jesus ever came to baths like these (this complex was constructed after His time), He did visit the Decapolis, and He did heal people of leprosy (Matthew 8:1–4).

*Lower Left: **Oval Pool.*** This large oval pool is the closest pool to the spring, making it the hottest of the baths. Bathers would not have stayed long in the very hot water with its high mineral content. The fountains along the sides were designed to provide a constant flow of water into the bath. The small chambers with arched roofs in the corners were bathing areas similar to modern hot tubs. Mineral water ran in constantly from the spring next door.

*Lower Right: **Hall of Fountains.*** The largest pool in the Hammat Gader complex was named the Hall of Fountains by archaeologists. This pool is more than 100 feet long. Many of the marble fountains are still in place. The hot water from the nearby spring ran through clay pipes and gushed out of the fountains into the pool. These 32 fountains originally had human or animal heads. Though the hall was constructed after Jesus' time, it represents the lifestyle of the people of the Decapolis.

Conclusion

Jesus deliberately confronted the evil powers of His time. He commanded His disciples to sail across the Sea of Galilee to the pagan Decapolis, a venture they must have dreaded. But Jesus knew there were people in the Decapolis who were Satan's captives. Rather than ignore them or avoid the place, Jesus used the power of God to defeat the power of evil. The demon-possessed men who met Jesus as He came ashore were among the first missionaries to the most pagan area of first-century Israel. Whether through the work of these early missionaries or through Jesus' teaching, many from the Decapolis came to believe in the Messiah.

As Christians, our calling and task are similar. We too must challenge the power of evil so prevalent in our society—we must not compromise with it or hide from it. Instead, we must seek it out, bringing the victorious power of the cross of Jesus to bear on it. As the formerly demon-possessed men did, we must testify to what God has done for us and what He can do for others. When it comes to sharing Christ's message, being a missionary is relatively simple. But it takes great conviction and courage to seek out and challenge evil in its lair.

Notes

1. Bargil Pixner's book *With Jesus Through Galilee According to the Fifth Gospel* (Rosh Pina, Israel: Corazin Publishing, 1992) provides an excellent treatment of the geographical and cultural setting of Jesus' teaching ministry. Pixner's description of the pagan Decapolis provides significant insight into Jesus' ministry there, especially His encounter with the men who were possessed by demons.

A FAR COUNTRY

The Decapolis is mentioned by name only three times in the New Testament. In addition to these three instances, on at least two other occasions, Jesus visited specific locations in the largely pagan league of cities to the east of the Sea of Galilee. While there is evidence of Jewish communities in these cities (most had synagogues, although these were constructed long after Jesus' time), it seems clear that this area was considered pagan by those Jews who were devoted to Israel's God and His Torah as the guide for their lives. Jesus' visits to the Decapolis can help us understand some aspects of His ministry that would not be as clear if they had occurred in Jerusalem, Capernaum, or some other "orthodox" Jewish site. There is a lot we do not know about the Decapolis, but we know enough to be enlightened concerning Jesus' visits to this Hellenistic area.

ORIGIN OF THE DECAPOLIS

Many of the cities that would come to be known as the "10 cities" (*Decapolis* in Greek) were founded by the Greek settler-soldiers of the Ptolemaic and Seleucid kingdoms. These kingdoms were sections of the empire of Alexander the Great, divided among his generals after his death. His dream of "Hellenizing" (making Greek) the entire world did not die with him. The dynasties that followed him were as devoted to Greek ideals as he was, each integrating the local customs and practices into their particular cultures.

The Seleucids settled in Persia and Syria, just to the north of Israel, and the Ptolemies settled to the south, in Egypt. The soldiers of these kingdoms founded many cities throughout Israel, and other cities simply became Hellenized due to their influence. The Maccabean revolt—and the support of this revolt by the Hasidim, those fiercely devoted to Yahweh and the Torah—was in large part a reaction to the attempts of these Greek-thinking kingdoms to convert the Jews to their pagan values and practices.

In 64-63 B.C., the Roman general Pompey brought the entire Near East under Rome's dominion. He incorporated the Greek cities east of the Sea of Galilee (and one city, Beth Shean—renamed Scythopolis—that was east of the Jordan River, just south of the sea) into a league of cities known as the Decapolis. Before that time, during the Maccabean period (167–63 B.C.), many of these cities had resented the attempts of religious Jews to convert them to their religion and practices. When Rome assumed control of the area, the pagans were pleased to finally receive autonomy from the religious fanatics. Though Caesar Augustus later gave two of the cities to Herod, the king of the Jews, for a little while, throughout New Testament times, these 10 cities remained a league of free city-states under the umbrella of Roman authority.

Although for much of its history the Decapolis actually comprised more than 10 cities, it retained its designation as the "10 cities." Many of the cities are familiar to the New Testament reader: Damascus, Philadelphia (modern Amman), Scythopolis (Beth Shean), Gadara (Gadarenes), Pella, and Gerasa (Geresenes). Hippos (Susita) was a major Decapolis city overlooking the Sea of Galilee from the east, but it is not directly mentioned in the New Testament. These cities, while joined as a league by the Romans to control the trade route that went from Arabia to Damascus and to provide protection for the eastern frontier, had a large measure of local autonomy. They minted their own coins, had jurisdiction over a large area, and ruled their own affairs. The culture of these prosperous cities was Hellenistic in all its Roman glory.

HELLENISM AND THE DECAPOLIS

Alexander the Great had a mission: He wanted the whole world to be under the influence of Greek culture in religion, language, philosophy, political structure, and values. He died before he could make his dream a reality, but his successors accomplished his goal to a large degree. Much of the known world, including many of the people of the land of Israel, adopted Greek ways, although they modified them with local beliefs. Greek cultural institutions were established in many cities, including Jerusalem. Theaters became common and popular. The rabbis of Israel forbade attendance at these theaters because their dramas portrayed the myths of Greek and Roman gods, contained erotic themes common to Hellenism, and were performed in connection with pagan religious festivals, which included sacrifices to the gods. Gymnasiums, the Greek educational institutions, appeared in many cities, including Jerusalem, not far from the Temple. In the gymnasium, the Greek ideal of training people's bodies and minds was put into practice. Students studied the philosophy of classical Greece, received athletic training, and competed—naked—in athletic events.

The Greek educational system was remarkably effective, instilling Greek ideals into entire generations of young Jewish people. Busts of Greek gods and heroes celebrated the ultimate ideal: the human form. Young Jews read Homer, Euripides, and Plato to absorb their values. They also learned to draw and sculpt, often creating the forms of Greek gods. Because Greek mythology offered heroes and role models who competed with the Jew's biblical ancestors, the Pharisees, devoted to keeping God's people faithful to Torah, constantly admonished young Jews intrigued by Greek culture.

Hellenistic cities had stadiums for the public display of athletic contests. Temples were built to honor local gods, and festivals were held to celebrate pagan holidays. In the midst of these attractions, the faithful Jewish population struggled to maintain its beliefs. The latest architecture and artistic designs made the Hellenized cities of the Decapolis seem very attractive and modern. People from the small villages of Galilee must have been awed by the marble streets, mosaic floors, running water, and fountains. In these cities and even in nearby regions, Hellenism influenced much of everyday life. In fact, the Greek language became the common tongue of the economic world.

Few people did more to bring these Hellenistic ideas to the Jews than

Herod the Great and his sons. Though they kept a few Jewish "rules" to pacify their religious subjects (e.g., they did not put their "images" on coins and apparently avoided eating pork), the Herods built theaters, stadiums, and gymnasiums. It fell to the faithful Jews to resist these cultural institutions and the values they brought. As a result, the Pharisees adopted increasingly detailed laws to remain faithful to Torah; the Zealots resisted Hellenism more and more violently; and the Essenes withdrew into isolated communities. By contrast, the Sadducees, while maintaining the prescribed Temple ceremonies, often became as Hellenistic as the pagans. Supporters of the Herods, the Herodians, also enjoyed the Hellenistic lifestyle their overlords created.

The Decapolis city-states were satisfied with their freedom under Roman authority. They could enjoy their Greek practices, from sacrificing in their temples to eating pork (also used for sacrifices). Rome provided support for their cultural practices and helped them resist the seemingly outdated worldview of the Jews. One of the most magnificent of the Decapolis cities, Hippos, sitting high on a hill, could be clearly seen across the Sea of Galilee by the fishermen of Capernaum and other villages around the sea. Ironically, this area would become a vital center for the early church.

At its core, Hellenism was humanism. It glorified human beings above all other creatures and portrayed the human body as the ultimate in physical beauty. Truth could be known only through the human mind, and pleasure was a crucial goal in life. Hellenism's values permeated the gymnasium and its excellent system of education, the theater, and the games in the arena. The majestic Romanized forms of Hellenistic architecture must have seemed harmless enough, but its temples glorified the excesses of pleasure.

The religious Jews of Galilee struggled against this pagan worldview. Seeing the exceptionally modern perspective of Hellenism can help us understand their struggle. It can also help us understand (not excuse) the legalistic excesses of some of the Pharisees. (How many parents make a multitude of rules to help their children avoid the temptations of modern society?) The glorification of sexuality, violence, wealth, and the human form, and the view that only what the human mind can understand and formulate can possibly be true, is the value system of humanism. The followers of Jesus today still wrestle with this worldview. In the process of struggling against its seductive power, some Christians become pharisaic; others escape to small, "safe" communities; some even resort to violence.

But Jesus wants us to follow His example. He sailed across the sea and confronted evil directly to bring His message of love to the Hellenistic Decapolis.

THE DECAPOLIS AND RELIGIOUS JEWS

It is clear from ancient records that the religious Jews of Jesus' day opposed the values and practices of Hellenism. The struggle of the Pharisees to avoid all uncleanness, while often creating a lack of love for those who were suffering, at heart may have included a desire to resist the pagan views of their neighbors. (The problem of the Pharisees was that they often hated the sinner along with the sin—a dilemma that is not entirely ancient.) The presence of pigs in the Decapolis (Mark 5:11) would certainly have made the area offensive and off-limits to those who followed Torah.

Bargil Pixner, a noted scholar on Galilee, has pointed out an ancient religious tradition that helps clarify the Jewish view of the pagan Decapolis.[1] He noted that in the Talmud and in the writings of the church fathers, the people of this area were described as belonging to the seven pagan Canaanite nations driven out of the Promised Land by Joshua and the Israelites (Joshua 3:10; Acts 13:19). These nations worshiped Baal and ate (and sacrificed) pigs (Isaiah 65:3–5, 66:3). Apparently, the pagan practices of the people of the Decapolis and their anti-God values seemed to be continuations of the practices of the Canaanites, who used sexual perversions and even child sacrifice in their worship. It is probable that the people of Jesus' day, who took their Scriptures seriously, viewed the Decapolis as very pagan. Although we do not know how many Jews actually believed that the people of the Decapolis were the descendants of the Canaanites, the fact that there is a link between the blasphemous practices of these two peoples helps establish the validity of this Jewish view.

JESUS AND THE DECAPOLIS

The Bible records two of Jesus' visits to the Decapolis. It also mentions crowds of people from the Decapolis following Jesus. Understanding the pagan world represented by these city-states helps us see the significance of Jesus' response to it. His message clearly was for the inhabitants of the Decapolis, for they heard and followed. He confronted the darkness of the pagan world in choosing to visit its people.

Given the Jewish view of the paganism of the Decapolis, it probably was not surprising to the disciples that as soon as He landed there, Jesus met a man (Matthew referred to two men) possessed with a "legion" of demons (Matthew 8:28–34; Mark 5:1–20; Luke 8:26–39). Jesus had just stilled the storm, which the disciples probably also believed was fueled by the powers of evil connected to the depths of the sea (Luke 8:31; Revelation 13:1). The devil was unable to prevent Jesus from crossing the sea to enter the pagan territory, so his demonic power confronted Jesus when He came ashore. But Jesus pierced the power of darkness that lay over the demon-possessed man.

When Jesus had cast out the demons, He commanded the man to return home to tell others what God had done for him. The territory to which Jesus sent the man was certainly one of the most challenging mission fields to which He ever called anyone. Later, crowds from the Decapolis followed Jesus. This crowd of followers was perhaps a testimony to the effectiveness of the healed man's witness. (Mark 7:31–36 and Matthew 15:30 record the same event. Matthew referred to crowds of people, but he did not mention the place.)

It is possible that the "distant" country Jesus referred to in His parable of the prodigal son was the Decapolis (Luke 15:11–32). Certainly, it was distant in its values and beliefs. It was definitely a place for "wild living," and it had plenty of pigs that needed to be fed. For the son, it would be only a short walk from the Decapolis back home to his forgiving father. No one knows whether this is the country Jesus had in mind in the parable, but certainly the lifestyle of the Decapolis fits the parable's description.

CONCLUSION

Many visitors to Galilee are amazed at how close Jesus' area of ministry was to the pagan Decapolis. Jesus did not avoid the people living in darkness (Matthew 4:16). He went to them and pierced the darkness of their sinful lifestyle with the light of God's message of salvation and love.

Jesus wants us to follow His example in confronting the darkness in our own world. The power of Satan and his demons seems overwhelming. It would be easy for us to isolate ourselves in safe, rule-bound communities and just let the outside world destroy itself. But even though rules can be good and community is necessary for Christian living, Jesus used neither as an escape. He modeled another way for us as His followers. He left the familiarity of His community and confronted evil on its own turf.

Such a display of God's power still can and does happen today, when we confront the darkness in our society with the message of what God, through Jesus, has done for us (Mark 5:19).

NOTES

1. Bargil Pixner's book *With Jesus Through Galilee According to the Fifth Gospel* (Rosh Pina, Israel: Corazin Publishing, 1992) provides an excellent treatment of the ministry of Jesus in the geographical and cultural setting of Galilee. It is highly recommended for anyone who wants to better understand the significance of Jesus' teaching. The meaning of Jesus' confrontation with the demons of the Decapolis, found in this handout, is based on Pixner's work.

GATES OF HELL

For the Teacher

The Christian community is often ineffective in facing and challenging the problems in the society around us. Sometimes we hide in safe, secure groups and try to avoid the challenges. At other times, we compromise with evil, in effect joining with the forces of evil and losing all our influence. This study reviews the last truth Jesus taught His disciples before He left for Jerusalem to die: His church—His community—would overcome the very gates of hell if its faith remained in Jesus the Messiah and if its methods were His methods. Christians need to take this lesson to heart as we struggle to maintain our values. We are to be on the offensive if we follow Jesus.

Ask your students if they have ever confronted particular sins or evil in their communities. If they have examples, ask a few students to share them with the rest of the class. Help draw out students' answers by asking questions such as, "What was the effect of your confrontation?" and, "Did that experience change your life in any way?" Remind your students of heroes like Elijah, David, Esther, Martin Luther, Dietrich Bonhoeffer, and others who made a significant impact by confronting evil in God's name. If you can, think of someone in your own community who acted against evil (e.g., pornography, abortion, crime, or racism) and made a difference. When you have pointed out and discussed these examples with your students, tell them that such confrontation is the focus of this study: We are called to boldly challenge evil in Jesus' name. In the power of His Word, we can be effective.

Your Objectives for This Lesson

At the completion of this section, you will want your students:

To Know/Understand

1. The geography of northern Israel.
2. The history and geography of Caesarea Philippi.
3. The religious practices found at Caesarea Philippi in Jesus' time.
4. How the location of Jesus' teaching helps us picture the rock on which the church is built and the task of the church to confront the gates of hell.
5. How Jesus challenged the power of the devil.
6. Why the Savior is called Jesus Christ.

To Do

1. Determine if their faith is in Jesus Christ (Messiah) as He revealed Himself.
2. Be committed to recognizing evil and challenging it in Jesus' name.
3. Choose a particular form of evil to confront, and develop a strategy to meet it.
4. Learn to use the self-sacrificing method Jesus did.
5. Become more skilled in the use of the weapons Jesus gave us for this battle.

How to Plan for This Lesson

Because of the volume of material in this lesson, you may need to divide it into several class sessions. To help you determine how to do that, the lesson has been broken into segments. Note that the time needed may vary significantly, depending on elements such as the leader, the size of the class, and the interest level of the class.

If you wish to cover the entire lesson in one session, you should complete Unit One. This unit provides a guided discussion covering the major points in the video. It does not go into great depth. If you wish greater depth on any of the points in Unit One, they are covered more thoroughly in the remainder of the material.

How to Prepare for This Lesson

Materials Needed

Student copies of the maps:	"Land of Jesus' Ministry" "Galilee of Jesus' Ministry" "The Roman World"
Overhead transparencies:	"Land of Jesus' Ministry" "Galilee of Jesus' Ministry" "The Roman World"

Student copies of the handout: "The Fertility Cults of Canaan"

Video: **Gates of Hell**

Overhead projector, screen, TV, VCR

1. Make copies of the maps listed above for your students.

2. Prepare the overhead transparencies listed above. (You'll find them at the back of the book.)

3. Make copies of the handout listed above for your students. (If possible, students should receive and read this handout before the lesson.)

4. Review the geography of the lands of the Bible from the "Introduction."

5. Determine which **unit** and which **Digging Deeper** sections, if any, you want to use in your class session(s). NOTE: You can use these sections in any order you wish (e.g., you might want to use **Digging Deeper III**, but not **Digging Deeper I** or **Digging Deeper II**).

6. Prepare your classroom ahead of time, setting up and testing an overhead projector and screen (for the overhead transparencies) and a TV and VCR. If you plan to hand out biblical references for your students to look up and read aloud, prepare 3x5 cards (one reference per card) to distribute before class.

Lesson Plan

UNIT ONE: Video Review

1. Introductory Comments

This lesson explores Jesus' teaching that the church will be built on a rock and the gates of hell will not overcome it. The emphasis of this lesson is on being rooted in Jesus as Christ (Messiah) and being committed to going out to meet the evil of our world and to defeat it by the power of Jesus' name. The geographical setting of Jesus' teaching helps us picture more clearly His intended meaning for the disciples and for our lives. It is possible that Jesus' choice of location was designed to give His disciples a picture of His lesson to them. This picture should become clear for each of you as you seek to follow Jesus the Messiah.

2. Show the Video *Gates of Hell* (19 minutes)

3. Map Study: Caesarea Philippi

HINT: *Begin this map study session by reviewing the geography of the overall region and working down to the city the lesson is dealing with—Caesarea Philippi.*

Using the overhead transparency "Land of Jesus' Ministry," point out the following areas, and have your students locate them on their maps.

> Jerusalem
> Nazareth
> Capernaum
> Galilee
> Sea of Galilee
> Caesarea Philippi
> Mount Hermon
> Decapolis

Using the overhead transparency "Galilee of Jesus' Ministry," point out the following areas, and have your students locate them on their maps.

> Sea of Galilee
> Capernaum
> Jordan River (north of the Sea of Galilee)
> Jordan River (south of the Sea of Galilee)
> Caesarea Philippi
> Dan
> Mount Hermon

4. Guided Discussion: Jesus and Caesarea Philippi

Caesarea Philippi was a thoroughly pagan place, complete with temples to the god Pan and other gods. The strong belief in pagan gods in this area was due in part to the great mountain cliff on which the city stood and the great spring that ran out of a cave in that cliff. This water and its underground source fit the ancient belief that the gods were in the underworld. This cave possibly was seen as the "gateway" to that world. Jesus came here to challenge the pagan view so that His disciples would recognize Him as Messiah and accept His way of redeeming a broken world.

a. Have your students read Matthew 16:13; Mark 8:27; 1 Kings 12:25–30. Then ask them to answer the following questions:

   1. Where did Jesus take the disciples?

   2. What did Jesus choose to do when they got to this place?

   Point out that this was a thoroughly pagan area. The fertility god Pan was worshiped not far from where King Jeroboam of Israel had set up a golden calf many years before.

b. Have your students read Matthew 16:13–20; Mark 8:27–30; Luke 9:18–21. Then ask them to answer the following questions:

   1. Why do you think Jesus asked His disciples this question? What was the significance of Peter's response (on behalf of all the disciples)? NOTE: This was the first time during Jesus' teaching ministry that the disciples professed that He was the Messiah.

   2. Have you ever professed that Jesus is God's Christ and your Messiah? *(Messiah* and *Christ* mean the same thing.)* If so, what impact has that profession had in your life?

c. Have your students read Jeremiah 10:1–5; Matthew 16:16. Then ask them to answer the following questions:

   1. According to these verses, what are some major differences between God and the idols of the pagan nations surrounding Israel?

   2. Why was Caesarea Philippi, with its location and its many idols, an appropriate place for Peter to declare Jesus the Son of the living God? How does the location help you understand this reality?

   3. What are some of the "gods" of your culture? Are they living? How do you know your God is "living"?

d. Have your students read Matthew 16:13–20. Then ask them to answer the following questions:

   1. On what did Jesus promise to build His church? What is this rock that Jesus spoke of? NOTE: Different church traditions hold different views regarding the identity of this rock. In the opinion of the author, each tradition is emphasizing a different aspect of the rock image. Two major viewpoints are listed below.

      • Peter (representing all the disciples) is the rock—Ephesians 2:20–21
      • Peter's profession that Jesus is the Christ, the Son of the living God, is the rock—1 Corinthians 3:10–14; Acts 4:11

   2. How will the church on its rock replace the gods on the rock where Jesus taught the lesson? (Possible answer: God will enable the church to destroy the power of evil and replace it with the truth of Jesus.)

   3. What challenge will the church be faced with? NOTE: The term *Hades* is used to refer to more than one thing in the Bible. By Jesus' time, it probably referred to evil forces arrayed against God. If this is the case, "the gates of Hades" would refer to the power of hell or of Satan (or the devil). (Some versions translate it as the "gates of hell.")

   4. Who will win this confrontation?

   5. What is the significance of the imagery used here when you consider what gates do? Do they ever attack? If the gates of Hades will not overcome (some versions say " . . . will not be

stronger than . . ."), who is attacking whom? What, then, is Jesus' mission for His church? For you personally?

6. Is today's Christian community on the offensive against sin and evil, or does it take a defensive position? Give some examples to support your answer. Why do you think the church takes the position it does? What position should we be taking?

7. Where do you meet the "gates of Hades" in your life? What do you do when you are confronted by this evil? Do you think you have the correct response?

8. Think of specific sins and evils you could be confronting in your own community. Discuss your examples with the rest of the class. What would you have to do to challenge this evil? What can you do?

9. Read 1 John 2:13–14, 3:7–8, and 4:4. How do these verses encourage you?

10. Why do you think Jesus chose such a pagan place to teach this lesson?

e. Have your students read Matthew 16:18–28; Luke 10:17–18; Hebrews 4:12. Then ask them to answer the following questions:

1. What did Jesus begin to teach immediately after He taught the disciples about the rock? What is the connection between the two lessons?

2. What was Jesus' method of defeating Satan and sin and death (the "gates of Hades")?

3. What are the method and source of strength we've been given?

f. Spend a few moments in prayer. Ask God to confirm Jesus as Messiah, Son of the living God, to you. If you want to, take this moment to tell God that you believe Jesus is the Christ. Ask God to give you the courage and wisdom you need to recognize the "gates of Hades," the presence of sin and evil around you. Pray that you will have the insight you need to know how to challenge sin and evil, using Jesus' methods.

UNIT TWO
Step One: "Caesarea Philippi—A Religious Place"

1. Introductory Comments

Certain places in the ancient Near East were considered religious. Jerusalem has been a religious center since Solomon built the first Temple there. Bethel took on religious significance when Jacob had a dream revealing God's presence in that place (Genesis 28:10–22). The location where the video *Gates of Hell* was filmed, Caesarea Philippi, was also a very religious place, but it was generally the pagan religions that made it important. The combination of natural springs and historical events created a sense of sacredness in the northern part of the land of Israel. This study investigates that sense of sacredness, along with Jesus' choice to come to this area to give His final instructions to His disciples before He went to Jerusalem to die. The next study will explore those instructions themselves in more detail.

2. Show the Video *Gates of Hell* (19 minutes)

3. Map Study: Caesarea Philippi

HINT: *Begin this map study session by reviewing the geography of the overall region and working down to the city the lesson is dealing with—Caesarea Philippi.*

Using the overhead transparency "The Roman World," point out the following areas, and have your students locate them on their maps.

> Rome
> Mediterranean Sea
> Egypt
> Judea
> Caesarea

Using the overhead transparency "Land of Jesus' Ministry," point out the following areas, and have your students locate them on their maps.

> Jerusalem
> Nazareth
> Capernaum
> Galilee
> Sea of Galilee
> Caesarea Philippi
> Mount Hermon
> Decapolis
> Dan

Using the overhead transparency "Galilee of Jesus' Ministry," point out the following areas, and have your students locate them on their maps.

> Sea of Galilee
> Decapolis
> Capernaum
> Chorazin
> Bethsaida
> Gamla
> Tiberias
> Jordan River (north of the Sea of Galilee)
> Jordan River (south of the Sea of Galilee)
> Caesarea Philippi

OPTIONAL — Digging Deeper I: The Religious History of Dan and Caesarea Philippi *(15–30 minutes)*

A. Preparation

Students should read the handout "The Fertility Cults of Canaan" before beginning this study.

B. Introduction

The religious importance of Caesarea Philippi was partly related to the history of the city of Dan, only three miles away. Its history takes us back to the Old Testament. **HINT:** *For teachers who* *have the optional overhead-transparency packets from Sets 1 and 2 of this series, the following transparencies give further detail on the city of Dan: Set 1—Overhead Transparencies 10, 11, 12, 13, and 15; Set 2—Overhead Transparency 18.*

C. Guided Discussion: The History of Idolatry in Northern Israel

1. Read Judges 18:1–2,11–17,27–31. Point out the following information, and ask students to answer the questions listed:

   - God gave the tribe of Dan the territory in the Shephelah between the Philistines and the tribe of Judah, but they did not capture this land. They decided to go to a place other than where God had placed them.

   - They brought idols with them and set up a worship center for them.

     a. What happens when people do not complete the task to which God has called them?

     b. How do you think the failure of the tribe of Dan to follow God's assignment for them was related to their idol worship?

   - The city of Dan, at the northern border of Israel, was the first city to fall to the nations God sent to punish His people for idol worship (1 Kings 15:20); so, in fact, Dan's suffering was increased by the tribe's failure to follow God.

2. After Solomon's death, the nation of Israel split into two kingdoms: Israel in the north and Judah in the south. Read 1 Kings 12:25–30. Point out the following information:

   - The Canaanite people put symbols of their gods on the backs of calves or bulls. Jeroboam tried to combine this Canaanite practice with the worship of Yahweh by using the statue of a calf but not putting a god image on it.

     a. Read 1 Kings 20:25,34; 16:18–19,26,31; 22:52–53; and 2 Kings 10:31; 13:2,11; 14:24; 15:9,18,24,28.

   - The calf worship Jeroboam established in Dan (and Bethel) opened the door to Baal worship throughout Israel. Dan remained a center of idolatry and a symbol of the worship of Canaan's fertility gods.

OPTIONAL — Digging Deeper II: The Physical Setting of Idolatry in Northern Israel *(15–30 minutes)*

A. Lecture

Baal, the fertility god of the Canaanites, was believed to be the supreme god because he had defeated the sea god. Baal was in control of fertility in particular because of his power over the weather. He is often depicted with a lightning bolt in his hand. One source describes him as the "one who rides on the clouds." (In Psalm 68:4, Yahweh is described in the same way, demonstrating His superiority over Baal). Baal's supposed ability to provide rain in a dry country was the main attraction for his worshipers. God often displayed His power to control water and rain, possibly to show the people that Yahweh, not Baal, is God.

B. Guided Discussion

Read the following passages, and point out the accompanying information to your students.

- Joshua 3:15–17—God showed His power over the Jordan River when it was at flood stage due to spring rains that the Canaanites thought Baal had caused.

- 1 Kings 17:1,24; 18:38,41–45—God displayed His control over the rain. Remember that ancient peoples believed that lightning was fire from heaven.

- Judges 5:19–21—Deborah defeated the Canaanites, and again God showed His power over the floodwaters.

- 2 Kings 2:8,11–14—Through the power of God, Elijah and Elisha divided the waters of the Jordan River.

Convey the following information to your students, and ask them to answer (individually or in small groups) the accompanying questions.

1. Near the city of Dan lies a fountainhead of the Jordan River. Its enormous freshwater springs attracted Baal worshipers because they believed Baal had provided them. Naturally, they would want to worship their fertility god near such an abundance of life-giving water.

   - In our day and age, are there certain physical settings that lend themselves to pagan practices? If so, where?

   - Have you seen God's power demonstrate itself in these places? Explain.

   - Considering that God intended Israel to defeat Baal and gain possession of Dan and the area surrounding it, what can we learn about our responsibility to reclaim our world for God? Can you think of an example of someone who reclaimed a part of our world for God? Discuss your answer with the class.

2. The cult center at Dan, dating from the time of the judges, remained a place to worship until New Testament times. Three miles away, at Caesarea Philippi, another fertility god was worshiped near a spring that was also a source of the Jordan River.

4. Caesarea Philippi and the Pagan God Pan

a. Lecture

A cave dedicated to Pan, fertility god of mountains and forests, was near Caesarea Philippi around 200 B.C. The people of this region probably considered Pan to be the supreme god. The ancient name of Caesarea Philippi was Panias, named after Pan. Later, Herod built a temple near the cave in honor of Augustus. After Herod's death, the territory was given to Herod Philip. Philip founded a city here, which he named Caesarea. Since there was another Caesarea on the Mediterranean (built by his father), he called his city Caesarea of Philip, or Caesarea Philippi. The town (there may have been several other towns or residential areas nearby) was built around several sacred shrines to Pan.

Caesarea Philippi was located at the foot of one of the ridges of Mount Hermon. A rock cliff formed a backdrop to the town. In the face of the cliff was a large cave from which an underground river emerged, soon becoming the Jordan River. It was on the flat area in front of this cliff that Pan was worshiped. It is possible that this is the place where Baal of the Old Testament was worshiped as well (Joshua 11:17, 12:7). The huge stream gushing from the cave would certainly have made the place appealing to Baal worshipers as an entrance to the underworld, since they believed he went there every year, causing the dry season. The Greeks who worshiped Pan apparently believed the same thing. Idols of Pan, Athena, and Aphrodite have been unearthed here. This indicates that the fertility rituals continued into New Testament times. On the cliff face, niches (small, scalloped openings for statues or idols) had been carved for images of Pan, his nymphs, and the goddesses of the fertility cults (including Nemesis from Phoenicia, the home of Asherah and Baal). An ancient Jewish legend claims that a gate here would fall with the coming of the Messiah and the water would turn to blood. This is probably based on rituals performed at the Pan shrine and temple and the pagan belief that the cave was the gate to the underworld.

b. Guided Discussion

Point out the following information to your students.

- Caesarea Philippi was a very pagan city. The worship practices of the Old Testament Canaanites were continued here during New Testament times, though under different names.

- The cliff or rock face had at least two temples against it, with many niches for the gods and goddesses.

- The people established a religious center here, apparently because of the water that gushed from the cave.

Ask your students to read Matthew 16:13 and Mark 8:27. Then point out the following information and have your students answer the question.

- The Bible does not say that Jesus went directly to the religious shrine at Caesarea Philippi, but Mark's reference to "villages around Caesarea Philippi" probably indicates that Jesus was nearby. The area of Caesarea Philippi is fairly small, so Jesus certainly must have been close to Pan's cave. Why do you think Jesus would go to such a pagan area? (There is no certain answer. He may have wanted to escape the crowds. Also, the message He gave His disciples here fits well in this pagan place.)

c. Prayer

Spend a few moments in prayer. Ask God for the courage to face the pagan values that exist in our culture without compromising our commitment to Jesus.

Step Two: "The Church Will Prevail"

1. Lecture

Jesus brought His disciples to pagan Caesarea Philippi to give them one of the most profound lessons He would teach them. In a way, it was the climax of His teaching ministry. From this point on, Jesus' path took Him to Jerusalem, where He would die. Hearing Jesus' words in this ungodly area probably made even more of an impact on His audience. The geographical setting helps us to understand the calling Jesus gave to every disciple who would follow Him.

2. Guided Discussion: Peter's Confession

Jesus left the religious area of Galilee and went to Caesarea Philippi. It is important to remember that this was a thoroughly pagan place, devoted to the worship of pagan gods since Old Testament times.

a. Ask your students to read Matthew 16:13–20; Mark 8:27–30; Luke 9:18–21. Then have them answer the following questions.

- How do you think the disciples felt when Jesus asked this question? Why do you think Peter answered the way he did on behalf of himself and the other disciples?

- Read Luke 9:7–8. How significant is the contrast between Peter's confession and the information Herod Antipas received?

b. Ask your students to read Matthew 11:2–3; Luke 2:11, 2:26, 4:41; John 4:29. Then point out the following information and have them answer the questions.

- The events described in the passages above took place before Jesus' visit to Caesarea Philippi. Who had recognized Jesus as Messiah?

- Read John 1:41. This is the only other place where someone—in this case, Jesus' disciple Andrew—recognized Him as Messiah.

- Read Mark 1:34 and Luke 4:41. Jesus would not allow the demons to speak because they knew He was the Christ. Jesus apparently wanted to hide the fact that He was Messiah, either because people (like the Zealots) might not understand the kind of king He was (John 6:15) or because He wanted to *demonstrate* that He was Messiah (John 10:38).

- Read Matthew 16:16. It appears that this is the first time (after Andrew's comment noted above) that Jesus' disciples professed that He was Messiah. NOTE: There are earlier references to Jesus Christ, but these are the assertions of the Gospel writers, some years after the events took place, and not of the people who were involved at the time.

- Read Matthew 16:21. After Peter's profession that Jesus was the Christ, what did Jesus do? Why would Peter's profession lead into Christ's redemptive work? What can you learn from this example? (Possible answer: Professing Jesus as Messiah must precede being used of Him and becoming an instrument of His redemptive power.)

Ask students to talk about their own experiences of professing Jesus as Messiah. Ask them to tell what resulted from their experiences.

- Read Jeremiah 10:1–5 and Matthew 16:16. Pan was in charge of all gods, many of whom had been worshiped at Caesarea Philippi for centuries. What is the difference between God and an idol like Pan?

- Read Matthew 16:16 again. The events in this passage took place in the very pagan area of Caesarea Philippi, near the shrine, niches, and statues of Pan and other gods. Knowing that, which word in the passage do you think should be accented? (Have someone read the verse stressing the word *living*.) How does the location help you to see more clearly the meaning of Peter's confession? (Answer: Not only is Jesus the Christ [Messiah], but He's also the Son of the living God.) What are some of the "gods" of our culture? Are they living? What leads you to answer the way you do? What evidence can you point to that proves your God is living? How can you share that conviction?

Thought to Ponder: Pagan worship centers were located at Caesarea Philippi because a river ran out of the cave there. Pagans related this "living" water to the power and vitality of their own gods, who were actually dead. When we see flowing streams, they should remind us of the source of our "living water," Jesus Christ (John 4:14).

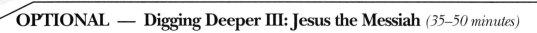

OPTIONAL — Digging Deeper III: Jesus the Messiah *(35–50 minutes)*

A. Guided Discussion

As English-speaking Christians, we refer to our Savior as Jesus Christ. Although we use these two names with all the respect and devotion God's Son deserves, many of us miss the richness of the meaning behind them because we do not understand their cultural background.

1. *Jesus* is the English form of the name found in Greek versions of the New Testament. The Hebrew name for "Jesus" was *Yeshua,* a shortened version of the word *Y'hoshua.* The word means "Yahweh saves" and is translated in English as *Joshua.* The Hebrew word *yoshia* means "He will save" and is also related to *Yeshua,* the name Jesus went by among His contemporaries. Today many Jewish Christians call the Savior "Yeshua" to emphasize His Jewish nature and the Jewish setting of the New Testament.

   Ask your students to read the following passages and answer the questions:

   * Matthew 1:21 (see also Luke 1:31). How does understanding the Hebrew version of Jesus' name help you to understand this passage better? How did Jesus (*Yeshua*) live up to His name?

2. *Christ* is the English translation of the Greek word *Christos. Christos* means the same thing as the Hebrew *Mashiach,* which in English is "Messiah." Therefore, "Messiah" and "Christ" are the same. Although "Christ" is used more often, "Messiah" reflects the Hebrew setting of Jesus' ministry.

   The word *messiah,* or *christ,* means "anointed" and is rooted in the Old Testament. It refers to the pouring (anointing) of oil on those marked by God as uniquely qualified for a task or office. This anointing was a symbol of the authority a person received from God. Every anointed person (e.g., prophets, priests, and kings) was in that sense *a* messiah. The prophets predicted that one day God would send His deliverer as "the ultimate Messiah," combining the roles of prophet, priest, and king.

   In Jesus' day, it was the kingly role of Messiah that was emphasized. The people longed for a military leader like David, who would deliver them from the political oppression they endured under the Romans, the Herods, and their supporters. This is probably the reason Jesus hid His identity as Messiah. It also explains the learning process the disciples went through: from identifying Jesus' messianic office as military and political to seeing His role as the suffering servant, bringing about His kingdom in God's way. It is in suffering that Jesus fulfilled the task for which God had anointed Him (Messiah—Christ).

   Ask your students to read the following passages and answer the questions:

   * 1 Kings 19:16; 1 Samuel 16:6,13; Exodus 29:7–9. What types of people were anointed in Old Testament times?

   * Zechariah 6:13. What roles would *the* Messiah fill?

   * Micah 5:2 and Matthew 2:4–6. Where would the Messiah be born?

   * Matthew 3:16–17. What might Jesus' baptism mean with regard to His role as Messiah? (Messiah is equipped for a task and given God's authority.)

   * John 1:41 and 4:25. Only twice did the writers of the Greek manuscripts retain the Hebrew word for "anointed." What conclusions can you draw about the people speaking in these two passages?

   * Luke 24:45–46; Acts 10:36–38; Acts 1:6–7. How did the disciples learn that the Messiah was sent by God to suffer? How do you know they learned it?

- Matthew 16:16,21–22. Peter (speaking for the other disciples) recognized Jesus as Christ (Messiah). At that point, did he understand God's way? How do you know? Why do you think Jesus picked this moment to begin explaining His need to suffer?

- Isaiah 53:1–12. What kind of life did the Old Testament prophets predict the Messiah would have? Why was it so difficult, then, for the people of Jesus' day (including the disciples) to understand what the Messiah was called to do?

- Mark 9:33–37, 10:41–45; John 13:14–17; Matthew 5:39, 10:38. As followers of Messiah, how are we called to live?

3. The disciples had a hard time accepting a suffering Messiah who served others and even gave His life for them. As His followers, we are called to be like Him. Our acceptance of Jesus as the Messiah God declared Him to be is manifested in our willingness to be salt and light to the world by serving others. This call to emulate Jesus seems obvious but is difficult for us to fulfill. Have your students answer the following questions:

- Do you believe Jesus is Messiah (Christ) as God revealed Him? If so, how should your life show your faith in Him? How well does your life show it?

- Give some examples of people who truly accept Jesus as Christ and who show this acceptance by their willingness to follow Him in serving and suffering for others. Discuss your answers with the class. Think of some ways you could show a serving attitude toward others. Ask God to help you take these steps to follow Christ's example.

B. Conclusion

To believe in Jesus (*Yeshua*) is to accept His work of saving sinners from sin. To believe in Christ (Messiah, *Mashiach*) is to confess that He was chosen and equipped by God for His office as prophet, priest, and king. Jesus accomplished the task He was sent to do by serving others and suffering for them, even unto death. Following Christ means accepting His command to suffer for Him and to serve others on His behalf. When we do these things, we truly are Christian ("Christlike").

3. Guided Discussion: "On This Rock . . ."

The "rock" on which the church is built has been the subject of many writings throughout the history of Christianity. The purpose of this study is not to explore deeply the various opinions on this subject but to consider an additional metaphor that Caesarea Philippi provides for the rock of Jesus' church.

a. Read Matthew 16:13–20, emphasizing verse 18.

b. There are two viewpoints within the traditional understanding of the meaning of the "rock" (foundation) upon which Jesus built His church:

1. The rock is the confession of Peter that Jesus is Christ (i.e., the Christ, Son of the living God, is the foundation of the church).

   Read 1 Corinthians 3:10–14 and Acts 4:11. What does it mean that Jesus is the foundation, or cornerstone, of His church?

   Read Psalm 18:2. In what ways is God your rock? (NOTE: See the leader's guide for Set 3, Lesson 12 ["My Rock and My Fortress"], of this curriculum series, for a more in-depth study of this concept.) What does this viewpoint mean for your life?

2. The rock is Peter, whose confession recognizes the truth that Jesus is Messiah (some would include the other disciples because Peter spoke for them as well).

Read Ephesians 2:20–21. In what ways are the apostles and prophets (Peter as one of them) the foundation of the church?

Read Isaiah 51:1–2. Who was the rock on which the nation of Israel was built? What parallels can you draw between this rock and Peter as the foundation of the church? What does this viewpoint mean for your life?

c. Here is another metaphor for the "rock" upon which the church is being built. Point out the following information to your students:

- Caesarea Philippi was located at the foot of the highest mountain in Israel: Mount Hermon.

- Caesarea Philippi stood on a plateau against a solid rock cliff, which dominated the city.

- Carved into the cliff were niches for the pagan gods.

Read Matthew 16:18. Emphasize the word *this*. Point out the following information to your students:

- The rock visible from all around Caesarea Philippi provided a physical picture of a "great" rock, illustrating the solid foundation of the church.

- The rock was covered with shrines to "dead" pagan gods. Jesus, the Son of the living God, would build on solid rock. His living faith would replace the pagan practices devoted to "dead" gods. In this sense, Jesus' church would *replace, or be built over or on,* the shrines to pagan gods.

This symbolism assures us that God's way through the Messiah, Jesus, will ultimately overcome and destroy the values and lifestyles of paganism. His call then is for us to challenge the "dead" gods of our age and to replace their values with those of God. The idea that the mission of the church is to confront and destroy pagan values is highlighted by Jesus' claim that even the gates of hell would not stand against His people (see Guided Discussion 4 below).

Ask your students to answer the following questions:

1. In what sense does the community of Jesus (Christians) simply coexist with the "gods" of our world? Why?

2. What does it mean to you that your mission in life is to challenge the evil of our world for Jesus? Do you know people who are doing this? Are they effective?

OPTIONAL — Digging Deeper IV: Caesarea Philippi (40–60 minutes)

(This section requires the use of the optional full-color overhead-transparency packet. For information on ordering it, see page 307.)

A. Lecture

The area around Caesarea Philippi is among the most beautiful locations in Israel. The majesty of Mount Hermon, the beauty of the Hula Valley, the many waterfalls in the area, and the greenery near the spring that begins the Jordan River make this an awe-inspiring and fertile region. It is probably because of its beauty and fertility that this area became the center for pagan religious practices throughout biblical times. Dan, a nearby city that sat on another of the three sources of the Jordan, was chosen by King Jeroboam as a religious shrine for the calf worship he introduced (1 Kings 12:28–30). Caesarea Philippi, built by Herod Philip, had an extensive shrine dedicated to the fertility god Pan. Jesus came to the city to teach His disciples that His church would confront the very power of evil. This visual study helps students picture the location where Jesus taught that lesson.

B. Visual Insights

Overhead Transparency 25. Mount Hermon. This high mountain range reaches more than 9,000 feet above sea level, is 28 miles in length, and is more than 10 miles wide. It is covered with snow for more than eight months a year. Water from melting snow is the main source of water for the Jordan River, both through the runoff that flows into the Hula Valley (as the Great Rift Valley is called to the west of Mount Hermon) and through the water that gushes from springs at the foot of the mountains, at Dan and Caesarea Philippi.

In the Bible, Mount Hermon is noted for its dew (Psalm 133:3) and its height (Psalm 42:6). It was always a religious place, probably because of the abundance of water, the fertile fields on its lower slopes, and the springs at its base (Judges 3:3 indicates that it had its own god of fertility). In Roman times, there were temples on its slopes, including one at Caesarea Philippi and one on its summit. The lesson Jesus taught at Caesarea Philippi, near the foot of Mount Hermon, was high-lighted by the mountain's massive rock peaks, its beautiful snow-covered slopes, its rushing streams, and its sacredness to the pagan population.

Jesus was at Caesarea Philippi, about seven miles west (left) from this photograph, immediately before His transfiguration. Many scholars believe the "high mountain" mentioned in the account of the transfiguration was Mount Hermon (Matthew 17:1). Although the name is not mentioned in the Bible, this site seems far more likely than other possibilities many miles away.

This photo illustrates the beauty of Mount Hermon. The apple blossoms and flowers indicate its fertility. The village on its slopes, called Majdal Shams, captures the ancient look that villages like Caesarea Philippi had in Jesus' time, though Caesarea Philippi is much lower in the valley to the west.

Overhead Transparency 26. The Grotto of Pan. Against this cliff and in the large cave on the left, in the third century B.C., was a cult center to the fertility god Pan. This center probably was built to compete with the high place at Dan, about three miles away. The presence of the spring forming the large stream, called the Banias River, fit well with the belief that the fertility gods provided water. Its sudden emergence from the ground at the foot of the cliff, a long rock face more than 100 feet high, supported the pagan belief that the gods went to the underworld (Hades) and reemerged each year. Originally, the spring gushed from the large cave, probably persuading the people of the area that the cave provided an entrance to the underworld itself. An earthquake in the nineteenth century collapsed the roof of the cave, and the water now gushes from the cliff below the cave. Josephus described the cave as a deep cavern filled with water, the bottom of which no one had ever reached. The water from the spring may have been collected first in a "sacred lake" before it flowed west, joining with two other spring-fed streams (including one from near Dan) to become the Jordan River. A natural terrace against the cliff was the platform for the temple to Pan. The opening to the right of the cave is cut into the rock and leads to a niche in which an idol stood. This niche was probably in the sacred area and allowed the priests to engage in ritualistic water ceremonies. The entire area covered more than 3,000 square yards. In the cliff face to the right of the opening are more niches to house the statues of gods. Herod also built a white marble temple nearby, to honor the Roman emperor Augustus. Because of the worship of Pan, the area was named Paneon, or Panias. It is still known today as Banyas, based on the Arabic pronunciation of Panias. King Herod Philip named the area Caesarea Philippi.

Jesus came here to call His disciples to challenge the gates of hell. Seeing the "living water" rush from the foot of the rock provides a picture of Jesus, the Son of the living God, whose community will be built on the solid rock of God's saving truth.

*Overhead Transparency 27. Scenes from Caesarea Philippi. Upper Left: **The Temple Podium.*** The reconstructed platform, or podium, near the cave at Caesarea Philippi was originally the base of a temple either to the Roman emperor Augustus or to Pan (or possibly both). The entrance to the Grotto (or Cave) of Pan is seen to the left of the podium. Niches in the cliff face originally held statues of Pan and other gods. The largest arched niche is next to the cave, from which a spring flowed. The temple next to the cave opened into the cave itself. The opening was probably used for religious ceremonies involving water. The temple may even have covered the entrance to the cave, with the water running beneath the temple floor. An open-air shrine to Pan was located to the right of the steps to the platform. Another temple was to the right of that shrine, though it has not yet been identified. Some evidence exists that it was a temple to Nemesis, a Phoenician fertility goddess. The presence of massive temples against this cliff and the fresh water gushing from the cave provide powerful images as a backdrop to Peter's confession that Jesus is the Messiah, the Son of the living God, and to Jesus' promise to build His church on the rock so that even the gates of hell will not overcome it (Matthew 16:13–19).

*Upper Right: **Niches.*** These niches originally held statues of the pagan gods worshiped at Caesarea Philippi. The largest is actually an artificial cave that leads to a niche in the cliff itself. This niche apparently held a statue of Pan. Above it is another niche with an inscription indicating that a priest named Victor dedicated the statue of the goddess in the niche to the god Pan. The statue is gone. Other niches are seen in the cliff around the cave. This rock cliff, against which the temples stood, could be viewed as the "rock of the gods." Jesus' church will replace these gods and their pagan practices, for His community will be built on the rock of Jesus Himself, God's Messiah. The temple that stood in front of the niches probably did not have a back wall but opened into the cave, which is to the left of the arched opening.

*Lower Left: **Pagan Gods.*** This photograph clearly shows a niche that originally contained a god or goddess. The idol, possibly made of silver or gold, stood on the pedestal inside the carved hollow. Archaeologists believe this niche dates to the time of Jesus.

*Lower Right: **Living Water.*** This stream is one of several that run out of the cliff at Caesarea Philippi. Originally, the springs ran from the cave known as the Grotto of Pan. The presence of a religious cult here is probably due to these springs of fresh water. Peter's confession that Jesus was "the Christ, the Son of the living God" (Matthew 16:16) and Jesus' reference to His own "living water" are in stark contrast to the lifeless idols worshiped here. This flowing water is a picture of the life that Jesus alone can give.

4. Guided Discussion: The Gates of Hell

a. Lecture

Read Matthew 16:13–20. Jesus promised Peter that His community, the church, would be built on "this rock." His promise ends with the strong words "The gates of Hades will not overcome it." Hearing this statement within the confines of pagan Caesarea Philippi—its gods the very tools of the devil— makes the words ring even more clearly. The ancient belief of idol worshipers that their gods went to the underworld through caves like the one near the temple at Caesarea Philippi illustrates Jesus' message further, for in that pagan sense, the cave was the "gates of Hades." This study will explore the meaning of Jesus' promise that the gates of hell would not overcome His church.

b. Guided Discussion

Read Matthew 16:18 again. Point out the following information to your students:

- The "gates of Hades" could be translated as "hell"; the Greek phrase here could be translated as "the gates of hell will not prove stronger than it" (see footnotes in the NIV).

- Hades (*Sheol* in the Old Testament) is the place where departed spirits live. Apparently, it was frequently used as a synonym for hell (Psalm 9:17, 55:15, 116:3). Here it seems to refer to the powers resisting Jesus, including Satan's ultimate weapon—death.

Ask your students to answer the following questions:

1. What comfort does Jesus' lesson here give you?

2. How does the geographical setting of pagan worship and a cave devoted to the powers of evil (Old Testament Baal, New Testament Beelzebub—Matthew 10:25, 12:24) add significance to Jesus' promise? Do the ruins of the temple provide imagery for Jesus' promise? How?

Matthew 16:18 has often been interpreted as describing a defensive church, resisting the attacks of Satan and his forces. Although there is a sense in which the church is under attack, limiting the application of this verse to a defensive stance ignores a significant part of the verse's meaning.

Ask your students the following questions:

1. What is the purpose of city gates?

2. If the gates of Hades (hell) will not *be stronger than* (overcome, prevail against) the church, who is on the attack? Who is under attack? Have you ever heard of gates attacking? (They defend.)

3. If the gates will not overcome the church, it must mean the gates of Hades themselves are under attack. Who will win? (See 1 John 4:4.)

4. What has been the mentality of the Christian community (the church)—offensive or defensive?

c. **Conclusion**

The church has often seen itself as a great fortress defending itself against the attacks of Satan and his demons. While there is a sense in which we defend against Satan's attacks (1 Peter 5:8), we also are called to bring the powerful Word of God to bear on the world around us. So, not only are we under attack, but, using Jesus' methods, we are also the *attackers!* The pagan values around us may appear to be dominant, but Jesus promised that the gates (defensive structures) of Hades will not prevail. They will not win in the struggle. We are called to bring the battle to hell itself.

Ask your students to answer (individually or in small groups) the following questions.

1. Where do you see the "gates of Hades" most clearly in your community? In your country? In your own life?

2. Do you hide from the struggle, or do you seek opportunities to confront the power of Satan whenever you can?

3. Should churches be fortresses or staging areas preparing people to resist or confront evil around them? Why or why not?

4. What are some examples of people or organizations that are confronting evil around them?

5. Are you ever tempted to hide rather than challenge evil? What would Jesus say about this approach?

6. Think of one specific example of evil in your life. What could you do to bring the power of Jesus Christ, the Son of the living God, to bear on this evil? Discuss your idea with the rest of the class.

7. Read 1 John 2:13–14, 3:7–8, 4:4. Do these verses encourage you? How? Why do you think Jesus chose such an evil, pagan place to teach the disciples this final lesson? Does the imagery of the surroundings make this lesson clearer to you? How?

d. Prayer

If you want to, spend a few moments in prayer, telling God that you will challenge the evil you face.

OPTIONAL — Digging Deeper V: City Gates *(10–18 minutes)*

A. Lecture: The Role of City Gates

The city gate was important in biblical times, principally because it protected the entrance to the city. Great energy was expended in the design and construction of this gateway. Often, the most significant remains found by modern archaeologists are the gateways of ancient cities. Because of its large size and the presence of soldiers and other government officials, the city gate became the "city hall" of the community. People went there to pay taxes, seek legal decisions, or make requests of the ruler of the town. The phrase "to sit in the gate" was a synonym for being a ruler, judge, or official. Merchants and vendors found the city gate to be a natural place to do business because of the crowds; consequently, it was the community center for many towns. City gates provide the setting or the imagery for many stories in the Bible.

B. Guided Discussion

For each of the following passages, ask your students to summarize (individually or in small groups) the story and then note the function taking place at the gate:

- Genesis 19 (especially verse 1). What does this tell us about Lot?
- Deuteronomy 21:18–21
- Ruth 4 (especially verses 1 and 11)
- 1 Samuel 4 (especially verse 18)
- 2 Samuel 15 (especially verse 2)
- 2 Samuel 19:1–8
- Esther 2 (especially verses 19 and 21)
- Luke 16:19–31 (especially verse 20)

If time allows, you may discuss the following: There is a tradition that the Eastern Gate (the so-called Beautiful, or Golden, Gate) of Jerusalem is the location for the Last Judgment (either symbolically or literally). This is based on the following scriptures: (1) The Judgment is in the Valley of Jehoshaphat, just east of Jerusalem (Joel 3:2,12). (2) Jerusalem will be established as the heavenly city by the power of God (Zechariah 14:1–11). (3) Following the Judgment, the saved will enter the gates of the heavenly city. Since the setting is on the east side of Jerusalem, the gate would be the Beautiful, or Eastern, Gate (Isaiah 62:10 and Revelation 21).

C. Visual Insights: City Gates of Israel

If you have the optional full-color overhead-transparency packet for Set 1 of this curriculum series, you may want to review **Digging Deeper VII** on page 14 of Lesson 1 ("Standing at the Crossroads").

5. Guided Discussion: Jesus Shows the Way

Jesus promised the disciples that His church would be stronger than the gates of Hades. He told them they must challenge the most pagan expressions of the power of evil as they lived and ministered in the world. They did challenge that power, even challenging Rome itself, and they were able to overcome the very power of Satan.

But Jesus didn't end the lesson with that promise. There was more to His message, and it is just as important.

Ask your students to read Matthew 16:18–28. Then have them answer the following questions.

- What did Jesus begin to explain after He made His great promise and challenge to the disciples?

- Why did the disciples (represented by Peter) have such a problem with Jesus' explanation?

- What did Jesus do to challenge the gates of hell (i.e., death and the power of the devil)?

Be sure your students recognize that Jesus challenged Satan by *suffering, dying, and being raised from the dead.* He overcame death and the devil and eventually all the evils of the world by serving others, even to the point of giving His life. That sacrifice was His way of confronting evil. He did not use armies or powerful weapons to challenge evil, but He defeated the greatest enemy we have—death (1 Corinthians 15:26–28).

Ask your students: What methods can we use to follow Jesus' example in confronting evil?

Read Ephesians 1:11–23; Acts 1:8, 19:20; Luke 10:17–18; Ephesians 6:10–18; Hebrews 4:12. Where does our power come from? What are our weapons?

6. Prayer

Ask God for the courage you need to challenge evil. Ask Him to keep you established on the Rock, Jesus the Messiah, as your foundation. Acknowledge that you need courage to *go out* to face the "gates of Hades" wherever you find them. Ask Jesus to fill you with the power of His Spirit so you will be able to follow His example—the example of self-sacrifice and love for others. Ask for the skills to use the weapons He has provided for us. Commit to Him that you will never run from the battle or hide in a fortress. Promise that you will seek opportunities to bring His Word to bear on the power of Satan. Ask for the ability to see the gates of hell fall before His power.

Conclusion

Jesus deliberately went to Caesarea Philippi, a pagan place where the gates of Hades were very real. There He taught His disciples to base their faith on the Messiah, Jesus Christ. He called them to face the evils of the world on the basis of that faith, knowing that the power of God would overcome evil. In conclusion, challenge your students to recognize the evil around them, cling to the power of Jesus Christ, and attack the power of evil with the weapons Jesus has provided.

THE FERTILITY CULTS OF CANAAN

Only recently have scholars begun to unravel the complex religious rituals of Israel's Canaanite neighbors. Much of our knowledge of the origins and character of these fertility cults remains tentative and widely debated. What we do know reveals dark, seductive practices that continued to entice the people God had chosen to be His witnesses.

THE ORIGINS OF JUDAISM

The people of Israel developed their faith in the wilderness. Abraham lived in the Negev desert, where God made His covenant of blood with him and sealed it with circumcision. Moses met God in a burning bush in the desert, where he learned the greatness of God's name and received his commission to bring the Hebrews out of Egypt. God spoke to His people on Mount Sinai and reestablished His covenant with them in the Ten Commandments. Throughout the Israelites' 40-year journey in the wilderness, their Lord accompanied them, protected them, fed them, and guided them to the Promised Land. There was no doubt that Yahweh was God of the wilderness.

YAHWEH OR BAAL?

When the Israelites entered Canaan, they found a land of farmers, not shepherds, as they had been in the wilderness. The land was fertile beyond anything the Hebrew nomads had ever seen. The Canaanites attributed this fertility to their god Baal—and that is where the Israelites' problems began. Could the God who had led them out of Egypt and through the wilderness also provide fertile farms in the Promised Land? Or would the fertility god of Canaan have to be honored? Maybe, to be safe, they should worship both— Yahweh and Baal.

An intense battle began for the minds and hearts of God's people. The book of Judges records the ongoing struggle: the Israelites' attraction to, and worship of, the Canaanite gods; God's disciplinary response; the people's repentance; and God's merciful forgiveness—until the next time the Israelites reached for Baal instead of Yahweh.

Under the kings, this spiritual battle continued. By the time of Ahab and Jezebel, the fertility cults appeared to have the official sanction of Israel's leaders. Ahab, with his wife's encouragement, built a temple to Baal at his capital, Samaria. All the while, prophets like Elijah (which means "Yahweh is God"), Hosea, Isaiah, and Jeremiah thundered that Yahweh alone deserved the people's allegiance. It took the Assyrian destruction of Israel and the Babylonian Captivity of Judah to convince the Israelites that there is only one omnipotent God.

This struggle to be totally committed to God is of vital importance to us today as well. We don't think of ourselves as idol worshipers, yet we struggle to serve only God in every part of our lives. It is easy (and seductive) to honor self, possessions, fun, relationships, fame, money, and a host of other potential "gods."

We need to learn from Israel's experience and respond to Jesus' command for total allegiance. One way we can accomplish this is to study the gods that attracted Yahweh's people 3,000 years ago.

CANAAN'S GODS

Baal

The earliest deity recognized by the peoples of the ancient Near East was the creator-god El. His mistress, the fertility goddess Asherah, gave birth to many gods, including a powerful god named Baal ("Lord"). There appears to have been only one Baal, who was manifested in lesser baals at different places and times. Over the years, Baal became the dominant deity, and the worship of El faded.

Baal won his dominance by defeating the other deities, including the god of the sea, the god of storms (also of rain, thunder, and lightning), and the god of death. Baal's victory over death was thought to be repeated each year when he returned from the land of death (underworld), bringing rain to renew the earth's fertility. Hebrew culture viewed the sea as evil and destructive, so Baal's promise to prevent storms and control the sea, as well as his ability to produce abundant harvests, made him attractive to the Israelites. It's hard to know why Yahweh's people failed to see that He alone had power over these things. Possibly, their desert origins led them to question God's sovereignty over fertile land. Or maybe it was simply the sinful pagan practices that attracted them to Baal.

Baal is portrayed as a man with the head and horns of a bull, an image similar to that in biblical accounts. His right hand (sometimes both hands) is raised, and he holds a lightning bolt, signifying both destruction and fertility. Baal has also been portrayed seated on a throne, possibly as the king or lord of the gods.

Asherah

Asherah was honored as the fertility goddess in various forms and with varying names (Judges 3:7). The Bible does not actually describe the goddess, but archaeologists have discovered figurines believed to be representations of her. She is portrayed as a nude female, sometimes pregnant, with exaggerated breasts that she holds out, apparently as symbols of the fertility she promises her followers. The Bible indicates that she was worshiped near trees and poles, called Asherah poles (Deuteronomy 7:5, 12:2–3; 2 Kings 16:4, 17:10; Jeremiah 3:6,13; Ezekiel 6:13).

CULTIC PRACTICES

Baal's worshipers appeased him by offering sacrifices, usually animals such as sheep or bulls (1 Kings 18:23). Some scholars believe that the Canaanites also sacrificed pigs and that God prohibited His people from eating pork in part to prevent this horrible cult from being established among them. (See Isaiah 65:1–5 for an example of Israel's participating in the pagan practices of the Canaanites.) At times of crisis, Baal's followers sacrificed their children, apparently the firstborn of the community, to gain personal prosperity. The Bible called this practice "detestable" (Deuteronomy 12:31, 18:9–10). God specifically appointed the tribe of Levi as His special servants, in place of the firstborn of the Israelites, so they had no excuse for offering their children (Numbers 3:11–13). The Bible's repeated condemnation of child sacrifice shows God's hatred of it, especially among His people.

Asherah was worshiped in various ways, including through ritual sex. Although she was believed to be Baal's mother, she was also his mistress. Pagans practiced "sympathetic magic"—that is, they believed they could influence the gods' actions by performing the behavior they wished the gods to demonstrate. Believing the sexual union of Baal and Asherah produced fertility, their worshipers engaged in immoral sex to cause the gods to join together, ensuring good harvests. This practice became the basis for religious prostitution (1 Kings 14:23–24). The priest or a male member of the community represented Baal. The priestess or a female member of the community represented Asherah. In this way, God's incredible gift of sexuality was perverted to the most obscene public prostitution. No wonder God's anger burned against His people and their leaders.

PAGAN RELIGIONS IN THE NEW TESTAMENT

Many, if not all, of the Old Testament gods had disappeared, at least in name, by the time of Jesus. Beelzebub, based on the Philistine god Baalzebul, had become a synonym for the prince of demons, Satan. Many of the ancient pagan deities lived on, however, now identified with the gods of the Greeks and Romans, the nations who controlled the people of Israel before and during New Testament times. It is not appropriate here to discuss all the gods and goddesses of the Greco-Roman pantheon; however, a few of them were significant in the first century, and some are even mentioned by name in the Bible.

The leader of the gods, Zeus (Jupiter to the Romans), took on the role of Baal, the god of weather or storms. Artemis, the goddess of childbirth and fertility, and Aphrodite, the goddess of love, continued the Asherah cults under a new name (Acts 19:35), but with worship practices that were as immoral as ever. It is said that in Corinth alone, there were more than 1,000 prostitutes in Aphrodite's temple. Hades, the Greek god of the underworld, became the namesake for the place of the dead and even for hell itself. In Matthew 16:18, Jesus referred to the gates of Hades, or the underworld, believed by some to be the grotto at Caesarea Philippi, from which one of the sources of the Jordan River came. The grotto itself was part of a temple complex used in the worship of the Greek god Pan.

Pan was depicted as an ugly man with the horns, legs, and ears of a goat. Most stories about him refer to sexual affairs. The worship practices of his followers were no different. Pan was associated with Dionysus, the Greek god of wine and orgies, whose worshipers continued many of the sexual rites of the Old Testament gods of the Baal cult. Dionysus was worshiped in the pagan Decapolis across the Sea of Galilee from the center of Jesus' ministry.

Clearly, though the names of the gods had changed, the people's worship practices had not. Only the child sacrifice of the Baal cult came to an end with the Greeks and Romans.

MAGIC AND THE OCCULT

Many ancient peoples practiced magic. They foretold the future by examining animal entrails or by watching flights of birds. The Greeks had oracles, shrines where gods supposedly communicated the future to priests and priestesses. Demon possession was a topic of much fascination. Many sorcerers claimed to have the ability to cast out demons (Acts 8:9–24, 13:6–12), as did some Pharisees. Because the Bible, in both the Old Testament and the New Testament, recognized the reality of the demonic world and condemned all of its practices (Deuteronomy 18:10–12,20; Micah 5:2; 1 Corinthians 10:20–21), we can be sure these practices continued and were a temptation to many.

Jesus provided the ultimate solution to resisting the seductiveness of pagan idol worship. He showed that He alone held power over the demons, sending them into the Abyss (Luke 8:31). He promised His disciples that His church would overcome all evil, even the gates of Hades itself.

CONCLUSION

Though today our gods—such as money, power, and possessions—are less "personalized" than in ancient times, the temptations for us are no less enticing. We would do well to remember the complete powerlessness of the pagan gods—from Baal, Canaan's bloodthirsty fertility god, to Hades, Greek god of the underworld—to prevail against the one true God and His Son, Jesus Christ.

CITY OF THE GREAT KING

For the Teacher

Jerusalem! There is no other place on earth that stirs the imagination like Jerusalem. It's been called the Holy City and the "center of the earth." It is a city whose origins date back 1,000 years before the birth of Jesus to the time when God gave this site to King David. Since then, Jerusalem has been the place of pivotal events for two religions, Judaism and Christianity, and has been significant in the history of Islam as well. To this day, a visit to Jerusalem is an emotionally powerful event. It is a vibrant city, alive with the sounds of people—shopkeepers, tourists, pilgrims, and religious people of many kinds, each one here to seek relationship with God as they believe He is to be known. For Christians, so much of great importance happened here. Abraham, David, Solomon, Hezekiah, Judah Maccabee, Herod, Jesus, the early church, Titus and the Romans, Mohammed, the Crusaders, the nation of Israel, and so many more have left their mark and have in turn been affected by this great city. It is especially the death, resurrection, and ascension of Jesus, our Messiah, that make Jerusalem so important to Christians. For Christians, the power in visiting Jerusalem is not so much in the mystique or "holiness" of this place—after all, the whole earth belongs to the Lord. Instead, a visit to Jerusalem provides an opportunity for Christians to remember the great redemptive work of God, to visualize it, and to understand it better.

The importance of Jerusalem to Christianity and other faiths presents significant problems for us in understanding its nature at the time of Jesus. So much has been destroyed or hidden by later building projects. Ancient traditions have obscured the appearance of Jerusalem at the time Jesus visited here. Fortunately, recent archaeological investigation has begun to open a window to Jerusalem's past. This study will explore Jerusalem as it appeared to the first-century pilgrim. The purpose of this lesson is not to inspire as much as to inform. For that reason, you will not find any "To Do" items in the section "Your Objectives for This Lesson." As we will discover, however, being informed about Jerusalem is itself inspiring. During this lesson, Bible events and passages that fit specific places and times will be noted with only brief comment. If anyone wishes to investigate the Bible further at any point, encourage him or her to do so. The material in this lesson also provides the background for the next four lessons, all of which focus on Jerusalem. The places where these events connect will be indicated.

Begin this study by asking your students for their impressions of and reactions to Jerusalem. To encourage discussion, ask probing questions like "Why do you feel this way?" or "What makes that important to you?" or "Can you give some examples?" A sense of excitement will grow as you mention that Jerusalem is sacred to three religions (Judaism, Christianity, and Islam), Abraham and David were there, Jesus went there often, Jesus' death and resurrection took place there, and the early church met there. In 1996, Jerusalem celebrated 3,000 years of history. Stress the fact that the history of Jerusalem is part of our history as Christians. This study examines the history of what our God has done for us. The more your students discover, the more grateful—and amazed—they will be and the more devoted they will be to following Jesus.

Your Objectives for This Lesson

At the completion of this section, you will want your students:

To Know/Understand

1. The topography of Jerusalem and its relationship to the development of the city.

2. The historical periods of Jerusalem.

3. The districts of Jerusalem in Jesus' time and how they shed light on the events that He was involved in.

4. The locations of several of the events during Jesus' last week and the meaning these locations add to His actions and words.

5. The organization and structure of the Temple Mount and its design, which was intended to provide relationship with God.

6. The ways key events in Jesus' life and the life of the early church fit the Temple location.

How to Plan for This Lesson

As the leader, you must review as much of the material as possible ahead of time. It would be wise for you to review the *entire* study before leading any part of it. This lesson contains a lot of information, but it is arranged logically, following the natural layout of the city itself. The more you understand about the relationships between the geography, topography, and history of this city, the more clearly you can present each part to your students.

Each student should have a Bible and a complete set of maps/diagrams and handouts. Using an overhead projector throughout this study is essential. While you are studying each location, reading the Bible passages listed in the Bible Connections will make Jerusalem "come alive" for your group, so be sure to take the time to read as much as possible. Some of these passages are accompanied by short explanations, while other passages are self-explanatory. Before class, it would be wise to distribute 3x5 cards with assigned passages written on them. Each student can read aloud the selection written on his or her card.

Lessons 23, 24, 25, and 26 focus on Jerusalem or nearby locations. Segments of this lesson form the background for each of those four. These specific areas of background are noted, and you should be sure to stress their importance to your students. In these sections, the Bible Connections are listed without explanation because you will explore them further in later lessons.

You may wish to view the video in its entirety during the first session. You may then choose to review the appropriate sections as you study the individual elements of the city's geography and history in later segments. Students should read the suggested handouts before this lesson if you plan to complete all or most of the lesson.

As in past lessons, Unit One provides a *very brief* overview. You may choose to use it if your time is limited. Each part of Unit One is covered in much greater detail in later sections.

How to Prepare for This Lesson

Materials Needed

Student copies of the maps/diagrams: "Topography of Jerusalem"
   "Jerusalem's Districts"
   "Land of Jesus' Ministry"

"Jerusalem of David and Solomon"
"Jerusalem of Jesus' Time"
"Temple Courts"
"The Temple Mount: A.D. 70"
"Development of the Temple Mount"
"Herod's Temple "

Overhead transparencies:

"Topography of Jerusalem"
"Jerusalem's Districts"
"Land of Jesus' Ministry"
"Jerusalem of David and Solomon"
"Jerusalem of Jesus' Time"
"Temple Courts"
"The Temple Mount: A.D. 70"
"Development of the Temple Mount"
"Herod's Temple"

Student copies of the handouts:

"Herod the Great"
"The Joy of Living Water: Jesus and the Feast of Sukkot"
"Pharisees or Sadducees?"
"The Jewish Revolts"

Video: **City of the Great King**

Overhead projector, screen, TV, VCR

1. Make copies of the maps/diagrams listed above for your students.

2. Prepare the overhead transparencies listed above. (You'll find them at the back of the book.)

3. Make copies of the handouts listed above for your students. (If possible, they should receive and read these handouts before the lesson.)

4. Determine which **unit** and which **Digging Deeper** sections, if any, you want to use in your class session(s). NOTE: In this lesson, the order of the sections is important. If you wish to change the order or skip some of the sections, be sure you review the material so you do not miss anything.

5. Prepare your classroom ahead of time, setting up and testing an overhead projector and screen (for the overhead transparencies) and a TV and VCR. If you plan to hand out biblical references for your students to look up and read aloud, prepare 3x5 cards (one reference per card) to distribute before class.

6. For some of the sections, there are transparencies in the optional full-color overhead-transparency packet that apply. The descriptions for these transparencies are collected at the end of this lesson (pages 117–126). For information on ordering the packet, see page 307.

7. It may be helpful for you to use one or two resources as you prepare for this lesson and lead your students through it. A helpful resource is Dan Bahat's *The Illustrated Atlas of Jerusalem* (New York: Simon & Schuster, 1990).

8. If you have the optional full-color overhead-transparency packets from Sets 1 and 2 of this curriculum series, you might want to use the following transparencies and their descriptions:

> Set 1—Overhead Transparency 8
> Set 2—Overhead Transparencies 11 and 21–24

Lesson Plan

UNIT ONE: Video Review

1. Introductory Comments

To understand the history of Jerusalem is to understand God's great acts of redemption. This study is designed to help people picture the city, its structures, its people, and its activity. As the life and ministry of Jesus are studied in the context in which God originally placed them, His message and work become even more vibrant and alive. This study also provides the background for the next four lessons, all of which are set in Jerusalem:

> Lesson 23—Mount of Olives
> Lesson 24—Garden of Gethsemane
> Lesson 25—Garden Tomb
> Lesson 26—Temple Stairs

2. Show the Video *City of the Great King* (43 minutes)

3. Map Study: Topography of Jerusalem

Using the overhead transparency "Topography of Jerusalem," point out the following areas, and have your students locate them on their maps.

> Mount of Olives
> Gethsemane (traditional)
> Kidron Valley
> David's City
> Spring of Gihon
> Hezekiah's Tunnel
> Temple Mount
> Tyropoeon Valley
> Pool of Siloam
> Western Hill
> Hinnom Valley

4. The History of Jerusalem

Using the overhead transparencies "Topography of Jerusalem," "Jerusalem of David and Solomon," and "Jerusalem of Jesus' Time," point out the following areas, and have your students locate them on their maps/diagrams. As you point out the areas, use the information below to highlight the significance of each area.

a. Abraham was sent to the Moriah area to sacrifice Isaac (approximately 2000 B.C.). Jerusalem was built on the mountain ridge called Moriah. *(Topography of Jerusalem)*

b. David captured Jerusalem in approximately 1000 B.C. and made it his religious and political capital. While he was king, David selected the location where the Temple should be built. *(Jerusalem of David and Solomon)*

c. Solomon built the Temple (ca. 950 B.C.) on the threshing floor of Araunah on Mount Moriah, the location chosen by David at God's leading. Solomon built a palace, apparently between the

Temple and David's City. Like the Temple, this palace was dramatic in construction and furnishings. At this time, the city covered approximately 30 acres and had a population of about 4,500 people. (*Jerusalem of David and Solomon*)

d. Hezekiah expanded Jerusalem in approximately 705 B.C. During his reign over Judah, the northern kingdom of Israel was destroyed by the Assyrians. The city expanded to the west across the Tyropoeon Valley onto the Western Hill. (*Topography of Jerusalem. Note the Western Hill.*)

e. In approximately 500 B.C., the Babylonians destroyed the Temple, and many of the people were taken into captivity. After 70 years, Cyrus, king of Persia, decreed that the people of Israel might return to Jerusalem. The Israelites returned from exile and rebuilt the Temple under the leadership of Ezra and Nehemiah. Over the next 100 years, the Temple was restored and the city was rebuilt, though on a smaller scale (530–400 B.C.).

f. Jerusalem became part of Alexander the Great's empire in 322 B.C. The city suffered through more than a century of conflict between the successors of Alexander. The Maccabean revolt (165 B.C.) brought Jerusalem back under Jewish control. The descendants of the Maccabees, the Hasmonaean dynasty, expanded Jerusalem. The Western Hill was enclosed within the city, the Temple Mount was expanded, and the fortress Baris (later the Antonia) was constructed. The city now covered 175 acres and had a population of more than 30,000 people. (*Jerusalem of Jesus' Time. Note that this diagram is based on Jerusalem several years after the Hasmonaeans, but the items are in the same places.*)

5. Herod's Jerusalem—Its Fullest Glory

Herod ruled from 37–4 B.C. He expanded the Temple Mount greatly, fortified the city with a citadel and an expanded fortress renamed the Antonia, built many structures (including a theater and a hippodrome), and fortified the walls. His greatest accomplishment was the lavish expansion and embellishment of the Temple and its platform. At this point, the city was spectacular, one of the wonders of the ancient world. The city had expanded to nearly 250 acres and had a population of 45,000. It was now ready for the ministry of Jesus, the Messiah.

Using the overhead transparency "Jerusalem of Jesus' Time," point out the following areas, and have your students locate them on their maps.

> Temple Mount and Temple
> Antonia fortress
> Hasmonaean palace
> Herod's palace
> theater
> first wall
> second wall

6. The City of Jesus' Time

a. The Temple Mount

Using the overhead transparency "Jerusalem's Districts," point out the following areas, and have your students locate them on their maps.

> Temple
> Temple Mount
> Eastern Gate
> Southern Stairs (possibly the site of the Christian Pentecost—see Lesson 26)

royal stoa (where Jesus drove out the buyers and sellers)
Robinson's Arch
Wilson's Arch
Tyropoeon Street
Warren's Gate
Antonia fortress (one possible site of Jesus' trial before Pilate)
Tadi (Sheep) Gate
Pool of Bethesda (where Jesus healed the lame man in John 5:1–15)

b. Temple Courts

The Temple platform was enormous. It was more than 900 feet wide from east to west (approximately 915 feet on the south end and approximately 1,030 feet on the north end) and more than 1,500 feet long from north to south (approximately 1,535 feet on the east end and approximately 1,590 feet on the west end). It was by far the largest temple area in the ancient world. Hundreds of thousands of pilgrims could be on the Mount at the same time. (Josephus claimed that the Passover pilgrims numbered more than 2 million people.) Herod trained 1,000 priests as masons to work on the Temple itself. Ten thousand highly skilled laborers, using 1,000 wagons, worked for years to construct it. The finished platform was divided into separate courts, which were increasingly more sacred the closer they were to the Temple itself. This study begins with the courts on the outer edge of the platform and gradually moves toward the Temple itself.

Using the overhead transparencies "Temple Courts" and "The Temple Mount: A.D. 70," point out the following areas, and have your students locate them on their diagrams.

> Temple
> Gentile Court (colonnade around the outside)
> royal stoa (where Jesus drove out the buyers and sellers)
> Solomon's Colonnade (where the early church met)
> Soreq (wall that kept out the Gentiles)

Using the overhead transparency "Temple Courts," point out the following areas, and have your students locate them on their diagrams.

> Women's Court (where the people gathered for worship)
> Court of the Israelites
> Priests' Court
> altar
> Temple
> holy place
> Holy of Holies

c. Districts of the City

Using the overhead transparencies "Jerusalem's Districts" and "Jerusalem of Jesus' Time," point out the following areas, and have your students locate them on their maps.

1. **David's City.** This was the Jerusalem of David's time. In Jesus' day, this area was home to many Jews (along with the Lower City).

2. **Lower City.** The home of most of the common people in Jesus' day, this area was built on the slope of the Western Hill, from the Tyropoeon up to the west. Located here is the Pool of Siloam, where Jesus sent the blind man to wash the mud from his eyes so he could see.

3. **Upper City.** This part of the city was located on the Western Hill (today called Mount Zion) and was the highest area in Jerusalem. Herod's palace was located here, as were several other large

structures. The population of this area was probably more Hellenistic than in the Lower City, and the people were certainly wealthier. Caiaphas's house, where Jesus may have been questioned by the Sanhedrin, and the theater are located here as well.

4. **Business District.** This appellation was chosen for the section of the city inside the Second Wall because of the many shops and markets located here. Ancient sources do not refer to this area by this name.

Using the overhead transparencies "Jerusalem of Jesus' Time" and "Jerusalem's Districts," point out the following areas, and have your students locate them on their maps.

> David's City
> Lower City
> Upper City
> Herod's palace
> first wall
> second wall
> business district
> Garden Gate
> Towers (Damascus) Gate

5. **New City.** The city of Jerusalem expanded to the north during and after Jesus' time on earth. The area of expansion was called the New City and was populated by many wealthy people. It was not walled until the time of Herod Agrippa some 30 or more years after Jesus' crucifixion.

Using the overhead transparency "Jerusalem's Districts," point out the following areas, and have your students locate them on their maps.

> second wall
> New City
> Garden Gate
> Towers (Damascus) Gate
> Golgotha (traditional)
> garden tomb (Protestant Golgotha)

UNIT TWO

NOTE TO THE TEACHER: *In this unit, we will explore the city of Jerusalem as Jesus knew it. Step One will cover the topography of the area and give a brief history of the city. Step Two will highlight the various districts of Jerusalem, beginning with the Temple Mount and moving clockwise around the city. It would be helpful for the teacher to review the topography ("Topography of Jerusalem") and all the districts ("Jerusalem's Districts") before beginning each section. The overhead transparency "Jerusalem of Jesus' Time" should be used with each section, along with other transparencies as noted. The descriptions for transparencies in the optional full-color overhead-transparency packet have been collected under the heading "Transparencies" at the end of this lesson. (For information on ordering the packet for this set or any other set mentioned below, see page 307.) Bible verses appropriate to each location will be listed as Bible Connections. Where there is a "faith lesson" to be learned based on the study, it will be presented as Thoughts to Ponder. If the teacher wishes to study Jerusalem without reviewing the Bible material for discussion, the Bible Connections and Thoughts to Ponder exercises should be omitted. Where another lesson in this series applies to the information being presented, it will be pointed out as well. Understanding Jerusalem, the city God chose as the home of kings David, Solomon, Hezekiah, and Jesus, will enhance your students' understanding of the events of the Bible and make the life, death, and resurrection of Jesus increasingly vivid to them.*

Step One: "A City of Kings"

1. Introductory Comments

Moses commanded the people of Israel to appear before the Lord three times each year (Deuteronomy 16:16). In fulfillment of this command, every year thousands of pilgrims came to Jerusalem on Passover, Pentecost (Shavuot, as the Jews called it), and the Feast of Tabernacles (Sukkot). Jesus made these pilgrimages, first with His parents, then with His disciples, and finally to be crucified. The yearly pilgrimages, the festive crowds in the city, and the ceremonies of the Temple were important parts of His ministry.

But the history of Jerusalem began more than 1,000 years before Jesus walked on the earth. The city had been built and destroyed more than once already. Its boundaries had spread to their greatest point. For Jews, the names connected with Jerusalem stirred emotions. The Mount of Olives, the Kidron Valley, Mount Zion, the Temple—they rang with history and religious meaning. Every child knew where these locations were and what had happened at each one.

But though they knew their history, few pictured what God had in mind for a hill just outside the city. Of all the cities in the world, God had chosen the city of King David, rebuilt by King Hezekiah and expanded to its fullest glory by King Herod, as the location for the greatest act of love and redemption the world would ever know. Here the King of the universe ascended His throne by way of a cross. To the Jewish followers of Christ, the choice of location must have made sense; they knew the meaning of Jerusalem and they could connect the final work of Jesus to its history. It had been the city of great kings. Now it became the city of the greatest King.

Tell your students that this study will explore Jerusalem's past so they can know some of what Jews knew in Jesus' day. With this knowledge, your students can marvel again at God's great work through His Son, Jesus, the Messiah.

(NOTE: If your students say that the details given in the video move too quickly, assure them that there will be added depth as you continue your study.)

2. Show the Video *City of the Great King* (43 minutes)

3. Student Preparation

Students should read the handouts "Herod the Great," "The Joy of Living Water: Jesus and the Feast of Sukkot," "Pharisees or Sadducees?" and "The Jewish Revolts" before beginning this unit.

4. The Topography of Jerusalem

HINT: *You may want to use Overhead Transparency 28 ("Modern-day Jerusalem from the South") in the optional full-color overhead-transparency packet for Set 4 to supplement your teaching in this section.*

Students should be given the maps "Land of Jesus' Ministry" and "Topography of Jerusalem." The teacher will need the overhead transparencies "Land of Jesus' Ministry" and "Topography of Jerusalem."

a. Location in the Judea Mountains

Using the overhead transparency "Land of Jesus' Ministry," point out the following areas, and have your students locate them on their maps.

> Mediterranean Sea
> Judea Mountains
> Sea of Galilee
> Judea Wilderness

Capernaum
Bethlehem
Jericho
Jerusalem

Explain the following points to your students:

- Jerusalem is on a high plateau in the Judea Mountains, 30 miles east of the Mediterranean Sea and 20 miles from the Dead Sea.

- The Dead Sea is 1,300 feet below sea level, making the mountains around Jerusalem seem higher than they are.

- The mountains around Jerusalem are 2,700 feet above sea level. The mountains on which Jerusalem is built are 2,400 feet above sea level.

- Jerusalem is six miles from Bethlehem, where Jesus was born; 60 miles (as the crow flies) from Nazareth, where He grew up; and 75 miles (as the crow flies) from Capernaum, where He centered His ministry.

- Because Jerusalem was in the mountains, going there meant climbing from nearly everywhere else in the country.

Bible Connection

Use the following passages to show your students how the topography and geography of Jerusalem connect with the Scriptures.

Psalm 87:1—Zion is built on a holy mountain.

Psalm 122:1–4—People go up to God's house, the Temple.

Psalm 125:2—Jerusalem is surrounded by mountains.

Isaiah 2:2–3—People will go up to the mountain of the Lord's house.

b. The Mount of Olives
HINT: *You may want to use Overhead Transparency 29 ("The Mount of Olives") in the optional full-color overhead-transparency packet for Set 4 to supplement your teaching in this section.*

Using the overhead transparency "Topography of Jerusalem," point out the following areas, and have your students locate them on their maps.

Mount of Olives
Kidron Valley

Explain the following points to your students:

- The ridge of the Mount of Olives is 2,650 feet above sea level and two miles long.

- To the east of the Mount of Olives is Bethany. Beyond that is the Judea Wilderness.

- On the slopes of the Mount of Olives are the traditional Garden of Gethsemane, an ancient Jewish cemetery, and the Kidron Valley.

Bible Connection

Use the following passages to show your students how the topography and geography of the Mount of Olives connect with the Scriptures.

2 Samuel 15:13–37—David fled Jerusalem to escape Absalom's revolt. David wept as he crossed the Mount of Olives. At the summit of the Mount of Olives was an ancient worship shrine.

Zechariah 14:7—In this description of Jesus' second coming, He is standing on the Mount of Olives as it splits in two.

Matthew 21:1–11; Luke 19:28–44—In His triumphal entry, Jesus entered Jerusalem from the Mount of Olives.

Matthew 24:3–25:46—In this passage, Jesus gave His final teaching session on the Mount of Olives, overlooking Jerusalem, whose destruction He predicted.

Luke 24:50–52; Acts 1:6–12—Jesus ascended from the Mount of Olives back to His Father in heaven.

c. The Kidron Valley

HINT: *If you have the optional full-color overhead-transparency packets for Sets 2 and 4, you may want to use Overhead Transparency 21 ("The Temple Mount at Jerusalem") in Set 2 and Overhead Transparency 29 ("The Mount of Olives") in Set 4 to supplement your teaching in this section.*

Using the overhead transparency "Topography of Jerusalem," point out the following areas, and have your students locate them on their maps.

> Mount of Olives
> Kidron Valley
> David's City
> Temple Mount

Explain the following points to your students:

- The Kidron Valley is a wadi about three miles long, between David's City and the Mount of Olives. Eventually, this wadi empties into the Dead Sea.

- The Spring of Gihon, ancient Jerusalem's water supply, is on the western side of the Kidron Valley.

- The Kidron Valley most likely is also the Valley of Jehoshaphat, the scene of the final judgment.

- The Garden of Gethsemane (traditional) is on the eastern edge of the Kidron Valley.

Bible Connection

Use the following passages to show your students how the Kidron Valley connects with the Scriptures.

2 Samuel 15:13–24—David crossed the Kidron Valley as he fled from Absalom.

1 Kings 2:36–38—Solomon refused to allow Shimei to cross the Kidron Valley.

1 Kings 15:11–15; 2 Kings 23:4–7,12–14; 2 Chronicles 15:16–18, 29:15–17, 30:13–14—Several reforming kings destroyed idols and pagan objects in the Kidron Valley.

Jeremiah 31:38–40—The prophet Jeremiah predicted that even the Kidron Valley, with all its dead bodies, would be holy to the Lord.

John 18:1—Jesus crossed the Kidron Valley on His way to Gethsemane, just before He was arrested.

Joel 3:1–21—The Valley of Jehoshaphat, where the nations will be judged (*Jehoshaphat* means "God will judge"), is believed to be part or all of the Kidron Valley; hence the cemetery on the Mount of Olives above it.

2 Samuel 18:18—Absalom placed a pillar (standing stone) in his own honor in the King's Valley. This is believed to have been another name for the Kidron Valley.

d. David's City (Ophel)

HINT: *If you have the optional full-color overhead-transparency packets for Sets 2 and 4, you may want to use Overhead Transparencies 22 ("The Cave of the Spring of Gihon"), 23 ("Hezekiah's Water Tunnel"), and 24 ("The Midway Point in Hezekiah's Water Tunnel Where the Workers Met") in Set 2 and Overhead Transparency 28 ("Modern-day Jerusalem from the South") in Set 4 to supplement your teaching in this section.*

Using the overhead transparency "Topography of Jerusalem," point out the following areas, and have your students locate them on their maps.

> Kidron Valley
> David's City
> Temple Mount
> Tyropoeon Valley
> Spring of Gihon
> Hezekiah's Tunnel

Explain the following points to your students:

- David's Jerusalem was a narrow strip of land—Mount Moriah—composed of approximately nine to 10 acres of land and populated by about 1,500 people.

- Mount Moriah was naturally defended by the Kidron Valley on the east and the Tyropoeon Valley on the west.

- The Spring of Gihon was an excellent source of water for this area, one of the main reasons the city was located here.

- This part of the city was originally called Zion.

- Solomon expanded the city to the north on the ridge called Mount Moriah, to build the Temple to Yahweh. This First Temple, Nehemiah's reconstruction, and Herod's Temple all stood in exactly the same place.

- Hezekiah expanded the city across the Tyropoeon Valley onto the Western Hill. He commissioned the construction of a tunnel from the Spring of Gihon, under David's City, to the Pool of Siloam.

Bible Connection

Use the following passages to show your students how David's City connects with the Scriptures.

> Genesis 22:1,2,14—Abraham brought Isaac to Mount Moriah to sacrifice him.

> 2 Samuel 5:6–12—David captured Jerusalem and made it his political capital.

> 2 Samuel 6:12–19—David brought the ark to Jerusalem, and the city became the religious center of Israel.

> 2 Samuel 24:1,16,18–25—David purchased the threshing floor of Araunah, which became the future site of the Temple.

> 2 Chronicles 3:1–2—Solomon built the Temple on Mount Moriah, the Temple Mount.

e. The Tyropoeon Valley

HINT: *If you have the optional full-color overhead-transparency packets for Sets 2 and 4, you may want to use Overhead Transparencies 22 ("The Cave of the Spring of Gihon"), 23 ("Hezekiah's Water Tunnel"), and 24 ("The Midway Point in Hezekiah's Water Tunnel Where the Workers Met") in Set 2 and Overhead Transparency 28 ("Modern-day Jerusalem from the South") in Set 4 to supplement your teaching in this section.*

Using the overhead transparency "Topography of Jerusalem," point out the following areas, and have your students locate them on their maps.

> David's City
> Temple Mount
> Tyropoeon Valley
> Pool of Siloam

Explain the following points to your students:

- The Tyropoeon Valley runs between David's City and the Western Hill. It was the western border of David's City in the Old Testament.

- The Tyropoeon Valley is never mentioned by name in the Bible.

- Josephus did mention the valley by name. *Tyropoeon* means "cheesemakers," possibly referring to the activities that took place there.

- The Tyropoeon Valley always was much shallower than the Kidron or the Hinnom. Because it was shallow, expansion across it was possible. The first expansion occurred at the time of Hezekiah. Today the valley is nearly filled with debris from the many destructions of Jerusalem.

- The Pool of Siloam was in this valley.

- The western wall of Herod's Temple Mount stood in this valley. This is the reason for its massive stones and gigantic walls.

- In Jesus' day, a bridge crossed the Tyropoeon, going from the Western Hill to the Temple Mount on Wilson's Arch.

Bible Connection

Use the following passages to show your students how the Tyropoeon Valley connects with the Scriptures.

> 2 Kings 20:20; 2 Chronicles 32:2–8—Hezekiah commissioned the building of the tunnel that ran from the Spring of Gihon to the Pool of Siloam in the Tyropoeon Valley.

> Nehemiah 3:15—Nehemiah repaired the wall near the Pool of Siloam.

> John 9:1–12—Jesus sent a blind man to the Pool of Siloam to wash the mud from his eyes, whereupon the man regained his sight.

f. The Western Hill (Mount Zion)
HINT: *You may want to use Overhead Transparencies 28 ("Modern-day Jerusalem from the South") and 30 ("The Western Hill") in the optional full-color overhead-transparency packet for Set 4 to supplement your teaching in this section.*

Using the overhead transparency "Topography of Jerusalem," point out the following areas, and have your students locate them on their maps.

> Tyropoeon Valley
> Western Hill
> Hinnom Valley

Explain the following points to your students:

- The Western Hill was originally outside Jerusalem's walls. Hezekiah apparently was the first to expand the city across the Tyropoeon Valley to this hill.

- In Jesus' time, this entire hill was within the city walls and was called the Upper City.

- Herod's palace, the Hasmonaean palace, and probably the Upper Room (where the last supper took place) were located on this hill.

- The Lower City was located on the slope of the Western Hill, reaching into the Tyropoeon Valley.

- Today this hill is called Mount Zion. The name change came fairly recently. In the Bible, Zion usually refers to David's City, though it sometimes refers to the Temple, the whole city of Jerusalem, the whole nation, or the heavenly Jerusalem.

Bible Connection

Use the following passages to show your students how the Western Hill connects with the Scriptures.

Matthew 2:1–2; Luke 23:6–7—These events in Jesus' life probably took place in Herod's palace, located on the Western Hill.

Luke 22:7–13; Acts 1:12–13—There is solid evidence that the Upper Room was on the Western Hill.

g. The Hinnom Valley

HINT: *You may want to use Overhead Transparency 30 ("The Western Hill") in the optional full-color overhead-transparency packet for Set 4 to supplement your teaching in this section.*

Using the overhead transparency "Topography of Jerusalem," point out the following areas, and have your students locate them on their maps.

> Western Hill
> Hinnom Valley

Explain the following points to your students:

- The Hinnom Valley formed the western boundary of the Western Hill and the Upper City of Jesus' time.

- The Hinnom Valley is very short, beginning along the Western Hill and ending where the Tyropoeon and the Kidron Valleys meet.

- The kings of Judah sacrificed their children in the Hinnom Valley.

Bible Connection

Use the following passages to show your students how the Hinnom Valley connects with the Scriptures.

2 Kings 23:10; 2 Chronicles 28:3–4, 33:6; Jeremiah 7:31, 19:5–6, 32:35—The Hinnom Valley (or the Valley of Ben Hinnom—"the sons of Hinnom") was the location where the kings and people of Judah chose to sacrifice their children to Baal. **HINT:** *See Lesson Six, in Set 2 of this series, for more information on this topic.*

- Matthew 5:22,29, 10:28, 23:33, 18:9; Mark 9:43–48; James 3:6—The Hebrew word for the Hinnom Valley could be written *ge-hinnom*. This word becomes *gehenna* in Greek. In the time between the Old Testament and the New Testament, the term *gehenna* was used to describe the fire of hell in the last judgment. By Jesus' time, *gehenna* was a synonym for hell. Thus the English versions of the Bible translate Valley of Hinnom in the New Testament as "hell." The horrifying practices of people who placed infants on red-hot metal idols and watched their charred bodies drop into the fire was so evil that it could only be a picture of hell itself. In addition, this valley became the perpetually burning garbage dump and sewer of the city, further portraying the rotting, burning filth that depicted hell.

h. Review the Topography of Jerusalem

Using the overhead transparency "Topography of Jerusalem," point out the following areas, and have your students locate them on their maps.

> Mount of Olives
> Gethsemane (traditional)
> Kidron Valley
> David's City
> Spring of Gihon
> Hezekiah's Tunnel
> Temple Mount
> Tyropoeon Valley
> Pool of Siloam
> Western Hill
> Hinnom Valley

5. The History of Jerusalem

Use the overhead transparencies "Topography of Jerusalem," "Jerusalem of David and Solomon," and "Jerusalem of Jesus' Time" as you outline the history of Jerusalem. Discuss the Bible Connections and Thoughts to Ponder throughout the material.

a. The Jerusalem of David and Solomon

1. Using the overhead transparencies "Topography of Jerusalem" and "Jerusalem of David and Solomon," point out the following information to your students:

   • Abraham was sent to the Moriah area to sacrifice Isaac approximately 2000 B.C.

   • Jerusalem was built on the mountain ridge called Moriah.

   Bible Connection

   Use the following passages to show your students how Mount Moriah connects with the Scriptures.

   Genesis 22:1–14 (Note especially verses 2 and 14.)

   1 Chronicles 21:18–19, 22:1

   2 Chronicles 3:1

   Matthew 27:32–33 (The exact location is unknown, but it is near Jerusalem on Mount Moriah.)

   Thoughts to Ponder: On this one mountain (probably within an area of a few hundred yards), God provided a substitute for Isaac, and the Israelites offered sacrifices pointing to their "substitute," from Solomon's time until Jesus' time, when God sent Jesus as our substitute to be sacrificed.

   Have your students answer the following questions:

   1. Why would God choose this same location for all three events?

   2. How might this location link God's work in the Old and New Testaments?

2. Using the overhead transparencies "Topography of Jerusalem" and "Jerusalem of David and Solomon," point out the following areas. **HINT:** *You may want to use Overhead Transparency 39 ("Ancient Jerusalem from the North") in the optional full-color overhead-transparency packet for Set 4 to supplement your teaching in this section.*

David's City
Spring of Gihon

Point out the following information to your students:

- David captured Jerusalem (then the Canaanite city of Jebus) in 1000 B.C. and made it his capital.

- Jebus had a population of approximately 2,000 people and covered 10 acres. It was nearly the same in size and location as David's Jerusalem.

- Apparently, David and his men entered the city by a "water shaft," though scholars debate the exact meaning of the Hebrew word used to describe it.

- David called it the City of David, and it became a royal city.

- Later David brought the ark of the covenant here, and the city became a holy city, the city where God chose to place His name.

- David fortified the city, making it very strong, and he also built his palace here.

- David's City apparently was already called Zion.

- David wanted to build God's house here, but that task was reserved for his son Solomon.

- David selected the location for the Temple and built an altar there. His choice was affirmed by God.

Bible Connection

Use the following passages to show your students how David's Jerusalem connects with the Scriptures.

Judges 19:10–11

2 Samuel 5:6

2 Samuel 5:8

1 Chronicles 11:4–9

2 Samuel 5:9–11

2 Samuel 6:1–19 (also 1 Chronicles 16)

Psalm 46:4 (also Psalm 48)

1 Chronicles 21:18–22:1; 2 Chronicles 3:1

1 Chronicles 28:4–7

Thoughts to Ponder: David's palace was apparently very beautiful, constructed of cedar and stone. Its recorded history is not pleasant. Read the following passages to discover some of the events that happened there.

- 1 Chronicles 15:27–29; 2 Samuel 6:16–23—David's wife Michal saw him dancing before the Lord. Michal thought that David was inappropriately clothed, and therefore she "despised him." She remained childless throughout her life.

- 2 Samuel 11:2–5—David was tempted by what he saw from the roof of his palace, and he fell into serious sin with Bathsheba.

- 2 Samuel 16:15–22—Absalom, David's son, led a revolt against his father. To indicate his assumption of power and complete disrespect of his father, he engaged publicly in intercourse with David's concubines (mistresses) on the roof of the palace.

Have your students answer the following questions:

1. Why do you think such a godly man had such troubles in his family?

2. What can you learn from the fact that these problems took place in and around David's palace? **HINT:** *Let students give their personal reactions to this fact—there is no set answer, but it is important for us to learn from the failures of the heroes of faith. You may want to point out Psalm 51, David's own expression of his reaction to his sin with Bathsheba.*

3. Using the overhead transparencies "Jerusalem of David and Solomon" and "Topography of Jerusalem," highlight the history of the building of the Temple by Solomon. **HINT:** *If you have the optional full-color overhead-transparency packets for Sets 2 and 4, you may want to use Overhead Transparency 11 ("The First Temple at Jerusalem") in Set 2 and Overhead Transparency 39 ("Ancient Jerusalem from the North") in Set 4 to supplement your teaching in this section.*

Point out the following information to your students:

- Solomon built the Temple approximately 950 B.C. on the threshing floor of Araunah on Mount Moriah, the location chosen by David at God's leading.

- It took seven years to build the Temple. No hammer or chisel was used on the site, for all stones were prepared at the quarry. The preparations were extensive, and the materials were magnificent.

- God honored the Temple and promised to live among the Israelites by placing His name and presence in the Temple.

- Solomon built a palace that was apparently between the Temple and David's City. It too was dramatic in construction and furnishings. Jerusalem now covered approximately 30 acres and had a population of 4,500.

Using the overhead transparencies "Jerusalem of David and Solomon" and "Topography of Jerusalem," point out the following:

> The Temple and its location (This is important because the location of the Temple remained the same for more than 1,000 years.)
> Solomon's palace and its location
> expansion of the city to the north

Bible Connection

Use the following passages to show your students how the construction of Jerusalem connects with the Scriptures.

1 Kings 6; 2 Chronicles 3—Solomon built the Temple.

1 Kings 7:13–51; 2 Chronicles 4—The Temple was precisely and luxuriously furnished.

1 Kings 8:1–21; 2 Chronicles 5—The ark was brought to the city and housed in the Temple.

1 Kings 8:22–66; 2 Chronicles 6—The Temple was dedicated to God.

2 Chronicles 5:13–14, 7:1–3—God's presence entered the Temple.

1 Kings 7:1–12—Solomon built a magnificent palace.

Thoughts to Ponder: Have your students read the following passages to see that God lived among His people.

- 1 Kings 6:11–13, 8:10; 2 Chronicles 5:13–14—God promised to live among His people, and

His glory entered the Temple.

- 2 Chronicles 7:1–3—God used fire to represent His presence and glory (*Shekineh* in Hebrew).

- Exodus 19:18, 24:17, 40:34–38; 1 Chronicles 21:26; 1 Kings 18:38; Revelation 1:14–15—God often used fire to represent the glory of His presence.

- Acts 2:3; 1 Corinthians 3:16–17—After Jesus' death and resurrection, on the Jewish feast of Pentecost, God's presence was symbolized by fire as it moved from the Temple to the new temples—the apostles.

Have your students answer the following questions:

1. Does this help you understand the meaning of that day of Pentecost? How?

2. How does your awareness of God's presence within you affect your life? NOTE: Lesson 26 covers this topic in greater detail.

b. Hezekiah's Expansion

HINT: *You may want to use Overhead Transparency 30 ("The Western Hill") in the optional full-color overhead-transparency packet for Set 4 to supplement your teaching in this section.*

Using the overhead transparencies "Topography of Jerusalem" and "Jerusalem of Jesus' Time," point out the following information to your students:

- During Hezekiah's reign over Judah, the northern kingdom of Israel was destroyed by the Assyrians (722 B.C.). Around 700 B.C., Jerusalem expanded to the west, across the Tyropoeon Valley and onto the Western Hill. No one knows exactly how much of this territory was included in the city. Assyria attacked Jerusalem in 701 B.C.

- Hezekiah fortified Jerusalem against the Babylonian threat. He built walls, tore down houses to expand fortifications, and added a tunnel to bring water into the city.

Using the overhead transparency " Topography of Jerusalem," point out the following areas, and have your students locate them on their maps.

> David's City
> Tyropoeon Valley
> Western Hill
> Spring of Gihon
> Hezekiah's Tunnel

Using the overhead transparency "Jerusalem of Jesus' Time," point out that the city of Jerusalem was on the Western Hill during Jesus' time. Though it is unlikely that Hezekiah's expansion spread this far west, this information gives us an idea of how the city grew across the Tyropoeon Valley up the slope of the hill. At this point, Jerusalem probably covered more than 100 acres and had a population of 24,000 people.

Bible Connection

Use the following passages to show your students how Hezekiah's expansion of Jerusalem connects with the Scriptures.

> 2 Kings 17:5–6—Israel was destroyed by Assyria.

> 2 Chronicles 32:1–5—Hezekiah fortified Jerusalem.

> Isaiah 22:10—Houses were torn down so the Israelites could expand the wall. (An example has been found in the Upper City of Jerusalem.)

Thoughts to Ponder: When Hezekiah had prepared for the Assyrian attack, he trusted God for the results. (Note Hezekiah's motive: "So that all kingdoms on earth may know that you alone, O Lord, are God"—Isaiah 37:20. This, of course, is the basis for the title of this series, *That the World May Know*.) Have your students read the following passages to discover how Hezekiah responded to the threat of Assyria.

- Isaiah 36:1—Assyria, a powerful nation, destroyed the northern kingdom of Israel and many cities of Judah, threatening the very existence of God's people.
- 2 Chronicles 29:1,31,35–36, 31:1,20–21—Hezekiah was a God-fearing king through much of his reign. He brought the nation of Israel back to God.
- 2 Chronicles 32:1–5—Hezekiah did everything he could do to prepare for the Assyrian attack.
- Isaiah 37:14–20—Hezekiah trusts God to deliver his people from the Assyrians.

Have your students answer the following questions:

1. What steps did Hezekiah take to deal with the great threat he faced?
2. Can you apply these steps to your life and the problems you face? How?

c. The Return from Exile: Ezra and Nehemiah

Using the overhead transparency "Topography of Jerusalem," point out the following information to your students.

- In 586 B.C., the Temple at Jerusalem was destroyed by the Babylonians, and many of the people were exiled. While they were in exile, though, they never lost sight of the importance of their city and Temple.
- Approximately 500 B.C., Cyrus, king of Persia, decreed that the Israelites could return to Jerusalem. The Temple was restored and the city was rebuilt over the next 100 years (530–400 B.C.), though on a smaller scale.

Using the overhead transparency "Topography of Jerusalem," point out the Temple Mount, where the Temple, called the Second Temple at this time, was rebuilt.

Bible Connection

Use the following passages to show your students that the Israelites never forgot Jerusalem and that when they returned, they immediately rebuilt the city.

Psalm 137:4–6; Lamentations 1:1,8, 5:20–21—The people remembered Jerusalem while they were in exile.

Ezra 1:1–4, 3:7–13, 6:15—The Israelites rebuilt the Temple, but there was no ark of the covenant, so the Holy of Holies was left empty.

Nehemiah 2:1–8, 3, 12:27–47—The city walls were restored and dedicated.

Thoughts to Ponder: God never forgets His people. After the Israelites had been in exile and the Temple had been in ruins for 70 years, the people began to rebuild the Temple, and after nearly 100 more years, they finished rebuilding the city. The people could then resume worshiping their God.

Have your students answer the following questions:

1. How does it help you to understand how God remembered Israel?
2. What is one reason God wanted a Temple in Jerusalem so Jews from around the world could come each year to worship? (See Acts 2:5–11.)
3. How can God's careful planning encourage you?

d. The Hasmonaeans: Jerusalem Expands Again

HINT: *You may want to use Overhead Transparency 42 ("Scenes from the City of Jesus' Day") in the optional full-color overhead-transparency packet for Set 4 to supplement your teaching in this section.*

Using the overhead transparencies "Topography of Jerusalem" and "Jerusalem of Jesus' Time," point out the following information to your students:

- Jerusalem, which was rebuilt during the time of Ezra, became part of Alexander the Great's empire in 322 B.C. The city suffered through more than a century of conflict between the successors of Alexander. The Maccabean revolt (approximately 165 B.C.) brought Jerusalem again under Jewish control.

- The cleansing and rededication of the Temple was celebrated in the Feast of Dedication (Hanukkah—see John 10:22).

- The descendants of the Maccabees, the Hasmonaean dynasty, expanded Jerusalem.

- The Western Hill was enclosed within the city, the Temple Mount was expanded, and the fortress Baris (later the Antonia) was constructed. The city now covered 175 acres and was home to more than 30,000 people.

Display the overhead transparency "Jerusalem of Jesus' Time" (note that this transparency is of Herod's Jerusalem, but it is quite similar to the Hasmonaean city). Point out the following locations, and have your students find them on their maps.

> Temple Mount
> Antonia fortress
> Hasmonaean palace

Using the overhead transparency "Topography of Jerusalem," point out the enclosed Western Hill.

e. Herod's Jerusalem: Its Fullest Glory

HINT: *You may want to use Overhead Transparencies 31–42 in the optional full-color overhead-transparency packet for Set 4 to supplement your teaching in this section.*

Using the overhead transparencies "Topography of Jerusalem," "Jerusalem's Districts," and "Jerusalem of Jesus' Time," point out the following information to your students:

- In 63 B.C., the Romans under Pompey took Jerusalem from the Hasmonaeans. Eventually, the Romans put the city and the country under Herod's control.

- Herod ruled from 37–4 B.C. He expanded the Temple Mount greatly, fortified the city with a citadel and an expanded fortress renamed the Antonia, built many structures, including a theater and a hippodrome, and fortified the walls. His greatest accomplishment was the lavish expansion and embellishment of the Temple and its platform. The city was spectacular, one of the wonders of the ancient world.

- The city had now expanded to cover nearly 250 acres and had a population of 45,000. It was ready for the ministry of Jesus, the Messiah.

Using the overhead transparency "Jerusalem of Jesus' Time," point out the following locations, and have your students find them on their maps.

> Temple Mount and Temple
> Antonia fortress
> Hasmonaean palace
> Herod's palace
> theater

first wall
second wall

Using the overhead transparency "Jerusalem's Districts," point out the following locations, and have your students find them on their maps.

Temple Mount
David's City
Lower City
Upper City
business district
New City

Using the overhead transparency "Topography of Jerusalem," review the following:

David's City
Temple Mount
Kidron Valley
Mount of Olives
Tyropoeon Valley
Western Hill
Hinnom Valley

Step Two: "The City of Jesus' Time"

1. Map Study: Jerusalem

Using the overhead transparency "Jerusalem of Jesus' Time," point out the following areas, and have your students locate them on their maps.

Temple Mount
Kidron Valley
David's City
Tyropoeon Valley

Using the overhead transparency "Jerusalem's Districts," point out the following areas, and have your students locate them on their maps.

Temple Mount
Southern Stairs
David's City
Temple Mount
Antonia fortress

2. Preparation

For the following study, you'll need to prepare the overhead transparencies "Jerusalem of David and Solomon," "Development of the Temple Mount," "Jerusalem of Jesus' Time," "The Temple Mount: A.D. 70," "Temple Courts," and "Herod's Temple."

3. The Temple Mount

God chose to put His name and presence in the Temple in Jerusalem, making it the focus of the worship of the Israelite people. The location of the Temple—on a high point of the ridge known as David's City, just to the north of the original Jerusalem—did not change in a period of 1,000 years, from the time of Solomon until the Temple was destroyed by the Romans in A.D. 70. The sacred area known as the Temple Mount gradually expanded throughout history. The Temple, though, standing in the center of the Mount, remained in the same location. Investigating the Temple and its structures and practices brings us to the very heart of God's plan of salvation for His people.

a. Development of the Temple Platform

HINT: *You may want to use Overhead Transparencies 31 ("The Western Wall"), 33 ("The Southern Stairs"), 36 ("Ancient Jerusalem from the South"), and 37 ("The Upper City") in the optional full-color overhead-transparency packet for Set 4 to supplement your teaching in this section.*

With God's direction, David chose a flat area (threshing floor) on Mount Moriah, and later Solomon built the Temple there. Apparently, this threshing floor, where David had built an altar, was large enough for the Temple and its courts.

1. **Location.** Using the overhead transparency "Jerusalem of David and Solomon," point out the location of the Temple Mount from David's time. No definite remains of this place have been found. Temples in the ancient world were built within sacred areas, usually on the highest points in their regions. Solomon's Temple was no exception: This sacred area was on the highest point of the ridge.

   Bible Connection

   Use the following passage to show your students how the development of the Temple Mount connects with the Scriptures.

   > 2 Chronicles 3:1

   Little is known of any changes to the Temple Mount after the time of Ezra and Nehemiah. It is assumed that in rebuilding the Temple, they worked within the original boundaries of Solomon's Temple.

2. **Hasmonaean Expansion.** Using the overhead transparency "Development of the Temple Mount," show the expansion of the Hasmonaeans, pointing out the following information:

   - The original square Temple Mount was built to provide a flat area on the top of the mountain. Remains of this structure have not been found.

   - The Hasmonaean expansion is on the right side of the transparency. (Note the tunnels providing access to the Mount.)

3. **Herod's Expansion.** Using the overhead transparency "Development of the Temple Mount," show the expansion of this area by Herod, pointing out the following information:

   - The extension to the south included tunnels.

   - The extension to the west in the Tyropoeon Valley demanded enormous retaining walls on both the south and the west.

   - The Antonia was built on a flat rock.

   - The eastern wall followed the original line from the times of Solomon, Ezra, and the Hasmonaeans.

   - The base for this Temple was the largest in the ancient world. A small section of it, located between Barclay's Gate and Wilson's Arch, is called the Western Wall, or Wailing Wall.

- The retaining walls of this mount contain massive stones, each weighing more than 500 tons. The Temple platform was more than 900 feet wide and 1,200 feet long.

b. The Temple Mount of Jesus' Time

1. The Outside Walls (East, South, West, North)

- **The East Wall**

HINT: *If you have the optional full-color overhead-transparency packets for Sets 1, 2, and 4, see Overhead Transparency 8 ("The Eastern Gate of Jerusalem") in Set 1, Overhead Transparency 21 ("The Temple Mount at Jerusalem") in Set 2, and Overhead Transparency 32 ("Scenes of the Temple Mount") in Set 4.*

Using the overhead transparencies "Jerusalem of Jesus' Time" and "Temple Courts," point out the Golden Gate to your students.

The east wall of the Temple Mount followed nearly the same line it did in Solomon's time. The main feature in the wall was the Eastern Gate, sometimes referred to as the Shushan Gate. Today the gate built over that gate is known as the Golden Gate.

This gate was probably the original eastern entrance to the Temple Mount. According to historical records, this gate was used to bring the Red Heifer to the Mount of Olives to be sacrificed. On Yom Kippur, the scapegoat was probably taken through this gate to the wilderness east of Jerusalem.

Bible Connection

Use the following passages to show your students how the east wall connects with the Scriptures.

> Numbers 19:1–10; Leviticus 16
> Matthew 4:5

Some people believe Jesus passed through this gate in His triumphal entry because it was a main ceremonial entrance. If He did enter here, it would have highlighted His kingship. Other gates, though, are more likely to have been on Jesus' route. NOTE: Lesson 23 covers this topic in greater detail.

Herod expanded this wall to the north and to the south. Some scholars believe that the high southeast corner of this wall is the pinnacle corner. At this point, the walls of the Temple were more than 225 feet above the bottom of the Kidron Valley. Others, however, place the pinnacle corner on the southwest corner of the wall.

- **The South Wall**

HINT: *If you have the optional full-color overhead-transparency packet for Set 4, see Overhead Transparencies 33 ("The Southern Stairs"), 34 ("Scenes from the Southern Stairs"), 36 ("Ancient Jerusalem from the South"), and 42 ("Scenes from the City of Jesus' Day").*

Using the overhead transparencies "Jerusalem of Jesus' Time" and "The Temple Mount: A.D. 70," point out the following structures and places, and have your students locate them on their maps/diagrams.

> Southern Stairs
> south wall
> royal stoa
> opening of entrance tunnels on Temple Mount floor

Using the overhead transparency "The Temple Mount: A.D. 70," point out the following locations, and have your students find them on their diagrams.

Double Gates (also called the Huldah Gates—entrance for pilgrims)
Triple Gates (probably an entrance for priests)
ritual baths
plaza

This south wall is probably the most impressive of all the walls of the Temple Mount. It is more than 900 feet long and more than 150 feet high. Pilgrims (including Jesus and the disciples) entered the Temple primarily through this entrance after washing in a ritual bath called a *mikveh* (pl. *mikvoth*). On feast days (Passover, Pentecost, and Sukkot), literally hundreds of thousands of people made their way up the Southern Stairs and into the Temple courts. It is probable that the New Testament Pentecost events happened here or nearby. NOTE: Lesson 26 covers this setting in more detail.

Bible Connection

Use the following passage to show your students how the south wall connects with the Scriptures.

Acts 2

- ### The West Wall
HINT: *If you have the optional full-color overhead-transparency packet for Set 4, see Overhead Transparencies 31 ("The Western Wall"), 32 ("Scenes of the Temple Mount"), 37 ("The Upper City"), and 42 ("Scenes from the City of Jesus' Day").*

Help students appreciate the stunning beauty of the Temple Mount, as well as its magnitude. It was twice as large as the largest temple enclosure in Rome at that time.

Using the overhead transparency "The Temple Mount: A.D. 70," point out the following locations, and have your students find them on their diagrams.

Robinson's Arch
royal stoa
Barclay's Gate
Wilson's Arch
Warren's Gate
Temple
Place of Trumpeting (above Robinson's Arch)
Tyropoeon Street

Using the overhead transparency "Jerusalem of Jesus' Time," point out the following locations, and have your students find them on their maps.

Temple Mount
Robinson's Arch
Barclay's Gate
Wilson's Arch and bridge
Warren's Gate
Tyropoeon Street

Robinson's Arch was named after the British explorer who discovered it. Rising 75 feet above the street and measuring more than 45 feet across, it was one of the largest masonry arches in the ancient world. It supported a massive staircase that ran from the Tyropoeon Valley and the Lower City to the royal stoa (the place of buying and selling, the place where the Sanhedrin met, and the place where the treasury of the Temple was located). Robinson's Arch also had a tower where the trumpet was blown to indicate the beginning or end of religious celebrations (especially the Sabbath).

Barclay's Gate was named after the American missionary who discovered it. It has an enormous lintel over it, which is more than 25 feet long and 7 feet high. This gate provided access to the Temple courts (Gentile Court) from Tyropoeon Street.

Wilson's Arch was named after a British explorer. It supported a bridge that extended from the Upper City, the home of the Sadducees and others. Like Robinson's Arch, Wilson's Arch was one of the largest arches of its kind ever constructed. It still stands, though it was probably reconstructed after the Roman destruction of the Temple in A.D. 70. Today the area beneath the arch is used as a synagogue.

Warren's Gate provided direct access to the Temple courts. Some have suggested that its location, just west of the Temple, may indicate that it was an entrance for priests into the inner courts. Warren's Gate was also probably reconstructed, but it still gives evidence of the enormous, spectacularly beautiful gates Herod built.

The *massive ashlars* in this course (or row of large, hand-shaped stones) are nearly impossible to describe. The largest of these stones is more than 10 feet high, 11 to 14 feet thick, and 45 feet long, and weighs nearly 600 tons. It was brought from a quarry nearly a mile away. There are four such stones here. Whether there are more where the wall has not been excavated is unknown, but seeing these stones helps us understand what a spectacular masterpiece the Temple of Herod was. These massive ashlars may be the stones the disciples marveled at (see Mark 13:1–2; Luke 21:5), though the thousands of regular stones on the Temple weighed many tons themselves.

Tyropoeon Street may not have had this name officially, but it did follow the Tyropoeon Valley. This street, one of the busiest in the city, was lined with shops and markets (called the upper and lower markets by Josephus). It ran past the entrance to the Antonia, the Roman fortress built by Herod and named after Mark Antony, his patron. Some believe that Jesus was taken to the Antonia to be tried. If so, He probably walked on this street.

Bible Connection

Use the following passages to show your students how the west wall connects with the Scriptures.

> Mark 13:1–2
> Luke 21:5

Thoughts to Ponder: Herod's Temple (as well as the whole city of Jerusalem) was one of the most spectacular sights in the ancient world. People today are still amazed at the Temple's magnitude and beauty. Jesus often visited Jerusalem, yet, unlike Herod, He left no buildings or writings, even though He was an even greater king than Herod.

Have your students answer the following questions:

1. Why might people have found it hard to believe that Jesus was the Messiah? Why do you think God often seems to use that which appears weak? (See John 2:19–22; Matthew 26:60–61, 27:40; Mark 14:57–59.)

2. What made Jesus' claim seem so impossible, so blasphemous?

- **The North Wall**

HINT: *If you have the optional full-color overhead-transparency packet for Set 4, see Overhead Transparencies 38 ("The New City") and 39 ("Ancient Jerusalem from the North").*

Using the overhead transparency "Jerusalem of Jesus' Time," point out the Antonia fortress, and have your students find it on their maps.

The *Antonia* was built by Herod the Great. In Nehemiah's time, there was a fortress or citadel on or near the Temple (Nehemiah 2:8). Later, the Hasmonaeans built a fortress on the northern end of the Temple Mount. This fortress was called Baris (meaning "birch" in Hebrew). It was probably built over the citadel. Herod the Great removed the Baris and built a large fortress-palace, called the Antonia, in this location.

The Antonia was on a rock plateau 150 feet by 400 feet in size and 80 feet higher than the surrounding area. The plateau had been cut so its slopes were nearly vertical. The walls of the fortress were an additional 65 feet high. Three of its corner towers were 80 feet high, and the fourth was more than 110 feet high. According to Josephus, the Antonia had bathhouses, broad courtyards, and many rooms.

Herod built the Antonia to guard the northern side of Jerusalem. (NOTE: A fortress was needed on the north because there are valleys on the east, west, and south.) It also provided a place for the Roman troops, stationed here in Jesus' time, to watch the activities taking place in the Temple courts. During festival times (Passover, Pentecost, and Sukkot), the spirit of revolt often ran high. The fortress was connected by entrances—some apparently secret—to the Temple courts.

The high priest's sacred robes were kept in the Antonia and were given out only during festivals so as to keep the high priest submissive to the Romans.

Paul was probably brought to the Antonia after his arrest. He defended himself on the steps (Acts 21:35) that apparently led to the fortress.

Bible Connection

Use the following passages to show your students how the north wall and the Antonia fortress connect with the Scriptures.

> Acts 21:27–40, 22:22–25

Tradition and some scholars claim that Jesus was tried here by Pilate, while others believe the trial took place either in Herod's palace or the Hasmonaean palace. Wherever it was, the Bible describes a place quite similar to the Antonia.

> Mark 15:16—Here the location is referred to as a palace and the praetorium (soldiers' quarters).

> Matthew 27:19; John 19:13—Pilate sat on a judgment seat that was on a paved area.

All these biblical details were true of the Antonia and probably other locations as well. It is not important for us to know exactly where Jesus' trial took place, but it is helpful for us to understand the nature of the location.

Thoughts to Ponder: Rome was the greatest of the ancient empires. Its powerful military machine kept the world relatively peaceful throughout the time of Jesus and the beginning of the church. It was Roman legionaries, though, who put Jesus to death.

Have your students answer the following questions:

1. How does understanding the nature of the Roman empire help you appreciate the careful preparations God made for the coming of Jesus?

2. Read John 18:37, 19:8–11. How does understanding the power of Rome, displayed by fortresses like the Antonia, help you understand what Jesus was saying in these passages?

NOTE: This topic is covered in more detail in Lesson 25.

Using the overhead transparency "Jerusalem of Jesus' Time," point out the following areas and have your students locate them on their maps.

Antonia fortress
Temple
Tadi (Sheep) Gate
Pool of Bethesda (also known as Sheep Pool)

The *Tadi Gate* is in the same location Nehemiah placed the "Sheep Gate" (Nehemiah 3:1, 32). This indicates that these two names probably refer to the same gate. This gate was built by priests, which indicates a connection to the Temple itself. Many believe this was the entrance through which the sacrificial animals went into the Temple.

Some believe Jesus entered this gate after His triumphal entry. This would emphasize His choice to make His entrance at the time the Passover lamb was selected (Exodus 12:2–3). Since He was the "Lamb of God, who takes away the sin of the world" (John 1:29), it is an intriguing possibility that He entered the city on the day of lamb selection and entered through the "Sheep Gate." The Bible does not specify which gate He entered.

Near the Tadi Gate was the *Pool of Bethesda* (John 5:2). Some early sources call it "Sheep Pool" as well, because sheep were washed here (or near here) before they were brought into the Temple courts, about 300 feet away. There were two pools (parts of which have been found) that had colonnades around the outside and between them.

People apparently believed that the pools held healing power. This is clearly indicated in the Bible (see John 5:3) and in the presence of a small Roman temple to the god of healing nearby.

Bible Connection

Use the following passage to show your students how the Tadi Gate and the Pool of Bethesda connect with the Scriptures.

John 5:1–14

- Note the reference to Sheep Gate.
- It is clear that people believed in the healing power of the pool.
- The pool was surrounded by five colonnades.
- Later, Jesus was in the Temple courts, which were nearby.

Thoughts to Ponder: Have your students answer the following questions:

1. Why would the man who was miraculously healed be in the Temple so soon afterward?

2. How do you show your gratitude for the things God provides for you?

3. Have you ever experienced an unusual blessing from God that at first you did not realize came from Him? (NOTE: At first the man did not even know who Jesus was.) How did you discover it was God's blessing? Discuss your experience with the rest of the class.

- **Review of the Outside Walls of the Temple Mount**
  Using the overhead transparency "Jerusalem of Jesus' Time," review the following:

  Temple
  Temple Mount
  Eastern Gate
  Southern Stairs
  Double Gates
  Triple Gates
  royal stoa
  Robinson's Arch

Barclay's Gate
Wilson's Arch
Tyropoeon Street
Warren's Gate
Antonia fortress
Tadi (Sheep) Gate
Pool of Bethesda

2. The Temple Courts (Gentile Court, Royal Stoa, Women's Court, Court of the Israelites, Priests' Court)

HINT: *If you have the optional full-color overhead-transparency packet for Set 4, see Overhead Transparencies 40 ("The Temple Mount") and 41 ("The Temple").*

The Temple platform was enormous. It was more than 900 feet wide from east to west (915 feet on the south end, and 1,030 feet on the north end) and more than 1,500 feet long from north to south (1,535 feet on the east end, and 1,590 feet on the west end). It was by far the largest temple area in the ancient world. Hundreds of thousands of pilgrims could be on the mount at the same time. (Josephus claimed that the Passover pilgrims numbered more than 2 million people.) Herod trained 1,000 priests as masons to work on the Temple itself. Ten thousand highly skilled laborers, using 1,000 wagons, worked for years to construct it. The finished platform was divided into separate courts, which were increasingly more sacred the closer they were to the Temple itself. This section begins with the courts on the outer edge of the platform and gradually moves toward the Temple itself.

Using the overhead transparencies "The Temple Mount: A.D. 70" and "Temple Courts," point out the following areas, and have your students locate them on their diagrams.

Temple
Gentile Court
royal stoa
Solomon's Colonnade
Priests' Court
Court of the Israelites
Women's Court
Southern Stairs

Review the material below with your students.

a. The Gentile Court

The *Gentile Court* was the large open area around the sacred courts of the Temple. Anyone could enter this area. This court was also intended to be a place of prayer for Gentiles.

Locate the *colonnade* around the outer edge of the court. On three sides, the colonnade was more than 45 feet wide and 40 feet high. It had a flat roof that rested on the outer wall on one edge and on two rows of massive columns on the other. This colonnade gave the mount great splendor and also provided a place for teaching and assembly.

Locate *Solomon's Colonnade.* This apparently was the oldest of the colonnades. Josephus attributed it to Solomon, although it probably wasn't that old. This colonnade often provided a place of meeting. It was a favorite teaching spot of Jesus, and the place where the early church met.

Bible Connection

Use the following passages to show your students how the Gentile Court connects with the Scriptures.

Matthew 26:55; Mark 11:27, 12:35; Luke 2:46, 20:1; John 7:14, 8:2—Jesus regularly taught in the Temple courts, which were most likely the areas beneath the colonnade on the east, west, or north.

Acts 2:46, 5:20–21,42—The first Christians, almost all Jewish, met regularly in the Temple courts, most likely in this same location beneath the colonnade.

John 10:22–23—Jesus confronted the crowd with His message in Solomon's Colonnade.

Acts 3:1–16—Peter healed a man at the Beautiful Gate (the entrance to the Women's Court just west of Solomon's Colonnade), and a crowd came to hear his teaching in Solomon's Colonnade.

Acts 5:12–14—The early believers met regularly in Solomon's Colonnade, and the group grew quickly.

Thoughts to Ponder: Have your students answer the following questions:

1. What can we learn from the fact that the early Christians met in the Temple courts?

2. Why would Jesus have come here to teach? (Possible answers: There were large crowds, people sought God here, the Temple symbolized the presence of God, Jesus would fulfill the means of forgiveness that people were looking for at the Temple, God's people were here.) NOTE: Encourage your students to think of other reasons. Help them see that Jesus, the disciples, and the early church all centralized their teaching in the Temple courts. Remind your students that we must never forget our Jewish roots or neglect to share Jesus with Jewish people.

3. What lesson can be found in the fact that it was referred to as Solomon's Colonnade?

b. The Royal Stoa (Portico)

The southern end of the Temple platform was one of the most beautiful buildings in the world, according to Josephus. The stoa had a central hall with aisles on each side. It also had 162 columns, each one more than 50 feet high and so large in circumference (according to Josephus) that three men with outstretched arms could barely reach around it.

The Sanhedrin met on the eastern end of the stoa, beginning shortly before Jesus' death. It is possible that some of the confrontations between the early Christians and the Sanhedrin occurred here.

Bible Connection

Use the following passages to show your students how the royal stoa connects with the Scriptures.

Acts 5:21—The Sanhedrin met and questioned the disciples.

- The royal stoa became the area where merchandise needed for the Temple was bought and sold. The marketplace spread from the stoa into the Gentile Court and up to the Soreq Valley, the wall that marked the boundary of the sacred area.

Matthew 21:12–16; Mark 11:15–18; Luke 19:45–47; John 2:13–22—Jesus drove the merchants out of the Temple. (Note Matthew 21:13. This is a quote from Isaiah 56:7. In the context of Isaiah, this refers to the nations—Gentiles—who will come to serve the Lord in Jerusalem.)

- Apparently, before Jesus' time, another rabbi had driven thousands of sheep into the Temple to protest the way the sacrificial system was conducted. (It may have happened during Passover season, as Jesus' confrontation did.)

- Jesus drove the merchants from the Temple because people were being cheated (Matthew 21:13) and because the area intended for Gentile prayer (worship) was being used as a marketplace by the Jews. Jesus would not allow the Temple authorities to prevent the Gentiles from having a place to worship God.

Thoughts to Ponder: Have your students answer the following questions:

1. In what ways are we sometimes insensitive to the spiritual needs of those who are different from us?

2. How can we demonstrate that God wants all people to have opportunities to find Him?

3. Jesus' greatest anger was with the religious community, who were uncaring about the hurting, sinful, broken, outcast, and Gentile people of His day. What might we do in our day that would bring the same anger?

4. What are some specific ways we can become more sensitive to those in need around us?

The *Soreq* was a stone wall that surrounded the consecrated Temple area. It was five feet high and had Greek and Latin signs on it, forbidding Gentiles from passing that point on the pain of death. Remains of two of these plaques have been found and are displayed in the Rockefeller Museum in Jerusalem.

Bible Connection

Use the following passages to show your students how the Soreq connects with the Scriptures.

Acts 21:27–35—Paul was accused of bringing a Gentile into the inner court, past the Soreq. He denied the charge.

Ephesians 2:14—Paul said the "dividing wall of hostility" (translated in the King James as "middle wall of partition," which is closer to the original Greek) must come down between Jews and Gentiles (along with all other dividing walls—between races, men and women, etc.) if people are to experience the peace of God. The Gentiles were to be allowed *in* to experience the blessings the Jews always had. Though the wall has been broken down by Jesus, it is important for us to identify and embrace our religious history. Reclaiming our Jewish roots can enhance our relationship with God.

Thoughts to Ponder: Have your students answer the following questions:

1. What walls divide you from others?

2. What can you do to break down the walls?

3. Why do we know so little about the Jewish roots of our faith? What can you do to learn more about your religious history as a Christian? To help others learn?

c. The Women's Court

This large area (more than 40,000 square feet) was where the communal worship activities took place. The Levites read the Psalms of Ascent (Psalms 120–134) from the semicircular staircase overlooking the court. The crowd gathered here as the sacrifices were made on the altar in the inner court.

Using the overhead transparencies "The Temple Mount: A.D. 70" and "Temple Courts," point out the following locations, and have your students find them on their diagrams. Then review the information given below.

Women's Court
Beautiful Gate and Nicanor Gate

Chamber of Nazirites
Chamber of Wood
Chamber of Lepers
Chamber of Oil
steps
Temple

Inside the Gentile Court and the Soreq was an elevated terrace or rampart called *Chel.* This raised area contained the sacred inner courts of the Temple. It was open only to Jews who were ritually clean and who had washed in a *mikveh.* This inner court had a wall around it and was divided into two parts. The eastern section was known as the *Women's Court* because it marked the limits beyond which women could not pass.

It is not clear whether the *Beautiful Gate* and the *Nicanor Gate* were the actual names of these gates. The main eastern gate to the Women's Court, here called Beautiful, was more than 115 feet high, so it makes it a likely candidate for that name, but the Nicanor Gate was covered with artistic brass plating, so it too could be called beautiful.

Bible Connection

Use the following passage to show your students how the Women's Court and Beautiful Gate connect with the Scriptures.

> Acts 3:1–11—Peter and John healed a crippled man. He immediately entered the Temple courts, praising God, running and jumping. This account seems to suggest that the Beautiful Gate was the eastern entrance to the Women's Court.

Under the *colonnades* around the outside of the Women's Court were "trumpet-shaped" *offering boxes* for required gifts. Seven of these boxes received specific offerings such as "Bird Offering," while the other six were for free-will offerings. Women would gather on the balcony on the feast of Sukkot to watch the celebration of the water drawing. This area was probably the Temple treasury.

Bible Connection

Use the following passages to show your students how the trumpet-shaped offering boxes connect with the Scriptures.

> Luke 2:21–38—Joseph would have presented the firstborn offering for Jesus at the gate at the top of the stairs in the Women's Court. Mary and Joseph would have requested an offering of birds (verse 24) and placed the required money in the third trumpet-shaped offering box. In this court, Simeon met the family (verse 27) and Anna spent her days (verse 37) in the Temple. (Women could go no farther than the Women's Court.)
>
> Mark 12:41–43—Jesus was in the Women's Court when the widow placed her offering in the appropriate offering box.

In the four corners of the Women's Court were chambers: (1) the Chamber of the Nazirites, (2) the Chamber of Wood, (3) the Chamber of Lepers, and (4) the Chamber of Oil.

Nazirites took a vow of separation for God for a set period of time or for life. (NOTE: Samson was a Nazirite for life, but many Nazirites were not.) In the *Chamber of the Nazirites,* the Nazirites could take their vows of separation, or complete them and have their hair cut. If they cut their hair somewhere else, they brought their hair to this chamber to complete their vows. After appropriate offerings, the hair was burned. The offering was eaten, and the Nazirite had finished his vow.

Bible Connection

Use the following passages to show your students how the Nazirites and their chamber connect with the Scriptures.

Numbers 6:1–21—The Nazirites took vows of total devotion to God.

Acts 18:18, 21:22–24—Some of the early Christians, including Paul, took Nazirite vows. They would have been completed in this chamber.

Thoughts to Ponder: Have your students answer the following questions:

1. Why would Paul and others make such a vow to God?

2. How might you show such total commitment to God?

In the *Chamber of Wood,* priests would carefully inspect the wood used for altar fires to make sure it was not wormy or rotten.

In the *Chamber of the Lepers,* lepers would ritually purify themselves before presenting themselves to the priests and then making the appropriate offerings at the Nicanor Gate.

Bible Connection

Use the following passage to show your students how the Chamber of Lepers connects with the Scriptures.

Matthew 8:1–4

The *Chamber of Oil* was the room in which the oil and wine for offerings were prepared and stored.

Four golden *menorahs* (lampstands) stood in the Women's Court. These were lit in connection with the feasts of Sukkot and Hanukkah (Dedication). These lampstands were more than 75 feet high. The wicks for the oil were made from the worn-out clothes of the priests. The light of these lamps could be seen throughout Jerusalem.

Crowds would gather in the Women's Court for all religious services. Noteworthy is the water drawing of Sukkot: Each day for seven days, a priestly procession went to the Pool of Siloam and brought water in a pitcher to the altar in the Priests' Court. The people, carrying the *lulavim* (branches of palm and other trees), filled the court, chanting the Hosanna (Psalm 118:25–26): "Lord, save us! Blessed is he who comes in the name of the Lord! From the house of the Lord, we bless you! The Lord is God, and he has made his light shine upon us. With boughs in hand, join in the festal procession up to the horns of the altar!"

The noise was deafening, and the sight of thousands of people waving their branches was astounding. As the people shouted, the priest poured the water into a funnel and into the altar. On the seventh day of the feast, this ceremony reached a crescendo. The passion and joy of the worshipers were indescribable as they sought God's salvation and the blessing of rain. On that evening of the seventh day, the great menorahs were lit, completing the celebration.

Bible Connection

Use the following passages to show your students how the water-drawing ceremony and menorahs connect with the Scriptures.

John 7:1,14,37–39—Jesus went to the feast of Sukkot celebration in the Women's Court. On the last day, as the ceremony reached its highest intensity, He shouted, "If anyone is thirsty, let him come to me."

John 8:12—At the same festival, Jesus said, "I am the light of the world." The lights from the Temple menorahs probably provided the backdrop for this message.

Thoughts to Ponder: Have your students answer the following questions:

1. Do these events help you understand Jesus' teaching style? What have you learned?

2. What kind of reaction do you think the massive crowd had to Jesus' shouting?

3. How can we show the kind of passion and joy for the Lord in our worship that the Israelites showed in theirs?

d. The Court of the Israelites

Using the overhead transparency "Temple Courts," point out the following locations, and have your students find them on their diagrams.

> Temple
> Court of the Israelites
> Priests' Court

The *Court of the Israelites* was more than 200 feet wide and 20 feet deep. It was divided from the *Priests' Court* by blocks of polished stone. People crowded this area on festival days (such as Passover and Sukkot). The main purpose of this court was for the Jewish men to place their hands on the animals to be slaughtered before offering them.

Bible Connection

Use the following passage to show your students how the Court of the Israelites connects with the Scriptures.

> Luke 2:41–42—In this account, Jesus, now considered an adult, would have placed His hands on the head of a lamb for the first time. (Some scholars believe that on Passover, the worshipers actually killed their own lambs, but this is debated.)

Thoughts to Ponder: Have your students answer the following question:

1. What do you think it meant to Jesus to be a regular part of the sacrificial ceremonies of slaughter when He knew He was to replace all offerings as "the lamb of God" (John 1:29)?

e. The Priests' Court

Using the overhead transparency "Temple Courts," point out the following locations, and have your students find them on their diagrams.

> Temple
> Court of the Israelites
> Priests' Court
> altar
> laver
> place of slaughter
> Chamber of Hewn Stone

The *Priests' Court* was for the sacrificial service. The *altar* was on the south side and was 48 feet square and possibly 24 feet high. It had a ramp and no steps (Exodus 20:26). On one corner were drains for the blood, which eventually reached the Kidron Valley to the east. On the corners of the altar were the funnels where the water and drink offerings were poured. At least three fires were kept burning on the altar. A ledge around the outside allowed the priests to walk around the altar to tend the sacrifices. The *laver* was where the priests washed their hands and feet.

The *place of slaughter* had six rows of four rings, into which the heads of the sacrificial animals were placed. Next to these rings were marble pillars with cedar beams. These beams had hooks attached, on which the carcasses were hung while they were skinned. Nearby were marble tables for cutting up the animals for the sacrifice itself. The blood was sprinkled on the altar or around its base, depending on the offering.

The *Chamber of Hewn Stone* was the place where the priests gathered each morning to cast lots for the privilege of performing the religious duties of that day, including slaughtering the sacrifice for the nation, caring for the Temple menorahs, and offering the incense. During this time, the Ten Commandments were read, the Shema was prayed (Deuteronomy 6:4–6), benedictions were pronounced, and the day's services were begun (at dawn).

As the incense offering was made (the last part of the service), the crowd gathered outside to pray. After the incense offering, the priests stood and together blessed the people with the benediction of Aaron (Numbers 6:24–26), and the service was ended. The afternoon service (at 3:00) was the same as the morning service, except a new priest was chosen to make the incense offering. The Sanhedrin also met in this chamber until about A.D. 30, when they began meeting in the royal stoa.

Bible Connection

Use the following passage to show your students how the Chamber of Hewn Stone connects with the Scriptures.

Luke 1:5–22

In the Chamber of Hewn Stone, Zechariah was chosen by lot to make the incense offering. There were several hundred priests in each course group. (There were 24 groups, each serving two weeks at a time.) Zechariah was of the priests in the course of Abijah. Whoever was selected to make the offering would not have the privilege again until *all* the other priests in the course had had an opportunity. This meant that most priests had this honor only once or twice in their lifetimes, if at all.

Zechariah was making the prayer offering as the people prayed. Suddenly an angel appeared to Zechariah in the chamber. The people outside began to wonder what was taking Zechariah so long. He finally came out but could not bless the people because he could not speak.

Thoughts to Ponder: Have your students answer the following question:

1. The angel Gabriel appeared as Zechariah offered the offering of prayer. What prayers were answered in this event?

Around the outside of the inner court were additional chambers for various functions, including storage of priests' vestments, the salt for the offerings, the shewbread, *mikvoth* (sing. *mikveh)* for the priests, incense, and a sleeping room for the priests who were part of the night watch.

3. The Temple Building

HINT: *If you have the optional full-color overhead-transparency packet for Set 4, see Overhead Transparencies 40 ("The Temple Mount") and 41 ("The Temple").*

Using the overhead transparencies "Temple Courts" and "Herod's Temple," point out the following locations, and have your students find them on their diagrams. Then relay the information given below.

porch

holy place (sanctuary)

most holy place (Holy of Holies)
veil

The Temple itself was 170 feet high and 170 feet wide in front and 110 feet wide in the back (the west side). The Temple faced east. Josephus wrote that it was built of large blocks of white marble.

The *porch* was an enormous entrance chamber without a door. It had two huge columns on each side. Hanging from these columns was a great golden vine, a gift from Herod. On it hung gold grape clusters Josephus described as "as tall as a man." Only priests and Levites could enter the Temple building.

The first chamber, the *holy place,* was 68 feet long and 35 feet wide. In it were the menorah (the seven-branched candlestick), the table of shewbread, and the golden altar of incense. The walls were plated with gold.

Bible Connection

Use the following passage to show your students how the elements described above connect with the Scriptures.

> Luke 1:5–22

The inner chamber—the *most holy place,* or *Holy of Holies*—was 33 feet square and was empty during Jesus' time because the ark of the covenant had disappeared during Old Testament times. Here the very presence of God had been manifested for hundreds of years (2 Chronicles 5:13–14).

A double *veil* separated the Holy of Holies from the holy place. One side of the veil was fastened on the south end and the other side on the north. Once a year, on Yom Kippur, the high priest entered the Holy of Holies and sought forgiveness in God's presence.

Bible Connection

Use the following passages to show your students how the Holy of Holies and the veil connect with the Scriptures.

> Matthew 27:51 (See also Hebrews 9:1–14, 10:14–22.)
> 2 Chronicles 5:13–14; Acts 2:1–3; 1 Corinthians 3:16–17

Thoughts to Ponder: Have your students answer the following questions:

1. What was the symbolism of the veil being torn at the moment of Jesus' death?

2. What does it mean to you to have access to God without the sacrificial system?

3. In the Old Testament, the presence of God was revealed in the Temple. Where is God's Temple now? What do the torn veil and the "shaking house" represent in this context? NOTE: Lesson 26 covers this subject in more detail.

4. **Jerusalem's Districts**

   a. **David's City**
   HINT: *If you have the optional full-color overhead-transparency packet for Set 4, see Overhead Transparencies 28 ("Modern-day Jerusalem from the South"), 36 ("Ancient Jerusalem from the South"), and 37 ("The Upper City").*

   This was the Jerusalem of David's time. In Jesus' day, David's City was home to many Jews (as was the Lower City).

   Using the overhead transparency "Jerusalem's Districts," point out the following locations, and have your students find them on their diagrams.

David's City
Southern Stairs
Spring of Gihon

Bible Connection

Use the following passages to show your students how David's City connects with the Scriptures.

> 2 Kings 20:20
> 2 Chronicles 32:30—Hezekiah tunneled through David's City to the Tyropoeon Valley to bring water into Jerusalem.

HINT: *You may want to refer to the overhead transparencies and study materials in Lesson 7, Set 2, for more information on this subject.*

b. The Lower City

HINT: *If you have the optional full-color overhead-transparency packet for Set 4, see Overhead Transparencies 30 ("The Western Hill"), 36 ("Ancient Jerusalem from the South"), and 37 ("The Upper City").*

The home of most of the common people in Jesus' day, the Lower City was built on the slope of the Western Hill, running from the Tyropoeon up to the west.

Using the overhead transparencies "Jerusalem of Jesus' Day" and "Jerusalem's Districts," point out the Pool of Siloam. This pool was filled by the water flowing through Hezekiah's Tunnel. Here water was drawn for the Sukkot water ceremony.

Bible Connection

Use the following passage to show your students how the Pool of Siloam connects with the Scriptures.

> John 8:58–9:12

Jesus sent the blind man with mud on his eyes to the Pool of Siloam to wash. The word *Siloam* means "sent." Apparently, the blind man was near the Temple (John 8:58). If so, the walk along the Tyropoeon would have been difficult because of the many steps down to the pool.

Thoughts to Ponder: Have your students answer the following questions:

1. Why would Jesus put mud on a blind man's eyes and then ask him to walk such a long, difficult path to be healed?

2. When God works in your life, does He ask you to show your faith and obedience? How?

3. Why is it important to step out in faith when you ask God to work in and through you?

c. The Upper City

HINT: *If you have the optional full-color overhead-transparency packet for Set 4, see Overhead Transparencies 30 ("The Western Hill"), 35 ("Mansions on the Western Hill"), 36 ("Ancient Jerusalem from the South"), 37 ("The Upper City"), and 42 ("Scenes from the City of Jesus' Day").*

The Upper City was located on the Western Hill (today called Mount Zion) and was the highest area of Jerusalem. Herod's palace was located here, as were several other large structures. The population here was probably more Hellenistic, and certainly wealthier, than the population of the Lower City.

Using the overhead transparencies "Jerusalem of Jesus' Time" and "Jerusalem's Districts," point out the following areas, and have your students find them on their maps. Then review the material given below.

Upper City
Lower City
Hinnom Valley
first wall
theater
Herod's palace
citadel
Essene Quarter
mansions

A large Hellenistic *theater* was built in the Upper City during Herod's time. Building this theater was probably part of Herod's attempt to shape the culture of the Jewish people. The theater would have been offensive to religious Jews, particularly the Pharisees. Ruins of this theater have not been found.

Herod's palace was one of the most beautiful structures in Jerusalem. It was located on the highest part of the Western Hill and covered nearly five acres. It had two wings, each with accommodations for hundreds of guests. Each wing had banquet halls, gardens, and porticoes. Throughout the rest of the palace were gardens, fountains, and groves of trees.

This was Herod's main palace. After his death, it became the seat of the Roman government. It was protected by the citadel, with its massive towers.

Bible Connection

Use the following passages to show your students how Herod's palace connects with the Scriptures.

Matthew 2:1–8

It is probable that the wise men came here, looking for the King of the Jews.

John 18:28, 19:13; Matthew 27:27; Mark 15:16; Luke 23:7

Some scholars believe this is the place where Jesus was tried by Pilate and had an audience with Herod Antipas. Others place these events at the praetorium in the Antonia or in the Hasmonaean palace. NOTE: For the Bible background for these events, see the study covering the Antonia in the section "The North Wall" above.

Thoughts to Ponder: Have your students answer the following questions:

1. How do you think the wise men reacted when they were sent from one of the most beautiful palaces in the world to a stable?

2. Why was it such an act of faith for the wise men to recognize Jesus as the Messiah?

3. Can you think of an example in which God chose an unexpected "instrument" for His work? When have you seen God at work in ordinary people?

The *citadel* was a triangular fortress defended by three massive towers named Hippicus (after one of Herod's friends), Phasael (after Herod's brother who, after being captured by his enemies, committed suicide by banging his head against his cell wall), and Mariamne (also Miriam; after Herod's beloved wife, whom he executed for an alleged affair). The highest tower (Phasael) was more than 145 feet high.

It is believed that the *Essene Quarter* is where the Essenes lived according to their laws. It is a small area in the southwestern corner of the Upper City near the Essene Gate and the latrines, outside the city wall. It is probable there were no women in this section of the city. Many believe the Upper Room was near or even in this area.

Bible Connection

Use the following passage to show your students how the Essene Quarter connects with the Scriptures.

> Luke 22:10—The oddity of a man carrying water (that was women's work in that place and time) might indicate that the Upper Room was in the Essene area. If so, this location is an interesting connection between the Essenes and the early Christians. NOTE: For more information on this topic, see Lesson 13 in Set 3 of this series.

Several *mansions* discovered in the Upper City are believed to have been the homes of priestly families and wealthy nobility. These large houses were decorated with frescoes on their walls and elaborate mosaic floors. Beautiful stoneware jars and other bowls and plates archaeologists believe are ritually clean also suggest a priestly class.

The largest mansion is more than 6,000 square feet. It contains many bathrooms, *mikvoth* (ritual baths), and banquet halls. Its close proximity to the bridge over Wilson's Arch and to the Temple Mount has led some scholars to identify it as the home of Annas.

The houses in this section of the city were burned in the great fire set by the Romans when Jerusalem was destroyed in A.D. 70. Many people were killed.

Bible Connection

Use the following passages to show your students how the mansions connect with the Scriptures.

> Matthew 26:57–58,69
>
> Mark 14:53–54,66
>
> Luke 22:54–61
>
> John 18:12–15,18

Whether these mansions belonged to the family of Annas or to his son-in-law Caiaphas is uncertain. Regardless of whom they belonged to, they do help us picture the wealth and luxury of the Sadducees, who were so threatened by Jesus that they plotted to have Him killed (John 11:45–53). The stark contrast between Jesus, a poor Galilean rabbi, and the members of the Sanhedrin, with their riches and power, is startling.

Thoughts to Ponder: Have your students answer the following questions:

1. Why do you think wealth and power so easily corrupt people?

2. The Sadducees gained wealth and power by controlling the Temple's economy and functions. Why do you think Jesus was so threatening to them?

3. How can you prevent your possessions or influence from distorting what God wants you to do and say?

4. Who are some examples of Christians whose wealth and power led them to distort God's message or disgrace His name?

d. The Business District

HINT: *If you have the optional full-color overhead-transparency packet for Set 4, see Overhead Transparencies 38 ("The New City"), 39 ("Ancient Jerusalem from the North"), and 42 ("Scenes from the City of Jesus' Day").*

This description was chosen for the section of the city inside the second wall because of the many shops and markets located there. This name was not used in ancient sources.

Using the overhead transparencies "Jerusalem of Jesus' Time" and "Jerusalem's Districts," point out the following locations, and have your students find them on their maps. Then review the information given below.

> David's City
> Lower City
> Upper City
> Herod's palace
> first wall
> second wall
> business district
> Garden (Gennath) Gate
> Northern (Damascus) Gate
> entrance to the Antonia

The *Garden,* or *Gennath, Gate* led out of Jerusalem to the area called the New City (which was not walled until after Jesus' time). The name *Gennath* comes from the Hebrew word meaning "garden." Just outside the gate was an old quarry.

Tradition holds that the location of Jesus' crucifixion was in this area. The execution definitely took place outside the city walls, and the presence of a gate called "Garden" fits the Bible description of a location near a garden. The quarry here could have provided rock faces for tombs (which were also located outside the city walls). Whether this is the correct site or, as Protestants believe, the garden tomb (which retains an appearance much closer to the original) was actually the place does not really matter. The important fact is that Jesus was taken outside the city of Jerusalem, where He died for the sins of the world.

Bible Connection

Use the following passages to show your students how the features described above connect with the Scriptures.

> John 19:17,41–42, 20:10–15
>
> Mark 15:22
>
> Matthew 27:33,39

Jesus was crucified *outside* the city walls, near a well-traveled road, and was buried in a new tomb in a nearby garden.

Thoughts to Ponder: Have your students answer the following questions:

1. Read Hebrews 13:13. In Bible times, to be "outside the camp (or city)" meant rejection by the community and was a sign of uncleanness. (See Numbers 5:1–4.) What does it mean to you that Jesus went "outside the city" to die? Why would He face such total rejection?

2. When have you felt rejected?

3. How does it encourage you to know that Jesus was totally forsaken so that you will never be alone?

NOTE: Jesus' crucifixion, burial, and resurrection are covered in more detail in Lesson 25.

The *Northern*, or *Damascus, Gate* was probably called the Towers Gate in Jesus' time. It was the main northern entrance into the city and was the beginning point of Tyropoeon Street, with its many shops.

After the Roman destruction of Jerusalem, the Damascus Gate was rebuilt into one of the most beautiful gates in the city. It is possible that the gate was beautiful in Jesus' time as well.

If Jesus' trial took place at the Antonia, the crowd gathered somewhere near its entrance (John 18:28), because they would not enter a Gentile's home and become ritually unclean.

e. The New City

HINT: *If you have the optional full-color overhead-transparency packet for Set 4, see Overhead Transparencies 38 ("The New City"), 39 ("Ancient Jerusalem from the North"), and 42 ("Scenes from the City of Jesus' Day").*

The city of Jerusalem expanded north during and after the time of Jesus. This expanded area was called the New City and was populated by many wealthy people. It was not walled until the time of Herod Agrippa II some 30 or more years after Jesus' crucifixion.

Using the overhead transparencies "Jerusalem of Jesus' Time" and "Jerusalem's Districts," point out the following features, and have your students locate them on their maps.

> second wall
> New City
> Pool of Bethesda
> Garden Gate
> Towers (Damascus) Gate
> Golgotha (traditional)
> garden tomb (Protestant Golgotha)

Point out that both the *traditional Golgotha* and the *garden tomb* were near a gate (outside the city), on a main street, near a quarry (which may have been a place for stoning), and in an area where there were tombs.

NOTE: Jesus' crucifixion, burial, and resurrection are covered in more detail in Lesson 25.

Conclusion

The city of Jerusalem was the focal point of God's dealings with His people for more than 1,000 years before Jesus arrived. God placed His name and His presence in the Temple and heard the prayers of thousands of people who loved Him. His anger burned here at those who rejected His ways and worshiped pagan gods, often in the same places where the faithful worshiped Yahweh.

Because of their sin, the Israelites were removed from Jerusalem and exiled to Babylon. Seventy years passed before God faithfully returned His people to David's City. The Temple was rebuilt, and the faithful again sought the blessings of Yahweh.

Many years later, Jesus arrived in Jerusalem to seek His heavenly Father. He visited the city both as a child and as a man, going to the Temple and worshiping with others. It was through Jesus' final acts of ministry that Jerusalem fulfilled its purpose: Near a hill outside the city, God accepted one final "lamb" as an offering, and forgiveness became complete.

The impact of Christ on Jerusalem did not end with His sacrifice, however. The followers of Jesus continued to live and worship in this city. The Holy Spirit revealed to believers the presence of God in their hearts and lives, and the world was never the same. The city that knew so many great kings, both good and evil, will always be known as the city of the Eternal King—our Messiah, Jesus.

Jerusalem symbolizes both the way to God and the presence of God. By studying different aspects of this city, we will be able to better understand the power and love of God as He reaches down to pull us to Himself. Jerusalem also gives us a picture of a greater city to come: the heavenly Jerusalem. Here God's faithful will live forever in His presence. Until then, Jesus' followers must bring His love to a broken world, much as God did to Jerusalem throughout history. We must become "Jerusalems" to those around us, touching their lives with God's presence, power, and forgiveness through Jesus' death.

Transparencies

(The following transparencies are all in the optional full-color overhead-transparency packet. For information on ordering it, see page 307.)

Overhead Transparency 28. Modern-day Jerusalem from the South. This photograph shows Jerusalem as it appears to someone looking north from some distance away. From this view, it is clear that Jerusalem is set in the mountains, which tower around it. The Golden Dome, also called the Dome of the Rock, stands where the temples of Solomon and Herod once stood. The southern wall of the Temple Mount is clearly visible here.

The mountain ridge on the right, with the three towers on the summit and the cemetery on the side, is the Mount of Olives. At 2,650 feet above sea level, it is the highest peak in the area. Beyond the Mount of Olives to the right is the Judea Wilderness. On the side of the mount, below the cemetery, is a grove of trees, the location of the traditional Garden of Gethsemane.

The deep valley between the Mount of Olives and the Temple Mount is the Kidron Valley. In the Kidron is the Spring of Gihon, the main fresh-water source of ancient Jerusalem.

Extending toward us from the Temple Mount is a narrow strip of land that comes to a point beyond the hill in the foreground. This is the City of David, or David's City. This area encompassed all of Jerusalem until Solomon added the Temple Mount to the north.

The Tyropoeon Valley is to the left of the ridge, though it has been filled with the debris of past civilizations. At one time, this valley formed the western border of David and Solomon's Jerusalem. In the New Testament, the Pool of Siloam was in the valley, near the point of David's City. Hezekiah's Tunnel brought water from the Spring of Gihon in the Kidron Valley, through David's City, to the Pool of Siloam.

The slope of the Western Hill can be seen on the right; part of the hill is not in the picture. In the first century, this hill was the location of the Upper City. The slope of the hill was the location for the Lower City.

At the right-center in the foreground of the photograph is a ridge with a grove of trees on top. This ridge is called the Mount of Offense and the Hill of Evil Counsel because here Solomon placed pagan worship shrines to his wives' many gods (1 Kings 11:7; 2 Kings 23:13).

Overhead Transparency 29. The Mount of Olives. This photograph shows the Mount of Olives as it appears to someone looking east from the Temple Mount. The Mount of Olives is 2,650 feet above sea level. The ridge is two miles long. Beyond the Mount of Olives is the Judea Wilderness. The Old Testament predicted that the Messiah would come from the east through the wilderness and would enter Jerusalem. Jesus took this route in His triumphal entry. (See Isaiah 40:3; Ezekiel 43:1–2; Luke 19:1,28–44.) The Mount of Olives may be the location for His return as well. (See Zechariah 14:4; Acts 1:11.)

The cemetery on the western slope is an ancient one, though it is still used for Jewish burials. Some of the tombs along the bottom of the ridge were already old in Jesus' time. Part of the reason Jewish people are buried here is the belief that the valley in the foreground, the Kidron, is also the Valley of Jehoshaphat (Joel 3:2,12), where the final judgment before the Lord will take place.

The olive grove on the left is part of the traditional Garden of Gethsemane. Whether this or some other place was the actual location of Gethsemane and the garden (the Bible mentions "Gethsemane" and "the garden," but not "the Garden *of* Gethsemane"), the location was definitely on the slope of this mountain. Probably the entire ridge was covered with olives in the first century. (See Matthew 26:36; Mark 14:26,32; Luke 22:39; John 18:1.)

The small dome of the Dominus Flevit ("Lord Wept") Church can be seen halfway up the hill on the left. To the right of it is a walled road. Tradition holds that Jesus' triumphal entry into Jerusalem happened on this road. When He reached the area of the church, He stopped to weep over the city.

The exact location of this event is not given in the Scriptures, but this road does portray what the actual path looked like, and the church is in a location where the view of Jerusalem is spectacular. If not here, wherever Jesus did stop to weep, the location must have been similar. (See Matthew 21:1–9; Mark 11:1–10; Luke 19:29–41; John 12:12–15.)

Overhead Transparency 30. The Western Hill. This photograph was taken from the Mount of Olives, looking west across the Kidron and Tyropoeon Valleys at the Western Hill. The cemetery in the foreground is on the slope of the Mount of Olives. The valley just beyond the cemetery is the Kidron. The slope of the hill beyond the Kidron is the ridge of David's City. The remains of an excavated wall that probably dates back to David's time are visible against this slope. The Spring of Gihon is just below the wall, though it is out of sight in a cave.

The many homes on the hill in the foreground, just beyond the Kidron Valley, are in David's City.

The Tyropoeon Valley is not visible in this photograph because it is largely filled in. It is between the houses and the blue-roofed church on the left side of the photo. Notice the wall against the slope of the hill beyond. That wall closely follows the line of the Tyropoeon Valley. The Lower City of Jesus' time was on the slope of the hill rising in the background. There are few buildings there today.

The high, broad Western Hill is clearly visible in the background. On its summit is a large, stone church tower with a smaller, higher tower next to it. This is near the traditional site of the Upper Room. The Western Hill extends to the right, where today's (fifteenth-century) city wall cuts across it. In Jesus' time, the entire hill was inside the city walls. Herod's palace was beyond the church.

On the left side of the photograph, going around the west side of the Western Hill, is the Hinnom Valley. It has a steep bank, and the hill beyond it is visible. To the left, the Hinnom Valley meets the Kidron and the Tyropoeon. To the right, it continues around the Western Hill, forming its boundary with the hills of Judea beyond. Here the kings of Judah sacrificed their children to Baal.

Overhead Transparency 31. The Western Wall. This section of the Temple Mount wall dates from the time of Herod. The Temple stood on the floor above the wall shown here. This particular wall would have been more than 40 feet above the street in Jesus' day. The Roman destruction of the Temple and later construction here have filled in the area beneath the plaza.

The wall with the arched opening is a later addition and is clearly made from smaller stones. If you enter through this arch, you soon come to Wilson's Arch, which supported a bridge extending from the Upper City to the Temple Mount above. This area was a place of public gathering in Jesus' time as well, though on a lower level than the plaza of today. For many years the Jewish people came to this place to pray and to mourn the loss of their Temple and the city of Jerusalem. At that time, this section of wall was known as the Wailing Wall. Today the Jews have returned to Jerusalem, and so this section of the wall is now called the Western Wall. It is an important place for prayers, as shown here.

This is also a location for bar mitzvahs, in which boys take on the adult responsibilities of faith at age 12 (similar to Jesus' first Passover, described in Luke 2:41–50). The women and men are separated by a dividing wall, as the Jews and Gentiles were separated at the Temple in Jesus' time. Many of the men in this picture are wearing prayer shawls (*tallits*) with tassels on the corners, similar to those on the hem of Jesus' garment (Matthew 9:20).

Though the stones of the Temple Mount are weathered, they still stand as powerful reminders of the awesome glory of the Temple complex of Jesus' time.

Overhead Transparency 32. Scenes of the Temple Mount. *Upper Left:* ***The Eastern Gate.*** This was the main gate on the eastern side of the Temple Mount of Herod. The gate seen here is a later construction from the sixteenth century. Several years ago, the Herodian ruins were accidentally discovered in one of the graves against the gate, indicating that today's gate was built over the remains from Jesus' time.

Just inside this gate is the area known as Solomon's Colonnade, where Jesus taught (John 10:23) and the first believers met (Acts 5:12). Today this gate is known as the Golden Gate, a name from more recent times.

Because the Bible prophesied the Messiah's entrance through this gate, the gate was blocked by the Muslim authorities on the Temple Mount (a sacred location to Islam), and a cemetery was placed in front of it since a Jew would be ritually unclean if he or she touched a tomb.

The best archaeological evidence seems to indicate that the Temple stood where the Dome of the Rock stands today. Its golden dome with the Islamic crescent on top is visible to the left of the gate. It is also possible that the entrance to the Temple Mount from Solomon's time was in this area, since the eastern wall of the Temple Mount has always been in the same location.

Upper Right: **Robinson's Arch.** The beginning of this arch, named after the British explorer who discovered it, still stands on the stones of Herod's retaining wall of the Temple Mount. Herod's distinctive style is demonstrated by the massive stones of the courses below the arch. The arch originally extended more than 45 feet from the wall and rested on a large foundation pier that has been discovered. The arch supported a massive staircase that passed over the arch, turned 90 degrees, and descended toward the viewer into the Tyropoeon Valley below. Above the arch was a high tower on which a priest would blow the trumpet to announce the beginning and end of the Sabbath day. The Roman soldiers dismantled the structures, including the tower, in A.D. 70, and threw the debris onto the street below, fulfilling Jesus' prophecy (Matthew 24:1–2).

The enormity of Herod's project is illustrated by the long stone in the foreground. It is more than 22 feet long, 40 inches high, and nearly six feet thick. It is dressed (cut) with the distinctive border (margin) and the protruding center (boss) that Herod used. Stones this size were cut so precisely that they were fit together without mortar. The lower courses, though covered with debris from Roman times, still look nearly new. The channels (cut later) were for clay pipes carrying water to the platform above.

Lower Left: **Wilson's Arch.** Located below the Old City of modern-day Jerusalem, Wilson's Arch extended high above the street in Jesus' time. The arch (the larger one in the background) supported a bridge across the Tyropoeon Valley from the Upper City on the Western Hill. Like Robinson's Arch (both of these arches were named after the explorers who discovered them in the nineteenth century), Wilson's Arch was one of the largest free-standing masonry arches in the world. It extended 75 feet above the valley floor below and covered a span of 45 feet. The arch has probably been restored. In this photograph, the floor on which the people are praying is on the debris from the Roman destruction of the city and later construction, and the arch is now only 20 feet above the pavement. Its majestic size and the enormous stones testify to Herod's magnificent aspirations. The wall in the background was a later addition. Today the area beneath the arch functions as a prayer area for religious Jews.

Lower Right: **The Temple Mount Colonnade.** The enormous Temple Mount of Herod had a 45-foot-wide colonnade around it. The eastern colonnade was called Solomon's Colonnade and was used by Jesus and the early Christians as a place of meeting and teaching (John 10:23; Acts 5:12). More than 40 feet high, the roof of the colonnade rested on the outside wall of the platform on one end and on two rows of columns on the other. The southern colonnade was much larger and more than three stories tall. It was called the royal stoa. The Sanhedrin met on the eastern end of the stoa. The remainder was the commercial center for the Temple. It was probably in the royal stoa where Jesus confronted the merchants and disrupted their market because they were cheating the people and intruding upon the Gentiles' place of prayer (Matthew 21:12–13).

This colonnade, much smaller and with stone piers instead of massive columns, is on the western side of the Temple Mount today. Of much later construction, it gives some idea of what the colonnade of Jesus' time looked like and shows why it would have been an attractive place to sit and discuss, worship, teach, and preach.

Overhead Transparency 33. The Southern Stairs. This photograph shows the southern end of Herod's massive Temple platform as viewed from the east on the Mount of Olives, looking west.

On the right side of the photo is a straight joint in the wall. This is the beginning of Herod's extension of the Mount to the south (left), which enlarged the Mount by more than 100 feet. The less-crafted stones to the right are clearly visible, showing the contrast between the old Temple Mount and Herod's extension. The massive stones of Herod's construction also contrast sharply with the smaller stones laid above them later in history.

The silver dome is part of the El Aqsa Mosque, constructed early in the eighth century. Herod built the magnificent royal stoa across the entire southern end of the Mount, making it nearly as wide as the mosque of today (right to left, or north to south) and considerably higher, and covering the entire end of the Mount. This dome was one of the most beautiful elements of Herod's Temple, built in basilica style with a central hall and side aisles. Four rows of columns, 50 feet high, supported the roof.

Below the Temple Mount, in David's City, the remains of the main pilgrim entrance to the Temple Mount can be seen. The partially reconstructed "broad staircase," also called the Southern Stairs, led to the massive Double Gates. Pilgrims entered these gates and went through magnificent passageways leading to the floor of the Mount above. The width of these stairs was more than 200 feet! The staircase was composed of 30 steps, with a landing after each step. This layout probably made the ascent slow and respectful. Part of the staircase has not been reconstructed so we can see the structures beneath it. The perpendicular wall covering the steps was a later addition.

On the foreground side of the steps were ritual baths—*mikvoth* (one of them can be seen just on this side of the middle of the steps)—where worshipers could bathe to be ceremonially clean before worship. After the baths was another smaller stairway (no longer existing), which led to smaller gates, the Triple Gates, believed to have been for priests to enter the storerooms located under the Temple Mount floor on this corner of the platform.

Archaeologists believe there was a large plaza at the foot of the staircase to handle the traffic of literally millions of pilgrims during the major festivals. One can imagine the people, including families with children, joyfully climbing the stairs to the Gentile Court above and then to the Temple itself. The view from the Mount of Olives, where this picture was taken, must have been spectacular as throngs of pilgrims went up the stairs to worship God. Jesus was among this crowd, both as a boy and as a rabbi with His students.

It has been suggested that the Christian fulfillment of the Jewish feast of Pentecost (Shavuot) may have occurred on these steps (Acts 2). Since it was 9:00 A.M. on a holy day, the time of morning prayer, large crowds would have been entering the Temple. The disciples went daily to the Temple Courts (Luke 24:53), so they too would have been arriving for morning worship. This staircase was also used by other rabbis as a place to teach. There were baths nearby, where the baptism of the 3,000 converts could have taken place. In his sermon, Peter referred to David's tomb, which was in the city nearby. Wherever the miraculous events of Acts 2 occurred, the large crowds of pilgrims who came to Jerusalem for the festival did hear the disciples' message and believed that Jesus had come as God's Messiah. At that moment, the disciples were filled with God's Spirit and became His new, living, growing Temple (1 Corinthians 3:16–17).

Overhead Transparency 34. Scenes from the Southern Stairs. Upper Left: The Broad Staircase. This massive staircase was built as the main pilgrim entrance into the Temple Mount above. Below the steps was a large plaza where pilgrims could gather. The staircase, more than 200 feet wide and 30 steps high, led to large gates called the Huldah Gates, now referred to as the Double Gates. After passing through these gates, pilgrims went through a passageway leading up to the Gentile Court. The wall on the left was added by the Crusaders in the Middle Ages, when they used this entrance as part of a city gate.

Each step on the staircase is followed by a landing. This layout probably made for a measured, respectful ascent. Somewhere in the vicinity of the Temple, God sent the Holy Spirit on the Jewish feast of Shavuot (Pentecost). It is possible that this staircase is the location. If you look closely at it, you can distinguish the original stone slabs from those that have been reconstructed.

*Upper Right: **The Original Steps.*** These stair treads are original to Herod's Temple and stood in place when Jesus and His disciples entered the Temple Mount on the Southern Stairs. The treads are more than six inches thick, and some are six or more feet long and three to four feet wide. Many of the treads were either plundered by later builders who used them on other structures in the city, or moved when other buildings were constructed in this area.

Lower Left: A **Mikveh.** This ritual bath, with its steps and plastered sides, is located next to the broad staircase leading to the Temple Mount. This *mikveh* (pl. *mikvoth)* is one of many discovered here. Jewish law required that worshipers be ritually clean before entering God's presence. That requirement prevented certain people (like lepers) or people at certain times (women just after childbirth) from entering at all (Numbers 5:1–3; Leviticus 15). Others would enter a *mikveh* and wash to indicate their ritual purity before entering the Temple grounds. Surely, Jesus and His disciples used installations like this one. A *mikveh* had to be watertight so no impurity could enter it. It had to contain a minimum amount of water (about 200 gallons), which had to be "living"—water that flowed freely into the chamber. This practice of washing before entering the Temple developed from the large bronze Sea in the First Temple of Solomon (1 Kings 7:23–40).

The *mikveh* shown here was for the common people. There were special *mikvoth* on the Temple Mount for priests, the high priest, and even lepers. Some scholars have suggested that the 3,000 converts who were baptized on the Christian fulfillment of Shavuot (Pentecost) probably were baptized in *mikvoth.* Since the event must have happened near the Temple (it was 9:00 in the morning on a holy day, the time when prayers and worship in the Temple began), the many *mikvoth* near the stairs, including this one, are possible candidates.

*Lower Right: **The Ruins.*** Jesus predicted that "not one stone here will be left on another" (Matthew 24:2). In fulfillment of that prediction, the Roman army destroyed Jerusalem in A.D. 70 (and again in A.D. 134), systematically tearing down as well Herod's magnificent buildings on the Mount above. These enormous stones, now broken, were thrown from the tower near the royal stoa and landed on the street below. The street can be seen on the left. The stones give silent testimony to the rage and violence of the Roman destruction of Jerusalem. When Jesus anticipated this event, He was moved to tears (Luke 19:41–44). If you look carefully, you can see the work of the craftsmen on the stones, which are being uncovered every day by archaeologists. Soon people will be able to walk on the original street again.

Overhead Transparency 35. Mansions on the Western Hill. *Upper Left: **Burnt House.*** The ruins of this house on Jerusalem's Western Hill were uncovered in the 1970s. This home belonged to the Kathros family, who were known from Jewish history and lived here at the time of Jesus. The Kathros were one of many priestly families (Sadducees) who lived along the edge of the Western Hill, overlooking the Temple where they served. In keeping with the character of many of the Sadducees in the New Testament (e.g., Caiaphas—see John 11:49–50), the Kathros were known as dishonest people who abused their position for personal gain (Mark 11:15–18). Their house was burned by the Roman soldiers who captured Jerusalem in A.D. 70. During this destruction of Jerusalem, according to Josephus, the alleys were choked with corpses and the city was deluged in blood.

The elegant stone table with small bowls and cups and the large storage jar, also made of stone, indicate the wealth of these people. Stoneware was very expensive, but it was convenient because it did not become ritually unclean (Leviticus 11:33). In this home, a spear point was found leaning against the wall. The skeletal arm of a young woman was found grasping at a step, where she had died in the fire. The broken pots in the background and the blackened walls give testimony to the horror of that day Jesus had predicted (Luke 1:41–44).

*Upper Right: **Mosaic Floor.*** In a mansion near the burnt house described above, the opulence of the people of this part of the city (many were Sadducees) is revealed. The beautiful mosaic in the floor, made from thousands of tiny bits of stones of various colors, displays the typical geometric designs used by religious Jews because images and pictures violated the second commandment (Exodus 20:4–6). The stone storage jars, stone tables, and stone tray (with bowls prepared for serving guests) were available only to the wealthy and were used because stone did not become ritually unclean.

The stone jars were probably used to store fresh water for household use. They are about the same size as those described in the biblical account of Jesus' miracle of turning water to wine (John 2:1–11). These jars were probably covered by lids.

This mansion was also destroyed by the Romans. The eminent Israeli archaeologist Nahman Avigad has suggested that this house may have belonged to a high priest (perhaps Annas or Caiaphas). Certainly, Jesus was questioned before Annas, Caiaphas, and the Sanhedrin (John 18:12–27) in a mansion of such luxury.

*Lower Left: **Bathroom.*** The luxury of the mansions on the Western Hill is highlighted by this mosaic-floored bathroom. On the left, a bathtub, found partially ruined, has been restored. Many of the mansions in this area had several beautiful baths as well as *mikvoth* for ritual cleansing.

*Lower Right: **Scorched Fresco.*** This beautiful wall in one of the Western Hill mansions is decorated with fresco panels painted red and yellow. This design is typical of those used among the wealthy (probably Sadducees) in the time of Jesus. The blackened areas are the result of the fires the Romans set to destroy Jerusalem after they had torn down the Temple. They captured the area of the Upper City in September of A.D. 70.

NOTE: The next seven transparencies are all taken from the model of ancient Jerusalem at the Holy Land Hotel. This model is built on a scale of 1:50 (1 inch = 1 foot) and is made from the same materials from which the original city was made in A.D. 60. Based on the Bible, Jewish history, Josephus, and archaeological research, this model is considered to be a fairly accurate representation of Jerusalem at the time.

Overhead Transparency 36. Ancient Jerusalem from the South. This view of Jerusalem is looking north toward the Temple Mount. The Mount of Olives would be off the photograph to the right. The Kidron Valley would be where the path is on the right. The Tyropoeon Valley is in the center of the photo where the colonnaded hallway runs.

In the distance is the Temple Mount. The Southern Stairs, where the pilgrims entered, are immediately in front of the Temple Mount. The royal stoa is across the end of the Temple Mount, on top of the platform. The marble Temple is visible here.

In the distance, the square towers of the Antonia, the Roman fortress, are visible. On the left side of the Mount are the two great arches. Robinson's Arch at the corner has a staircase that descends into the Tyropoeon Valley. Wilson's Arch is beyond Robinson's Arch and supports the bridge that extends to the Upper City.

The City of David is in the foreground, to the right of the Temple Mount. The Lower City rises up the slope of the Western Hill on the left. The Pool of Siloam is on the lower right. The Upper City, with its mansions, can be seen on the far left.

Overhead Transparency 37. The Upper City. This view of Jerusalem is from the southwest, looking northeast over the Upper City. In the foreground is the Upper City on the Western Hill. Here the wealthy, Hellenistic citizens of Jerusalem lived, including the Sadducees. The section of the city to the right of the monument (below the stone ledge) is the Essene Quarter. Apparently, the Upper Room was in or near this area.

Tradition holds that the mansion to the left of the monument was that of Caiaphas, the high priest who plotted against Jesus. Regardless of who it belonged to, this mansion is typical of those owned by priests who had become wealthy from the Temple economy. Jesus was questioned in a place like this, and Peter denied Him here.

Along the left side of the photo, inside the wall with the towers, is the palace of Herod. The large, beautiful tower beyond the palace is called Mariamne, named after the beloved wife Herod executed. It is likely that the wise men came to this palace, looking for the king of the Jews. Jesus may have faced Herod Antipas (and possibly Pilate) in this palace.

Beyond the Upper City is the Temple Mount. Its immense size and magnificence are evident even from this distance. The Antonia, the Roman fortress, is the structure with the four towers to the right of the Temple Mount. The marble Temple stands majestically in the center. The royal stoa is on the south end. Below it are the massive Southern Stairs, where pilgrims entered the Temple. David's City stretches south (to the right of the Temple).

In the Upper City, the theater (semicircular structure) overlooks the Lower City. The palace of the Hasmonaeans is near the Temple. Two round, pointed towers mark the front of it. This palace is another possible location of Jesus' trial.

Overhead Transparency 38. The New City. This view is from the northwest looking southeast across the New City. Jerusalem expanded to the north in Jesus' time, to the area in the foreground called the New City. The wall in the center is the second wall, and the area inside is the business district. In the distance, the Temple Mount is clearly visible.

The four massive towers of the Antonia are on the left of the Temple Mount. Jesus may have faced Pilate here. The Mount extends to the right of the Antonia. The marble Temple is obvious. The royal stoa can be seen on the far right.

Jesus was probably crucified in this section of the city. There are two traditional locations: The first is the Catholic Church of the Holy Sepulchre, which has superior historical and archaeological evidence. The church is near the right gate in the second wall (directly in line with the Temple). To its left was an abandoned quarry (a place of execution and a location for tombs), and there were gardens nearby.

The second location is the Protestant garden tomb, which is much closer in appearance to the actual place described in the Bible. It is just outside the left gate in the second wall, today called the Damascus Gate (called the Towers Gate in Jesus' time). This area extends out between two towers, and the roadway goes along the wall. The site is just to the left of the road.

The exact location of Jesus' crucifixion is not important. What is important is the fact that He was crucified outside the city and near busy roads.

Overhead Transparency 39. Ancient Jerusalem from the North. This view is of Jerusalem from the northeastern corner, looking almost directly south. The Temple Mount is on the left in the distance. The royal stoa is visible along its southern edge. The marble Temple stands at the center, within the city's inner walls.

Above the Temple stands the Antonia fortress, the Roman garrison's headquarters. Herod built this fort to defend the northern side of Jerusalem. Some believe that Jesus faced Pilate here. Later, Roman soldiers, observing the crowds in the Temple Courts (where problems often began), rescued Paul from a mob and brought him to the Antonia.

The Tadi (Sheep) Gate is in the shadow where the road meets the Temple Mount. The sacrificial animals entered here. It is possible that Jesus, God's Lamb, making His triumphal entry at the time the lamb was chosen for Passover, entered the Temple through this gate, where He drove out the merchants.

In the foreground is the Pool of Bethesda. Represented here are the two separate pools with five colonnades (four on the sides, one in the middle) as described in the Bible. Here (or near here) the sheep for the Temple sacrifices were washed. Apparently, the pool was believed to have healing power, for the sick gathered here. Jesus healed a lame man here, who immediately entered the Temple to worship God (John 5:1–15).

Overhead Transparency 40. The Temple Mount. This view is of the Temple Mount, looking west. The royal stoa can be seen on the left (southern edge) of this enormous platform. Here is where Jesus drove out the merchants.

The outer wall was in the form of a colonnade, which can be seen on the stoa and on the west wall across the platform. Under the colonnade, people would gather to hear rabbis teach. Under the colonnade on the eastern side (not visible in this photograph but similar to the one on the west), Jesus taught and the early Christians met. This colonnade was called Solomon's Colonnade (John 10:23; Acts 5:12).

The entrance from the Southern Stairs is barely visible in the shadow of the stoa (just to the left of the tower of the inner courts of the Temple). Around the inner courts (inside the walls) was a low wall called the Soreq. It was designed to keep Gentiles and other "unclean" people out of the Temple. The wall can be seen at the bottom of the steps. Archaeologists have found two plaques from this wall indicating that anyone improperly crossing here would be responsible for his or her own death.

The visitor to the Temple continued to "go up to God" as he or she approached the Temple itself. The inner courts are on a platform called Chel, seen here. The first court inside the gate is the Women's Court, which was as far as Jewish women could go. Beyond this court is the Priests' Court (also at the top of another stairway). The great altar can be seen through the inner wall on the left of the Women's Court.

The gate in the foreground allowed entrance into the Women's Court (inside the walls in the foreground). This gate was probably the Beautiful Gate, where Peter and John healed a man (Acts 3:2–10). The gate in the background, leading to the Court of the Israelites (at the top of the semicircular stairs), was called the Nicanor Gate. Only Jewish men could enter here.

The chambers in the corners of the Women's Court are visible in this photograph. On the upper left is the Chamber of Oil (for the offerings). On the lower left, barely visible, is the Chamber of the Nazirites (those separated in devotion to God). On the upper right is the Chamber of Lepers (where lepers could be inspected by the priests if they were healed). On the lower right (just behind the tower) is the Chamber of Wood (where priests inspected the wood to be used on the altar).

The Women's Court was where most of the people gathered for worship. The Levites chanted the Psalms of Ascent (Psalms 120–134) on the semicircular staircase. There were 13 trumpet-shaped offering boxes around the outside of this court. Jesus once pointed out to His disciples a widow who threw all she had into one of these boxes (Luke 21:1–4).

The balcony around the outside was used by the women so they could watch the water-pouring ceremony on Sukkot (and other holiday ceremonies). In the court (not visible here) were four enormous lampstands (menorahs), which were lit on Sukkot and Hanukkah. It was during Sukkot when Jesus announced, "I am the light of the world" (John 8:12).

In the background is the great marble Temple. Only priests and those from the tribe of Levi could enter it. Here God revealed His presence to His people for more than 1,000 years.

Overhead Transparency 41. The Temple. This view is of the Temple, looking west. The Temple was one of the greatest buildings commissioned by Herod. The front of it was 170 feet high and 170 feet wide. The back portion was 170 feet high and 115 feet wide.

The building was made of white marble, and the inside was covered with gold. The door was overlaid with gold, and there was gold on the roof spires. Josephus claimed that people could not look at the Temple when the sun was reflecting off the gold on the roof. The Temple's beauty was indescribable. No part of the Temple was left standing after the Romans destroyed it in A.D. 70.

This building symbolized the presence of the glory of God Himself. When Jesus died, the veil to the inner chamber (Holy of Holies) was torn from top to bottom, symbolizing the access all believers now have to God's presence through Jesus. On the Christian fulfillment of Pentecost, God took up residence in a new temple—His community of believers (1 Corinthians 3:16–17).

Overhead Transparency 42. Scenes from the City of Jesus' Day. *Upper Left:* **The Western Wall of the Temple Mount.** This photograph is of the western retaining wall Herod constructed to support the Temple platform. The marble building above is the Temple. In the distance on the left is the Antonia fortress, the home of the Roman garrison in Jerusalem. The end of the royal stoa is visible on the right.

The large arch on the left is Wilson's Arch. It supported a bridge that extended from the Upper City across the Tyropoeon Valley to the Temple Mount. An aqueduct bringing water to the Temple also went across this bridge. The arch on the right is Robinson's Arch. It supported a large staircase that went down into the Tyropoeon Valley. The arrow on the wall between the arches marks the location of today's Western Wall, formerly known as the Wailing Wall. **HINT:** *At this time, you may want to display Overhead Transparency 32 ("Scenes of the Temple Mount") again. Point out to your students the areas of the model (in Overhead Transparency 42) as they compare with the actual areas in the modern-day photograph (in Overhead Transparency 32).*

Upper Right: **The Southern Stairs.** This massive stairway, more than 200 feet wide, was the main pilgrim entrance onto the Temple Mount above. At the top of the stairs are the Huldah Gates. The gates on the right should actually be triple, not double, gates. Many believe that the gates on the right were for priests to enter the storerooms located within the Mount itself and supported by massive arches. Between the two stairways is a building that contained *mikvoth*—ritual baths used by the worshipers before they went up to the Temple. **HINT:** *At this time, you may want to display Overhead Transparencies 33 ("The Southern Stairs") and 34 ("Scenes from the Southern Stairs") again. Point out to your students the areas of the model (in Overhead Transparency 42) as they compare with the actual areas in the modern-day photographs (in Overhead Transparencies 33 and 34).*

Lower Left: **The Hasmonaean Palace.** This palace was originally built by the Hasmonaean (Maccabean) kings, who ruled Israel before Jesus' time. It was later used by some of the Herods, including Herod Antipas. It stood on the edge of the Western Hill, providing a magnificent view of the Temple Mount. The large open square in front of the palace was the Xystus, probably built over the Hellenistic gymnasium of the Hasmonaeans, which was no longer used. It became a place where large crowds assembled to hear speeches from the roof of the palace. It has been suggested by some that Jesus was interrogated by Herod Antipas in this palace. If so, the mob probably gathered in this open area. At least one scholar suggests that the coming of the Holy Spirit on Pentecost also occurred here. The event was certainly close to the Temple, given the crowd and the time of day (9:00 A.M., the time of morning worship in the Temple), as is this plaza. Others, though, say the event took place on the Southern Stairs.

Lower Right: **The Antonia.** The massive size of the fortress Herod named after Mark Antony is obvious in this photograph. Built to house the garrison of soldiers who watched Jerusalem for the Roman governors, this fortress was adjacent to the Temple Mount (only the right edge of the Mount is visible here). The Antonia's highest tower rose more than 120 feet above the rock plateau on which the fortress stood. Many believe that this is the place where Jesus faced Pilate. If so, the crowd would have gathered outside on the massive stairs in the foreground (John 18:28–29), for they would have refused to enter a Gentile's home lest they become unclean for Passover.

HEROD THE GREAT

Lesson Twenty-two
Handout #1

King Herod is known as Herod the Great, with good reason. He was "great" in everything he did, whether it was good or bad. He was able to attain the continual support of the powerful Roman empire by an endless variety of ingenious means. This meant that he ruled with relatively little real opposition over more territory than almost all Jewish kings who had ruled before him.

Yet Herod saw threats in every corner and was cruel in suppressing any resistance, real or imagined, among his Jewish subjects and even within his own family. The slaughter of the babies of Bethlehem, so central to the Bible story, was so small in comparison with his other crimes that it is not even mentioned by Josephus, who left a detailed record of Herod's life, exalting his triumphs and not hiding his failures.

Hated by some of his subjects and loved by others, Herod was one of the greatest visionaries Israel had ever known. Christian travelers to modern-day Israel soon discover that though they may have come to Israel to find the Messiah, there is significantly more physical evidence of Herod than of Jesus. That can be disturbing. Yet there are profound lessons in seeing Herod and Jesus on the same stage of history. Herod may have left the greater physical record, but what he stood for and believed in lies in ruins, whereas the King who was born in a Bethlehem manger lives on, and His kingdom has no end.

ALEXANDER THE GREAT AND HELLENISM

More than 300 years before Jesus and Herod, Alexander and his Greek army swept away the remnants of the Persian empire, which had kept the Jews under loose control since the time of Ezra. Alexander's dream was to bring the culture of the Greeks, called Hellenism, to the known world, leaving a legacy that would not soon be forgotten. In almost every way, he succeeded. Hellenism became the philosophy of most of the secular world. Its emphasis on the importance of the human being as the center of reality, its glorification of human accomplishment, its fascination with the human form in the gymnasium and stadium, and its delight in the erotic and bawdy in the theater made it seductive if not remarkably modern. Hellenism was the antithesis of the God-centered, self-denying religion of the Jews, who took their Bible seriously and refused pagan gods, images, and public nudity and sexuality, focusing instead on a lifetime of obedience. The two world-views would surely clash, as they have since Satan tempted Adam and Eve to put themselves ahead of the word of God. The most that can be said is that the spread of the Greek language became the tool used in God's plan to simplify and enhance the spread of the gospel. Thanks to the pagan Hellenists, nearly everyone spoke Greek. But Alexander did not live to see his dream become reality. He died when it had just begun.

His generals divided his empire among themselves. The territory along the eastern shore of the Mediterranean became the Hellenistic kingdoms of

Egypt and Syria. The land of the Jews, located on the trade route between the two, became a prize both kingdoms desired, leaving the Jews in the middle as they had always been. For more than 100 years, the Egyptians controlled Judea, as it was now called, ruled by a dynasty of kings called Ptolemies (after the general who received this part of Alexander's empire). They were benevolent kings who allowed much freedom to the Jews, especially in matters of religion. Apparently, they believed that the attractiveness of Hellenism would serve as its own marketing.

About two centuries before Jesus' birth, the Syrian kingdom, under the rule of the Seleucids (named after another of Alexander's generals), defeated the Ptolemies, and the Jews saw another side to the struggle between Hellenism and biblical faith. Antiochus, a Seleucid king, was determined to forcibly Hellenize his subjects, which for the Jews meant outlawing the Torah. (God's Word is always dangerous to those who would make human beings the center of the universe.) Antiochus also forbade the Sabbath observance, circumcision, and other important practices in Jewish faith. Revolt was inevitable for a people who believed that obeying God takes priority over all other matters in life.

THE HASMONAEANS AND FREEDOM

The Jewish revolt was led by an old priest from the Hasmonaean family and his five sons. The strongest, Judah, nicknamed Maccabee, led a miraculously successful revolt and gave his people freedom, commemorated in the feast called Hanukkah. After Maccabee's death, his brothers, and then their descendants, ruled as kings over the Jews. The faithful followers of Torah, called Hasidim, prevailed over the humanism of the Greeks.

The Hasidim ruled effectively for more than 100 years. The tiny Judean state grew in size and strength to include Samaria, Galilee, Peraea (east of the Jordan), and even areas east of the Sea of Galilee (today called the Golan Heights). In the region known as the Negev (in the south), the Idumaeans were conquered and forced to convert to the Jewish faith. This was to have a dramatic effect on the Jewish people in the days ahead.

But all was not well for God's people under their own rule. The priestly Hasmonaean family became as fascinated by Hellenism as the Greeks had been. They brought its practices, architecture, and moral values into official status. A gymnasium, a combination school and athletic club for nude athletic events, was built near the holy Temple. And worse, these now-Hellenized priests took for themselves the highest religious office, that of high priest.

The country grew fragmented, and new movements began. The Hasidim, fervent followers of Torah, spawned the Pharisees, who believed that obedience to God was the greatest value; the Zealots, who violently resisted anything that violated their view of Torah; the Sadducees, who were generally Hellenistic and concerned with the Temple practices; and the Essenes, who were so enraged that they separated from the world to wait for the Messiah to come to obliterate the heretics in the Temple. The country had a series of Hasmonaeans trying to make alliances with whatever group seemed to be in power, and assassination became the means of selecting rulers.

Two brothers, Hyrcanus and Aristobulus, rivals for the throne, sought the support of the rapidly growing Roman empire. Hyrcanus built an alliance with the Idumaean ruler, Antipater, and his son Herod. After near civil war, through the support of Julius Caesar (who was grateful for the support of Hyrcanus and Antipater in his war with Pompey), Hyrcanus prevailed and Antipater became procurator of Judea. Antipater's son Herod, barely 20 years old, was made governor of Galilee, and his brother Phasael was given Jerusalem.

THE HEROD DYNASTY BEGINS

Galilee was home to a fiercely independent people known for taking the law into their own hands. In a campaign that set the tone for his reign, Herod showed no mercy in stamping out the opposition. He caught one of the rebel leaders (Ezekias) and many of his supporters and brutally executed all of them, creating a climate for religious rebellion that would still be fierce when Jesus ministered here (note Ezekias's son is mentioned in the Bible— Acts 5:37). For this, Herod was summoned to Jerusalem to be tried by the Jewish religious council, the Sanhedrin. The elders could have sentenced Herod to death, but apparently they were frightened by his growing power. Fearful of a plot against him, Herod fled the country and appealed to his friend Julius Caesar for help. Unfortunately, he lost his patron when Caesar was murdered and Rome fell into turmoil. His father's rivals, sensing that Hyrcanus and Antipater were weakened by this loss of support, rebelled and murdered Herod's father. Hyrcanus, the Hasmonaean on the throne, sought Herod's support against his rival Antigonus (also a Hasmonaean). To convince Herod to support him, Hyrcanus offered him his granddaughter, the beautiful Miriamne (Miriam), as his wife. Herod divorced the wife he had and expelled her and their son from the country.

The Roman power was taken by Mark Antony, who, desperate for support, appointed Hyrcanus ruler of the Jews and continued Herod and Phasael as governors. Herod's paranoid nature led him to fear Antony's lover, Cleopatra from Egypt, on Herod's border. Some of his huge fortresses probably provided Herod the security of an escape route should Antony give in to Cleopatra's wish for Herod's territory.

Meanwhile, Hyrcanus's rival Antigonus invaded Jerusalem with an army from Parthia (the land to the east of Palestine, from India to Mesopotamia). Hyrcanus was arrested and had his ears cut off so he could never be high priest again (Leviticus 21:16–23). Phasael, knowing he would be tortured, committed suicide, reportedly by bashing his head against his cell wall. Herod, as he always seemed to do, escaped and went to Rome with a huge sum of money to beg for Antony's support. Antony saw Herod as a defense against the Parthian threat and a fiercely loyal king whose brutal tactics could keep the peace in Judea.

With renewed Roman support, Herod sailed home. He landed at Acre in the north and proceeded to Galilee. He burned Sepphoris and broke the resistance of the rebels near the Sea of Galilee. The remaining rebels and their families hid in caves in the cliffs along Mount Arbel, overlooking the sea. Herod was so determined to destroy any opposition that he commanded his troops to make platforms to be let down with ropes to the openings of the caves, and there they lit fires. Refugees who came out for air were pulled out with long poles with hooks on them and dropped down the sheer cliff. One old man killed his seven children and his wife before leaping to his own death. Herod's reign began in blood.

Antony now gave Herod two additional legions who marched south and laid siege to Jerusalem. For weeks the Jews held out until the city wall was breached. Many retreated to the Temple, a walled enclosure, and held out longer. Herod recognized the importance of the Temple to the Jewish people and begged the Romans to spare it, but it was too late. The Temple and Upper City were breached. The slaughter was beyond description. Women were raped and slaughtered, children were brutally killed, and soldiers were tortured and chopped to pieces. The Hasmonaean dynasty ended; in 37 B.C. Herod took his throne.

Now he would have to keep it. The battle for Jerusalem made it impossible to ever win the support of many of the God-fearing Jewish people he would rule. Herod would need the might of Rome, the support of the Temple authorities, and the favor of the Hellenistic Jews of the land to stay in power. Any threat would be ruthlessly destroyed, as parents in Bethlehem were to discover (Matthew 2:16).

HEROD'S REIGN OF TERROR

Herod now embarked on a campaign to make his throne secure and assure his place as the greatest of kings. To accomplish the former, he executed 45 of the 70 Sanhedrin members who had resisted him. Their property enriched his family's fortune considerably. He promised the Pharisees that they could have their religious freedom if they would stay out of the political matters of the nation. They regularly denounced him as a foreigner (Deuteronomy 17:15) but commanded their followers to obey his rule.

Pressured by the Jews in Jerusalem, Herod appointed one of the Hasmonaean family (his beloved Miriamne's brother) high priest. Though only 17, Aristobulus soon became popular because of his link to the Hasmonaean family line. Herod quickly became frightened of a potential rival, so he invited Aristobulus to the palace in Jericho. After filling him with much imported wine, Herod suggested a swim in the palace pool. Herod's friends, apparently following his plan, drowned the unfortunate young priest and claimed it was an accident. Though the family reported the matter, Rome did nothing because of their need for Herod's skills to keep the peace in his part of the world. Herod also executed his brother-in-law for a supposed affair with Miriamne, with whom he was passionately in love.

The civil war continued in Rome. Herod's master, Antony, committed suicide with his Egyptian lover. Octavian, soon to be Caesar Augustus, became the ruler of the Roman world. Herod, fearing a plot, executed his old friend Hyrcanus, who had given him his start. Then he journeyed to Rome to plead with Augustus, leaving orders that his beloved Miriamne should be killed if he was executed, as Herod could not bear the thought of her marrying another.

Herod returned to his throne with even greater support from Rome. However, his mother convinced him that Miriamne had been unfaithful, so he had Miriamne executed. Miriamne's mother plotted revenge, so Herod had her killed as well. Hundreds of friends and family members, along with supporters of these last of the Hasmonaeans, were slaughtered on the slightest of accusations.

Herod had two sons from Miriamne whom he favored greatly—Alexander and Aristobulus. He sent them to Rome to get the best Hellenistic education available. Apparently, they were being prepared to be Herod's successors. Herod's sister began to plot against them and spread vicious rumors about their desires to take Herod's throne before he died. Herod recalled his divorced wife, Doris, and their son, Antipater, whom he had exiled years earlier and presented Antipater as his successor.

Even by Herod's cruel standards, his life descended into madness. He took nine wives, apparently hoping he would find happiness and an heir he could trust. Each marriage added to the plotting and hatred found in his palace. Over the next years, countless members of his family and court were tortured. Under the pain of being torn apart, they accused guilty and innocent alike. Finally, after years of accusation, Herod's two sons were accused for the last time. Their accusers were tortured and beaten to death in a public display, along with more than 200 soldiers who expressed support for the brothers. Then Alexander and Aristobulus were strangled and buried with honor—marking the end of Herod's love for Miriamne.

Antipater appeared to be the chosen heir to Herod's throne. But a new wave of intrigue swept the palaces Herod had built. He appointed a series of high priests and then quickly deposed them because he feared their popularity. He weakened the office to "chief priest." Accusations and torture continued as a regular part of life. Antipater was imprisoned and appeared doomed. Herod determined to give his throne to another son, Antipas.

Then Herod became ill. Some believe he had a sexually transmitted disease; others believe it was a disease of the digestive system. Josephus's description is unclear. Herod was in great pain with gangrene, rotting of his sexual organs, and convulsions. Sensing his weakness, two important Pharisees, disregarding their nonpolitical status, encouraged their students to chop down the hated Roman eagle Herod had placed over the Temple gate years before, because it violated the commandment against graven images (Exodus 20:4). Forty students were captured. The teachers who instigated the plot and the students who had actually cut the eagle down were burned alive; the others were executed more humanely.

To compound matters, the Pharisees spread the belief that Herod was king of the Jews only by Roman decree and that he was not of the house of David. Therefore, he and his family were unfit for the throne. Messianic "prophets" predicted a bizarre list of upcoming events that would occur as the kingdom was taken from Herod and given to God's anointed. This stirred even more paranoia in Herod, and many more lost their lives as a result.

Into this web of hatred and suspicion, "Magi from the east came . . . and asked, 'Where is the one who has been born king of the Jews?' . . . When King Herod heard this he was disturbed" (Matthew 2:1–3). His deception of the wise men and his subsequent order to kill the infant boys of Bethlehem were only small additions to the bloody list of Herod's accomplishments.

THE MASTER BUILDER

There was another side to Herod. His visionary building programs, his ingenious development of trade with the rest of the world, and his advancement of the interests of his nation are legendary. Many of his building projects were designed to strengthen the loyalty of his subjects, a goal he never achieved. Most seem to have been built to strengthen his relationship with Rome and to establish himself as the greatest king the Jews had ever had. Herod built on a magnificent and grandiose scale. His building projects included:

Jerusalem: The Temple was rebuilt in a splendid setting unsurpassed in the ancient world. Some of the limestone blocks of the supporting platform weigh more than 500 tons. The Temple, made of marble and gold, was taller than a 15-story building. On the Western Hill of the city, Herod built a spectacular palace complex that contained reception halls, royal apartments, a fortress for his personal guard, fountains, gardens, and baths. The Antonia, a huge fortress as luxurious as Herod's own palace, defended the city. Some scholars believe it was the site of Jesus' trial. A Greek theater and hippodrome provided the Hellenistic emphasis Herod appreciated. Streets were paved, sewers were built, and water carriers were constructed to make Jerusalem one of the great cities of the world.

Masada: Part of a line of fortresses that included the Alexandrion, the Herodion, and Machaerus, Masada was one of the wonders of the ancient world. Perched atop a plateau in the Judea Wilderness with a spectacular view of the Dead Sea nearly 2,000 feet below, it was a luxurious fortress-palace combining all the essential elements of a Herod project. A three-tiered palace hung precariously from one end of the plateau, almost defying gravity. The western portion contained hot and cold baths, mosaic floors, and plastered walls. Masada also boasted swimming pools, barracks for soldiers, huge storehouses with supplies for outlasting years of siege, and cisterns holding millions of gallons of water.

The Herodion: This mountain fortress overlooked the town of Bethlehem. Standing on a high hill, the upper fortress was round and more than 200 feet in diameter. Originally, it was seven stories high, with an eastern tower that stood more than 40 feet higher. Packed dirt covered the first four stories, giving the upper fortress a cone shape. Inside were a peristyle garden, reception hall, Roman baths, and countless apartments. The lower palace included an enormous pool, a colonnaded garden, a 600-foot-long terrace, and a building more than 400 feet long. The Herodion was the third-largest palace in the ancient world.

Jericho: This palace was built on both sides of a deep wadi (dry streambed), with a bridge across the bed. One wing contained a huge, marble-floored hall where Herod received guests. Next to it were peristyle gardens, dining halls, and a complete Roman bath. Across the wadi, Herod built another monumental building with baths, a swimming pool, and gardens.

Caesarea: Herod needed contact with the Roman world for its military support and its market for the spice trade and other goods his people controlled. Thus he built Caesarea, on the Mediterranean coast, into one of the most spectacular seaports of the ancient world. Founded in 22 B.C., the city housed a large theater, an amphitheater, a hippodrome, and a massive temple to Augustus. Caesarea was almost completely covered with imported marble. It had an elaborate sewer system designed to be cleansed by the sea.

The glory of Caesarea was its man-made harbor spanning more than 40 acres. An enormous lighthouse stood near the narrow entrance, able to be seen from great distances at sea. This harbor welcomed the Roman legions, the marble and granite for Herod's projects, and the Hellenistic culture so dear to him. From it, ships carried spices, olive oil, grain, and, most important, the gospel to the far reaches of the world.

The visitor cannot help being impressed with Herod's vision and ingenuity. However, all that remain are spectacular ruins, because Herod lived for Herod. By contrast, another builder, a humble carpenter born in Bethlehem, used a different material than did Herod (Matthew 16:18; 1 Peter 2:4–8). Jesus' buildings continue to grow because He built for the glory of God. Like David (1 Samuel 17:46), Elijah (1 Kings 18:36), and Hezekiah (Isaiah 37:20), He lived so that the world may know that Yahweh, the God of Israel, is truly God. His construction projects will last forever because He built for the glory of God the Father.

THE DEATH OF THE KING

Herod went to Jericho to die in agony, hated even by his family. Truly mad and fearing that no one would mourn his death, he commanded his troops to arrest important people from across the land, lock them in the hippodrome, and execute them after he died—if people would not mourn him, at least they would mourn. At the last moment, Herod ordered the execution of his son Antipater and changed his will, dividing his kingdom between three other sons: Archelaus, Philip, and Antipas. Finally, the bloody, brilliant reign of this king of the Jews came to an end. Although the King of the world was born during his reign, Herod never knew Him.

Why was Herod never accepted by his own people? Was it his cruelty? That is possible. Was it his commitment to the pagan values of Hellenism? That is probable. But there is another important factor to understand. Herod was a Gentile, an Idumaean (called Edomite in the Old Testament). And God's Word made clear that no Gentile could ever be king over His people (Deuteronomy 17:15). Regardless of Herod's power or greatness, his reign violated God's rules. Consequently, God-fearing people could not accept him.

In addition, God's Word frequently predicted that the descendants of twin brothers Jacob and Esau would be in conflict. Ultimately, a ruler would emerge from Jacob who would overpower Esau and be God's Messiah (Genesis 25:23; Numbers 24:17–19; Obadiah 17–18; Amos 9:12). The

Messiah must be from Jacob (Israel) and must rule over Esau (Edom, or Idumaea). To the follower of God's Word, Herod could not be Messiah, or God's king.

But could Jesus be Messiah? How could He be Messiah if He (Jacob's descendant) was in a manger while Herod (Esau's descendant) sat in power in a fortress? This dilemma helps us understand why it was so difficult for people to accept Jesus as Messiah, for every appearance said otherwise. Esau was in control. Rabbis referred to Herod's city of Caesarea as the "daughter of Edom" (probably a reference both to Herod's Idumaean origins and to Rome's symbolic identification as Edom, the nation rejected by God). How could Jesus be the star of Jacob if Herod was in power? Second, this dilemma helps us understand the tremendous faith the Christmas story demanded of the Jewish people and of us today. They were (and we are) asked to accept by faith the fact that, contrary to appearance, it was not Herod who was in control but the boy in the stable. If someone had (or has) the faith to believe in Jesus as Messiah, he or she has recognized God's reality.

Today it may sometimes appear as if Jesus is not at the right hand of God, Lord of heaven and earth (Ephesians 1:18–22). Look around you and it may seem as if the evil descendants of Herod (the followers of the devil) are the dominant power. In times like these, just as in Jesus' day, God asks us to commit to and live by the reality that Jesus is Lord. Be encouraged. Evil may appear strong, but God is in control. Herod appeared all-powerful, but God was in the manger.

THE JOY OF LIVING WATER: JESUS AND THE FEAST OF SUKKOT

With joy you will draw water from the wells of salvation.

—Isaiah 12:3

Water was of great importance to the people of the Bible. They lived in a dry country, completely dependent on the seasonal rains. Fresh water was not available everywhere, and the task of digging wells and cisterns was difficult. Such an important resource as fresh water would naturally be a picture, or symbol, of spiritual reality as well. God frequently made use of common cultural phenomena to teach the truths of faith. He was Shepherd, Potter, and King. The people were sheep, clay, and subjects. Water became symbolic as well.

LIVING WATER

Different types of water were found in the land of Israel. Cistern water was rainwater trapped in pits dug into rock and plastered to prevent leakage. Most homes and public buildings had such pits. The water was often dirty, having flowed from roofs or streets into the cistern. This source of water was not dependable because one season it might not rain, or the plaster might leak and the water seep away.

Running water, especially springwater, was different. It stayed fresh and clean. And most springs were dependable, providing water year round. This constant fresh source of water was called "living water," probably portraying its life-giving qualities as well as its constant freshness. God provides (and is described as) living water (Psalm 107:9; Isaiah 35:6–7, 58:11; Jeremiah 2:13; Zechariah 14:8; John 4:13–14, 7:37–38). Living water was cleansing (Leviticus 15:1–3). The ritual bath of Jesus' day, the *mikveh*—used before coming into the presence of God at the Temple or to the synagogue worship service—contained flowing water, or living water. John the Baptist's choice of the Jordan River for his symbolic cleansing likely was based on the need for fresh, moving water to symbolize cleansing. Jesus described Himself as living water (John 4:13–14, 7:37–38), and the people of His day understood the meaning. Only God could provide living water. It would not fail to satisfy any thirst. But it was the connection between living water and the feast of Sukkot that gave Jesus' image of living water the clearest meaning. He chose that feast day to reveal that He was living water.

THE FEAST OF SUKKOT

In the Old Testament, God instituted a religious calendar for the Israelites to follow. The seventh day, the seventh year, and the end of seven "seven years" were significant to Him. Within each year, there were seven specified feasts (Leviticus 23). In the spring, three feasts were celebrated together: Passover, Unleavened Bread, and Firstfruits. These feasts remembered, respectively, Israel's deliverance from Egypt, God's gift of the Promised Land, and the spring harvest. Fifty days after Passover came Shavuot, sometimes called Pentecost, which celebrated the end of the grain harvest and the anniversary of the giving of the Torah on Mount Sinai. In the fall were the holy days of Rosh Hashanah, or the Feast of Trumpets, and Yom Kippur, the day of atonement when Israel went before the Lord and asked forgiveness to escape His judgment. Immediately after these two feast days came the most joyous one of all, the only feast God commanded the people to "rejoice before him" (Leviticus 23:40)—Sukkot, or the Feast of Tabernacles, as it would come to be known. And rejoice they did.

The weeklong celebration began after the fall harvest (figs, pomegranates, dates, and grapes) had been gathered and the olives hung heavy on the trees. Now was the time to be glad. Following God's command, the people built booths of olive, palm, and myrtle branches (Nehemiah 8:15). The booths provided shade, but there needed to be enough space in the branches so the people could see the sky, reminding them of their years in the wilderness. These booths, or *sukkot* (sing. *sukkah),* gave the feast its name.

For seven days, the people ate, lived, and slept in these booths. Since this was one of the three feasts in which everyone was commanded to come to Jerusalem (Passover and Shavuot are the others), thousands of people crowded the streets of the city, and there were *sukkot* everywhere. The children loved it, and so did the adults. It was a time to praise God for the past gifts of freedom, land, and bountiful harvests.

The Pharisees had adopted another custom based on God's commands in Leviticus 23:40. They took the branches of the three trees—olive, palm, and myrtle—and tied them together. Holding this cluster of branches (called *lulav*; pl. *lulavim*) in one hand and a citron (the fruit they decided was mentioned in Leviticus 23:40) in the other, they carried them to the Temple for each of the seven days of the festival (as religious Jews still do today). Here the people, and even the youngest children, would wave their *lulavim* joyously, as they danced, sang, and chanted the *Hallel* (Psalms 113–118) in a time of great celebration rivaling any holiday the world has ever known. A procession of priests—who made the festive sacrifices (literally hundreds of animals were offered) and carried water and wine to be poured into the silver funnels on the altar as drink offerings—would lead the men and boys around the altar in the Priests' Court in front of the Temple. Whenever they came to the Hosanna (Psalm 118:25), they waved their *lulavim* toward the altar as they sang, "O Lord, save us! O Lord, grant us success!" After several hours of intense rejoicing before the Lord, the people returned to their booths to rest, eat, and prepare for the next day's celebration.

SUKKOT IN HISTORY

The commands in Leviticus 23 leave little doubt about the importance of this great celebration to God. But three historical events added even more to the joy the people felt on this great fall festival. The first, described in

2 Chronicles 5–7, was the dedication of the Temple of Solomon (2 Chronicles 5:3, 7:9), which took place during Sukkot. For seven days, the nation of Israel celebrated and rejoiced because God had chosen to live among them. The ark, the resting place of God's glorious presence, was moved into the Temple, God's earthly home, in a spectacular display of His glory (2 Chronicles 5:13–14). After the people said an impassioned prayer for God's presence (2 Chronicles 6), God sent fire from heaven to consume the sacrifices, a stunning display of His power and love (2 Chronicles 7:1–3). On the day the Temple was dedicated, Solomon and the people offered more than 140,000 sacrifices, a measure of their joy. Afterward, everyone went home filled with happiness (2 Chronicles 7:10). The people of Jesus' day, though Solomon's Temple had been destroyed and the ark had disappeared, remembered their joy and celebrated God's presence in the Temple of Herod, still in the same location. Their jubilation was no less than in Solomon's time.

The second event was the celebration of Sukkot following the reconstruction of Solomon's Temple (destroyed by the Babylonians) by the exiles after their return from Babylon. Though this building was not as glorious as the first, the people's devotion to their God was stronger than ever. When the Torah was read and the feast of Sukkot described, Nehemiah, the high priest, commanded that it be celebrated again (Nehemiah 8:13–18), and the people's joy was "very great" (Nehemiah 8:17). As the people of Jesus' time remembered this ancient celebration, their joy grew greater, for God had not forgotten them.

The third event is not mentioned directly in the Bible. Between the Old and New Testaments, the Jews were severely oppressed by the Hellenistic Greeks from Syria. Antiochus, the king of the Syrians, was determined to Hellenize the Jews, so he outlawed the Sabbath, circumcision, and the study of Torah. Sacrifices were ordered to the pagan king, even in the Temple itself. The great altar of the Temple was defiled by the offering of pigs on it. The entrails of these unclean animals were dragged around the Temple courts, defiling them as well. A statue of the king was placed in the Temple. It was a time of great anguish for the Jewish people.

But God sent deliverance. An old priest, Mattathias, began a revolt by refusing to make the royal sacrifice in a small town near Jerusalem. His son, known as Judah Maccabee, led a group of freedom fighters against the far stronger Greek army. Trusting God, these rebels miraculously defeated the army of Antiochus and reclaimed the city of Jerusalem. Reaching the Temple, Judah ordered a complete cleansing and rededication of the building, and the altar was rebuilt.

The menorah, or eternal light, in the Holy of Holies had been extinguished while Jerusalem was under Syrian control. Though only a small supply of sacred oil remained, Judah ordered the lamp lit. Miraculously, it burned for eight days, the entire time of the rededication of the Temple, when new oil was purified. The celebration of this great deliverance of God became known as the Feast of Dedication, or Hanukkah (which Jesus also celebrated—see John 10:22–23). It was celebrated after Sukkot that year.

But Judah and the religious leaders were concerned. Sukkot was the celebration of God's goodness and the time to pray for His future blessings, especially for the fall rains. Judah ordered Sukkot to be held even though the time was past (2 Maccabees 10:5–8). So the Sukkot celebration took on even greater happiness as it recalled God's miraculous deliverance and preservation of His people and His Temple for a third time. Several Sukkot and Hanukkah customs became intertwined. The palm branch became the symbol of political as well as religious freedom. The chant of Hosanna (or "O Lord, save us!") now was understood to mean not only the salvation of deliverance from Egypt, the provision of rain for next year's harvest, and the forgiveness requested by the sacrifices, but it also was a prayer for political freedom. (This connection, along with the waving of palm branches, was to have interesting application in the ministry of Jesus—see Luke 19:28–44.)

Four great menorahs (more than 75 feet high), placed in the Women's Court in remembrance of the miraculous unending supply of oil on Hanukkah, were also lit on Sukkot, commemorating God's deliverance of His people from the Syrians. (The bowls on top of the branched candles held more than 10 gallons of oil. The wicks were made from the worn-out breeches of the priests.) The light of the candles could be seen in every house in Jerusalem. Tradition records that the people, upon seeing the light, sang these words: "Our ancestors turned their backs on the Temple of the Lord, but our eyes are on the Lord." Truly, the feast of Sukkot was one of great celebration. A rabbi once said, "Whoever has not seen Sukkot has not witnessed real joy."

SUKKOT AND LIVING WATER

There was another special element to the celebration of Sukkot, and it involved living water. Sukkot took place at the end of the dry season. The rains needed to begin immediately to ensure a harvest the following year. Thus the celebration of God's harvest was coupled with fervent prayer for next year's rains. Some believe this custom came from Solomon's prayer at the Sukkot dedication of the Temple (2 Chronicles 6). He prayed that God would forgive the sins of the people when they prayed toward the Temple and that He would not withhold the rains (2 Chronicles 6:26–27). The people knew that no rain meant no life. So the priests added a ceremony that included a prayer for rain. They may have based this ceremony on Isaiah 12:3: "With joy you will draw water from the wells of salvation."

This part of the ceremony involved a procession of priests, accompanied by flutes, marching from the Temple to the Pool of Siloam, which was fed by the Spring of Gihon. One of the priests filled a golden pitcher (more than a quart) with water, and the procession returned to the Temple. They arrived just after the sacrifices were laid on the altar. The priest carrying the pitcher entered the Priests' Court through the Water Gate and, to the blast of the shofar, approached the altar. He made one circle around the altar as the crowd sang the *Hallel*. Then the priest climbed the ramp and stood near the top of the altar. Here there were two silver funnels leading into the stone altar for the daily drink offerings. As the crowd grew silent, the priest solemnly poured the water into one of the funnels. Again the people, accompanied by the Levitical choir, began to chant the *Hallel.* The sound was deafening because of the thousands of pilgrims jammed into the Temple courts. In this way, they asked God for life-giving rain. The living water they used apparently acknowledged it was God who brought rain and life. The chant of the Hosanna—"O Lord, save us!"—now meant "Save us by sending rain as well."

It seems hardly possible, but the celebration became even more intense as the week drew to a close. When the seventh day of the feast arrived, the courts of the Temple were packed with worshipers. Chants of praise were heard throughout the city, and thousands of *lulavim* waved in the air. The priestly procession went to the living water of the Pool of Siloam. As the massive crowd waited expectantly, the sacrifices were offered, and the priests chanted, "O Lord, save us! O Lord, grant us success!" (Psalm 118:25).

The procession returned and entered the Court of the Gentiles, then went through the Water Gate into the Priests' Court. As hundreds of priests chanted the Hosanna ("Deliver us! Save us!") and thousands of people jammed into the Temple courts, the procession circled the altar seven times (remembering the walls of Jericho, which fell after seven circuits because of God's great power). Then there were three blasts on the trumpets, and the crowd grew still as the priest poured the living water into the funnel. Now the chanting became even more intense: "Save us, hosanna! Help us, hosanna!" and the next verse: "Blessed is he who comes in the name of the LORD" (Psalm 118:26). The waving of the *lulavim* reached a frenzy as branches were beaten against the ground until the leaves fell off.

Gradually, the people fell silent as they returned, exhausted, to dismantle their booths before journeying home. God had blessed them. They had celebrated joyously His presence, thanking Him for His gift of land and the bountiful harvest. They had begged for His continued blessing of the rains and had pleaded for political freedom as well. They were now prepared to face another year.

JESUS' TEACHING

In the context of Sukkot, the water ceremony, and the menorah blazing with light, Jesus dramatically presented the message of His new kingdom. It was during the last week of His life on earth. He had gone to Jerusalem for Sukkot (John 7:10) and had spent time teaching the great crowds who thronged the Temple (John 7:14). On the "last and greatest day of the Feast" (John 7:37), in the midst of the water ceremony, the chanted prayers, and the plea through the offering of living water, Jesus stood and said, "If anyone is thirsty, let him come to me and drink. Whoever believes in me, as the Scripture has said, streams of living water will flow from within him" (John 7:37–38).

Did He say this during the silence that fell as the priest poured the water? Was His shout heard above the chants of "Save us"? Or was it as the crowd began to leave that Jesus explained His ministry in the symbol of living water, streams that flow from within those who believe? Did Jewish tradition support His teaching that living water represented God's Spirit (John 7:39)? It is not stated in the Bible. But the setting Jesus chose to give this lesson, and the similarity of His meaning to Jewish tradition, meant that His shouted promise in the Temple must have had stunning impact. "Let him come to *Me!*"

John's gospel also recorded another teaching during the time of Sukkot. Though it is not placed on the exact days of the feast, it is during Jesus' visit to Jerusalem for Sukkot. In the context of a joyous feast, ended each day with the blazing candles in the Temple courts, Jesus said, "I am the light of the world" (John 8:12). The crowd, having just seen how the Temple candles had lit up the city, must have been strongly affected by Jesus' words, the mastery of His teaching, and the Old Testament background. Jesus is "living water," as taught during the water ceremony, and He is the "light of the world," in the context of the great Temple lights.

CONCLUSION

The importance of the Jewish background to Jesus' work cannot be exaggerated. It gave Him the context He needed to make His teachings relevant, powerful, and practical. The feast of Sukkot has additional lessons. It was (and is) a feast of great joy. Jesus experienced that emotional celebration of God's goodness. In many ways, the Christians of today have exchanged the ability to celebrate before the Lord for the shallow "happiness" of the secular world or for the always somber mentality of worship. There were solemn times in Temple worship, reminding the Jewish people to be sober, holy, and serious about their faith. But they also had Sukkot. It reminded them that God wants His people (including us) to celebrate before Him (Leviticus 23:40). How many modern-day Christians truly celebrate with this kind of joy before the Lord?

A second lesson can only be suggested here. The seven Jewish feasts also became the outline for Jesus' ministry. He died on Passover, was buried on the Feast of Unleavened Bread, and was raised on the Feast of Firstfruits. He sent the Holy Spirit on Shavuot (Pentecost). Rosh Hashanah (the trumpet call to judgment) and Yom Kippur (judgment day) in some sense will be fulfilled upon Jesus' return, though He has already fulfilled some elements of these two feasts.

And what comes after the final judgment? Heaven! The new Promised Land! Sukkot is the feast that celebrated the Promised Land, God's deliverance, living water, and God's blessing. Sukkot is a feast that will be fully realized in heaven. There will be living water (Revelation 7:17), the eternal presence of God (Revelation 21:22), and the light (Revelation 22:5).

Sukkot taught the Jewish people to be joyful, in anticipation of heaven. Take the most joyful celebration that ever existed and imagine it lasting forever. That is heaven. No wonder some Jewish Christians (and some Gentile ones, too) celebrate Sukkot.

PHARISEES OR SADDUCEES?

THE ORIGIN OF THE PHARISEES

The Maccabees' struggle against oppression by the Seleucid Greeks was ultimately a triumph of God's people over those who exalted human beings as supreme (167 B.C.). Among the Maccabees' strongest supporters was a group called the Hasidim, or the "pious ones." These Torah teachers and scholars joined Judah Maccabee and his rebels because the Seleucid authorities had outlawed the study of Torah. The Hasidim are called the "mighty warriors in Israel" in 1 Maccabees. Though noted for their fierceness in battle, ultimately they were devoted to obeying God alone in everything they did.

After the Maccabee victory and the cleansing of the Temple, the Maccabees' successors, known by the family name Hasmonaean, soon became as Hellenized as the Greeks they had fought earlier. That presented a problem for these "mighty warriors." Some apparently opted to continue to battle the influence of paganism, whether it belonged to Jews or to pagans such as the Romans, who came in 63 B.C. Around the time of Jesus' birth, this rebel group became a formal movement under the leadership of Judah of Gamla. They called themselves the Zealots.

Others decided that violence would not work. They believed that God had allowed (even caused) the foreign oppression because of the failure of His people to obey the Torah. This group believed that one should devote oneself to complete obedience to every detail of law—and to separating oneself from all influences or people that might interfere with that devotion. These Jews took the name "separated" or "the separatists" (*perushim*)—"Pharisee" in English. They committed themselves totally to God and assumed the responsibility to lead Israel back to Him.

THE BELIEFS OF THE PHARISEES

The Torah was of great importance to the Pharisees. It was the focus of every part of their lives. They believed that Moses had given a two-part law: the written law of the Torah itself and additional oral commandments that had been passed through generations to help the faithful understand and apply the written law. The Pharisees continued to interpret and expand the Torah to cover every possible occurrence of unfaithfulness to the written law. This oral law became a complex guide to everyday life often beyond the comprehension of the average person. Yet its intent was to help people understand Torah, much as a creed or catechism is intended to help summarize and interpret the Bible today. It is important to recognize that the word *law* can mean either (or both) of these "Torahs" when used in the Bible. It is often the oral Torah that Jesus criticized, though He kept it in many respects.

The Pharisees had many beliefs in common with Jesus and the New Testament. They believed in the physical resurrection of the dead (the Sadducees did not) and a coming day of judgment followed by reward or punishment. They anticipated the Messiah at any moment. They believed in angels. They recognized a combination of free choice and divine control in human life. They thought of God as all-wise, all-knowing, just, and merciful. They taught that He loved His people, calling them to a life of obedience. The Pharisees believed that everyone had the power to choose good or evil, and the Torah must be his or her guide.

Because their lives revolved around the study of the Torah, the Pharisees made the synagogue their community center, though they supported the Temple as well. There were more than 6,000 Pharisees by Jesus' time, and they were the dominant influence on the people's spiritual lives. The "yoke of Torah" (or method of obeying) taught by the Pharisees was a heavy burden, sometimes obscuring the very law they sought to obey. The Pharisees desired to raise the spiritual character of the Jewish people to help them draw nearer to God (Psalm 73:28, 34:18; see also James 4:8 for a New Testament expression of the same idea).

HYPOCRITES AMONG THE PHARISEES

Most of the Pharisees were godly men who tried to be totally devoted to God in a hostile world without resorting to the violence of the Zealots. They were greatly persecuted by the Hasmonaeans and Herods, and they disagreed strongly with the Sadduccees, whose theology and Hellenistic lifestyle conflicted with the Pharisees' desire to submit totally to God.

Among the Pharisees, not all were godly and righteous. Though they set high moral standards, not all of them measured up. The Misnah, the written record of their oral law, contains many criticisms of the "sore spots" among them who were "plagues of the Pharisaic party" (Mishnah Sot. 3:4, 22b). Some were so zealous for their oral interpretations that they violated the very letter of Torah. Others were so focused on obedience that they did not notice or care about the needs of those around them (a problem still significant in many churches today). This overemphasis on tiny details of obedience, particularly to human tradition, at the expense of the care and concern for others that the Torah itself demanded (Deuteronomy 10:19), was harshly condemned by the truly faithful among the Pharisees.

It is quite unfortunate, then, that history perceives this group as hypocrites and stubborn, uncaring religious fanatics who rejected Jesus. Though it is unlikely this view will ever change, it is important to note both Jesus' strong condemnation of certain Pharisees and the specific application of that condemnation. Jesus never criticized anyone for *being* a Pharisee. He criticized "hypocritical Pharisees" (Matthew 23) and those who were "leaven" among the Pharisees and spoiled the whole group (Matthew 16:6,11). Jesus instructed His followers to *obey* what the Pharisees taught (Matthew 23:2–3) but not to practice their hypocrisy (Matthew 23:3–7). Many Pharisees supported Jesus, frequently inviting

Him to their homes (Luke 7:36, 14:1, 11:34) and even warning Him that Herod wanted Him killed (Luke 13:31). Some were not far from the kingdom of God (Mark 12:34), and others entered it as Pharisees (Acts 15:5). Paul spoke and wrote proudly, "I am a Pharisee, the son of a Pharisee" (Acts 23:6; Philippians 3:5).

This should not be interpreted as defending those who rejected and hated Jesus or worked for His arrest and conviction. Nor does it deny that Jesus strongly condemned the hypocritical Pharisees (most references to them make this point). It is intended to say that Jesus pointed out sin, especially hypocrisy, wherever He found it. To paint all Pharisees with the brush of legalism and hypocrisy is unfair and incorrect. Many of them were a powerful force for good among God's people. In many (perhaps most) respects, the theology of early Christians was similar to that of the Pharisees, including the fact that both groups worshiped in synagogues.

THE ORIGIN OF THE SADDUCEES

The Sadducees also had their roots in the time of the Hasmonaean dynasty. After the Israelites returned from the Babylonian Captivity, it was the tradition that the high priest must be of the tribe of Levi, the family of Aaron, and the family of Zadok, Solomon's high priest (1 Kings 2:35; Ezekiel 40:46). Descendants of this family (called *Zedukim,* or "Sadducee" in English) were the Temple authorities throughout the time before Jesus was born. Descendants of Zadok and their supporters, many of them priests, were also called Sadducees. They were wealthy and politically active (having the favor of the Romans and the Herods), and they were a large majority on the Sanhedrin. This gave them far greater influence than their small numbers justified (some scholars believe there were fewer than 1,000 actual Sadducees). They also controlled the economy of the Temple, for which they were criticized by the Essenes and confronted by an angry Jesus. Apparently, many were Hellenistic in lifestyle, though faithful to the Temple rituals.

THE BELIEFS OF THE SADDUCEES

The Sadducees were definitely the conservatives of the time. They held that only the written Torah was authoritative, rejecting the oral law completely—even holding the prophets and other writings of less value than Torah. They opposed the Pharisees in every way they could up to the time the Temple was destroyed in A.D. 70. They denied a bodily resurrection and most of the Pharisaic doctrine of angels and spirits. They held completely to the letter of Torah, with no room for the creative applications of the Pharisees. This was especially true in cases involving the death penalty. Extenuating circumstances made no difference.

The Sadducees' authority was one of position and birth, unlike the Pharisees, whose authority was based on piety and knowledge. They hated the Pharisees, believing that the Temple ritual was undermined by the synagogue and study of the Torah and its interpretations as a form of worship. The Sadducees frequently dealt brutally with anyone who undermined the Temple, its economy (their income), and its ritual—and with Roman support they were capable of severe punishment. The Sadducees offered worship that brought God down to the people. In their eyes, worship was an act of homage to the divine ruler, not an exercise in understanding. Their power was largely based in Jerusalem and Judea through the Sanhedrin, the ruling religious council, used by the Romans and Herods as the instrument to govern the Jewish people.

The Sadducees had the most to lose because of Jesus. Any popular movement jeopardized not only their place as the majority on the Sanhedrin, but also the support of the Romans who ruled through it (John 11:49–53), a fact that would have profound consequences. This was the one group most likely to wish Jesus removed from the scene.

The early church, now a growing movement, faced a similar reaction from the Sadducees (Acts 4:1, 5:17), although a large number of priests who became believers in Jesus probably were Sadducees (Acts 6:7).

When the Temple in Jerusalem was destroyed, the Sadducees ceased to exist as a group.

THE JEWISH REVOLTS

Jewish people of Jesus' day passionately desired freedom from Rome and the oppressive Herod dynasty that had ruled them for years. Revolt seethed continuously, mostly underground, for more than 100 years—from the time Herod became king (37 B.C.) until the Romans destroyed Jerusalem and the Temple (A.D. 70).

It is helpful to realize that this underlying struggle is the backdrop for Jesus' ministry and the reason so many hoped He would be a conquering king. This helps us understand why the adulation of the crowds during the triumphal entry reduced Jesus to tears, and probably why many people rejected His message.

THE RISING STORM

Ever since the Romans arrived on the scene in 64 B.C., the Jewish people were divided over how to respond to the rule of their often-corrupt governors or the Herod family who served them. The religious community, particularly the Pharisees, believed the Jewish people were to be God's instruments on earth, from whom the Messiah would come to institute that glorious age when Israel would be a great and free nation. Many others, especially the secular community and apparently some of the Sadducees, noted the present reality of the rule of Rome and determined that cooperation was the best policy. The contrast between the situation at hand and the messianic hopes was heightened by Rome's tyrannical rule and the paganism of its culture. This difference produced increasing fragmentation of the people, and several movements developed in response.

The *Zealots,* an ultra-nationalistic group, proclaimed revolution to be God's solution (Acts 5:37). The *Essenes* withdrew, waiting anxiously for the Messiah to lead a violent overthrow of the Romans and their Jewish supporters. The *Sadducees* apparently practiced a form of cooperation since it was Rome who kept them securely in their position over the Temple and therefore over the people (John 11:49–50). The *Herodians* appeared satisfied with the Herod dynasty (Matthew 22:16). The *Pharisees,* condemning Rome's pagan excesses, were removed from politics and viewed the foreign oppressors as God's hand punishing His people for their unfaithfulness to the Torah. The country was in turmoil, each faction longing in a different way for the freedom they desired. To this climate of confusion, hatred, and division, many so-called messiahs came, each preaching his own brand of salvation (Acts 21:38). During feast days, especially Passover, tensions reached fever pitch, and the Romans increased their military presence to prevent open revolt. The climate existed, however, for revolution to begin.

About this time, Jesus presented His unique message of salvation. The Sadducees, fearful of losing their power over the people, had Jesus crucified around A.D. 30.

After Herod Agrippa I, grandson of Herod the Great, died in A.D. 44 (Acts 12:19–23), the Romans appointed a series of governors called procurators, each more corrupt and cruel than the previous ruler. Groups of rebel *sicarii* (assassins) were everywhere, killing Romans and the Jews who cooperated with them. Jonathan the high priest was assassinated. During this time, Paul was arrested (Acts 21:27–37) and accused of being one of the rebels (Acts 21:38). Popular support for the Zealots grew. The priesthood became more dependent on the Romans for security and support, and in so doing, they grew increasingly corrupt. This drove the common people toward the radical approach of the Zealots.

Felix (Acts 24) was replaced by Festus (Acts 25) as governor. Both were brutal but ineffective in their attempts to quell the rising revolt. Festus died after a short time. The high priest, Ananus, took this opportunity to murder his opponents, including Jesus' brother James and many others in the Christian community. Ananus was deposed and replaced with a man named Jesus and then another priest named Jesus. These two were in such opposition that their followers fought in the streets.

The Roman administration was in disorder, and the Zealots and *sicarii* flourished. Florus, another governor, attempted to stop the violence by flogging and crucifying hundreds of people. The time was ripe. The Jewish people's desperate hope of a messiah who would bring freedom from political oppression was ready to bear fruit.

THE REVOLT BEGINS

While Christians and Jews were thrown to the wild animals by the emperor Nero in Rome, violence flared in Judea. In Caesarea, a conflict between Jews and Gentiles over activities next to the synagogue had been brewing for some time. In A.D. 66, on the Sabbath day, a Gentile offered a "pagan" sacrifice next to the entrance to the synagogue. There was an outcry from the citizens of Caesarea. The authorities in Jerusalem decided to end all foreign sacrifices, including the one for Caesar himself, in the Temple. Florus the governor, who lived in Caesarea, came to Jerusalem with troops, entered the Temple treasury, and took a large amount of gold. When people gathered to protest, Florus unleashed his soldiers on innocent civilians of the city. Hundreds of women were raped, whipped, and crucified. More than 3,500 people were killed, including women and children.

The reaction was outrage. Mobs swarmed the streets, driving the outnumbered soldiers out of the city. The people stormed the Antonia (the Roman fort) and burned the archives, destroying records of debts. The revolt spread. The Zealots surprised the Roman garrison and occupied the fortress of Masada. From this fortress, huge supplies of weapons were distributed. Though there were voices urging calm, even the nonpolitical Pharisees joined the Zealot movement in droves.[1]

The violence mounted within the rebel movement. The Zealot leader Menahem was assassinated by another Zealot leader, Eleazar, who then ordered the slaughter of the Roman prisoners remaining in the city. There was no turning back.

A BLOODY REBELLION

The Gentiles in Caesarea, hearing of the violence against fellow Romans in Jerusalem, rose against the Jews of that town. Within a day, 20,000 Jews were killed. This slaughter of men, women, and children, young and old, was repeated in many places in the country and throughout the empire, including Syria and Egypt. Fifty thousand were killed in Alexandria alone. The land ran with blood.

Gallus, the governor of Syria, advanced on Jerusalem with the twelfth legion. But he was ambushed by Zealots in the mountain pass of Beth Horon, and his force was destroyed. The Romans had lost their advantage, and the Jews gained their national freedom (albeit temporarily) and the weapons of an imperial legion.

Nero acted quickly. He ordered his leading general, Vespasian, to end the Jewish problem once and for all.

Vespasian began his campaign in A.D. 67 in Galilee, where a young priest, Joseph, was in command. His army numbered more than 50,000 men. Vespasian took Sepphoris, Jotapata (where Joseph surrendered to the general and became the Roman scribe Josephus), and several other towns with brutal force. He also destroyed Gamla, where the Zealot movement began, putting 10,000 people to the sword. Most of the towns of the region were left as smoking ruins. Many men were executed, often crucified, and the women and children were sold into slavery. A few were saved for the games in the arena. Galilee was again Roman.

Vespasian then conquered the coast, including Joppa, and the lands to the east of Judea. He took Jericho, which guarded the eastern approach to Jerusalem, and Emmaus, which guarded the western. Jerusalem was now isolated.

In A.D. 68, the campaign halted due to Nero's suicide. As Josephus had predicted (a prediction that apparently spared his life), Vespasian became emperor. He left his son Titus to complete the campaign against Jerusalem.

The situation in Jerusalem was horrible. Several factions of Zealots converged on the city, having been defeated elsewhere. They blamed each other for their defeats. One group controlled the Temple Mount and appointed its own priest. When the Sadducee priests resisted, they were slaughtered, along with 8,500 of their supporters. The sewers of the city ran with Jewish blood. Simon Bar Giora, another self-proclaimed messiah, entered the city and fought the Zealots. Confusion and terror reigned. Jerusalem was divided into three sections, each fighting the other as the Romans tightened the noose. Apparently, the Christian community, possibly remembering Jesus' words (Matthew 24:15–16), fled to the mountains east of the country, beginning the long separation of Jew and Christian that would bear terrible consequences later.

In the spring of A.D. 70, Titus arrived outside Jerusalem. His army now numbered 80,000 or more. Titus breached the third wall near the end of May and slaughtered the people of that part of the city. Five days later, the second wall fell. Half of the city belonged to the Romans. In July the Romans built a siege wall around the city to prevent escape and to starve the citizenry.

Unbelievably, the killing between Jewish factions continued. People killed each other over scraps of food. Anyone suspected of contemplating surrender was killed. Because some Jews had swallowed gold coins before trying to escape, their fellow citizens began to disembowel those they caught, looking for money. In one night, 2,000 were ripped open. No one bothered to bury the dead. Many who did surrender were crucified just outside the walls so the hapless defenders could watch their agony. Josephus records that the Roman soldiers nailed people in various positions for their own amusement until they couldn't find enough crosses for the victims.

The famine took its toll as well. Josephus reports that 600,000 bodies were thrown out of the city. This may be an exaggeration, but it gives a sense of the carnage.

THE END OF THE REVOLT

The Antonia fell in mid-July. On August 6, the sacrifices ceased in the Temple. The Temple itself was burned and destroyed on the ninth of the Jewish month of Ab (the end of August), the same day it had been destroyed by the Babylonians more than 600 years before. It has never been rebuilt.

On August 30, the Lower City fell, and in September the Upper City did. Titus ordered all buildings leveled, except for three towers in Herod's palace, which were left as evidence of his former strength. All the citizens of the city were executed, sold into slavery, or saved for the games in the arena. The slaughter was beyond description. Infants were thrown to their deaths from the city walls, and people were burned alive; the alleys were choked with corpses. Eleven thousand prisoners died of starvation waiting for their execution. Josephus records that more than 1 million perished and nearly 100,000 were sold into slavery. The Jews' holy city was gone and their Temple destroyed.

A few Zealots took refuge at Herod's fortress of Masada. Here they hoped to outlast the Romans. One can only imagine the state of mind of these people, some of whom had seen Jerusalem fall. Titus left their fate in the hands of Silva, the new governor. The tenth legion laid siege to Masada in A.D. 72. A wall six feet high and more than two miles in length, was built by Jewish slaves around the base of the enormous mountain plateau. But there was little chance of starving out the defenders because Herod's extensive storehouses were still filled with food and weapons and his cisterns with water. The Zealots apparently felt safe here.

Over the next seven months, the Romans built a siege ramp against the western side of the mountain. When the ramp was finished, a battering ram was winched to the top, and Roman soldiers smashed a hole in the fortress wall. The Zealots fortified their wall with timbers, but these were set on fire.

That night the Zealots met. Their leader, Eleazar from Gamla, argued forcefully that suicide was the only honorable action. They had seen what the Romans would do to them, their wives, and their children. They had lived their lives for freedom and the opportunity to serve God alone. Now they must remove all possibility of serving anyone else.

Every man killed his family. Ten men were chosen to kill the Jewish soldiers; one killed the other nine and then committed suicide. In so doing, the Zealots stole the final victory from the Romans. But the revolt was ended. Two old women and five children survived to share the story with the world.

POSTSCRIPT

The Romans eventually built a temple to Jupiter on the Temple Mount. Emperor Hadrian (A.D. 117–138) desired to remake Jerusalem as a Roman city named Aelia Capitolina. The few Jews who remained held to their desire for freedom and their hopes of a conquering messiah. When Simon Bar Kochba, a descendant of David and apparently a charismatic leader, began a new resistance, the religious community declared him messiah. Open rebellion (the Second Jewish Revolt) began in A.D. 131, and the Jews rallied around Bar Kochba's leadership.

The Romans were surprised and initially defeated, but their follow-up was swift and devastating. The Roman commander Julius Severus, and even Hadrian himself, responded with overwhelming force. Nearly a thousand villages were destroyed, and Bar Kochba was killed. In A.D. 135, the Second Jewish Revolt ended. Any Jews who had not fled the land were killed or enslaved. Jerusalem became Hadrian's Roman city, the Jewish religion was outlawed, and Judea became Palestine. The Jews were a people without a land.

Out of this disaster came two new religious movements: Christianity and rabbinic Judaism. The revolt drove Christianity to the ends of the earth, and it soon became a largely Gentile faith. Only today are its Jewish roots being fully appreciated. Rabbinic Judaism became the Orthodox faith of Jewish people today, the descendants of the Pharisees. The Sadducees, the Essenes, and the Zealots are no more.

JESUS AND THE REVOLTS

The First and Second Jewish Revolts were a disaster for God's people. The agony suffered over two millennia can be traced to those events. Jesus was crucified (by the same Romans) nearly 40 years before the first revolt. Understanding the climate that led to the revolt and His anticipation of that event makes Jesus' teaching clearer.

Often people saw in Jesus a Davidic king, a military conqueror who would rescue them from the Romans (John 6:15; Acts 1:6). But His kingdom was not the kingdom of the Zealot or the sword (Matthew 26:51–52), though He had a Zealot disciple (Matthew 10:4). Jesus frequently commanded those He taught or healed not to tell anyone, possibly because they would misunderstand, given the political climate of the day (Mark 1:44, 7:36, 3:12, 5:43; Matthew 8:4, 9:30, 12:16; Luke 8:56). When we remember how many messiahs proclaimed their message during this time, we can understand the uniqueness of Christ's message and the reticence of His audience.

Clearly, Jesus predicted the destruction that would result from the revolt (Matthew 24:1–2). It led Him to weep on one occasion as He described exactly what would happen (Luke 19:41–44). It seems that Jesus was saddened because His fellow Jews looked for military solutions to their problems rather than spiritual ones—to a political messiah rather than the Lamb of God. He warned His followers not to take part in that method of bringing in God's kingdom. The coming destruction can be seen as the natural result of human beings seeking salvation through their own political and military might. Jesus' method was the opposite of such an approach.

While we cannot fully understand God's reasons for shaping history the way He has, we must be able to weep with Jesus, because the destruction wrought by the two Jewish revolts resulted from people seeking God in the wrong places and ways. We must be devoted to Jesus the Messiah's message, for He truly is God's hope of peace (Luke 2:14).

NOTES

1. Judah of Gamla apparently revolted against a census ordered by Quirinius, governor of Syria, and was executed by Herod Antipas (who also executed John the Baptist). Judah probably founded the Zealot party, though not the movement. His sons Jacob and Simon were executed by the Romans for resistance, and his son (possibly grandson) Menahem was a leader in the First Jewish Revolt.

THE LAMB OF GOD

For the Teacher

Many descriptions of Jesus have been written over the last 2,000 years. He has been called a revolutionary, a prophet, a great man, a teacher, a miracle worker, and a peasant. Some descriptions have focused only on His divine nature, and others only on His human nature. It seems as if everyone has some idea of who Jesus was (and is). The Bible is clear that Jesus was born to a virgin, worked miracles, claimed to be God's Son, died, was raised from the dead, and ascended into heaven. He was God's Anointed (*Messiah* in Hebrew). The exact nature of His messianic work and the kingdom He came to establish was a matter of great debate during His ministry and has been ever since. Never did Jesus proclaim His messianic identity more clearly, or display the method He would use to bring in His kingdom more pointedly, than in His triumphal entry into Jerusalem just five days before His death. This lesson will explore that event in its context.

Ask your students to think of words that describe who Jesus was and who He is. Encourage them to give several examples, without labeling their answers right or wrong. Note how many different—and true—pictures there are of the person Jesus. Explain to your students that in this lesson, you will consider who Jesus presented Himself to be on Palm Sunday.

Your Objectives for This Lesson

At the completion of this section, you will want your students:

To Know/Understand

1. The route Jesus took from Galilee to Jerusalem before He died.

2. The reason the east was believed to be the direction from which the Messiah would come.

3. Why Passover was a dangerous time in the first century.

4. That Jesus chose to enter Jerusalem on a donkey on the Sunday before Passover for specific reasons.

5. What palm branches and the Hosanna meant in Jewish culture and why they were used to welcome Jesus.

6. The two times the Bible tells us Jesus wept and how they were different.

7. Why Bethphage was the location where Jesus began His ride into Jerusalem.

To Do

1. Reflect on their own commitment to Jesus as Messiah.

2. Determine the types of tears Jesus sheds for them.

3. Make specific plans to become more sensitive to those who do not know Jesus or who reject Him.

4. Evaluate whether they have accepted Jesus as He proclaimed Himself to them.

5. Learn to say "Hosanna" to Jesus for salvation available only through His blood.

How to Plan for This Lesson

Because of the volume of material in this lesson, you may need to divide it into several class sessions. To help you determine how to do that, the lesson has been broken into segments. Note, however, that the time needed may vary significantly, depending on elements such as the leader, the size of the class, and the interest level of the class.

If you wish to cover the entire lesson in one session, you should complete Unit One. This unit provides a guided discussion covering the major points in the video. It does not go into great depth. If you wish to go into greater depth on any of the points in Unit One, they are covered more thoroughly in the remainder of the material.

How to Prepare for This Lesson

Materials Needed

Student copies of the maps/diagrams:	"Topography of Jerusalem" "Jerusalem's Districts" "Temple Courts" "The Roman World" "Land of Jesus' Ministry"
Overhead transparencies:	"Topography of Jerusalem" "Jerusalem's Districts" "Temple Courts" "The Roman World" "Land of Jesus' Ministry" "New Testament Chronology"
Student copies of the handouts:	"Pharisees or Sadducees?" (Lesson 22) "The Joy of Living Water: Jesus and the Feast of Sukkot" (Lesson 22) "The Jewish Revolts" (Lesson 22)

*Video: **The Lamb of God***

Overhead projector, screen, TV, VCR

1. Make copies of the maps/diagrams listed above for your students.

2. Prepare the overhead transparencies listed above. (You'll find them at the back of the book.)

3. Make copies of the handouts listed above for your students. (If possible, students should receive and read these handouts before the lesson.)

4. Review the geography of the lands of the Bible from the "Introduction."

5. Determine which **unit** and which **Digging Deeper** sections, if any, you want to use in your class session(s). NOTE: You can use these sections in any order you wish (e.g., you might want to use **Digging Deeper III,** but not **Digging Deeper I** or **Digging Deeper II**).

6. Prepare your classroom ahead of time, setting up and testing an overhead projector and screen (for the overhead transparencies) and a TV and VCR. If you plan to hand out biblical references for your students to look up and read aloud, prepare 3x5 cards (one reference per card) to distribute before class.

Lesson Plan

UNIT ONE: Video Review

1. Introductory Comments

Jesus walked from Galilee to Jericho, then to Jerusalem. When He arrived at the outskirts of Jerusalem, at Bethany, He waited until the next day to continue His journey. Then He walked halfway to Jerusalem on Sunday. When He got to Bethphage, He rode on a donkey down the Mount of Olives and into the city of Jerusalem. That event—Jesus' triumphal entry—stirred the whole city of Jerusalem at the time and has stirred Christians for centuries ever since. In this lesson, we will seek to discover what affected those who were there for Jesus' triumphal entry, and we'll examine what they may have missed so we may be stirred again by the Lamb of God.

2. Show the Video *The Lamb of God* (20 minutes)

3. Map Study: Jerusalem

HINT: *Begin this map study session by reviewing the geography of the overall region and working down to the city the lesson is dealing with—Jerusalem.*

Using the overhead transparency "Topography of Jerusalem," point out the following areas, and have your students locate them on their maps.

> Mount of Olives
> Kidron Valley
> Temple Mount

Using the overhead transparency "Jerusalem's Districts," point out the following areas, and have your students locate them on their diagrams.

> Mount of Olives (toward the east)
> Kidron Valley
> Temple Mount

4. Guided Discussion: Jesus' Last Journey

Have your students (individually or in small groups) read the following passages and answer the questions.

a. Matthew 16:21–22; Matthew 17:22–23; Matthew 20:17–27.

   1. Jesus taught His disciples that He must go to Jerusalem to die, but they did not seem to understand what He meant. Why do you think the disciples didn't seem to learn this lesson? What were the disciples' expectations of Jesus?

b. Luke 19:28–44; John 12:13; Isaiah 40:3 (the Messiah's way is in the wilderness east of Jerusalem).

   1. On His way to Jerusalem, Jesus walked through the Judea Wilderness, passing up many opportunities to escape. He reached the Mount of Olives and was triumphantly acclaimed by the people of Jerusalem as He entered the city. Because they were familiar with Old Testament prophecy, how do you think the direction of Jesus' arrival would have affected the people of the city?

c. Exodus 12:1–6,12–15; John 12:1,2.

1. Jesus entered the city on Passover. What did the Jews celebrate on Passover?

2. Why do you think Jesus chose this time to enter the city the way He did?

3. How did the people react? (NOTE: See John 6:3–15 for an account of another Passover celebration when the people tried to make Jesus king.)

4. Why was Passover considered to be a dangerous time by the Romans (and Jews)? (Remember what Jewish people celebrated on Passover.)

5. Read John 1:29. Point out that Sunday was the tenth day of the month, the day the Passover lamb was to be chosen. What does it mean that Jesus chose to appear as Messiah on the day the lamb was chosen? What was He asking of people?

d. Zechariah 9:9–10; Matthew 21:1–6.

1. According to the rabbis, Bethphage marked the city limit of Jerusalem. What was Jesus saying by getting on the donkey as soon as He arrived at the edge of Jerusalem?

2. By arriving in Jerusalem at the time the Passover lamb was chosen, what was Jesus showing that He would do to be God's King? (Answer: He would become God's sacrificial lamb.)

3. Did the people seem to understand the kind of messiah He was?

e. John 12:16; John 12:13; Matthew 21:9.

1. The palm branches and the shouts of "Hosanna!" ("O Lord, save us!"; from Psalm 118:25–26) had taken on political meaning after the time of the Maccabees. It is likely that many of the people who chanted and waved branches to Jesus were proclaiming Jesus a military savior. What indications are there that even the disciples did not understand what kind of Messiah Jesus was?

f. Luke 19:41–44. As a result of the people's response to Him, Jesus wept!

1. Why did Jesus weep as the crowd shouted, "Blessed is the king who comes in the name of the Lord"?

2. How is Jesus' prediction of the destruction of Jerusalem related to His weeping? (NOTE: The destruction of Jerusalem would be the result of looking for peace by military power.)

3. What are some ways people today miss who Jesus really is?

4. Why is it so natural for people to want to make Jesus into the kind of messiah they want, with the kind of kingdom they think He should have?

5. Do you think Jesus still weeps for those who miss Him and His message? Do you?

6. Read John 11:33–35. On another occasion, Jesus wept at the tomb of His friend Lazarus. He didn't weep for Lazarus, for He had already indicated that He would raise him up. He wept for the pain Lazarus's death had caused his friends. Do you think Jesus still "weeps" (feels compassion) for those whom He loves when they experience pain and sorrow?

7. Do Jesus' tears on these occasions give you comfort? Have you experienced Jesus' great compassion? Explain.

8. Conclusion: Jesus weeps for everyone. Either He weeps with you over your hurts and sorrow, or He weeps because you have missed Him and His message. Ask yourself today, "Why does Jesus weep for me?"

g. Spend a few moments in prayer. Ask God to give you the ability to recognize Jesus as the King He claimed to be. Ask Him for the wisdom you need to see that true deliverance can be found only in the sacrifice of the Lamb of God. Ask for sensitivity to those who still look for salvation elsewhere. Thank God for His tears of compassion for those whom He loves.

UNIT TWO
Step One: "The Road to the Cross"

1. Introductory Comments

When the disciples had finally recognized that Jesus was Messiah, He immediately began to teach them about the way He would carry out His mission to bring in God's kingdom. The disciples did not want to hear about suffering and death, and when Jesus told them anyway, they did not understand, but Jesus was determined. Nothing could dissuade Him from completing His divine mission and from equipping His disciples to spread His message after He was gone. In the process, He provided the model for the kingdom that we must learn to follow. Most important, through His suffering and death, He provided the power for us to follow His example. This study explores the road Jesus intentionally took to Jerusalem to face the cross.

2. Map Study: The Mount of Olives

HINT: *Begin this map study session by reviewing the geography of the overall region and working down to the area the lesson is dealing with—the Mount of Olives.*

Using the overhead transparency "The Roman World," point out the following areas, and have your students locate them on their maps.

> Rome
> Mediterranean Sea
> Judea
> Caesarea

Using the overhead transparency "Land of Jesus' Ministry," point out the following areas, and have your students locate them on their maps.

> Sea of Galilee
> Galilee
> Capernaum
> Gamla
> Caesarea Philippi
> Decapolis
> Perea
> Jericho
> Judea Wilderness
> Jerusalem
> Jesus' route to Jerusalem: From the Sea of Galilee to Caesarea Philippi
>   From Caesarea Philippi to Perea
>   From Perea to Jericho
>   From Jericho to Jerusalem

3. Review the Overhead Transparency "New Testament Chronology"

Using the overhead transparency "New Testament Chronology," highlight the following dates for your students:

63 B.C.	Roman conquest of Judea
37 B.C.	Herod's reign begins
ca. A.D. 27–30	Jesus' ministry
A.D. 66–73	First Jewish Revolt against Rome
A.D. 70	Jerusalem is destroyed

4. Show the Video *The Lamb of God* (20 minutes)

5. Guided Discussion: "Jesus Resolutely Set Out for Jerusalem"

The last time Jesus traveled from Galilee to Jerusalem was one of the most significant teaching periods of His entire ministry. Help your students recognize that Jesus presented the following information knowing He was going to His death.

a. Read Matthew 16:16–26.

　1. In this passage, what did the disciples finally recognize (assuming Peter spoke for all of them)?

　2. What promise did Jesus make?

　3. How did Jesus' teaching change from this point on?

　4. How did the disciples react to the new focus of Jesus' teaching (verses 22–24)?

　5. What is the very specific calling Jesus gave the disciples (verses 24–26)?

　6. What does that calling mean for your life?

　7. What do you think it means to "take up your cross"? How do you follow this commission? (NOTE: At the very least, it means being totally committed to Christ.)

b. From that point on, Jesus' ministry changed. His new focus was on Jerusalem and the cross. Have your students form groups of three to five people. In their groups, have them read the following passages. Ask the people in each group to explain the theme of each passage after they have read it. As they read, have your students note how clear Jesus was about His goal, how little the disciples seemed to understand, and how determined Jesus was to complete His work.

- Matthew 17:22—Jesus explained again that He had to go to Jerusalem to die.

- Luke 9:51—The Greek literally says, "He strengthened His face for Jerusalem." It means He was absolutely determined—He would not go to the right or left.

- Matthew 19:1—He set out for Jerusalem by way of Perea.

- Matthew 20:17–19—He explained His coming death and resurrection again.

- Luke 10:5–7—Jesus described the strategy the disciples were to follow after He was gone.

- Luke 13:22—Jesus continued to teach the disciples, even as He made His way to Jerusalem to die.

- Luke 18:31–33—Jesus privately stressed the suffering and death He would endure in Jerusalem.

- Matthew 20:29–30—Jesus continued His journey to Jerusalem by way of Jericho.

- Matthew 21:1—Jesus arrived in Jerusalem.

- Matthew 21–25 —Jesus stayed in Jerusalem, in the Temple courts, confronting His opponents.

- Matthew 26:1—Jesus taught about His death and resurrection again.

- Matthew 26:10–12—Jesus prepared His disciples for His death.

- Matthew 26:31–32—Jesus explained His coming death and resurrection the night He was to be arrested.

Have the groups come back together as a class, and ask them to answer the following questions.

1. Why do you think Jesus was so determined to go to Jerusalem to die? (See John 12:27.)

2. What does it mean to you that He was so committed to His mission?

3. What can you learn from His actions, and how can you apply them to your life? (Possible answers: Be dedicated, love others, don't be distracted from my purpose, be totally committed, live to serve others.)

c. The disciples did not seem to understand Jesus' new teaching. The vision of a suffering Messiah who would give His very life to defeat the "gates of hell" and provide true freedom for His followers was just too foreign to their mind-set. Also, the idea of following Jesus' example by giving themselves as servants to others must have been too shocking for them to even consider.

Have your students form small groups of three to five people. In their groups, have them look up the following passages, and have them answer these questions after they read each passage: (1) What was Jesus teaching (through His words or actions) in this passage? (2) What were the disciples thinking (based on their words or actions)? (Remind your students to check the context if they are not sure how to answer the questions.)

- Matthew 16:22–23

- Matthew 17:23

- Matthew 20:20–27 (Point out that as the disciples argued about who was number one, Jesus was on His final walk to Jerusalem, where He would die.)

- Matthew 26:50–54

- Luke 18:34

- Luke 20:1–6, 11–12

Ask your students the following questions, and have them discuss their answers within their groups.

1. How can you explain the disciples' inability to understand Jesus' clear teaching?

2. If you were one of them, do you think you would have understood what Jesus was teaching? Why or why not?

3. Read Luke 24:45–48. Do these verses help you understand the disciples' failure to grasp Jesus' teaching?

Have the groups come back together as a class. Ask them the following questions.

1. Why did Jesus' message seem so strange to the disciples? What were they supposed to learn from it?

2. Can you think of ways in which Jesus does not fit our ideas of what the Messiah should be? How do people reinterpret Jesus to be what they want Him to be? What are some specific examples?

3. What method did Jesus use to carry out His mission as Messiah? (Answer: He sacrificed Himself for others.)

4. What were the disciples supposed to learn from Jesus' sacrificial death? Did they learn the lesson? Explain.

5. What should we learn from the method Jesus chose to carry out His mission as Messiah?

6. How did Jesus change the world? Using the "servant" model, can you change your community? Your world? The people you interact with every day?

Spend a few moments in prayer, asking God to help you see areas in your life where you have misunderstood Jesus' teaching. Ask for His help in becoming a servant to others as Jesus was.

OPTIONAL — Digging Deeper I: Becoming Servants *(15–30 minutes)*

A. Lecture

Part of the reason the disciples couldn't understand Jesus' strategy of bringing the kingdom of God was His insistence that He would accomplish His mission by suffering, serving others (especially the undesirables of His world), and even dying for those who did not deserve it (or who may not have even cared). His prayer "Father, forgive them" is remarkable—He never diverted from His selfless sacrifice, even at the very end.

B. Guided Discussion

Read each of the passages listed below. As you read each one, have your students consider what Jesus wanted His disciples to be and what *they* desired to be.

- Matthew 5:14
- Matthew 5:43–47
- Matthew 18:1–6
- Matthew 18:21–35
- Matthew 19:13–14
- Matthew 20:20–28
- Luke 22:24–30

1. How was Jesus a model for His disciples? How is He our example?

2. What implications did Jesus' method have for the disciples' own actions?

3. Can you be Jesus' disciple if you are not a servant to others? Why or why not?

4. What does this service look like? Are you a servant? How? Whom do you serve?

5. Why was it so natural for the disciples to want power, authority, and control (Matthew 20:21)? Why is it so natural for us?

6. What was Jesus' answer to this desire? (See Matthew 20:26–28.)

C. Conclusion

Ask your students to answer the following questions:

1. Do you know anyone who lives a life of true servanthood? Discuss your answer with the others.

2. How does the principle of "being a servant" apply to your family relationships, your church, your community, and your ability to change your culture?

OPTIONAL — Digging Deeper II: Tempted Again? *(20–40 minutes)*

A. Lecture: The Jericho Road

According to Jewish history and belief, the wilderness was both a place of escape and a place where evil lurked. Jesus walked from Jericho to Jerusalem (along the Jericho Road), through 10 to 12 miles of the Judea Wilderness. The entire route was filled with places to hide or escape. This wilderness is also the place where Jesus had been tempted by Satan years earlier. Perhaps it was a final temptation for Him to walk past so many opportunities to flee, knowing that if He kept going, He would face jeering crowds, the betrayal of His friends, a Roman cross, and finally the rejection of His own Father while bearing the agony of hell for the very people who despised Him. Today when people walk this rugged, lonely road, many of them experience the depth of Jesus' love for them as they realize that He *chose* to stay on this path, rather than run off into the safety of the wilderness nearby. When we understand Jesus' resoluteness in wanting to save us from our own sin, His love seems truly remarkable.

B. Guided Discussion

To appreciate the commitment Jesus had as He walked to Jerusalem, look up these passages and answer the questions:

1. The wilderness as an escape.

    - 1 Samuel 23:14, 24:1
    - 1 Kings 19:3–5
    - Acts 21:38

    a. Why did Jesus continue walking to His death when He could have easily escaped?

    b. How does this affect your understanding of His love for you?

2. The wilderness as a place of temptation and evil.
    - Leviticus 16:8–10—The Hebrew word *Azazel* is translated "scapegoat." The word apparently came from the name of the goat-demon that was thought to live in the wilderness; hence the connection between the wilderness and evil. In this case, the goat bearing the sins of the people was sent into the wilderness.

    - Leviticus 17:7; 2 Chronicles 11:15; Isaiah 13:21—Goat-gods (satyrs) were believed to live in the wilderness. In Daniel 8:21, the pagan Greek king is symbolized by the satyr—the goat with one horn—and is described by the same word used for goat-gods. Jewish tradition before Jesus' time taught that the desert was inhabited by demons, including a fallen angel (1 Enoch 6–13).

- Luke 4:1–13

a. Why do you think the devil tempted Jesus in the wilderness?

b. Would you have been tempted to escape into the wilderness if you knew a cross awaited you in Jerusalem?

c. One scholar has suggested that Satan continued to tempt Jesus up to His death, to try to divert Him from God's plan. If so, Jesus' wilderness walk can be seen as another opportunity for Satan to try to pull Jesus down. Fortunately, Jesus chose not to escape but continued toward His destination: Golgotha.

3. Jesus' disciples did not share His burden.

- Mark 10:32–45

a. What was on Jesus' mind as He and His disciples walked on the wilderness road toward Jerusalem?

b. What was on the disciples' minds?

c. How would you have reacted if you had been on your way to die for the salvation of your friends and to demonstrate the model of the kingdom—serving others—and your friends were arguing about who would be number one? How did Jesus react?

d. Does Jesus love you? How do you know? Can you tell how much He loves you? Explain.

OPTIONAL — Digging Deeper III: Doubting Thomas (10–20 minutes)

A. Lecture

Many people are familiar with the expression "doubting Thomas," based on the disciple who would not believe that Jesus had been raised from the dead until he saw Him with his own eyes. Although this is the reputation Thomas is most noted for, there is another side to him.

B. Guided Discussion

Ask your students to read the following passages and answer the questions.

- John 20:19–31

1. Why did Thomas doubt what he was told?

2. How was he convinced?

3. Are you at all like Thomas? Explain.

4. Do you think Thomas deserved his reputation? Why or why not?

- John 11:7–8

1. What did Jesus tell His disciples in this passage? What was the danger in what Jesus said?

2. What was the disciples' reaction?

3. What would your reaction have been?

- John 11:16

1. What was Thomas's reaction?

2. What does this tell you about Thomas?

C. Conclusion

Ask your students to answer the following questions:

1. Why do you think we remember Thomas as doubting, rather than as courageous?

2. Why do you think we have a tendency to remember bad things about some people rather than good?

3. How do you feel, knowing that even courageous people have times of doubt and weak faith? Why do you feel this way?

OPTIONAL — Digging Deeper IV: The Road to Jerusalem *(10–20 minutes)*

(This section requires the use of the optional full-color overhead-transparency packet. For information on ordering it, see page 307.)

NOTE: For more in-depth information on this topic, see Overhead Transparency 17 ("The Oasis of Jericho"), along with its description in Set 1 of this series.

Overhead Transparency 43. The Road to Jerusalem. The roads leading to Jerusalem through the Judea Wilderness traverse some barren, desolate, and rugged areas. This path following a wadi is one such trail. Seeing this path can help us understand the parable Jesus told of a man who went down to Jericho from Jerusalem and was beaten by robbers (Luke 10:30). The photograph can also help us picture Jesus' final walk from Jericho—where He healed Bartimaeus (Mark 10:46–52) and visited Zacchaeus (Luke 19:1–10)—to Jerusalem, along a path like this one. Jesus had been tempted in this wilderness before (Matthew 4:1–11). It must have been a difficult walk for Him, knowing that a horrible death lay ahead of Him and that, if He chose to, He could easily escape into the safety of the wilderness nearby (Matthew 20:17–19,20–28). His pain and despair probably deepened at the sound of His disciples arguing about who would be number one when they reached Jerusalem. We should be eternally grateful when we realize that Jesus made that hot, difficult journey because of His great love for us.

Step Two: "The King — God's Lamb"

1. Lecture

Jesus' triumphal entry into Jerusalem on Palm Sunday is one of the most well-known events of the New Testament. Celebrated just a week before Easter, Palm Sunday is a time of great celebration of Jesus' kingship. Seen in its first-century context, Jesus' entrance into Jerusalem on a donkey highlights the true nature of His kingdom. This study will investigate the setting for this significant event, both geographically (He chose to enter Jerusalem from the east, as everyone knew the Messiah would do) and culturally (it was Passover, when Jewish longing for a messiah intensified).

Before each of the following sections, be sure to read the story of the triumphal entry, found in Matthew 21:1–11, Luke 19:28–44, and John 12:12–16.

2. Map Study: Jerusalem

Using the overhead transparency "Topography of Jerusalem," point out the following areas, and have your students locate them on their maps.

> Mount of Olives
> Kidron Valley
> Temple Mount

Using the overhead transparency "Jerusalem's Districts," point out the following areas, and have your students locate them on their diagrams.

> Mount of Olives (toward the east)
> Kidron Valley
> Temple Mount
> Eastern Gate
> Tadi (Sheep) Gate
> Huldah Gates
> royal stoa

HINT: *If you have the optional full-color overhead-transparency packet, you may want to view Overhead Transparencies 29 ("The Mount of Olives") and 33 ("The Southern Stairs"), and their descriptions, in Lesson 22 before beginning Guided Discussion 3 below. You may also want to use Overhead Transparency 8 ("The Eastern Gate of Jerusalem") in Set 1 and Overhead Transparency 21 ("The Temple Mount at Jerusalem") in Set 2 of this series.*

3. Guided Discussion: He Came from the East

You may have noticed that in His triumphal entry, Jesus chose to approach Jerusalem from the east. That fact added emphasis to the event. The east was important to the Jewish people. To the east of Jerusalem was the Judea Wilderness, which was also significant for the coming of the Messiah.

Have your students look up the following passages and discover the reasons the east and its wilderness were so important to the Jewish people.

a. Exodus 27:12–15 (Numbers 3:38); Ezekiel 8:16 and 11:1 (2 Chronicles 3:17). These passages may be difficult for your students to understand. Help them see that the Tabernacle and the Temple both faced east.

b. Joshua 3:1,15–17. Israel, with the ark symbolizing God's presence, entered the land from the east.

c. Ezekiel 10:4,18–19; Ezekiel 11:22–24. In Ezekiel's vision, the glory (presence) of the Lord left the corrupted Temple and departed to the east. (The mountain to the east is the Mount of Olives.)

d. Ezekiel 43:1–5. In this later vision, the glory of God (His presence) returned to the Temple from the east.

e. Matthew 2:1–2,9. Jesus' birth was announced in the east.

f. Acts 1:6–12. Jesus ascended into heaven from the Mount of Olives to the east of Jerusalem.

g. Zechariah 14:4 (Joel 3:2,12). Many people believe that this refers to part of the Kidron Valley east of Jerusalem, between Jerusalem and the Mount of Olives. This portrays Jesus' second coming in judgment as taking place on the Mount of Olives, east of Jerusalem.

h. Isaiah 40:3 (Matthew 3:3). The wilderness is east of Jerusalem, along the eastern side of Israel.

i. Acts 21:38. Other "messiahs" came to Jerusalem from the east. (The "deliverer" mentioned in

Acts 21 gathered his followers on the Mount of Olives and told them he would make the walls of Jerusalem fall. Needless to say, Felix, the Roman commander from the Antonia, sent out the legionaires, who slaughtered many people, although the messiah escaped into the desert from which he had come. This episode, which is representative of many others, highlighted the dangerous atmosphere that existed in Jerusalem, especially during festivals, none of which was more significant than Passover. One man named Theudas [apparently not the Theudas of Acts 5:36] went to the wilderness—probably during Passover—and gathered a following. The Romans killed him and his followers and placed Theudas's head on the Antonia fortress.)

Ask your students to answer the following questions.

1. Why do you think Jesus chose to enter Jerusalem from the east?

2. There were many viewpoints concerning what the Messiah was to be like. Did Jesus' journey east from the wilderness to the Mount of Olives, and riding on a donkey (Zechariah 9:9), force the people to make a decision? If so, what was the decision? (Answer: They had to decide not only if Jesus was the Messiah, but also what kind of Messiah He was.)

3. What characteristics about Jesus would have led people to believe He might be the Messiah?

4. What aspect of the triumphal entry would have confirmed that Jesus was the Messiah? Did anything occur that might have raised questions in people's minds?

5. Does it surprise you to discover that other individuals used the people's awareness of prophecy to declare themselves messiahs and gain a following? Does it help you understand (not excuse) the skepticism some people had concerning Jesus? How?

4. Guided Discussion: The Day of the Lamb

God planned carefully when He carried out His great work of salvation. Nothing was left to chance (Galatians 4:4). Jesus came to Jerusalem from the east, riding on a donkey, just as the prophets had predicted. The day He entered Jerusalem was also important to God's plan. This section investigates the significance of the day Jesus entered the city.

Ask your students to read the following passages and answer the questions.

a. John 12:1,12. Based on this passage, many people believe the triumphal entry took place on the Sunday before Passover. Regardless of the specific day, it certainly took place during Passover season.

b. Exodus 12:12–15,24–27; Exodus 23:15. Here Passover is called the Feast of Unleavened Bread.

c. Matthew 26:5. Passover was a dangerous time.

d. John 6:3–15. Crowds had tried to make Jesus a political king once before during Passover season.

   1. What was commemorated during the feast of Passover?

   2. What was the status of the Jews of Israel during Jesus' time?

   3. Why would this feast be a time of danger?

   4. Why would this be a time when people would be looking for the Messiah? (As evidence in support of the idea that Passover was always a time of messianic fervor, point out that Jewish tradition states that the Temple door should remain open on Passover eve in case the Messiah arrives. Also, many incidents involving bloodshed—by Archelaus as well as several Roman governors—occurred during Passover.)

   5. Given the situation the Jewish people were in, what kind of messiah would be attractive to them?

NOTE: Jesus chose to enter the city during Passover season, when messianic anticipation was at its highest. The Jews were looking for a messiah, and the Romans were ready for trouble.

    e. Zechariah 9:9–10. The promised king ("anointed," or *messiah*) would enter Jerusalem on a donkey.

    f. Matthew 21:1–6. Jesus began riding the donkey at Bethphage, the town the rabbis had decided was the city limit of Jerusalem (as part of the oral law). Jesus got on the donkey as soon as He reached the city. This way, the people knew He didn't just happen to be riding a donkey; He chose to enter the city on a donkey to fulfill Zechariah's prophecy.

        1. What part of this prophecy might the people have been drawn to?

        2. What part might not have appealed to them?

        3. Did Jesus proclaim Himself king, or did the people put the claim on Jesus? How do you know? (Jesus' act of getting on the donkey was clearly a claim to be Messiah.)

        4. Are there other details in the story that make it clear that the people wanted Jesus to be their predicted king, the anointed one? If so, what are they?

    g. Exodus 12:1–6. If Passover was on Saturday that year, the sacrificial lamb would have been killed on Friday. The lamb would have been selected on the Sunday before—the day Jesus entered Jerusalem.

    h. John 1:29,36; 1 Corinthians 5:7. Jesus is God's Lamb, our Passover Lamb.

        1. What does it mean to you that Jesus came to Passover and announced that He was Messiah at the time the people were to select their lambs? Do you think the people understood that Jesus was inviting them to choose Him as their Passover Lamb? Explain.

        2. How do the hopes of the people contrast with the true nature of Jesus' kingship? (See Matthew 16:21,28; Matthew 17:22–23; Matthew 20:17–19; Luke 17:20–21; John 18:37; Acts 2:36.)

        3. Jesus became King, God's Anointed, by being brutally executed on a cross. The sign of weakness, condemnation, and defeat became God's victory. Jesus came on Palm Sunday to declare Himself King—but He came on a donkey, meek and humble—God's sacrificial Lamb. In a real sense, He was announcing, "Yes, I am the Messiah you have been waiting for. But I come as a lamb for offering. Will you still accept Me as God's Anointed?"

Conclusion: Jesus entered Jerusalem at the time when the Passover lamb was chosen. He proclaimed Himself Messiah by coming from the east and riding a donkey into the city. But His true kingship would be as God's Lamb, our Passover Lamb. Palm Sunday should be a great time of invitation for Christians. Because it's the day the lamb was chosen for the Passover offering, we must choose our lamb. Just as in Jesus' day, some choose Him and some don't.

Prayer: Have you chosen Jesus as your Lamb? Let us pray together as we admit before God that we need an offering of forgiveness for our sins and that Jesus is our choice for that offering.

5. Guided Discussion: What Does "Hosanna" Mean?

To fully prepare for this section, students should read the handouts "Pharisees or Sadducees?" "The Joy of Living Water: Jesus and the Feast of Sukkot," and "The Jewish Revolts" before you begin this section.

In the last section, we established that Jesus clearly fulfilled messianic prophecies by His entrance into Jerusalem on Palm Sunday. We have also seen that He declared His kingship as God's Lamb. The crowds obviously understood that He was announcing His messianic title, but did they understand what He meant? Do we? We will explore these questions here.

a. Have your students (individually or in small groups) read the following passages and answer the questions.

- John 12:16; Acts 1:6. Did the disciples understand correctly the meaning of Jesus' triumphal entry? What were they hoping for?

- Luke 19:39. Do you think some of the Pharisees understood Jesus' point? Why?

- Luke 19:41. Why did Jesus weep over the people of Jerusalem?

b. The key to understanding the crowd's reaction to Jesus is to recognize that palm branches and "Hosanna," when used together, had a specific significance to the Jewish people of the time.

- Read Psalm 118:25–26. The word *Hosanna* comes from this passage and is composed of two Hebrew words: *hosha* and *na*. *Hosha* means "save," and *na* adds a sense of urgency. Transliterated, the word means "Please save!" or "Help, please!"

- Read Matthew 21:9. The crowd was shouting, "Please save us, O son of David!"

- John 12:13. The shouting crowd used palm branches.

The chant of "Hosanna" and the waving of palm branches are linked in the Jewish feast of Sukkot in the fall. This was originally a festival to give thanks for the protection God provided during the wilderness wandering and the gift of the Promised Land. The feast included the "Hosanna" prayer from Psalm 118:25–26 and palm branches. The people asked God to deliver, or save, them by providing the fall rains, which would soon begin.

When Judah Maccabee drove the pagan Greeks out of Jerusalem and cleansed the Temple, he immediately commanded the people to keep the feast of Sukkot, for it had been outlawed. As a result, the festival took on a political tone in prayers for freedom and deliverance from foreign rule. The palm soon became a symbol of Jewish national identity (e.g., on coins), and the "Hosanna" became more than a prayer for rain or spiritual salvation. It became a prayer for political deliverance as well.

Point out to your students that the crowd may have been even more agitated when Jesus immediately entered the Temple courts and cleansed them, just as Judah Maccabee had done. (See Matthew 21:12–15. NOTE: The children were still shouting, "Hosanna.")

- Read Luke 19:41–44. Jesus wept!

1. Why would Jesus weep when so many people recognized Him as Messiah?

2. What kind of messiah did some of the people in the crowd think Jesus was? Why? (Remember that even the disciples missed Jesus' point—see John 12:16.)

3. Read the context in which Jesus wept (John 12:42–44). (This is exactly what happened to those who sought a political-military messiah in Jerusalem.) Is it possible that some people shouted "Hosanna" and waved palms but totally missed who Jesus was? Do you think Jesus was weeping for them?

4. Do you think some people understood Jesus' message correctly? If so, who?

5. What do modern-day Christians mean when we say "Hosanna" to Jesus? Is it important to understand the meaning of this word? Why or why not?

6. The word *Hosanna* means "Please save!" but *save* can mean many different things. What should we mean when we say it?

7. What are some specific misconceptions people today have about Jesus? (Possible answers: Jesus was just a good man, Jesus was a revolutionary, Jesus was a member of a specific denomination.)

8. Have you ever missed the message of who Jesus really is? If so, when?

9. Do we ever misunderstand the nature of Jesus' kingdom? If so, how?

10. How do we determine who and what Jesus and His kingdom are?

Spend a few moments in prayer, asking God for guidance in knowing Jesus for who He claimed to be.

OPTIONAL — Digging Deeper V: Jesus Wept *(40–60 minutes)*

For those who have cherished the divine nature of Jesus, it may not be easy to think of Him as so human that He would weep. But the Bible presents an equally strong picture of Jesus the Man. Twice the Bible writers recorded Jesus' tears.

1. Read John 11:1–44.

   - verse 3—Lazarus was Jesus' close friend.
   - verses 1–3,14—Jesus knew ahead of time that Lazarus was sick.
   - verse 4—Jesus knew that He would raise Lazarus from the dead.
   - verses 20–23—Martha, a sister of Lazarus, went to Jesus. Jesus told her He would raise her brother from the dead.
   - verses 32–33—Mary, another sister of Lazarus, went to Jesus. She was grieving.
   - verse 33—Other Jews were also grieving.
   - verse 34—Jesus went to the grave.
   - verse 35—Jesus wept. The Greek word used here emphasizes the tears, which fell quietly. Jesus cried.

   Ask your students: Why did Jesus cry? Then point out the following information:

   - Jesus knew for a while that Lazarus was dead.
   - He had already said He would raise Lazarus from the dead.
   - Jesus was crying for the sisters and for the Jews because He had such compassion for their grief (verses 33–35).

   Jesus weeps for the hurts, sorrows, and pain of people whom He loves and who love Him. Ask students to discuss their reactions to knowing that Jesus weeps for their hurts. Ask if any of your students have experienced His great comfort as He helped bear their pain. If students are willing to talk about their experiences, allow them to tell them to the rest of the class. Ask students: Does it seem to make grief and sorrow more appropriate to know that Jesus shared in them? Why?

2. Read Luke 19:37–44.

   - verses 37–38—Jesus came into view of the city of Jerusalem. The crowd began to shout "Hosanna" and to wave palm branches (John 12:13).
   - verse 41—Jesus saw Jerusalem. He had heard the shouting and seen the palm branches.
   - verses 42–44—Jesus knew what would happen because the people were looking for the wrong kind of deliverance—political rather than spiritual—and the result would be terrible.

- verse 41—Jesus wept! The Greek word used emphasizes the deep mournfulness of weeping aloud. Jesus shook with anguished sobs.

  Ask your students: Why did Jesus cry? Then point out the following information:
    - The people were shouting "Hosanna," proclaiming Jesus the "son of David"—Messiah.
    - Many of the people missed the point of Jesus' message. They didn't want what He offered: the kingdom of God through the forgiveness of sins. Some wanted political freedom, and others probably didn't care.

3. Conclusion: Jesus cries deeply for those who do not recognize that He is the Messiah who offers redemption from sin.

Key Issue: Jesus weeps for each one of us. The question is, why does He weep? Does He weep because we hurt, suffer, or grieve? If so, we will know a most compassionate Messiah, for He will comfort us. Or does He weep because we are looking for something different from what He is offering us?

OPTIONAL — Digging Deeper VI: The Compassionate Jesus *(15–30 minutes)*

Students should read the handout "The Jewish Revolts" before beginning this study.

HINT: *If you have the optional full-color overhead-transparency packet, now would be an appropriate time to view Overhead Transparencies 32 ("Scenes of the Temple Mount"), 34 ("Scenes from the Southern Stairs"), and 35 ("Mansions on the Western Hill"), and their descriptions, in Lesson 22.*

Jesus wept as He predicted what would happen to the people who missed His message of peace because they were focused on their one wish for a political-military deliverer. Not accepting God for what He offers is very serious, as the passages below show.

- Isaiah 29:3; Ezekiel 4:1–3—Destruction had come to Jerusalem before because they had not followed God's way.

- Luke 19:42–44; Luke 21:20; Matthew 24:2—Jesus made predictions that similar things would happen to Jerusalem.

Many of Jesus' predictions about Jerusalem came true in the Roman destruction of the city in A.D. 70. The brutality of that destruction, which resulted when the Jews revolted against Rome, is beyond description. Hundreds of thousands of people were killed or starved to death, and thousands more were crucified (according to Josephus, 500 individuals per day during the siege). It was for these people that Jesus wept.

Ask your students: How can we develop the same compassion Jesus had for those who ignore, reject, or misinterpret Him and His message? As we weep for their future, what can we do to reach out to them?

Conclusion

It is tempting for people to look for a different kind of salvation or deliverance from what we desperately need: redemption from the penalty we face because of our sins. We may think success or fame, removal of hardships and suffering, or restored health are the solutions to our problems, but none of these would remove the brokenness created by our inherent sinfulness.

When Jesus came to Jerusalem, the people believed the solution to their problems was freedom from the Romans and their collaborators. Although Jesus certainly stands for freedom, it isn't the political freedom the Jews of His day sought. Like us, they were sinners—broken, condemned, and in desperate need of forgiveness and healing. But because they misidentified their deepest need, they misunderstood Jesus when He proclaimed that He was Messiah.

We, too, are in danger of misunderstanding Jesus and His message. We may want many appropriate things from Jesus. But first and foremost, He must be for us the Lamb of God who takes away the sin of the world. If we believe salvation is our greatest need, we will see Jesus for who He really is. If not, we will miss Him, or worse, misinterpret Him and mislead others.

THE WEIGHT OF THE WORLD

For the Teacher

It is impossible for us to comprehend Jesus' love for His followers and His devotion to God. Not only is it difficult for us to imagine loving someone as much as He does, but also the fact that the ones He loves don't deserve it makes it almost impossible to understand. The human mind cannot grasp the level of Jesus' devotion to His Father's will—He willingly went to His death on the cross. Yet Jesus did leave a record of His last hours of agony. Reading that record can help us begin to sense His love, and seeing that record in its proper setting can provide us with even more understanding.

Jesus faced not only the pressure of His walk to the cross, but also the realization that He would be forsaken there by everyone, including His heavenly Father. Before His crucifixion, He chose to face that burden in a place created to apply enormous pressure: a *gethsemane*—an olive press. This unit explores the hours Jesus spent at Gethsemane and how we can apply them to understand more about His love. This study should inspire you to be more dedicated to Him and willing to become more like Him.

Ask your students to talk about stressful experiences they've had recently. Ask them how they felt during those times, how they acted, and how God responded. When students are finished sharing, explain to the class that this lesson will focus on the tremendous stress Jesus faced as He went to the cross.

Your Objectives for This Lesson

At the completion of this section, you will want your students:

To Know/Understand

1. The location of Gethsemane and its relationship to Jerusalem.

2. What a *gethsemane* is and how it can help us picture Jesus' experience.

3. The importance of olive farming for the people of Israel.

4. The people who were instrumental in Jesus' arrest.

5. How Jesus spent the week in Jerusalem before He died.

6. The manner in which Jesus handled the anguish of His coming crucifixion.

To Do

1. Plan to face the pressure of suffering and sorrow in the same manner Jesus did in Gethsemane.

2. Thank God for the love and dedication Jesus showed by going to the cross.

3. Try to relate to God as a compassionate, caring Father, as Jesus did.

How to Plan for This Lesson

Because of the volume of material in this lesson, you may need to divide it into several class sessions. To help you determine how to do that, the lesson has been broken into segments. Note that the time needed may vary significantly, depending on elements such as the leader, the size of the class, and the interest level of the class.

If you wish to cover the entire lesson in one session, you should complete Unit One. This unit provides a guided discussion covering the major points in the video. It does not go into great depth. If you wish to go into greater depth on any of the points in Unit One, they are covered more thoroughly in the remainder of the material.

How to Prepare for This Lesson

Materials Needed

Student copies of the maps/diagrams:	"The Roman World"
	"Land of Jesus' Ministry"
	"Topography of Jerusalem"
	"Jerusalem's Districts"
Overhead transparencies:	"The Roman World"
	"Land of Jesus' Ministry"
	"Topography of Jerusalem"
	"Jerusalem's Districts"
	"The Olive Press"
Student copies of the handout:	"A Light to the World"

Video: **The Weight of the World**

Overhead projector, screen, TV, VCR

1. Make copies of the maps/diagrams listed above for your students.

2. Prepare the overhead transparencies listed above. (You'll find them at the back of the book.)

3. Make copies of the handout listed above for your students. (If possible, students should receive and read this handout before the lesson.)

4. Review the geography of the lands of the Bible from the "Introduction."

5. Determine which **unit** and which **Digging Deeper** sections, if any, you want to use in your class session(s). NOTE: You can use these sections in any order you wish (e.g., you might want to use **Digging Deeper III**, but not **Digging Deeper I** or **Digging Deeper II**).

6. Prepare your classroom ahead of time, setting up and testing an overhead projector and screen (for the overhead transparencies) and a TV and VCR. If you plan to hand out biblical references for your students to look up and read aloud, prepare 3x5 cards (one reference per card) to distribute before class.

Lesson Plan

UNIT ONE: Video Review

1. Introductory Comments

This lesson explores the agony Jesus faced as He willingly went to the cross because He loved us. He spent His last week focused on the needs and concerns of others, even as a few threatened leaders plotted His death. He spent His last meal encouraging His closest friends and teaching them about the importance of giving oneself for others. The song He sang is a message of trust in God and sure victory for those who follow His ways.

After the meal, Jesus walked to the very place where His betrayer would be sure to find Him. There He faced directly the reality of what He was about to do. On His knees in the garden, He expressed Himself openly to His Father—His fears, His despair, His agony. But in the end, Jesus submitted Himself completely to Him. The agony of those few hours should tear at our souls as we discover in the imagery of a *gethsemane* that it was because of us—our sin and His love for us—that Jesus faced the horrors of hell and even the rejection of God. We can truly see Jesus, the compassionate Savior, when we see His reaction to the weight of the world upon His shoulders.

2. Show the Video *The Weight of the World* (19 minutes)

3. Map Study: Capernaum and Jerusalem

HINT: *Begin this map study session by reviewing the geography of the overall region and working down to the cities the lesson is dealing with—Capernaum and Jerusalem.*

Using the overhead transparency "The Roman World," point out the following areas, and have your students locate them on their maps.

> Rome
> Mediterranean Sea
> Judea
> Jerusalem

Using the overhead transparency "Land of Jesus' Ministry," point out the following areas, and have your students locate them on their maps.

> Jerusalem
> Capernaum (location of a *gethsemane*)
> Sea of Galilee

Using the overhead transparency "Topography of Jerusalem," point out the following areas, and have your students locate them on their maps.

> Mount of Olives
> Kidron Valley
> Gethsemane (traditional)
> Temple Mount
> Western Hill

Using the overhead transparency "Jerusalem's Districts," point out the following areas, and have your students locate them on their diagrams.

Upper City
Mount of Olives

4. Guided Discussion: On the Way to the Olive Press

a. Read Matthew 26:30. Scholars believe the hymn that Jesus and His disciples sang was the *Hallel*, the normal Passover hymn, composed of lines from Psalms 113–118 and 136.

Read the following verses and remind students that Jesus sang them before He was arrested:

- Psalm 115:1
- Psalm 116:1–2
- Psalm 118:5–7
- Psalm 118:22–24

Ask your students to answer the following questions:

1. What do you think these words meant to Jesus on this occasion?

2. How can Jesus' use of these words help you understand how to prepare to handle great suffering or sorrow?

b. Read John 18:1 and Matthew 26:36. Note that John mentioned an olive grove, and Matthew called the place Gethsemane. These two locations are the same: A *gethsemane* was an olive press, usually found in or near an olive grove.

Ask your students to answer the following questions:

1. Why did Jesus go to Gethsemane? (See Luke 21:37, 22:39.)

2. How did Judas know where to find Him?

c. Displaying the overhead transparency "The Olive Press," explain the following information about Gethsemane.

- The word *gethsemane* comes from the Hebrew word *gat-shemanim*, which means "oil press." Apparently, there was an oil press near the olive grove Jesus went to.

- After they were picked, olives were placed in a large basin to be crushed.

- As the millstone was turned, it rolled over the olives, crushing them to a pulp.

- The pulp was collected in baskets and placed under a stone weight in a pit. A horizontal beam, with one end in a hole in the wall, was placed across the weight, and some other heavy stone weights were suspended from it, placing enormous pressure on the pulp.

- Under this great pressure, oil from the olives flowed out of the baskets and into a pit underneath.

- The great weights and the beam used for pressing the oil are the *gethsemane*.

d. Have your students read the following passages and answer the questions, to understand better the pressure Jesus experienced in Gethsemane.

- Matthew 26:37–38; Luke 22:44. What was Jesus' state of mind that night? Why?

- Matthew 26:39,42,44. What did Jesus pray? What was He asking?

- Matthew 26:40–44. Why was there such a contrast between Jesus' mind-set and that of the disciples?

- Luke 22:44. Why did this happen to Jesus? What was the "weight" on Him that caused such agony?

Explain that the imagery of the *gethsemane* provides a picture of Jesus' suffering the night before His crucifixion. The task Jesus knew lay before Him—rejection, suffering, and finally death on a cross to pay for the sin of humanity—pressed down upon Him like a heavy millstone. Jesus, straining under the pressure, was crushed like the olives in their baskets. His sweat, "like drops of blood falling to the ground," flowed from Him like olive oil, a precious gift from God.

Ask your students for their reactions to the fact that the weight on Jesus was the pressure of bearing our sin and its penalty. Then have them answer the following questions:

1. Who was responsible for Jesus' suffering? How does this help us relate to God?

2. How should Jesus' night of agony affect our lives? What can we learn from His anguish?

3. What can Jesus' response to the pressure He was under teach us about how we should respond to the needs of others? To the obligations God places on us?

e. Some final thoughts: What if Jesus had chosen to walk away into the night instead of facing His imminent arrest? Jesus wants us to love as He loves. Think about what this means for the attitude you have toward those God has placed in your life.

f. Conclusion: Spend some time in quiet prayer. Ask God to help you begin to appreciate the depth of the love Jesus has for you. Ask Him to help you realize that He was in agony because of your sin. Pray for a commitment to resist sin because of your appreciation for the price Jesus paid. Ask for assurance that His blood has fully paid the price for your sin, and admit that you need Him to give you enough compassion to face suffering and stress in order to love others and act according to what is best for them. Pray for the strength and wisdom you need to follow Jesus' pattern when you face the stress of sorrow and agony in your own life, turning honestly to God in complete devotion to His will.

UNIT TWO
"A Place Called Gethsemane"

1. Introductory Comments

This study is unusual because it involves a faith lesson based on two very different locations. One setting is the place called Gethsemane, located on the slope of the Mount of Olives to the east of Jerusalem. As we will discover, the reason for the name of this location is no longer found there. There is, however, a perfect example of a *gethsemane* in the town Jesus called home, in Galilee. So in this unit, we will move from the setting near Jerusalem to Galilee, to discover a powerful metaphor that provides a picture of Jesus' agonizing prayer in Gethsemane.

2. Show the Video *The Weight of the World* (19 minutes)

3. Map Study: Capernaum and Jerusalem

HINT: *Begin this map study session by reviewing the geography of the overall region and working down to the cities the lesson is dealing with—Capernaum and Jerusalem.*

Using the overhead transparency "The Roman World," point out the following areas, and have your students locate them on their maps.

> Rome
> Mediterranean Sea
> Egypt
> Judea
> Caesarea

Using the overhead transparency "Land of Jesus' Ministry," point out the following areas, and have your students locate them on their maps.

> Bethlehem
> Jerusalem
> Nazareth
> Capernaum (location of a *gethsemane*)
> Galilee
> Sea of Galilee
> Jerusalem

Using the overhead transparency "Topography of Jerusalem," point out the following areas, and have your students locate them on their maps.

> Mount of Olives
> Kidron Valley
> Gethsemane (traditional)
> Temple Mount
> Western Hill

Using the overhead transparency "Jerusalem's Districts," point out the following areas, and have your students locate them on their diagrams.

> Upper City
> Temple Mount
> Antonia fortress
> Herod's palace
> Golgotha (traditional)
> garden tomb
> Mount of Olives

4. OPTIONAL — Guided Discussion: Capernaum—Jesus' Adopted Home

During Jesus' ministry, His headquarters were in the Galilean town of Capernaum. This topic was explored extensively in Set 3 of this series, in the videos and in the leader's guide, especially Guided Discussion 5, Lesson 14, pages 88–90. Capernaum is one of the settings for this lesson because a *gethsemane* is found here and not in the traditional Garden of Gethsemane in Jerusalem. If you wish to study more about Jesus' ministry in Capernaum, you might consider covering the following information:

a. Jesus and the millstone: Matthew 18:1–6. (Note Matthew 17:24, where Matthew gives the location where this event occurred.)

Ask your students to answer the following questions:

1. How did Jesus respond when He was interrupted? How do you usually respond to interruptions?

2. What did Jesus mean when He described the fate of those who mislead "little ones"?

(NOTE: Some scholars believe that "little ones" means children, and it can also refer to people who are of no importance to others.)

3. What "little ones" are under your leadership or influence, directly or indirectly? What is your responsibility to them?

4. Why would Jesus use the analogy of the millstone and the sea here? (Note the location.)

5. Read Mark 9:33–42. What did Mark add to the story? Why is it so important for Christians always to act as Jesus would?

b. The following passages describe events in Jesus' life that took place at Capernaum. Review them to see how central this location was to His ministry.

- Matthew 4:13–16, 8:5–17, 9:1–34, 17:24–27
- Mark 1:16
- Luke 7:1–6, 17:2
- John 4:46–54, 6

HINT: *Overhead Transparency 40 ("Aerial View of Capernaum") in Set 3 is also set in Capernaum.*

5. Guided Discussion: The Last Week

It is impossible for us to study in detail here all the events of Jesus' last few days of ministry, but a review of the major events of those days can help us understand how clearly He was focused on His approaching death. All scholars do not agree on the specific days in which these events occurred, but the outline below is generally accepted.

Read each passage listed below, and reflect on the questions that follow. If you want further details on a location, refer to the lesson and study unit listed for that location.

a. Sunday—The Triumphal Entry

- Luke 19:29–44

1. Why were there such large crowds in Jerusalem at this time?

2. What made them so enthusiastic about Jesus?

3. Why did Jesus respond to the crowds as He did?

4. If you did not know how Jesus' life would end, would you have predicted that the crucifixion would occur, based on the events of that day?

For Further Study: See Lesson 22, Unit 2, Step 1, "The Mount of Olives," pages 85–86; and Lesson 23, Unit 2, Step 2, Guided Discussion 4 ("The Day of the Lamb"), pages 163–164, as well as the video for that lesson.

b. Monday—Cleansing the Temple

- Mark 11:12–19

1. Who was Jesus confronting most harshly in His challenge to the Temple merchants? (See verse 18; also John 11:45–53.)

2. What made Jesus so angry?

3. Why did this incident make people angry enough to plot to kill Jesus?

For Further Study: See Lesson 22, Unit 2, Step 2, "The Gentile Court" and "The Royal Stoa," pages 103–105.

c. **Tuesday and Wednesday—Confrontations in the Temple; The Widow's Offering (These events took place on either Tuesday or Wednesday.)**

- Matthew 21:23–27,45–46; Luke 21:5–24,37; Matthew 26:1–5,14–16

1. Where did Jesus do His teaching during His last week? Why would He go there?

2. What was the theme of His teaching? How did the people respond to what He said?

3. Why did some respond negatively to Jesus?

4. Why do you think Jesus' message always produced such strong reactions? Is this still true? Explain.

- Luke 21:1–4; Mark 12:41–44

1. Where was Jesus when He observed the widow? What is the significance of this location?

2. How was Jesus' lesson displayed in His own life?

3. How could you practice what He taught?

For Further Study: See Lesson 22, Unit 2, Step 2, "The Women's Court," pages 105–108.

d. **Thursday—The Passover**

NOTE: The Last Supper of Jesus is a topic beyond the range of this study. There are, however, many excellent studies available, both in video and in print. Teachers who wish to pursue this topic further are encouraged to make use of the resource materials listed in the "Introduction."

- Luke 22:7–30; John 13:1–17

1. What is most striking to you about the Passover celebration Jesus had with His disciples?

2. Knowing that Jesus would be crucified for the sin of the world the next day, why do you think the foot-washing was so significant?

3. Typically, the story of the Passover lamb in Egypt is recounted at the Passover meal, and although the Bible does not mention it, Jesus and His disciples probably kept up the tradition. Read John 1:29; 1 Corinthians 5:7. Why would recounting the story of the Passover lamb have been especially significant for Jesus?

For Further Study: See Lesson 22, Unit 2, Step 2, "The Upper City," pages 111–113.

OPTIONAL — Digging Deeper I: They Sang a Hymn *(15–30 minutes)*

Ask a student to read aloud Matthew 26:30. Scholars are certain that the Passover meal ended with the reciting of Psalms 113–118 and 136 (at least parts of them), a collection called the *Hallel* ("Praise").

Have students take turns reading aloud the following verses. Then ask them to reflect on what it means to them to picture Jesus saying those words, knowing He would soon face Gethsemane, arrest, torture, and execution.

- Psalm 115:1
- Psalm 116:1–2

- Psalm 116:3–4
- Psalm 116:12–14
- Psalm 118:1
- Psalm 118:5–7
- Psalm 118:13–14
- Psalm 118:22–24 (What was the specific day this passage referred to? Answer: It was the day the stone—Jesus—was made head of the corner.)

6. Guided Discussion: A Place Called Gethsemane

Few Christian visitors to Jerusalem miss the chance to go to the traditional Garden of Gethsemane, just east of the city. Its old olive trees and its location just below the city wall help people reflect on the agony Jesus faced when He prayed before His arrest. Many would be surprised to discover that the Bible does not mention a *Garden* of Gethsemane. Gethsemane was mentioned by two writers describing this event—one referred to the Mount of Olives, and the other to "an olive grove." Both descriptions are correct, and understanding their relationship can help us appreciate the intensity of Jesus' prayer.

Before beginning this study, your students should read one or more of the accounts of Jesus' prayer time in Gethsemane. These accounts are found in Matthew 26:36–56; Mark 14:32–51; Luke 22:39–53; and John 18:1–11.

a. The Place

Using the overhead transparencies "Topography of Jerusalem" and "Jerusalem's Districts," point out the following areas, and have your students locate them on their maps/diagrams.

> Upper City
> Kidron Valley
> Mount of Olives
> Garden of Gethsemane (traditional)
> the distance Jesus traveled to Gethsemane (NOTE: No one knows the route Jesus took to Gethsemane. He probably traveled from the Upper City, crossed the Kidron, and entered an olive grove on the Mount of Olives.)

Ask your students to read the following passages and answer the questions.

- Luke 21:37, 22:39

1. Why do you think Jesus stayed where He did during the week before His death? What does this location have to do with Gethsemane? With the fact that Judas knew how to find Jesus and His disciples? (See John 18:2.) NOTE: It is likely that more than 1 million pilgrims traveled to Jerusalem for some of the feasts. Every available place for miles around would have been loaned or rented to the travelers for the weeklong feast. It is likely that Jesus and His disciples stayed at a place called Gethsemane on the Mount of Olives during that week.

2. Read Luke 22:39 again. What does this verse tell us about the location to which Jesus went after the Passover meal?

- John 18:1

1. What does this passage tell you about the location to which Jesus went after the Last Supper? NOTE: The word translated "olive grove" means "cultivated plot of ground." Given the olive

groves lining the mount of that name and the presence of a *gethsemane*, it is very likely that this word referred to an olive grove.

- Matthew 26:36; Mark 14:32

1. What additional information is given in these passages about the place where Jesus went to pray? NOTE: The garden, or grove, itself is never called Gethsemane. Since *gethsemanes* were found near olive groves, it is probable that the olive grove (John 18:1) had a *gethsemane* in or near it. Apparently, the grove was enclosed, for Jesus and the disciples "entered it."

2. Why do you think Jesus went to this location that night? Is there anything in the story that indicates a reason?

b. The Olive Press

Students should read the handout "A Light to the World" before beginning this section.

The word *gethsemane* is the English transliteration of a Greek word. The Greek word comes from two Hebrew (or Aramaic) words. *Gat* or *Gath* means "a place for pressing oil (or wine)." *Shemanim* means "oils," probably referring to different qualities of oil. A *gethsemane*, therefore, was an olive (or oil) press. Apparently, the press near the olive grove where Jesus went was large enough that the area was known as "Gethsemane."

Oil presses in Israel were frequently found in caves. It is likely that the Gethsemane of Jesus' visit was also in a cave. This would help explain why Jesus stayed there during the cool nights of the Passover season. It would also explain why one disciple was wearing only a linen undergarment at the time of Jesus' arrest (Mark 14:51–52).[1]

Display the overhead transparency "The Olive Press" as you highlight the olive production process to your students:

1. Olives were harvested in October and early November. They were picked when they had blackened.

2. Those set aside for oil were placed in a crushing basin, in which a large millstone rolled in a circle, crushing the olives—pits and all—into pulp.

3. The pulp was placed in woven baskets (like rough burlap), which were stacked on top of each other, over (or in) a pit in the floor (usually solid rock—one reason caves were used).

4. Stone weights were used to press the pulp. In some cases, a large stone pillar was placed on the baskets, squeezing the pulp. A long pole across the beam, set in an opening in a nearby wall, was used to place the pillar on the olives. In other presses, the beam was laid across a smaller stone placed on the olives, and great stone weights were suspended from the beam, bringing even more weight down on the baskets.

5. The oil gradually flowed out of the baskets and into a pit or vat below. The first pressing produced the best oil. Anyone who has seen the streams of golden oil pouring from baskets in the many small presses used by mountain Arabs and Palestinians today can understand why it was a symbol of fertility. The rich, pungent odor saturates the air for miles.

6. Jesus went to an oil press like the one now being displayed to pray with His disciples. That press was in or near an olive grove. The press would have been idle at the time of Passover because it was springtime.

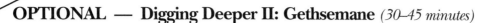

OPTIONAL — Digging Deeper II: Gethsemane *(30–45 minutes)*

(This section requires the use of the optional full-color overhead-transparency packet. For information on ordering it, see page 307.)

Israel has always been an agricultural country. The shepherds pastured their flocks in the wilderness areas and along the fringes of the tillable land. Farmers prayed for the rains necessary to raise a variety of crops in the interior of the country and along the coastal plain. No crop was more significant than the olives that grew almost everywhere in the country where there was rain. It is not by accident that the olive tree, its fruit, and olive oil were so frequently used in portraying God, His blessing, His people, and even His Messiah. The olive press that produced the oil was as common to the people of Jesus' time as the shopping mall is to us. These overhead transparencies will help us picture the olive-farming industry so familiar to the Israelites.

Overhead Transparency 44. Jerusalem from the Traditional Garden of Gethsemane. The Bible does not actually link the place of Gethsemane with a garden. It is called Gethsemane (Matthew 26:36) and an olive grove (in some versions, a garden; John 18:1). Both names are correct. Gethsemane (which means "oil[s] press") would have been located in or near an olive grove referred to as "a garden." Jesus apparently went to an olive press located near an olive grove.

This photograph was taken in the area traditionally called the Garden of Gethsemane. It is located on the western slope of the Mount of Olives (Luke 22:39), near the city of Jerusalem (John 18:1–3) and at the edge of the Kidron Valley (John 18:1). Only (twelfth- and thirteenth-century) tradition gives support to this specific location, but because it fits the biblical description, it helps give people a clearer picture of the appearance of the place where Jesus spent His last evening before the crucifixion. No remains of a *gethsemane* have been found on the grounds of this garden.

The olive trees on both sides of the path are ancient. Some have suggested the roots could even date to Jesus' time, and the trees are probably more than 1,000 years old. The flowers are a modern addition. Just beyond the stone wall is the bottom of the Kidron Valley. The slope of the hill on which Jerusalem is built, also covered by olive trees, is visible beyond the valley. The wall of Jerusalem (built in the fifteenth century) still maintains an ancient appearance and actually follows the line of the wall of Jesus' time. Beyond the wall is the Temple Mount. The Temple stood where the gold dome (the Dome of the Rock, a Muslim shrine) is on the left. The gold on this dome can help us envision the gold trimming on the Temple. The gate is now called the Golden Gate. It was the main eastern gate to the Temple Mount at the time of the Temple. It is probable that the guards sent by the Temple authorities came through this gate on their way to arrest Jesus. While it is not clear exactly where Gethsemane was, it must have been nearby. Jesus could have seen the mob that was coming for Him because of the proximity of Gethsemane to the city and the Temple. The guards were carrying torches in the dark night (John 18:3–4).

A cave nearby was recently identified as containing an ancient olive press. Early (sixth-century) tradition supports this cave as being Jesus' Gethsemane. Its location near Jerusalem, near the olive groves, close to the Kidron, and in a cave where pilgrims to Jerusalem might stay the night (Luke 22:39; Matthew 26:30,36) make it a possibility. Of course, regardless of whether it is the actual place where Jesus went to pray, its location and appearance in a large cave can help us picture Jesus enduring His night of agony. **HINT:** *If you have the optional full-color overhead-transparency packets for Sets 1 and 2, you may want to view Overhead Transparency 8 ("The Eastern Gate of Jerusalem"—Set 1) and Overhead Transparency 21 ("The Temple Mount at Jerusalem"—Set 2), along with their descriptions.*

Overhead Transparency 45. Olive Presses. There were several different types of olive presses in the first century. These photographs show the two most common types, although all presses followed the same sequence (as they do today) and functions.

Upper Left: An Olive Crusher. This olive installation is located at the modern-day city of Maresha in southern Judea. Its appearance and location in a cave are typical of ancient presses. Oil installations were commonly placed in caves because the more moderate temperatures improved the efficiency of olive production. It is likely that the *gethsemane* Jesus visited the night before His arrest was in a cave near an olive grove.

The ripe (black) olives were placed in a large, round basin (called *yam*, or "sea"). A donkey, blindfolded to prevent dizziness, walked around the basin, pushing the horizontal beam and rolling the wheel (called *memel*, or millstone) on the ripe fruit, crushing it into pulp. Smaller caves beyond the crusher may have been used to store the olive oil in clay jars, keeping it cool so it did not spoil.

Upper Right: A Basalt Crusher. The crusher in this photograph functioned just as the one to the left did, although the vertical post and horizontal beam are missing. This crusher is found at Capernaum, Jesus' home-base (Matthew 4:13), near the synagogue. The local basalt—a hard, volcanic black rock—made excellent crushers and other types of grinders. Jesus frequently saw crushers and millstones like this one. The basalt grinders are found in archaeological remains around the country. They were probably exported from the area of the Sea of Galilee. Jesus' teaching about being a proper influence on "little ones" or facing a fate worse than being thrown into the sea (the Sea of Galilee is barely 100 feet to the left) took place near here (Matthew 18:6).

*Lower Left: A **Gethsemane**.* This olive press is in the same cave as the crusher above. The crushed olive pulp was placed in baskets (about four inches thick and two feet in diameter), which were then stacked several high. These baskets are barely visible in the distance under the wooden beam, through the slot in the press. A heavy stone slab was placed on the top basket (not visible in this picture). The beam, with one end in a hole in the wall above the press, was positioned on the stone over the olive baskets. Great weights (visible in the foreground) were suspended by ropes from the end of the beam, placing enormous pressure on the olive pulp. These weights may have been lifted by a shorter beam placed in the hole in the wall above, on the left. Over time, the pressure squeezed the juice out of the pulp. The juice ran out of the baskets and into a pit below, where it separated into water and oil. The water was drained off, and the oil was collected and placed in clay jars. These jars were often stored in a cool area in the cave near the press (see above).

Olive oil had religious significance for the Israelites, both because it was connected with the fertility of the land (Deuteronomy 8:6–9) and because it was used for "anointing" (Genesis 28:18). The small niche (opening) to the right of the press may have held an idol to whom the press and the oil were dedicated. God's people brought olives to the Temple on Shavuot (Pentecost) to indicate their recognition that Yahweh, not the pagan gods, provided the gift of fertility.

Olive oil can have religious significance for us as Christians, too. A person who was anointed was a *mashiach* ("messiah" in English). This role was ultimately fulfilled by Jesus, God's Anointed. This imagery links Jesus to the olive tree and its rich fruit.

*Lower Right: A **Gethsemane** in **Capernaum**.* This press, slightly different from the one to the left, is part of the same installation as the crusher above. It was located in a building, not a cave. The pulp from the crusher was put in baskets and placed on the stone base under the large limestone pillar. Note the groove around the outside, which channeled the oil into the pit just to the left. The huge pillar was apparently lifted with a beam like the one on the press to the left, and placed on the olives, squeezing the oil from the fruit. This installation was also a familiar sight to Jesus and His disciples in Galilee, where they lived.

Jesus' visit to Gethsemane the night before His execution can be symbolized by olive presses like these. The great weight of His imminent crucifixion to pay for the sin of the world, His abandonment by His (sleeping) friends, and the knowledge that He would eventually be rejected by God, His Father, bore down on Him. There in Gethsemane, this burden, which He was willing to bear, squeezed from Him "sweat . . . like great drops of blood falling to the ground" (Luke 22:44). The burden, symbolized by the beam of the olive press, was the atoning death made necessary by our sin. We were the burden He bore, and His flowing blood was His "anointing" for us (2 Corinthians 1:21).

Overhead Transparency 46. Olive Farming. Upper Left: An Olive Grove. Olive trees rarely reach 20 feet high. This ancient tree, with its gnarled trunk, is still very productive after 100 or more years of bearing olives. The root system of olive trees spreads wide to obtain the necessary moisture in Israel's relatively dry climate. Because of this, trees in groves like this one in Galilee are far away from each other.

The olive tree is known for its beauty (Hosea 14:6), in part because its ancient trunk often has the look of a productive past. Its leaves are light green on the top and much lighter green on the bottom, so the leaves shimmer in the wind.

When olive trees get very old (often hundreds of years old), the branches are cut off. Soon new shoots grow out of the stump, and the tree begins producing olives again. The roots and the trunk can survive for centuries. This tree provides an image of Isaiah's prophecy, "A shoot will come up from the stump of Jesse; from His roots a Branch will bear fruit" (Isaiah 11:1). Jesus was the shoot from the stump of Jesse (David's father).

The old tree shown here helps illustrate God's plan of salvation. In Romans 11:11–24, Paul described Christians as either natural branches (those of Jewish background) or branches that have been grafted onto Jesus (Gentiles). As branches on this tree, our fruit is Jesus' fruit. We will bear fruit if we are attached to Him.

Upper Right: **Ripening Olives.** Flower blossoms develop in the springtime, and olives appear during the summer and ripen in the fall. Olive farmers harvest both green (unripe) olives, for pickling and for eating, and black (ripe) olives, for eating and for oil. A good tree may produce 50 pounds of olives a year and four to six pounds of oil. The olives of Israel were (and are) known for their high oil content.

Lower Left: **Olives.** This bowl contains both ripe and unripe olives. The green olives, pickled or salted, are an important part of the daily diet. The black ones may be salted or pickled for eating; or more likely, they may be crushed and pressed for oil.

Lower Right: **Olive Oil.** Olive oil was a significant part of the daily lives of the Israelites in the first century. It was eaten in or with other food (1 Kings 17:12), used for skin care (Ecclesiastes 9:7–8), used to fuel lamps, taken as medicine, and widely used in trade (1 Kings 5:11). It may also have been used as a lubricant, to keep leather soft (Isaiah 21:5), and to protect people from the sun. It was one of God's three blessings of the land (Deuteronomy 6:11). It was mixed with the morning burnt offerings (Exodus 29:40). It symbolized honor (Judges 9:9), joy (Psalm 45:8—applied to Jesus in Hebrews 1:9), favor (Deuteronomy 33:24), and love (Song of Songs 1:3). It was also a symbol of God's Spirit (James 5:14).

OPTIONAL — Digging Deeper III: The Traditional "Garden" of Gethsemane (5–10 minutes)

(This section requires the use of the optional full-color overhead-transparency packet. For information on ordering it, see page 307.)

The traditional Garden of Gethsemane is probably near the actual location for the "olive grove" (John 18:1) and the "Gethsemane" (Mark 14:32) where Jesus agonized in prayer before His arrest. At this point, you may want to review "The Mount of Olives" in Lesson 22, Unit 2, Step 1, pages

85–86; and/or Overhead Transparencies 28 ("Modern-day Jerusalem from the South") and 29 ("The Mount of Olives"), and their descriptions, in Lesson 22.

7. Guided Discussion: Jesus in Anguish

The agony Jesus faced in Gethsemane before His trial and execution provides a profound picture of God's love, Jesus' humanity, and the awful price to be paid for sin. In this section, we will explore Jesus in His anguish, particularly as it can be portrayed by the *gethsemane* where He was.

Ask your students to read the following passages and answer the questions:

a. Matthew 26:37–38; Mark 14:33–34; Luke 22:44

   1. Why did Jesus go to this place for His time of prayer?

   2. What was Jesus' outlook that night? Why?

   3. How does this help you understand His human nature? NOTE: Point out that while people frequently experience the emotion Jesus felt, what He faced could be endured only by God's Son.

   4. Have you ever experienced such anguish? If you feel comfortable doing so, discuss your answer with the rest of the class. What did you do in that situation?

b. Matthew 26:39,42,44; Mark 14:36; Luke 22:42

   1. What was Jesus asking in His prayer?

   2. Compare the word *cup* here with Matthew 20:22–23; Mark 10:38; Psalm 75:8. NOTE: This was a Jewish expression meaning "to share someone's fate."

   3. What temptations do you think Jesus faced at this time? (See Matthew 26:53.)

   4. To whom did Jesus address His prayer? NOTE: The word *Abba,* which is the Aramaic form, is close to the English word *Daddy.* Jewish children affectionately refer to their fathers as "Abba" to this day.

   5. What can you learn from Jesus' prayer?

   6. What does this prayer show us about Jesus' relationship with God? (See Romans 8:15–17.)

   7. How does this shape your understanding of God's love for us?

   8. What does this teach you about how to pray when you experience anguish and sorrow?

c. Matthew 26:40–45; Mark 14:37–41; Luke 22:45–46

   1. Why was the disciples' mind-set so different from that of Jesus? Why did they act the way they did?

   2. What did Jesus want the disciples to do? Why? How does the disciples' behavior relate to what Jesus was about to face? (See Isaiah 53:3.)

   3. What temptations were the disciples facing? (See Mark 14:51–52; Matthew 26:56.) How could they resist this temptation?

   4. Have you ever experienced a loss of support from your friends at a crucial time? If so, what happened?

   5. How can that experience help you understand Jesus' feelings as He faced His anguish alone?

   6. What can you learn from Jesus' example about resisting temptation?

d. Luke 22:44

    1. What happened to Jesus as a result of His agony? What made the weight on Him so extraordinary?

    2. Point out the following information to your students.

- Jesus was pressed by the weight of what He had to face: rejection by His friends, trial by His religious leaders, torture by Gentiles, brutal execution, death, and—worst of all—rejection by God the Father as He suffered the agonies of hell for those He loved. Jesus would face all this in the next few hours, even though He was completely innocent and those for whom He would die didn't deserve such love. It is impossible for us to understand the depth of His emotions at this time, but the weight of a *gethsemane* can provide some insight into His suffering.

- Jesus may be symbolized by the olives, the sign of God's blessing and anointing.

- The precious oil of anointing produced at Jesus' *gethsemane* was His sweat—the drops of blood that fell to the ground. This blood becomes our anointing, providing forgiveness, cleansing, and wholeness (Ephesians 1:7; Colossians 1:20; Hebrews 13:12; 1 John 1:7; Revelation 1:5; 19:13).

- Jesus was pressed at Gethsemane because He loves you!

e. Luke 22:42–43

    1. How do you know Jesus was completely submitted to God the Father?

    2. What was God's response?

    3. How can this help you face trouble?

Form groups of three to five people. Spend a few moments discussing with your group members the significance of what Jesus was willing to face on your behalf. Then answer the following questions:

1. How does Gethsemane help you appreciate Jesus' agony?

2. How can you respond to Jesus' great love for you?

3. What have you learned from this study?

OPTIONAL — Digging Deeper IV: Olives and the Bible *(30–40 minutes)*

Students should read the handout "A Light to the World" before beginning this section.

The Garden of Gethsemane was on the slopes of the Mount of Olives, which were covered with olive groves in Jesus' time. This location provides us with an opportunity to reflect on how the olive tree, its fruit, and the oil it produced are used symbolically in the Bible, particularly in relation to the Messiah.

Point out the following information to your students. Then have your students (individually or in small groups) answer the questions.

- Israel is like an olive tree God planted (see Jeremiah 11:16).
- God's followers are like olive trees (see Psalm 52:8, 128:3).

    1. What can you learn about God from these passages? About yourself?

    2. How can you be God's olive tree today? Do you know any people who live out the symbolism of the olive tree? Explain.

- God's relationship to His people is represented by the olive tree: (1) Unfruitful trees are cut down (see the description in Hosea 14:6 and apply it to Jeremiah 11:16), and the same judgment can fall on God's people today if they do not bear fruit (Matthew 3:10–12, 7:19). (2) God's olive tree would send out new shoots, and one would come from Jesse's stump (Isaiah 11:1–2; Jeremiah 23:5, 33:15; Zechariah 3:8, 6:12). (3) Believers are those who are naturally sprouting from or are grafted onto God's olive tree and Jesus, the Branch (Romans 11:11–24).

  1. What can you learn about God from this symbolism?

  2. What can you learn about yourself from the image of the olive tree?

  3. What is the fruit God desires today? What will happen if we bear no fruit? Do you know someone who "bears a lot of fruit"? What in his or her actions and lifestyle make this evident to you?

- God's Spirit is symbolized by olive oil and the process of anointing.
- People who had God's Spirit were anointed and brought great benefit to others (1 Samuel 10:1).
- Jesus, the Anointed One (Messiah), had God's Spirit (Acts 10:38).
- Jesus' followers, as His anointed ones, also had His Spirit (1 John 2:20).
- The prayers of Jesus' followers, if accompanied by the Spirit (oil is the sign of the Spirit), would bring healing (James 5:14).

  1. What can you learn about Jesus from the anointing process?

  2. What can you learn about yourself? Are you anointed? What does that mean to you?

- The olive tree provided oil for lighting lamps. Both God and God's people are symbolized by an olive tree. Jesus is an olive shoot, and we are olive branches.
- God is light (1 John 1:5).
- Jesus is the Light of the World (John 8:12).
- Jesus' followers are the light of the world (Matthew 5:14).

  1. How does this symbolism help you understand God? Jesus?

  2. How do you provide light where you live? Is this light related to the "oil" of anointing? How?

  3. Do you know anyone who truly is the light where he or she has been placed by God? Relate your example to the class.

8. Guided Discussion: Jesus' Arrest

All the Gospel writers describe Jesus' arrest, but they do not give many details about the people who arrested Him. Have students look up the following passages and discover what is known about Jesus' arrest.

- Matthew 26:31–56
- Mark 14:43–51
- John 18:1–11

1. What is significant about the people who arrested Jesus?

2. Why was Jesus arrested at night? What does this tell you about Jesus' guilt?

3. What does this imply about many of the common people (Matthew 26:3–5; Mark 11:18, 12:12; Luke 22:1–2)?

4. What did Jesus' disciples do when He was arrested? Why?

5. What is there in these passages that indicates whether Jesus' disciples understood the nature of Jesus' kingdom at this point?

6. Why did Jesus have to face death and God's judgment all alone (Matthew 27:46)?

Conclusion

Jesus faced complete rejection by His friends, the leaders of His religion, and even His Father, God Himself. As He faced that awful experience, He went first to find strength in prayer—in His own prayers to Abba, His Father, and in the prayers of His friends. His friends could not overcome their own weaknesses and left Him alone as He agonized over His coming fate.

Despite the emotion He felt, Jesus submitted Himself completely to His Father's will. He loved His own people so deeply that He would go to the cross alone for them because His Father said it was the way. The awareness of this reality led Him to such depths of anguish that His sweat became like blood. As a *gethsemane*'s enormous weight squeezes oil from olives, Jesus' mission pressed blood from Him.

By Jesus' blood we are restored to our Father and anointed by Him. Our guilt and its penalty were great, but Jesus' love for us and His devotion to His Father's will were greater.

Notes

1. An excellent article was recently published on the discovery of such a cave near the traditional location of the Garden of Gethsemane on the Mount of Olives. See Joan E. Taylor, "The Garden of Gethsemane: Not the Place of Jesus' Arrest," *Biblical Archaeology Review* (July/Aug. 1995). Taylor carefully compares the biblical material with the physical remains and concludes that it is likely that Jesus stayed, if not in this place, then in one similar to it.

A LIGHT TO THE WORLD

*Israel was called "an olive tree, leafy and fair,"
because they shed light on all.*

—*Ancient Jewish Commentary on Jeremiah 11:16*

Olive trees and the abundance of oil they produce were significant in the lives of the people of the Bible. A leading agricultural product, an important part of the diet, and a regular element of religious practices, the olive naturally became part of the imagery the Bible used to describe God and His people in relationship. Knowledge of the beautiful olive tree and its uses can enrich our understanding of God so that we may be—as the olive tree was believed to be—a "light to the world."

OLIVE TREES

The olive tree is one of the plants most frequently mentioned in the Bible. God called the land of Israel "a land with . . . olive oil and honey" (Deuteronomy 8:8). The importance of the olive tree was noted in Jotham's parable—other trees chose the olive tree to be king over them (Judges 9:8–9). As the Bible often notes, the olive tree is beautiful (Jeremiah 11:16; Hosea 14:6). The faithful followers of God are compared to vigorous olive trees (Psalm 52:8), and their children are said to be like the shoots that appear at the tree's roots, guaranteeing its survival (Psalm 128:3).

Olive trees have extensive root systems, spreading far beyond the reach of the leaves, to provide adequate moisture for them. Because their roots travel so far, these trees often stand alone, which accents their beauty. Olive leaves are gracefully narrow, light green on one side and an even lighter green on the other, and they shimmer beautifully in the wind.

The olive tree thrives throughout Israel. The ability of this tree to grow on rocky hills makes it well-suited to the terrain of Israel, a land "with oil from the flinty crag" (Deuteronomy 32:18). The tree grows exceptionally well on the cultivated hillside terraces of Judea and Samaria. Many of the hills of Upper and Lower Galilee are covered with olive trees to this day. They grow especially well in western Galilee, where the tribe of Asher lived.

Olive trees begin to produce olives when they are between six and 10 years old, and they reach their peak at about 40 to 50 years. Many continue to produce an abundance of olives even when they are *hundreds* of years old. When the trunk becomes large and old, the branches are trimmed off, leaving what appears to be a dead stump. But the next year, fresh shoots spring from the old stump, and soon a new and vigorous growth of branches again produces an abundance of olives.

This phenomenon provided some of the rich imagery of the Bible. Job compared human beings to the olive tree and noted that the olive tree did not die when cut down but sprang again to life, unlike people, who die and are gone (Job 14:7–9). The children of God's people are compared to the many small shoots that spring continually from the root system of the tree, ensuring the continued existence of the fruitful family (Psalm 128:3).

God used the metaphor of an olive tree (and sometimes other trees and vines) to describe His relationship to His people. He planted them as a farmer would plant a beautiful olive tree (Jeremiah 11:16–17; Psalm 52:8), but He said He would cut them down because the fruit they bore was the worship of Baal (Jeremiah 11:17). (Also see Matthew 3:10, 7:19; and Isaiah 5:1–7—the vineyard was the picture for the same point.) After God allowed His people to be "cut down," they appeared to be nothing but a dead stump. But God and faithful Israelites knew better: Out of that stump came new shoots.

The shoot of Jesse's stump was a special one because God's Spirit rested on Him (Isaiah 11:1–2). That shoot was Jesus, who was a citizen of Nazareth (meaning "branch"—Matthew 2:21–23). Many other prophecies also described the Messiah as a branch or a shoot, probably drawing on the image of the olive tree (Jeremiah 23:5, 33:15; Zechariah 3:8, 6:12). Jesus is the shoot from a stump in the olive grove of Israel. His fruit is obedience and fulfillment.

This beautiful picture of God's people and the Messiah as an olive tree was completed by Paul. Paul reversed the image of the Jewish farmer who grafted a cultivated olive shoot onto the root system of a wild tree to take advantage of its ability to withstand a harsher climate. Israel, God's cultivated tree, had had some of its branches removed. In their place, God has grafted the branches of believing Gentiles. This provides the basis for Paul to remind the Gentiles of their Jewish roots, affirm God's continued love and concern for His Jewish tree, and warn people that since God had removed *natural* branches for not bearing fruit, how easy it would be for Him to remove ones that had been grafted on (Romans 11:11–24).

The olive tree provides an excellent lesson for the Christian who is not Jewish. As Christians, we have Jewish roots, and Jesus is our Jewish Branch. When God broke down the wall separating Jews and Gentiles, He did not invite the Jews to become Gentiles; He invited the Gentiles to join the Jews, His people. The olive tree can be a constant reminder that Jesus is our source of life—He is our Branch. He sprang from Jewish roots, and so do we. The beautiful olive tree reminds us of God's love and His expectation that all His branches bear fruit in abundance.

FRUIT OF THE OLIVE TREE

The olives of Israel had an unusually high oil content, but some were used as part of the daily diet of the people. Olive trees blossomed in the spring and bore fruit throughout the fall (October through November). Olives were harvested either by beating the branches with poles or by stripping the fruit by hand. Often the olives that were to be eaten were hand-picked to prevent bruising. Some olives were picked while they were green (unripe), pickled in vinegar and salt, then eaten fresh, as were some of the ripe olives. Some green fruit was boiled, then dried and used throughout the year. The black (ripe) olives were the best for oil, often containing over 50 percent oil by volume.

During Old Testament times, the ripe olives were pounded to a pulp in pestles (Isaiah 17:6) or under people's feet (Micah 6:15). The pulp was collected in reed baskets, and the oil was allowed to drain off. This first oil, the finest, was called "beaten oil" (Leviticus 24:2; Exodus 29:40; 1 Kings 5:11). The people then extracted more oil by heating and pressing the pulp again.

During the time of Jesus, new olive-pressing systems were in use. In one system, the olives were placed in a large circular basin in which a great wheel-shaped millstone rolled in a circle. The stone was turned by an animal (e.g., a donkey) or by people. The pulp was then collected in baskets, which were stacked several layers high in (or over) stone pits. A stone weight was placed on top of the baskets, and a heavy wooden beam, with one end in a hole in the wall nearby (often these presses were found in caves) was placed across the pile of baskets. Stone weights were hung from the beam, applying enormous pressure to the olives and squeezing the oil from the pulp. In a similar method, a great stone pillar was placed directly on the olives to press the oil from the pulp. The oil ran through the baskets and into the pit below. The smell of the olive oil spread for miles during the fall of the year, when the oil was being pressed. The oil was collected in jars and placed in a cool place. It was sold or stored for use during the coming year.

Jesus spent the last few hours before His arrest in an olive grove (John 18:1) at a place called Gethsemane (Matthew 26:36). It is likely that this was a cave somewhere on the Mount of Olives (Luke 22:39) where the olives of the nearby groves were pressed. As Jesus reflected on the work He was about to do, He, too, was pressed. The great weight of the sin of the world and the coming rejection by His Father led Him to sweat drops of blood (Luke 22:44). The image of the great weight of a *gethsemane* on the precious olives can help us imagine the pressure Jesus felt as He contemplated the burden He was to bear. His blood became the symbol for the anointing He provides for those who love Him.

ANOINTING OIL

Olive oil had a great variety of practical uses in the Bible, including the following:[1]

> An element in food—1 Kings 17:12
> Fuel for lamps—Matthew 25:1–13
> Medicine—James 5:14; Luke 10:34; Isaiah 1:6
> Cosmetics—Ecclesiastes 9:7–8; Esther 2:12
> Temple (Tabernacle) menorah—Exodus 27:20
> Sacrifices—Exodus 29:40

Olive oil also had great symbolic value. It could indicate honor (Judges 9:9) and joy. Pouring oil on someone's head was to wish that person happiness (Psalm 23:5, 92:11, 45:7, 104:15). It was also a symbol of life. The recovered leper had to place oil on his or her right ear, right thumb, and right big toe after placing blood on those places. Oil was then poured on the leper's head, making "atonement for him before the Lord" (Leviticus 14:15–18). Jewish tradition indicates that the oil was a symbol of the leper coming back to life because he or she had been considered dead. Oil was also a symbol of divine blessing (Deuteronomy 7:13; Jeremiah 31:12; Joel 2:19), which God denied to people who were unfaithful (Micah 6:15; Joel 1:10).

Oil was linked symbolically to the coming of God's Spirit. God's Spirit bestows the "oil of gladness" on those who mourn (Isaiah 61:1–6). This image is probably also linked to the use of oil for anointing people for special tasks and appointments. Pouring oil on the chosen one symbolized God's equipping him or her with authority and His calling that person to a specific responsibility. Kings were anointed (1 Samuel 10:1; 1 Kings 1:39), as were priests (Leviticus 8:12; Exodus 30:30), holy things (Exodus 30:22–33), and places where God had acted (Genesis 28:18, 35:14). As God put His Spirit on the person called to serve Him, the oil used for the outward anointing increasingly came to symbolize the Spirit that accompanied that anointing (1 Samuel 16:13; Isaiah 61:1). By New Testament times, anointing had come to be seen primarily as the inner work of the Spirit on Jesus (Acts 10:38) and on His followers (1 John 2:20).

The Hebrew word for "anointed" is *mashiach*, from which we get our English word *Messiah*. Though many were anointed (messiahs) in the Old Testament and the believer is anointed by God's Spirit today, there is only one Messiah: Jesus, God's Anointed.

OIL AND LIGHT

Probably the most common use of olive oil was for lighting small household lamps. In this sense, olives and the oil they produced were the source of light for the people. The Temple menorah, the eternal flame, was lit by the oil of olives that were specially prepared for this sacred role. The light of this flame symbolized God's presence, which enlightened the world: The olive tree, which produced the oil for anointing, also produced the light that would light the world. It was only natural that Jesus, the Anointed One, would call Himself the "light of the world" (John 8:12). It is not surprising that those who have experienced His anointing should be called the "light of the world" as well (Matthew 5:14).

NOTES

1. There were other types of oil used in Bible times, but scholars normally understand the references to oil to mean olive oil.

ROLL AWAY THE STONE

For the Teacher

Most of your students will be quite familiar with the general details of this study: Jesus was arrested, tried, crucified, and buried, but He came back to life on the third day. This is a proper time to review those details, but this lesson will also explore other details of these astounding events. Ask your students if they know on what Jewish festivals Jesus was crucified, buried, and raised. Point out that knowing the meaning of those holidays as commanded by God in the Old Testament adds emphasis to the events of Jesus' atonement.

Many of your students will know that Jesus was buried in a new tomb owned by a man named Joseph of Arimathea. They may not realize the significance for Joseph of placing Jesus in the tomb, and they may not know what commitment Joseph made by doing so. These and other details in this lesson are designed to encourage your group to see Jesus' great acts of redemption in a more personal way, because it was for them that He submitted to the horrors of these events. Remind your students that they are the ones who benefit from Jesus' sacrifices—if they, like Jesus' disciples, recognize that the tomb is empty and that their Lord is alive.

Your Objectives for This Lesson

At the completion of this section, you will want your students:

To Know/Understand

1. What is known of the location of Jesus' crucifixion and burial.

2. The relationship of the Jewish festivals of Passover, Unleavened Bread, and Firstfruits to Jesus' death, burial, and resurrection.

3. The Roman laws of crucifixion and how Jesus' crucifixion fulfilled prophecy.

4. Burial customs of first-century Israel and the implications for Jesus' burial.

5. Why Jesus was totally rejected by everyone and crucified "outside" the city.

6. The importance of the veil in the Temple and why it ripped when Jesus died.

7. Why the stone was rolled away from Jesus' tomb.

To Do

1. Have a deepened sense of gratitude for the awful death Jesus endured on their behalf.

2. Become more confident in God's careful planning of the lives of His people as they understand the planning that preceded Jesus' life and death.

3. Learn from Jesus' rejection to be aware of His faithful presence at all times.

4. Be willing to face rejection in order to remain faithful to Jesus.

5. Plan to be more faithful in entering God's presence now that the veil has been removed.

6. Consider what they could do to show their total devotion to Jesus, and make specific plans to make such a commitment.

How to Plan for This Lesson

Because of the volume of material in this lesson, you may need to divide it into several class sessions. To help you determine how to do that, the lesson has been broken into segments. Note that the time needed may vary significantly, depending on elements such as the leader, the size of the class, and the interest level of the class.

If you wish to cover the entire lesson in one session, you should complete Unit One. This unit provides a guided discussion covering the major points in the video. It does not go into great depth. If you wish to go into greater depth on any of the points in Unit One, they are covered more thoroughly in the remainder of the material.

How to Prepare for This Lesson

Materials Needed

Student copies of the maps/diagrams:	"Jerusalem's Districts" "The Roman World"
Overhead transparencies:	"Jerusalem's Districts" "The Roman World"
Student copies of the handout:	"A New Tomb"

Video: **Roll Away the Stone**

Overhead projector, screen, TV, VCR

1. Make copies of the maps/diagrams listed above for your students.

2. Prepare the overhead transparencies listed above. (You'll find them at the back of the book.)

3. Make copies of the handout listed above for your students. (If possible, students should receive and read this handout before the lesson.)

4. Review the geography of the lands of the Bible from the "Introduction."

5. Determine which **unit** and which **Digging Deeper** sections, if any, you want to use in your class session(s). NOTE: You can use these sections in any order you wish (e.g., you might want to use **Digging Deeper III,** but not **Digging Deeper I** or **Digging Deeper II**).

6. Prepare your classroom ahead of time, setting up and testing an overhead projector and screen (for the overhead transparencies) and a TV and VCR. If you plan to hand out biblical references for your students to look up and read aloud, prepare 3x5 cards (one reference per card) to distribute before class.

Lesson Plan

UNIT ONE: Video Review

1. Introductory Comments

It is impossible to measure the love of God displayed in the events highlighted in this lesson. They were preceded by thousands of years of carefully detailed planning. Jesus created a small community of students and showed them how to continue after He was gone. He then suffered great humiliation, physical torture, and spiritual agony for people He loved, whether they loved Him or not. No one will ever reflect so much on these stories that the events will no longer humble, inspire, and lead him or her to a more grateful life. In this study, we will examine some of the cultural details surrounding the events of the last week of Jesus' life and begin to explore the depths of God's love.

2. Show the Video *Roll Away the Stone* (22 minutes)

3. Map Study: Jerusalem and the Garden Tomb

HINT: *Begin this map study session by reviewing the geography of the overall region and working down to the area the lesson is dealing with—the garden tomb.*

Using the overhead transparency "Jerusalem's Districts," point out the following areas, and have your students locate them on their diagrams.

> Upper City
> Herod's palace
> business district
> New City
> Antonia fortress
> Golgotha (traditional)
> garden tomb (traditional)
> possible routes Jesus took before He was crucified:

> > Gethsemane (across the Kidron Valley, on the Mount of Olives, where Jesus prayed and was arrested)
> > Antonia or Herod's palace (Jesus was tried before Pilate at one of these locations)
> > Golgotha or garden tomb (Jesus was crucified at one of these locations—the traditional Golgotha is probably the correct location, but it is inside the Church of the Holy Sepulchre, so the original appearance is lost. The garden tomb fits the description of the place well and helps us understand the appearance of the actual location. The *Roll Away the Stone* video was filmed at the garden tomb to help students appreciate what the location looked like.)

4. Guided Discussion: Jesus' Sacrifice

a. Jesus Is Crucified

Crucifixion was governed by specific rules laid out by the Romans to make this horrible execution practice as painful as possible and therefore provide the greatest example to others. This meant Jesus' physical suffering on the cross was dreadful, giving us a small sense of the even greater spiritual pain He experienced because of the Father's rejection. Crucifixion also served to fulfill prophecies regarding Jesus' death.

Have your students read the following passages and answer the questions.

- Psalm 22:16

  1. How did crucifixion fit God's plan?

- Matthew 27:32–33; Hebrews 13:12; Numbers 5:1–4—Unclean people were to be taken out-side the camp or city. Roman law dictated that crucifixion should take place outside the city.

  1. Where was Jesus crucified? Why?

  2. What does that mean for you?

- Matthew 27:35; Psalm 22:18—Soldiers kept the condemned person's possessions.

  1. Why did the writer of Psalm 22 seem to be familiar with Roman crucifixion? What does this say about how carefully God planned for these events?

- Exodus 12:1–6; John 1:29; 1 Corinthians 5:7; John 19:31; Luke 23:44-46

  1. What is the link between the Old Testament and the time of day when Jesus died?

  2. How does that help you understand Jesus' death?

- John 6:66; John 7:47–53; Matthew 26:14–16; Matthew 27:46

  1. In each of these passages above, who rejected Jesus?

  2. Why did Jesus have to face His death alone?

  3. What does the loneliness of Jesus' death mean for you? (See Matthew 28:20.)

  4. How do you feel, knowing you are never completely alone (even when you feel alone)?

- Matthew 27:50–51

  1. What happened at the moment of Jesus' death?

  2. What was the purpose of the veil in the Temple? (Answer: It separated the Holy of Holies, where God's presence was focused, from the people. See Exodus 26:31–35.)

- Hebrews 9:7,12

  1. What does the torn veil mean for you?

b. **Jesus Is Buried in a New Tomb**
   Have your students read the following passages and answer the questions.

- Matthew 27:57–61
- Luke 23:50–56

  1. What do these passages tell us about the tomb in which Jesus was buried?

- Mark 15:43–47
- John 19:38–42

  1. What do these passages tell us about Joseph?

  2. A new, hewn tomb was a very expensive item, costing the equivalent of $100,000 in present-day U.S. currency. What does it say about Joseph that he willingly gave his tomb to Jesus? NOTE: Some scholars believe that once Jesus was buried there, the tomb was unusable to Joseph's family. To use it again would violate Jewish law.

3. Have you ever made a great sacrifice for Jesus? What was it? What was the result?

4. How could you show the same level of devotion to Jesus that Joseph did? Discuss your answer with the class.

c. Jesus Is Risen!

The Sunday after Jesus' burial was the Feast of Firstfruits. During this festival, Jewish people brought the first of their barley harvest to the Temple as a way of thanking God and showing Him they trusted Him to provide the rest of the crop.

Have your students read the following passages and answer the questions.

- Luke 24:1-8

    1. When was Jesus raised from the dead?

    2. Why was Jesus raised on this day?

- 1 Corinthians 15:22–23

    1. What does the symbolism in these verses mean? What does Jesus' resurrection guarantee?

- Matthew 28:1–6—Note especially verse 6, which literally says, "He has already risen."

    1. The earthquake happened as the women came to the tomb, but Jesus had already risen. Why was the stone rolled away if Jesus didn't need to be "let out" of the tomb?

    2. What was the effect on the women (and the disciples later) when they saw that the stone had been rolled away?

    3. Why was it necessary for Jesus' followers to see His empty tomb?

    4. What would (or did) it mean to you to see the empty tomb?

    5. What in the passage tells you that the women understood the meaning of the empty tomb?

    6. What difference did it make when they met the living Jesus?

    7. How do you know when a person has experienced the empty tomb and met the living Jesus? Do you know someone who shows this every day? What is this person like? What impact does he or she have on the world?

Spend a few moments in prayer, asking God to roll away any "stones" in your life so you can see the empty tomb again. Tell Him you want to meet the living Jesus again.

d. Committing Yourself to Jesus' Love

The video ended with a time of commitment to the love Jesus showed us in His death and resurrection. In Jesus' day, a man and woman sealed their engagement by exchanging a cup of wine. While there are many other meanings involved in Jesus' giving the "cup" to His disciples and to us, in one sense, it was a declaration of His love for us and His invitation to us to be His spiritual bride.

Have your students read the following passages and answer the questions.

- Mark 2:19–20; Luke 22:20 Revelation 19:7–9; 2 Corinthians 11:2

    1. How does it help you understand Jesus' love to think of Him as the perfect spiritual husband?

    2. What does this commitment demand from us until we see Jesus face to face?

    3. The bride accepted the cup from her husband-to-be as an indication of her lifelong commitment to him. How has Jesus proved His love to you? Has He lived up to His commitment to you?

4. How have you indicated your total commitment to Jesus, who wants to be "engaged" to you?

5. How have you been faithful to Him? . . . unfaithful to Him?

Spend a few moments in prayer, asking God to help you accept His offer of love and be totally committed to Him.

UNIT TWO
Step One: "An Ancient Promise Kept"

1. Introductory Comments

History moves toward its finish, carefully directed by Almighty God. No event has been more central and more history-changing than the death and resurrection of Jesus, the Messiah. It is impossible for us to explore even a small percentage of the meaning and impact of that event. The purpose of this lesson is to highlight several key elements that rest on Bible concepts that were investigated in earlier lessons and that can be better understood in their geographical and historical setting. Stress to your students that this study does not claim to be complete. It simply presents God's work in Jesus as the empowering moment of our call to be His witnesses. As we bring the news and power of His sacrificial work to others, history will continue to be shaped according to God's plan. We cannot make an impact without the power of what Jesus did during those few days in Jerusalem. With His victory, nothing is impossible.

2. Show the Video *Roll Away the Stone* (22 minutes)

3. Map Study: Jerusalem and the Garden Tomb

HINT: *Begin this map study session by reviewing the geography of the overall region and working down to the area the lesson is dealing with—the garden tomb.*

Using the overhead transparency "The Roman World," point out the following areas, and have your students locate them on their maps.

> Rome
> Mediterranean Sea
> Judea
> Caesarea

Using the overhead transparency "Jerusalem's Districts," point out the following areas, and have your students locate them on their diagrams.

> Upper City
> Herod's palace
> business district
> New City
> Antonia fortress
> Golgotha (traditional)
> garden tomb (traditional)
> possible routes Jesus took before He was crucified:
>
>> Gethsemane (across the Kidron Valley, on the Mount of Olives, where Jesus prayed and was arrested)

Antonia or Herod's palace (Jesus was tried before Pilate at one of these locations) Golgotha or garden tomb (Jesus was crucified at one of these locations—the traditional Golgotha is probably the correct location, but it is inside the Church of the Holy Sepulchre, so the original appearance is lost. The garden tomb fits the description of the place well and helps us understand the appearance of the actual location. The video *Roll Away the Stone* was filmed at the garden tomb to help students appreciate what the location looked like.)

OPTIONAL — Digging Deeper I: The Time Would Come *(15–25 minutes)*

You may want to review the following sections in Lesson 22, Unit 2, Step 2: "The North Wall," especially the section on the Antonia (pages 100–102); "The Upper City" (pages 111–113); "The Business District" (pages 114–115); and "The New City" (page 115). If you have the optional full-color overhead-transparency packet, you may want to review Overhead Transparencies 35 ("Mansions on the Western Hill"), 37 ("The Upper City"), 38 ("The New City"), and 39 ("Ancient Jerusalem from the North"), along with their descriptions, also in Lesson 22.

4. Guided Discussion: Jesus' Crucifixion

a. Introduction

Jesus was crucified. Remind your students of some of the incredible implications of this event: Prophecies made thousands of years before were fulfilled. The blood of countless animals received its full meaning. A new community was born. Humanity received eternal hope. Millions would live forever in a glorious new creation.

We cannot possibly grasp all that God did in Jesus on the day of His crucifixion, but we can explore some of the implications for us.

b. Crucifixion: Its History and Practice

Centuries before the Romans came to Israel, the Persians practiced crucifixion by impaling their victims on stakes (Ezra 6:11; Esther 2:23). The ancient Jews believed those who were hanged were under God's curse (Deuteronomy 21:22–23).

The Romans brought crucifixion to Israel as the method of execution for non-Romans. The Romans crucified thousands of people during the 400 years they were in Palestine. General Varus crucified 2,000 people at one time; General Titus crucified 500 a day during the siege of Jerusalem; and the Hellenistic Jewish king Alexander Jannai had 800 Pharisees crucified as he and his mistresses watched.

The Rules

1. It had to take place outside the city (often a place associated with execution or curse), in a public location (Matthew 27:32–33; Hebrews 13:12; Matthew 27:35).

2. Normally, people were crucified naked (Matthew 27:39).

3. The preferred cross probably was in the shape of an uppercase T rather than a lowercase t. Crosses were quite low, only five to six feet off the ground (Matthew 27:48).

4. The condemned person was nailed to the cross through the wrists and ankles (John 20:27—the Greek word translated "hand" refers to the part of the arm from the palm to the wrist. Evidence indicates that the spikes were driven through the bones of the arm where they join at the wrist).

The Procedure

1. The condemned person was first flogged, which often left the prisoner near death (John 19:1; 1 Peter 2:24).

2. The crossbar (the *patibulum,* not the whole cross) was tied to the prisoner's shoulders, and he was paraded through the streets for humiliation and as an example. A soldier carried a sign (*titulus*) indicating the crime the person had committed (John 19:16–21).

3. At the place of execution, the prisoner's wrists were nailed to the crossbar, and the bar was lifted and placed on the stake (*stipe*), which was already in the ground. The condemned person's ankles were then nailed to the stake. Finally, the sign identifying the person's crime was attached to the stake. The prisoner, in excruciating pain, eventually died of asphyxiation and from loss of blood (John 19:19 [Psalm 22:16]).

4. Prisoners would sometimes remain conscious for days, able to talk only in short bursts because of the stress on their diaphragms. Sometimes the Romans would shorten prisoners' suffering by breaking their legs. Because their legs could no longer support the weight of their bodies, they suffocated faster. Jesus died without any broken bones (John 19:33 [Exodus 12:46, 34:20]).

   Following is a list of verses that record what Jesus said as He hung on the cross. Notice that the statements are short (even more so in Aramaic/Hebrew—Jesus' language).

   • Luke 23:34
   • Luke 23:42–43
   • John 19:25–27
   • Matthew 27:46 (See also Psalm 22:1.)
   • John 19:28 (See also Psalm 22:15, 69:21.)
   • John 19:30
   • Luke 23:46

5. The soldiers kept the victim's possessions (Matthew 27:35 [Psalm 22:18]).

c. **Reflection**

Ask your students to answer the following questions.

1. So many prophecies from hundreds of years before Jesus' death (before crucifixion even existed) were fulfilled in Jesus' method of execution. What does this teach you about God's planning?

2. Who executed Jesus? Why? Why did He choose to be executed?

3. Why did Jesus choose to die in such a horrible manner? NOTE: Some scholars have pointed out that the physical agony Jesus endured as He hung on the cross paralleled the spiritual agony He felt at being rejected by God the Father and bearing the penalty of our sin.

4. How does the reality of Jesus' execution affect your life? How *should* it affect you?

d. **Jesus' Crucifixion and the Old Testament**

Ask your students to read the following passages and answer the questions.

1. The normal method of Jewish execution was stoning, but prophecy indicated that Jesus would die by crucifixion (Psalm 22:16).

2. Read Exodus 12:1–6; John 1:29; 1 Corinthians 5:7; John 19:31. What is the link between the Old Testament and the time of Jesus' death?

3. Read Leviticus 23:5 (the word translated as "twilight" here is interpreted by the rabbis to mean "halfway through the second half of the day," or "3:00 in the afternoon" [Mishnah Pesahim 5:1]). Traditionally, the Passover sacrifice was slaughtered at 3:00 P.M. and offered at 3:30 P.M. after the daily sacrifice. Both the daily sacrifice and the Passover sacrifice were offered on behalf of the nation of Israel. Conclusion: The offering of a lamb for the nation of Israel occurred around 3:00 in the afternoon on Passover.

4. Read Mark 15:33–37; Luke 23:44–46. What time of day did Jesus die? Why do you think He died at exactly this time? Could the similarity between Jesus' death and the death of the Passover lamb be a coincidence? Remember that lambs had been killed at that time for hundreds, if not more than 1,000, years. What does this say about God's planning? About the Jewish background for Jesus' work?

5. It is possible that a trumpet was blown in the Temple courts to announce the afternoon sacrifice. Imagine Jesus on the cross, hearing that piercing sound, recognizing that the hour of sacrifice had come, and then saying, "It is finished." This link gives us a powerful picture of Jesus' death and its effect on our lives.

OPTIONAL — Digging Deeper II: Total Rejection (10–20 minutes)

Jesus was totally rejected by the people of His day, from His enemies to His friends.

1. Read Isaiah 53:3. What was predicted about Jesus?

2. Identify who rejected Jesus in each of the following passages:
   - John 6:66
   - John 7:47–53
   - Matthew 26:14–16
   - Matthew 26:56
   - Matthew 26:69–75
   - Matthew 27:46

3. Why did Jesus gradually lose all His supporters? Why did God the Father forsake Him? Why did He have to face death and spiritual agony all alone?

4. A significant part of Jesus' suffering was His rejection by those He loved. In the end, He faced His mission totally alone. Have you ever felt so alone? If so, when?

5. Read Matthew 28:20. What comfort can you draw from this verse? Is it possible for us to be forsaken as Jesus was? How does this encourage you as you seek to affect the world around you?

OPTIONAL — Digging Deeper III: Outside the Camp (15–30 minutes)

One symbol of the total rejection of Jesus by everyone, including the Father, was His execution outside the city walls. The basis of this location is in the Old Testament.

- Numbers 2:1–2—The people of Israel camped together around the Tabernacle, where God's presence was.

- Leviticus 13:46, 24:14; Numbers 5:1–4—People considered unclean or ritually unclean were to be placed outside the camp.

- Leviticus 16:6–10,20–22—On Yom Kippur, the priest entered the Holy of Holies of the Tabernacle (Temple) to ask forgiveness for the sins of the people in the presence of God Himself. Then he placed his hands on the head of a goat, symbolically transferring the sins of the people onto the goat. The goat was led into the desert to die, carrying the sins of the people outside the camp (city). In Jesus' time, there was a gate on the southeastern corner of the Temple Mount through which the "scapegoat" was led into the desert to die.

- Luke 23:26; Hebrews 13:11–13—Jesus was taken outside the city (camp) to die. This symbolized His uncleanness because He was bearing the sin of the world. He was shut off from the community because He was cursed.

Have your students (individually or in small groups) answer the following questions.

1. Why would Jesus face such total rejection and humiliation? How would the Jewish community of the day have viewed Him? How would God have viewed Him?

2. How does it affect you to see that Jesus was willing to be cursed and cast out of the community because He was bearing our sins?

OPTIONAL — Digging Deeper IV: Review — The Blood Path (*30–45 minutes*)

Ask your students to open their Bibles to Genesis 15. Read each verse, and have the students (individually or in small groups) answer the appropriate questions.

Verse 1: In what form did God come to Abram? What was God's promise to him?

Verse 2: What was Abram's reaction? Do you dare speak so directly (respectfully, of course) to God? Should you?

Verse 3: What was Abram's concern?

Verse 4: What was God's response?

Verse 5: What was the sign of God's promise?

Verse 6: What was Abram's response? God's reaction to Abram's faith? Would God react to your faith the same way today? How might you indicate that you are willing to take God at His word?

Verse 7: What did God recall from the past? Why did this establish God's right to make a covenant with Abram?

Verse 8: What was Abram's reaction? Again, note his directness. Put Abram's reaction in your own words (e.g., "Prove it!").

Verse 9: How did God react to Abram's request for proof? What is a heifer? How do you know that the ram was not a goat?

Verse 10: What did Abram do after he got the animals? How does this show you that he knew what was happening? NOTE: This ceremony was practiced by the culture and so was known to Abram. The animals were arranged so that the blood ran to the middle of the altar, forming a pool, or path of blood, between the two parties. Both parties, beginning with the greater one, would then walk through the "blood path" as a symbol of what would happen if they did not keep their word. This type of ceremony is called a self-maledictory oath: "May this be done to me if I break my word."

Verses 13–16: What did God promise?

Verse 17: What symbols passed between the pieces? How do you know that God was symbolized? What was God saying? From Abram's perspective, could God have broken the covenant? How do you know a covenant was made? (See verse 18.)

Notice the symbols that passed between the pieces: a smoking firepot and a blazing torch. When was fire a symbol of God (Exodus 2:2 and Acts 2:3)? When was smoke a symbol of God (Exodus 19:18 and Isaiah 6:4)?

With these two symbols, God made a covenant with Abram, which meant that Abram also was expected to put his life on the line for his obedience. That may explain the "thick and dreadful darkness" that came over Abram earlier that night (verse 12). If so, the image of this passage is God's willingness to pay the price for His own breaking of the covenant (which could not happen to a perfect God). The story also shows God's willingness to pay the price for Abram's (and his descendants') failure to keep the covenant.

Ask a student to read aloud Genesis 17:1–2. Then ask your students to answer the following questions.

1. In confirming the covenant (already made in chapter 15), what was Abram's responsibility (not mentioned in chapter 15)? Who was this covenant with? Could Abram and his descendants keep this covenant? By walking the blood path for Abram and his descendants, what was God promising? What does this have to do with Jesus?

2. How would God's walking the blood path help the Israelites understand the meaning of their sacrifices? Could the sacrifices have been reminders of God's promise to pay with His own life for breaking the covenant?

3. What does it mean to you that God was willing to pay the price for your sins? If you desire, relate your response to the class.

4. How does the realization of God's forgiveness help us to be His instruments to those around us? Think of a time when sin or guilt prevented you from being a witness. If you feel comfortable doing so, relate your example to the class.

5. How does the crucifixion of Jesus relate to God's promise to Abraham in the blood path? What can you learn about God, knowing that He made this promise so many years (more than 1,600) before Jesus' birth?

OPTIONAL — Digging Deeper V: The Temple Veil *(15–30 minutes)*

The Bible mentions that the Temple veil was torn in half when Jesus died. This event would have profound meaning for the Jews of Jesus' time.

1. Read Matthew 27:50–51. What occurred in the Temple at the moment of Jesus' death? What do you think this meant?

2. Read and summarize each of the following passages and answer the questions.

    Exodus 26:31–35; Exodus 25:10–22, 40:3; Numbers 7:89; 2 Chronicles 5:13b–14; Psalm 99:1;

Leviticus 16:2. Where did God make His presence known to the people of Israel? (Answer: In the inner part of the Temple—the Holy of Holies—on the ark of the covenant.)

Leviticus 16:1–2, 29–33, 23:26–32. When could the high priest go through the veil into the Holy of Holies? NOTE: In the time of the Second Temple, the ark was no longer in the Temple. God still revealed His presence in the Holy of Holies.

Ezekiel 43:4–7, 44:4; Hebrews 9:1–14 (especially verses 7 and 12), 10:14–22. What did Jesus' death accomplish? What was the significance of the torn veil? What practical meaning does it have for you? How does having direct access to the very presence of God affect your life? How can you make use of this fantastic privilege? If we are to be God's witnesses to our world and make a real impact on our culture, why is this such an important event?

Step Two: "The Firstfruits"

1. Introductory Comments

Jesus' crucifixion provided forgiveness for those who believe in Him as the Lamb of God. His burial and resurrection offer victory over death, the cruel result of sin. This section will explore when Jesus was buried, what the burial practices were in His day, and when He was raised from the dead. A fuller study of His resurrection would be inspiring, but it is outside the scope of this lesson.

2. Guided Discussion: A New Tomb

Students should read the handout "A New Tomb" before beginning this section.

Ask students to read the following passages and compile a list of what we know for certain about the tomb Joseph of Arimathea provided for Jesus.

- Matthew 27:57–61,66—The tomb belonged to a rich Jewish man.
- Matthew 28:2
- Mark 15:42–47—The tomb was cut from rock and sealed with a stone.
- Mark 16:1–5
- Luke 23:50–56—It was a new tomb.
- Luke 24:1–4,12—People had to bend down to see in, and it was large enough for more than one person.
- John 19:38–42—There was a garden nearby.
- John 20:1–8—People could see in the tomb without entering it.

Read the following passages and note what they teach us about Joseph of Arimathea.

- Mark 15:43–46
- Luke 23:50–54
- John 19:38–42

1. Why was Joseph so devoted to Jesus? How did he show his devotion?

2. Have you ever made such a generous gesture for Jesus? How? Could you do something this generous? What could you do?

3. Have you ever done something so dangerous for Jesus? Would you?

Read Leviticus 19:19; Deuteronomy 22:9–11. These laws were apparently in place to teach the Israelites that unlike things were not to be mixed. They may have provided object lessons to show that God's followers must not mix (i.e., intermarry) with pagan people (2 Corinthians 6:14). It is possible that this same logic—don't mix things that are by nature different—may lie behind the practice of placing only family members in the same tomb. If so, Joseph gave Jesus a tomb that he would never be able to use. How does this help you understand Joseph's devotion to Jesus? How could you indicate such devotion to Jesus?

Read the following passages and summarize what they teach us about Nicodemus.

- John 3:1–21
- John 7:45–52
- John 19:39–41

1. Was Nicodemus a believer? What did he do to show his devotion to Jesus?

2. Why are some public figures so hesitant to speak on Jesus' behalf? Why are others very bold?

3. Have you ever spoken out for Jesus in a setting where your views were unpopular? Discuss examples with the rest of the class.

4. How can we encourage each other to be more publicly outspoken about our commitment to Jesus, even if our views are not popular?

OPTIONAL — Digging Deeper VI: Burial Customs During New Testament Times *(30–50 minutes)*

(This section requires the use of the optional full-color overhead-transparency packet. For information on ordering it, see page 307.)

Overhead Transparency 47. The Garden Tomb. Just north of the Damascus Gate, the main northern entrance to Jerusalem, is a beautiful garden located against the side of a rocky cliff. It has been a place of interest to many Christian visitors because it is remarkably similar to the Bible's description of the place of the crucifixion and resurrection of Jesus. The atmosphere of this quiet place, along with the features that can help us picture the location, make it worth a visit, whether it is the actual location of those great events or not. (Archaeological evidence seems to indicate that it is not the original site.)

This photograph shows the cliff face in the garden, with a tomb cut into the rock. In front of the entrance to the tomb is a channel where originally a stone was rolled in front of the tomb to close it off after a burial (Mark 15:46, 16:1–3). Entering the tomb through the doorway—enlarged during the Crusades—one must look to the right to see the burial places, which were never finished. (John 19:41–42 describes a new tomb hewn in the rock. John 20:3–9 says the disciples had to look in to see the clothes where the body had been laid, and the tomb was large enough for more than one person to enter.) The small window lets light into the burial chamber, but it may have been added later. At some point, the entrance to this tomb was enlarged and later blocked in, so the opening was originally much taller.

Excavations indicate that this tomb was originally located in a garden—a large cistern and a winepress were found nearby (John 19:41, 20:15). The garden and the tomb are located outside the city walls of Jerusalem (Hebrews 13:12), near an old, abandoned quarry. It is not hard to imagine the sorrowful friends of Jesus coming to a place like this, seeing Jesus' body laid in a tomb and a great stone rolled across the entrance. Returning on the morning of Firstfruits, they discovered the tomb—open and empty (like this one in the photograph). Hurrying back to Jerusalem, they encountered Jesus, who had become the firstfruits of those who would be raised from the dead (1 Corinthians 15:23).

Overhead Transparency 48. Burial Customs. *Upper Left: Cliff at the Garden Tomb.* This cliff face is located just outside the garden tomb (see previous transparency). It was originally a quarry, but the rock quality was poor. It is just outside the city of Jerusalem, near the main gate. The area in front of the cliff was probably the place where people were stoned according to Jewish law. (Some suggest this is the place where Stephen was stoned. See Acts 7:54–60.) While there is no archaeological evidence that indicates this was the crucifixion site, this place can help us picture the location where Jesus was crucified, for it fits the biblical description. It is outside the city (Hebrews 13:12) and in a public place, as Roman law demanded. It is near a garden and tombs (John 19:41) and probably was a place of execution. The caves in the face of the cliff on the right side remind some people of a skull—two eyes with the bridge of a nose between. Though Jesus was crucified at Golgotha, the place of the skull (John 19:17), there is no certainty that these caves looked the same then or that the hill was called Golgotha because it looked like a skull. It is likely that if Golgotha was a hill, Jesus was crucified at its base, not on top, because the Romans wanted to keep victims as close to passersby as possible so they might serve as examples.

*Upper Right: **Channel for the Stone.*** This channel is found in front of the entrance to the garden tomb. It is likely that a large tombstone, round like a disc and probably about five feet high and 12 inches thick, rolled in this channel to seal the tomb. Since families continued to use tombs over several generations (storing the bones in ossuaries), they had to be able to open and close the burial site. Some of the wealthy who could afford this luxury had tombs carved out of the rock. A disc-shaped stone was cut, which rolled in a trench in front of the entrance. A small depression made the stone stop exactly where it closed the tomb. A rolling stone like the one here would weigh more than two tons (Mark 16:1–3). There is no way to know if this was Jesus' tomb, but it is not really important. This stone can help us understand how Jesus' tomb was sealed.

*Lower Left: **The Herod Family Tomb.*** This tomb to the west of Jerusalem was at one time thought to be the burial place of the Herod family. Later research indicated that it was not Herod's tomb. It is noted for the "rolling stone" still in place next to the entrance. This photograph was taken from the main entrance to the tomb. The steps descending into the tomb are visible in the foreground. The stone arch was originally part of an entire face of the tomb so that the round stone would have been completely hidden behind the wall. The stone is over five feet high and one and one-half feet thick and is perfectly round. One can understand how this well-preserved stone was pried loose and rolled to the left to its present position so people could descend into the rather large tomb.

After the burial had been completed, the stone was allowed to roll back down its "slot," covering the opening to the tomb. Wax or clay was sometimes placed between the rolling stone and the wall, and the owner's seal was impressed on it so people could determine if the tomb was opened or not. In Jesus' case, the tomb was sealed and guards were placed in front of it (Matthew 27:62–66). These extra precautions didn't matter: Jesus, by the power of God, came out of the tomb, the angels rolled the stone back, and Jesus' friends and disciples discovered an empty tomb.

*Lower Right: **Ossuaries.*** Beginning shortly before Jesus' time, Jewish people began to practice reburials. After the flesh had decayed from the bones of a person who was buried, the bones were collected and placed in a small box—an ossuary—like the ones shown here. These particular ossuaries were found in a tomb on the Mount of Olives. They were generally made of soft stone or limestone. Sometimes they were decorated with geometric designs, like the ones shown here. After they were filled, sometimes with the bones of several individuals, they were stored in small chambers (called *kokhim* in Hebrew) within the tomb (in the background). Sometimes the name of the family or one of the individuals within was carved on the outside. Among the ossuaries archaeologists have found is that of Joseph Bar Caiapha, (*Caiaphas* in Greek) possibly the high priest who plotted against Jesus.

No one knows exactly why the practice of using ossuaries began. Some believe it was due to the Pharisees' teaching that "flesh" is the location of the sinful nature and that it must decay so the bones can be raised in the resurrection of the righteous.

3. Guided Discussion: Jesus Is Buried

God planned carefully for Jesus' mission. As part of God's plan, this work of Jesus was conducted during the Jewish Passover. Seeing Jesus' crucifixion, burial, and resurrection in light of the celebrations that took place at that time can provide us with an object lesson of what He came to do.

Have your students read the following passages and answer the questions.

a. **Passover (on Friday that year)**

- Exodus 12:12–14; Leviticus 23:5. When was Passover to begin? What did it celebrate?

- John 18:28. When did Jesus die? Why?

- John 1:29; 1 Corinthians 5:7. How does this help you understand the meaning of Jesus' death? NOTE: See also "Jesus' Crucifixion and the Old Testament" on pages 198–199.

b. **Feast of Unleavened Bread (beginning on Saturday that year)**

- Leviticus 23:6. When did the Feast of Unleavened Bread begin? This feast was a reminder of the bread the Israelites ate as they left Egypt. Unleavened bread was made without yeast, which represented sin (1 Corinthians 5:7–8). This feast also commemorated God's provision during the exodus from Egypt.

- John 6:35, 12:24, 19:31—Sabbath was the day after Jesus' crucifixion. This day was also the Feast of Unleavened Bread (the day after Passover). What did Jesus call Himself? How was Jesus like unleavened bread? What had to occur for wheat ("bread") to come to life from the ground? When was Jesus buried? What symbolism does this provide? (Answer: He was our "grain," our bread, that had to come from the earth. He was like unleavened bread because He was without sin, and He was buried—planted—on the Feast of Unleavened Bread.)

Some scholars believe Jesus was buried on the Feast of Unleavened Bread to highlight His own nature as the "bread of life," which comes from the earth. First Corinthians 15:42–44 says that we, like Jesus, are sown (die and are buried) and raised to new life. How does this help you understand Jesus' burial? How does this understanding encourage you?

c. **Feast of Firstfruits (on Sunday that year)**

- Leviticus 23:10–11. When was the Feast of Firstfruits? (Answer: The feast was a celebration of the beginning of the year's harvest—in this case, the barley harvest. The "first part" of everything the Israelites were given was returned to God to indicate three things: (1) their thankfulness for the harvest; (2) their acknowledgment that God had given them these gifts; and (3) their faith that there was more to come because they gave the first part to God. The Feast of

Firstfruits was an act of faith that, just as God had given His people the "first part," He would surely provide them the rest.

- Exodus 23:19, 34:26; Numbers 15:17–21, 18:12–13; Deuteronomy 26:1–11; Luke 24:1–8. On what day of the week and during what feast was Jesus raised from the dead?

- 1 Corinthians 15:20–23. Jesus became the firstfruits of what spiritual "harvest"? (Answer: People who would be raised from the dead.) If Jesus was the firstfruits, what was the guarantee? How does understanding the Feast of Firstfruits help you understand what God was doing in Jesus' resurrection? What does Jesus' resurrection mean for your everyday life? How does it provide comfort for you? How can Jesus' resurrection help you touch the lives of others? Why do you think God planned for the resurrection to happen on that day?

d. Review

Point out to your students what Jesus did that year.

Passover	Jesus died as God's Lamb.
Feast of Unleavened Bread	Jesus was buried like wheat so He might come from the earth to provide life.
Feast of Firstfruits	Jesus came to life as God's Firstfruits, the guarantee that the rest would follow.

It is astonishing to realize that the Old Testament feasts were practiced for 1,200 years before they became object lessons for the work of Jesus. This links His work to the Old Testament Jewish community, reveals God's meticulous planning, and helps us better understand what Jesus accomplished on the cross.

The next feast celebrated that year was Shavuot (Pentecost). That will be the subject of Lesson 26.

4. Guided Discussion: The Stone Was Rolled Away

Ask your students to read the following passages and answer the questions.

- Matthew 28:1–10; Mark 16:1–8; Luke 24:1–12; John 20:1–18. Who came to the tomb, looking for Jesus' body? Why were they so shocked at what they found?

- John 20:9; Mark 8:31, 9:31, 10:33–34; Luke 18:32. Why was it so hard for the disciples to believe what had happened? Why was Jesus' resurrection the most difficult option to accept? Why do you think it's hard for people today to accept Jesus' resurrection?

- Matthew 28:1–6 (especially verse 6). The Greek could be translated "He has already risen." In other words, He rose before the stone was moved and before the earthquake, which happened as the women went to the tomb.

- Ephesians 1:18–20. Knowing what power raised Jesus from the dead, and knowing that a tombstone could not stand in His way, why do you think the stone was rolled away? (Answer: The stone was removed so the women and the disciples could look into the tomb to discover that it was empty.) Why did they need to be able to see into the tomb?

Through the experience of Jesus' followers, we can discover the empty tomb. The stone sealing the entrance has been rolled away so *we* can know that Jesus, the Messiah, has been raised from the dead. What would (or did) it mean to you to see the empty tomb? What effect does the reality of the resurrection have in your life? What does it mean to you that Jesus is alive? How does that affect you every day?

Conclusion

In Jesus' day, a man and woman sealed their engagement by exchanging a cup of wine. Though there are many other meanings involved in Jesus' giving the "cup" to His disciples and to us, in one sense it was a declaration of His love for us and His invitation to us to be His spiritual bride.

Have your students (individually or in small groups) read the following passages and answer the questions.

- Luke 22:20; Mark 2:19–20; Revelation 19:7–9; 2 Corinthians 11:2

1. How does it help you understand Jesus' love to think of Him as the perfect spiritual husband?

2. What does this commitment demand from us until we see Jesus face to face?

3. The bride accepted the cup from her husband-to-be as an indication of her lifelong commitment. How has Jesus proved His love to you? Has He lived up to His commitment to you?

4. How have you indicated your total commitment to Jesus, who wants to be "engaged" to you?

5. How have you been faithful to Him? Unfaithful to Him?

Spend a few moments in prayer, asking God to help you accept His offer of salvation and to make a total commitment to Him.

A NEW TOMB

Throughout Bible times, the burial ritual was regarded as very important. Jesus, sharing fully in our humanity (Hebrews 2:14), was given a typical, though hurried, burial. Understanding the burial customs and practices of first-century Israel can help us understand Jesus' experience and can underscore for us the commitment of those who provided Him with a proper tomb.

OLD TESTAMENT BURIAL

The Old Testament makes clear the importance of a proper burial. Abraham spent a great sum to purchase a tomb for his family (Genesis 23:1–20). His children and grandchildren were buried in this same family tomb (Genesis 49:30–31). Though little is known about specific Israelite burial customs (they appear to have been simple—e.g., only a few items such as pottery, clothes, weapons, jewelry, and so on, were buried with the dead—in sharp contrast, for instance, to the Egyptians), many of the biblical biographies conclude by mentioning people's burials, indicating that burial was an important part of life (1 Kings 2:10, 11:43; 2 Kings 21:18; 2 Chronicles 26:23).

It was considered important to bury someone near his or her home and family (Genesis 49:29, 50:25; 2 Samuel 19:37). Tombs were generally hewn from the rock just outside the village where people lived (probably so the living could avoid being defiled by the dead—Numbers 5:1–3). Families were buried in the same tombs for generations. The remains of those who had died before were carefully piled in one part of the tomb to make room for the newly deceased. This is probably the reason for the expression "He rested with his fathers" (1 Kings 2:10, 11:43; Genesis 47:30; 2 Chronicles 12:16) used to describe burial.

Burial apparently happened quite soon after death, possibly within one day (Deuteronomy 21:23). A sign of God's judgment on a person was that his or her body would remain unburied (Deuteronomy 28:26; 1 Kings 14:10–14, 21:23; 2 Kings 9:34–37). Though there is little discussion in the Bible of the people's belief in resurrection, the importance of burial to them indicates clearly that they believed life continued after death (Job 19:25–26).

FIRST-CENTURY BURIAL CUSTOMS

The Israelites began to use new burial practices in the first century A.D. Tombs were still cut into the rock around cities (e.g., Jerusalem), as they had been for generations. The new tombs generally had two chambers. There was an outer chamber where the body could be laid out to be prepared for burial. This chamber may have even served as a place for mourning the deceased shortly after death. A second inner chamber provided a place for the burial itself. Many tombs had a number of shelves, or niches, cut into the rock (*kokhim* in Hebrew).

After the flesh had decayed from the bones, the bones often were collected and placed in a small box, usually made of soft stone, called an ossuary. These boxes were usually about 20 inches long, 12 inches high, and 12 inches wide. In some cases, they were decorated with geometric designs. The ossuary was placed in a small niche cut into the rock on the side of the chamber. Over time, several people from the same family would be placed in the same ossuary. In many cases, the family name would be inscribed on the side. Occasionally, additional details might be included, such as the person's accomplishments or status.

Recent archaeological discoveries have included ossuaries. One of these was inscribed with the words "Simon, the builder of the Temple," apparently by the family of one who worked on the Temple of Herod. The most significant recent discovery was made in 1990. Construction workers accidentally broke open a tomb from the first century. Located in an area south of the city of Jerusalem, the tomb is one of many that have been found there. Several ossuaries were also found, all carved from stone and some highly decorated. The inscriptions indicate that they belonged to the family of Caiapha (*Caiaphas* in Greek).

On one of the highly decorated ossuaries was the name Joseph Bar Caiapha, the full name of the high priest who plotted Jesus' death (John 11:49–51; Matthew 26:57–66). Inside were the remains of several people, including an adult female, a child, two babies, and an adult male approximately 60 years of age. While an exact identification of the individuals is not possible, scholars believe the tomb, the ossuary, and the remains of the adult male are those of the high priest Caiaphas. The fact that there are remains in his tomb, while Jesus' tomb (even though it has never been conclusively identified) is empty, can help to illustrate the true nature of their conflict.

No one knows why the practice of using ossuaries began during Jesus' time. Some believe that the Pharisees' view that sin is of the "flesh" led them to adopt a practice by which the "flesh" would decay and the bones would be gathered for the resurrection to come (Romans 7:24; 1 Corinthians 15:50). Others believe the influence of the Pharisees' doctrine of the bodily resurrection led to the gathering of bones to be preserved for that day (Mark 12:18–27).

When someone died, his or her body was laid in the outer chamber of the tomb and prepared with various spices and perfumes. During this time, mourning ceremonies would take place. After the body had been carefully placed on one of the ledges around the chamber, the tomb was sealed with a large disc-shaped stone that rolled in a trench in front of the tomb. It remained closed until the family returned to collect the bones or to bury another family member. Jesus' tomb was sealed before the body was prepared (Matthew 27:57–66), and Jesus was raised before His friends returned to complete the burial (Matthew 28:1–6).

AN EXPENSIVE GIFT

Only the wealthy could afford large tombs cut into the rock. Their families were buried in these tombs for years (sometimes centuries). The tomb that Joseph of Arimathea provided for Jesus was such a tomb (Matthew

POWER TO THE PEOPLE

For the Teacher

There are few events more well known to Christians than God's gift of the Holy Spirit on Pentecost. Yet few Christians are aware that Pentecost was (and is) a Jewish feast instituted by God through Moses more than 1,200 years before its Christian fulfillment. The Jewish practices, those described in the Bible and those instituted in the culture, provided the background to the events in the early church. Understanding the history of the feast makes its Christian fulfillment more vivid and personal and issues a great challenge to bring the presence of God to a world that needs to know Him.

This study explores the Jewish setting of Acts 2 and the Pentecost story. Encourage your students to understand that this focus is not intended to diminish the meaning of Pentecost that Christians have always stressed—the miracle of tongues, the gifts of the Spirit, and Peter's empowered preaching. The intent is to *add* an element—Jewish tradition—to make its meaning even more vivid.

Begin by asking your class what Pentecost was. If no one mentions that it had Old Testament background, ask students when Pentecost began. If no one knows, simply continue the lesson. If someone is aware of its background, allow a couple of minutes for the class to discuss what that feast celebrated and how it was related to the story in the New Testament. Then watch the excitement grow as your students discover additional richness they may not have known is included in the story of Pentecost—their story. Help them understand that Pentecost is God's gift of power—His power—to His people. Your presentation may help empower your students to become God's witnesses to their world.

Your Objectives for This Lesson

At the completion of this section, you will want your students:

To Know/Understand

1. The location of the events that happened on Pentecost in Acts 2.

2. The purpose and practices of the Jewish feast of Pentecost and their relationship to the coming of the Holy Spirit.

3. The meaning of the symbolism in the Pentecost story.

4. That caring for those in need is one element of experiencing Pentecost.

5. That Pentecost empowered (and still empowers) the community of Jesus because it involved the very presence of God.

6. The beautiful parallel between the story in Acts 2 and the giving of the law on Mount Sinai.

7. How Jesus' work was symbolized in the feasts of the Torah.

To Do

1. Recognize the call to be God's witnesses, empowered by His Spirit.

2. Choose at least one person whose needs they could meet, and plan to reach out to that person.

3. Be inspired to express appreciation to God for His decision to live within His people and His community, the church.

How to Plan for This Lesson

Because of the volume of material in this lesson, you may need to divide it into several class sessions. To help you determine how to do that, the lesson has been broken into segments. Note that the time needed may vary significantly, depending on elements such as the leader, the size of the class, and the interest level of the class.

If you wish to cover the entire lesson in one session, you should complete Unit One. This unit provides a guided discussion covering the major points in the video. It does not go into great depth. If you wish to go into greater depth on any of the points in Unit One, they are covered more thoroughly in the remainder of the material.

How to Prepare for This Lesson

Materials Needed

Student copies of the maps/diagrams:	"Jerusalem's Districts"
	"The Roman World"
	"Land of Jesus' Ministry"
	"Topography of Jerusalem"
	"Jerusalem of David and Solomon"
	"Development of the Temple Mount"
	"Jerusalem of Jesus' Time"
	"The Temple Mount: A.D. 70"
	"Temple Courts"
Overhead transparencies:	"Jerusalem's Districts"
	"The Roman World"
	"Land of Jesus' Ministry"
	"New Testament Chronology"
	"Topography of Jerusalem"
	"Jerusalem of David and Solomon"
	"Development of the Temple Mount"
	"Jerusalem of Jesus' Time"
	"The Temple Mount: A.D. 70"
	"Temple Courts"
Student copies of the handout:	"Temple of the Spirit"

Video: **Power to the People**

Overhead projector, screen, TV, VCR

1. Make copies of the maps/diagrams listed above for your students.

2. Prepare the overhead transparencies listed above. (You'll find them at the back of the book.)

3. Make copies of the handout listed above for your students. (If possible, students should receive and read this handout before the lesson.)

4. Review the geography of the lands of the Bible from the "Introduction."

5. Determine which **unit** and which **Digging Deeper** sections, if any, you want to use in your class session(s). NOTE: You can use these sections in any order you wish (e.g., you might want to use **Digging Deeper III,** but not **Digging Deeper I** or **Digging Deeper II**).

6. Prepare your classroom ahead of time, setting up and testing an overhead projector and screen (for the overhead transparencies) and a TV and VCR. If you plan to hand out biblical references for your students to look up and read aloud, prepare 3x5 cards (one reference per card) to distribute before class.

Lesson Plan

UNIT ONE: Video Review

1. Introductory Comments

In the context God chose, the story of Pentecost takes on great meaning for Jesus' church. Not only is the Spirit the new Teacher of the believers, but God has also decided to live in the temple of the new community so the world may know Him through the members of that community. This study explores the Pentecost story in its context.

2. Show the Video *Power to the People* (17 *minutes*)

3. Map Study: The Southern Stairs

HINT: *Begin this map study session by reviewing the geography of the entire city and working down to the location the lesson is dealing with—the Southern Stairs.*

Using the overhead transparency "Jerusalem's Districts," point out the following locations, and have your students find them on their diagrams.

> David's City
> Kidron Valley
> Mount of Olives
> Tyropoeon Valley
> Temple Mount
> Southern Stairs (This is where the video for this lesson was filmed. Some believe that the fulfillment of Pentecost took place here. Others put this event elsewhere—for example, on the Temple Mount.)
> Temple

4. Guided Discussion: Pentecost at the Temple

The feast of Pentecost originated from God's revelation to Moses on Mount Sinai. The Jewish people had celebrated this festival for more than 1,200 years before God's Spirit appeared on the disciples. The original instructions for Pentecost are given in the following passages:

a. Read Leviticus 23:15–22; Deuteronomy 16:16.

Based on the Bible material:
- This feast was called the Feast of Weeks (*Shavuot* in Hebrew), or Pentecost, meaning "50 days," because it took place 50 days after Passover.
- This was one of three feasts at which all men were to appear at the Temple in Jerusalem.
- The Feast of Weeks celebrated the end of the wheat harvest, during the third month.

Based on Jewish tradition:
- The feast celebrated the giving of the Torah (the Law) on Mount Sinai.
- Exodus 19:1 indicated that the Israelites arrived at Mount Sinai in the third month, the month of Pentecost.
- The readings in the Temple on this day were from Exodus 19–20 and Ezekiel 1–2.
- The reading from Exodus was the story of the Ten Commandments, and the reading from Ezekiel described a vision of a fiery theophany (appearance of God).

b. Read Luke 24:50–53; Acts 2:1–15.
  1. What did the disciples do after Jesus' resurrection?
  2. Where would they be on a holy day (Pentecost)?
  3. What do you think "the house" referred to? (Point out that the Temple is often called "the house" in the Old Testament. See also Acts 7:47.)
  4. What time did the Holy Spirit come upon the disciples? (Point out that the Temple service of Pentecost occurred after the morning sacrifice, around 9:00 A.M.)
  5. Why were there so many people there from various backgrounds?

c. Remember that the crowd understood Pentecost to celebrate the giving of the Torah on Mount Sinai. Compare the following passages and answer the questions.
   - Acts 2:1–3; Exodus 19:16–19
  1. How are these two events similar?
   - Acts 2:38–41; Exodus 32:1–4,19–20,27–28—Because of their sin, about 3,000 people died when Moses was receiving the Torah. Because of their repentance, about 3,000 became believers when the Spirit came.
  1. How do these comparisons help you understand God's careful planning for the work of redemption to fulfill the Old Testament?
   - 2 Chronicles 5:7–8,13–14
  1. Where was God's presence for the people of Old Testament Israel?
   - Acts 2:1–4—The "house" (probably the Temple) was filled with the sound of wind, and fire rested on the disciples.
  1. Where was God's presence before this Pentecost?
  2. Where was it after the fulfillment?
   - 1 Corinthians 3:16–17, 6:19
  1. Where is God's presence today?
  2. What does it mean for your life that you are to be God's presence to others? How can you do that for your family? Your friends? Your community?

- Acts 1:8, 4:33—God gave His power to His people.

1. What is the responsibility of those who have God's Spirit?

2. What does it mean to you to know there is no greater power than the presence of God?

3. How can you obtain God's power? How can you be His witness?

4. How can you be to your world what the Temple was to the world of the Old Testament?

5. Think of someone who helps you see the presence of God. How is that person God's witness?

- Leviticus 23:16–17; Matthew 9:37–38—Pentecost (Weeks) was the feast that celebrated the wheat harvest.

1. What are some similarities between the fulfillment of Pentecost and the harvest?

2. How are you part of the harvest? If you have God's Spirit, you are commissioned to bring in the harvest, too. How can you do that?

- Leviticus 23:22; Acts 2:44–46—Pentecost (Weeks) was a holiday of thanksgiving. The evidence of thankfulness was caring for those in need. The fulfillment of Pentecost was no different. One mark of the experience of the Spirit on Pentecost was the concern for those in need.

1. What does it mean when someone claims to have God's Spirit and has no concern for those in need?

2. How does the Old Testament background to this feast make it impossible for Spirit-filled people to have no concern for others in need?

3. Do you know a Christian who truly cares for those who are in need? Give some examples.

4. What kinds of needs should we be concerned about meeting for others?

5. For whom should you show greater concern? How might you do that?

5. Conclusion

Celebrating Pentecost meant going to the Temple (the presence of God), bringing the first of the harvest, and showing concern for the poor. The Holy Spirit worked a great miracle on the day of Pentecost for the new community of Jesus. The presence of God entered a new "temple": the community of believers. The first of a great harvest (3,000 believers) was brought into the church. Once the community had truly experienced Pentecost, it immediately became concerned for the poor.

We are called to be *Pentecost* Christians. We must ask God to live in us so that we become witnesses to His presence in our world. We must bring the harvest to God as we introduce others to Him and His love. We must demonstrate that we are Spirit-filled by showing compassion for those in need.

6. Prayer

Spend a few moments in prayer. Ask God to live in your heart, your life, your church. Ask Him to give you the desire to be His witness and to fill you with a sense of power. Request that He give you a compassionate spirit, sensitive to those in need.

UNIT TWO
Step One: "Pentecost in Jerusalem"

1. Introduction: The Context of Pentecost

The Holy Spirit empowered the first believers on a Jewish feast day (in Hebrew, *Shavuot;* called Weeks or Pentecost in English) that had been celebrated for 1,200 years. The events of that fulfillment were dramatic. In typical Jewish fashion, they also provided "pictures" of their meanings. The location of the story of Acts 2 cannot be determined completely. It was, however, clearly related to the Temple and its courts. This study explores the city of Jerusalem and the Temple Mount in relationship to the pilgrims who came to celebrate Pentecost in that crucial year.

2. Map Study: Jerusalem and the Southern Stairs

HINT: *Begin this map study session by reviewing the geography of the overall region and working down to the areas the lesson is dealing with—Jerusalem and the Southern Stairs.*

Using the overhead transparency "The Roman World," point out the following areas, and have your students locate them on their maps.

> Rome
> Mediterranean Sea
> Egypt
> Judea
> Caesarea
> Parthian Empire
> Cappadocia
> Cyrene

Using the overhead transparency "Land of Jesus' Ministry," point out the following areas, and have your students locate them on their maps.

> Bethlehem
> Jerusalem
> Nazareth
> Capernaum
> Galilee
> Sea of Galilee

Using the overhead transparency "Jerusalem's Districts," point out the following areas, and have your students locate them on their diagrams.

> David's City
> Kidron Valley
> Mount of Olives
> Tyropoeon Valley
> Temple Mount
> Southern Stairs

3. Review the Overhead Transparency "New Testament Chronology"

Using the overhead transparency "New Testament Chronology," highlight the following dates for your students:

586 B.C.	Babylonian Captivity of Judah
ca. 500 B.C.	Return to Israel
37 B.C.	Herod's reign begins
4 B.C.	Herod's death
ca. 6 B.C.	Jesus' birth
ca. A.D. 27–30	Jesus' ministry
ca. A.D. 30	Jesus is crucified
A.D. 66–73	First Jewish Revolt against Rome
A.D. 70	Destruction of Jerusalem and the Temple

Point out the following information to your students.

- Not all the Jews returned after the captivity; many remained in the lands to which they had been exiled or had fled.

- The Pentecost when the Spirit was given was in approximately A.D. 30.

4. Show the Video *Power to the People* (17 minutes)

5. Guided Discussion: Pentecost Pilgrims Come to the Temple

a. Introduction

The physical features of Jerusalem and the Temple Mount are important to an understanding of the events of Pentecost. This section begins with the larger picture and works down to the specific area for our study of Pentecost. NOTE: The information that follows was taken from Lesson 22.

b. Topography of David's City and the Temple Mount

1. David's City

HINT: *If you have the optional full-color overhead-transparency packets for Sets 2 and 4, you may want to use Overhead Transparencies 22 ("The Cave of the Spring of Gihon"), 23 ("Hezekiah's Water Tunnel"), and 24 ("The Midway Point in Hezekiah's Water Tunnel Where the Workers Met"), and their descriptions, in Set 2, and Overhead Transparency 28 ("Modern-day Jerusalem from the South") in Set 4 to supplement your teaching in this section.*

Using the overhead transparency "Topography of Jerusalem," point out the following areas, and have your students locate them on their maps.

> Kidron Valley
> David's City
> Temple Mount
> Tyropoeon Valley
> Spring of Gihon
> Hezekiah's Tunnel

Explain the following points to your students.

- David's Jerusalem was a narrow strip of land—Mount Moriah—composed of approximately 9 to 10 acres of land and populated by about 1,500 people.

- Mount Moriah was naturally defended by the Kidron Valley on the east and the Tyropoeon Valley on the west.

- The Spring of Gihon was an excellent source of water for this area, one of the main reasons the city was located here.

- This part of the city was originally called Zion.

- Solomon expanded the city to the north on the ridge called Mount Moriah, to build the Temple to Yahweh. This First Temple, Nehemiah's reconstruction, and Herod's Temple all stood in exactly the same place.

- Hezekiah expanded the city across the Tyropoeon Valley onto the Western Hill. He commissioned the construction of a tunnel from the Spring of Gihon, under David's City, to the Pool of Siloam.

Bible Connection

Use the following passages to show your students how David's City connects with the Scriptures.

> Genesis 22:1,2,14—Abraham brought Isaac to Mount Moriah to sacrifice him.
>
> 2 Samuel 5:6–12—David captured Jerusalem and made it his political capital.
>
> 2 Samuel 6:12–19—David brought the ark to Jerusalem, and the city became the religious center of Israel.
>
> 2 Samuel 24:1,16,18–25—David purchased the threshing floor of Araunah, which became the future site of the Temple.
>
> 2 Chronicles 3:1–2—Solomon built the Temple on Mount Moriah, the Temple Mount.

HINT: *If you have the optional full-color overhead-transparency packet for Set 4, see Overhead Transparencies 28 ("Modern-day Jerusalem from the South"), 36 ("Ancient Jerusalem from the South"), and 37 ("The Upper City").*

This was the Jerusalem of David's time. In Jesus' day, David's City was home to many Jews (as was the Lower City).

Using the overhead transparency "Jerusalem's Districts," point out the following locations, and have your students find them on their diagrams.

> David's City
> Southern Stairs
> Spring of Gihon

Bible Connection

Use the following passages to show your students how David's City connects with the Scriptures.

> 2 Kings 20:20
> 2 Chronicles 32:30—Hezekiah tunneled through David's City to the Tyropoeon Valley to bring water into Jerusalem.

HINT: *You may want to refer to the overhead transparencies and study materials in Lesson 7, Set 2, for more information on this subject.*

2. The Temple Platform

HINT: *If you have the optional full-color overhead-transparency packet for Set 4, see Overhead Transparencies 31 ("The Western Wall"), 33 ("The Southern Stairs"), 36 ("Ancient Jerusalem from the South"), and 37 ("The Upper City").*

With God's direction, David chose a flat area (threshing floor) on Mount Moriah, and later Solomon built the Temple there. Apparently, this threshing floor, where David had built an altar, was large enough for the Temple and its courts.

a. Location. Using the overhead transparency "Jerusalem of David and Solomon," point out the location of the Temple Mount from David's time. No definite remains of this place have been found. Temples in the ancient world were built within sacred areas, usually on the highest points in their regions. Solomon's Temple was no exception: This sacred area was on the highest point of the ridge.

Bible Connection

Use the following passage to show your students how the development of the Temple platform connects with the Scriptures.

2 Chronicles 3:1

Little is known of any changes to the Temple Mount after the time of Ezra and Nehemiah. It is assumed that in rebuilding the Temple, they worked within the original boundaries of Solomon's Temple.

b. **Hasmonaean Expansion.** Using the overhead transparency "Development of the Temple Mount," show the expansion of the Hasmonaeans, pointing out the following information:

- The original square Temple Mount was built to provide a flat area on the top of the mountain. Remains of this structure have not been found.

- The Hasmonaean expansion is on the right side of the transparency. (Note the tunnels providing access to the Mount.)

c. **Herod's Expansion.** Using the overhead transparency "Development of the Temple Mount," show the expansion of this area by Herod, pointing out the following information:

- The extension to the south included tunnels.

- The extension to the west in the Tyropoeon Valley demanded enormous retaining walls on both the south and the west.

- The Antonia was built on a flat rock.

- The eastern wall followed the original line from the times of Solomon, Ezra, and the Hasmonaeans.

- The base for this Temple was the largest in the ancient world. A small section of it, located between Barclay's Gate and Wilson's Arch, is called the Western, or Wailing, Wall.

- The retaining walls of this Mount contain massive stones, each weighing more than 500 tons. The Temple platform was more than 900 feet wide and 1,200 feet long.

3. The Temple Mount

HINT: *If you have the optional full-color overhead-transparency packet for Set 4, see Overhead Transparencies 33 ("The Southern Stairs"), 34 ("Scenes from the Southern Stairs"), 36 ("Ancient Jerusalem from the South"), and 42 ("Scenes from the City of Jesus' Day").*

Using the overhead transparencies "Jerusalem of Jesus' Time" and "The Temple Mount: A.D. 70," point out the following structures and places, and have your students locate them on their maps/diagrams.

Southern Stairs
south wall
royal stoa
opening of entrance tunnels on Temple Mount floor

Using the overhead transparency "The Temple Mount: A.D. 70," point out the following locations, and have your students find them on their diagrams.

> Double Gates (also called the Huldah Gates—entrance for pilgrims)
> Triple Gates (probably an entrance for priests)
> ritual baths
> plaza

The south wall is probably the most impressive of all the walls of the Temple Mount. It is more than 900 feet long and more than 150 feet high. Pilgrims (including Jesus and the disciples) entered the Temple primarily through this entrance after washing in a ritual bath called a *mikveh* (pl. *mikvoth*). On feast days (Passover, Pentecost, and Sukkot), literally hundreds of thousands of people made their way up the Southern Stairs and into the Temple courts. It is probable that the New Testament Pentecost events happened here or nearby.

Bible Connection

Use the following passage to show your students how the south wall connects with the Scriptures.

> Acts 2

HINT: *If you have the optional full-color overhead-transparency packet for Set 4, see Overhead Transparencies 40 ("The Temple Mount") and 41 ("The Temple").*

The Temple platform was enormous. It was more than 900 feet wide from east to west (915 feet on the south end, and 1,030 feet on the north end) and more than 1,500 feet long from north to south (1,535 feet on the east end, and 1,590 feet on the west end). It was by far the largest temple area in the ancient world. Hundreds of thousands of pilgrims could be on the mount at the same time. (Josephus claimed that the Passover pilgrims numbered more than 2 million people.) Herod trained 1,000 priests as masons to work on the Temple itself. Ten thousand highly skilled laborers, using 1,000 wagons, worked for years to construct it. The finished platform was divided into separate courts, which were increasingly more sacred the closer they were to the Temple. This section begins with the courts on the outer edge of the platform and gradually moves toward the Temple itself.

Using the overhead transparencies "The Temple Mount: A.D. 70" and "Temple Courts," point out the following areas, and have your students locate them on their diagrams.

> Temple
> Gentile Court
> royal stoa
> Solomon's Colonnade
> Priests' Court
> Court of the Israelites
> Women's Court
> Southern Stairs

Review the material below with your students.

The *Gentile Court* was the large open area around the sacred courts of the Temple. Anyone could enter this area. This court was also intended to be a place of prayer for Gentiles.

Locate the *colonnade* around the outer edge of the court. On three sides, the colonnade was more than 45 feet wide and 40 feet high. It had a flat roof that rested on the outer wall on one edge and on two rows of massive columns on the other. This colonnade gave the Mount great splendor and also provided a place for teaching and assembly.

Locate *Solomon's Colonnade*. This apparently was the oldest of the colonnades. Josephus attributes it to Solomon, although it probably wasn't that old. This colonnade often provided a place of meeting. It was a favorite teaching spot of Jesus, and the place where the early church met.

Bible Connection

Use the following passages to show your students how the Temple courts, and particularly Solomon's Colonnade connect with the Scriptures.

> Matthew 26:55; Mark 11:27, 12:35; Luke 2:46, 20:1; John 7:14, 8:2—Jesus regularly taught in the Temple courts, which were most likely the areas beneath the colonnade on the east, west, or north.
>
> Acts 2:46, 5:20–21,42—The first Christians, almost all Jewish, met regularly in the Temple courts, most likely in this same location beneath the colonnade.
>
> John 10:22–23—Jesus confronted the crowd with His message in Solomon's Colonnade.
>
> Acts 3:1–16—Peter healed a man at the Beautiful Gate (the entrance to the Women's Court just west of Solomon's Colonnade), and a crowd came to hear his teaching in Solomon's Colonnade.
>
> Acts 5:12–14—The early believers met regularly in Solomon's Colonnade, and the group grew quickly.

Have your students answer the following questions:

1. What can we learn from the fact that the early Christians met in the Temple courts?

2. Why would Jesus have come here to teach? (Possible answers: There were large crowds, people sought God here, the Temple symbolized the presence of God, Jesus would fulfill the means of forgiveness that people were looking for at the Temple, God's people were there.) NOTE: Encourage your students to think of other reasons. Help them see that Jesus, the disciples, and the early church all centralized their teaching in the Temple courts. Remind your students that we must never forget our Jewish roots or neglect to share Jesus with Jewish people.

3. What lesson can be found in the fact that it was referred to as Solomon's Colonnade?

OPTIONAL — Digging Deeper I: The Southern Stairs (*20–40 minutes*)

(This section requires the use of the optional full-color overhead-transparency packet. For information on ordering it, see page 307.)

See Overhead Transparencies 28 ("Modern-day Jerusalem from the South"), 33 ("The Southern Stairs"), 34 ("Scenes from the Southern Stairs"), 36 ("Ancient Jerusalem from the South"), and 40 ("The Temple Mount"), and their descriptions, in Lesson 22.

Step Two: "Pentecost Fulfilled"

1. Introductory Comments

There is significant truth in the statement "Pentecost is the birthday of the church." On this day, the new community of Jesus' followers was empowered and began its mission to bring the kingdom of God to the world. But the statement is also an oversimplification. Pentecost did not occur in a historical or cultural vacuum. Point out the following details to your students.

- Pentecost was a festival, given by God to Israel at the time of Moses.
- It had been celebrated for more than 1,200 years by the time the fulfillment God promised occurred.
- It was one of three feasts that required the Jewish people to go to Jerusalem.
- Much of the symbolism of the fulfillment of Pentecost finds its meaning in the Jewish experience of the Hebrew Bible (the Old Testament).

This study will investigate the fulfillment of Pentecost in the context God created for it. The significance for all Christians will be enhanced as His Spirit continues to dwell in His community—the church. Students should read the handout "Temple of the Spirit" before beginning this study.

2. The Jewish Feast of Shavuot (Pentecost)

a. Old Testament Background

Ask your students to read Leviticus 23:15–22; Numbers 28:26–31; and Deuteronomy 16:9–12. Then point out the following information.

- This celebration was called the Feast of Weeks. This was the feast of the harvest.
- The Feast of Weeks was celebrated 50 days after Passover Sabbath (Leviticus 23:16). Because of this, it was called Pentecost, from the Greek word for "50 days" (Acts 2:1). This put it in the third month of their year Sivan.
- Pentecost was one of three feasts on which all men were required to appear before God at the Temple (Deuteronomy 16:16).
- This feast was celebrated at the end of the wheat harvest and included an offering of new grain (Leviticus 23:16).
- Those celebrating Pentecost were to show their concern for the poor by leaving the edges of their fields unharvested and leaving the grain they dropped on the ground so those in need could gather what was left (Leviticus 23:22; see also Leviticus 19:9–10).

b. The Jewish Tradition of Shavuot in Jesus' Time

The Jewish beliefs and practices of Shavuot from Jesus' time are well attested with some difference of opinion. In addition to the practices outlined above, these included interpretations of the Bible from the religious leaders. Some of those interpretations are listed below, along with the bases for the interpretations.

- Shavuot was believed to be the day God gave the Torah on Mount Sinai.
- Exodus 19:1 indicated that the Israelites arrived at Mount Sinai in the third month, the same month in which the Bible placed Shavuot.
- 2 Chronicles 15:10–13 described a covenant renewal (calling people back to Torah) in the third month, believed to be on Shavuot.

- Jewish writings from before the time of Jesus included specific reference to the Law being given on Shavuot (Jubilees 6:17), and the Essenes at Qumran celebrated a covenant renewal on that day for the same reason.

- The Bible readings for the synagogue and Temple on Shavuot were the following:

    Exodus 19:1–20:26—the story of God giving the Torah (the Law).
    Ezekiel 1:22–28—including a description of God's appearance with sound and fire.
    Ruth—a story set at harvest time.

c. Conclusion

It is clear that Shavuot (Pentecost) was a time of great celebration centered in Jerusalem and around the Temple. It was connected in the minds of the people with the giving of the Law, and its celebration included showing concern for the poor.

Ask your students the following questions:

1. What would have been the "mood" in Jerusalem on Shavuot?

2. Who would have been there?

3. Why were the disciples there? (See Acts 1:4.)

4. What would they be doing on Shavuot?

5. How does the Old Testament background add to your understanding of God's creation of the new community of Jesus?

6. Before this study, did you know that Pentecost had been a Jewish celebration for more than 1,200 years? Is it important to understand this information?

OPTIONAL — Digging Deeper II: Jesus and the Feasts *(20–40 minutes)*

God planned carefully for the work of Jesus. Included in His plan was a feast system, crucial to the Jewish people's relationship to Him, which also symbolized Jesus' work of redemption. Review the following information with your students. Point out that these are the first four of seven feasts God gave the Israelites.

1. **Passover.** Jesus' triumphal entrance into Jerusalem happened on the day the lamb was chosen, and He died at the time the Passover lamb was killed in the Temple. NOTE: For more information, see Lesson 23, Guided Discussion 4 (pages 163–164); Lesson 24, Guided Discussion 5 (pages 175–176); and Lesson 25, study a under Guided Discussion 3 (page 205). These studies cover in more detail the connection between Jesus and Passover.)

2. **Feast of Unleavened Bread.** Jesus was buried on the day this feast was celebrated. NOTE: For more information, see Lesson 25, study b under Guided Discussion 3 (page 205). It covers in more detail the connection between Jesus and the Feast of Unleavened Bread.

3. **Feast of Firstfruits.** Jesus rose from the dead on this day. NOTE: For more information, see Lesson 25, study c under Guided Discussion 3 (pages 205–206). It covers in more detail the connection between Jesus and the Feast of Firstfruits.

4. **Pentecost.** Jesus sent His Spirit on this day to indwell His community of believers, the church.

3. Guided Discussion: The Wind of God

This study will explore the meaning of the events in the fulfillment of the feast of Pentecost in the setting of the Temple in Jerusalem and in the context of the meaning of the festival for the Jewish people. In each section, read the passage, note the key points, and respond to the questions.

a. The Disciples Were in Jerusalem

- Acts 1:4–5; Luke 24:50–53

1. What were the disciples doing in Jerusalem? Why were they there? Would they be doing the same thing when Shavuot (Pentecost) arrived? Why or why not?

2. What does this activity tell you about the disciples? NOTE: Let your students reflect on this question. There are many answers, including "They continued their Jewish practices," "They obeyed Jesus," "They must have expected something to happen," and others.

b. The Day of Pentecost Arrived

- Acts 2:1–15

1. Where were the disciples? (Answer: They were all in one place—"the house"—where there were large crowds.)

2. In what location have people often assumed this great event took place?

Key Points: It is quite unlikely that the location was the Upper Room. There is not enough room there for such large crowds. More important, the Bible gives significant clues that the location was near or in the *Temple*. Point out the following evidence:

- Luke 24:53—The disciples were continually in the Temple.

- Acts 2:1,15—These events took place during Pentecost, one of the great religious festivals. During Pentecost, people went to the Temple for presentation of their offerings. Also, it was 9:00 A.M., the time when the morning ceremony was held in the Temple. (The daily service began at dawn with a sacrifice and continued for a considerable amount of time, ending with the offering of incense. Nine o'clock would have been near the end of the morning service.) It is likely that the specific offerings of Shavuot (two leavened loaves and animals—Leviticus 23:16–21) were being offered at 9:00. Certainly, the disciples—religious Jews who were continually in the Temple—would have been there for this service.

- Acts 2:2, 7:47—The Jews called the Temple "the house." (Many Old Testament passages simply referred to the Temple as "the house," although the English translation is "Temple." See Ezekiel 40:5, 42:15, and 43:10 for examples. The King James Version retains the literal translation, "the house.")

Using the overhead transparency "The Temple Mount: A.D. 70," point out the following highlights:

- The Temple in the middle of the Temple Platform
- The Southern Stairs, the main pilgrim entrance to the Temple (where the video for this lesson was filmed)
- The Gentile Court

Some scholars believe the events of Acts 2 took place on the Southern Stairs. That could be, because the stairs had been used in the past for public teaching and there were ceremonial baths nearby, convenient for baptism. The stairs were also the place where thousands of pilgrims would have been entering and leaving the Temple Mount.

Others believe the disciples were elsewhere in the Temple courts. No one knows for sure where they were in the Temple area.

Read the following passage and answer the questions.

- Acts 2:5—The people in the crowd were "from every nation under heaven."

1. Why would people have come from "every nation" at this time of year? NOTE: Remind the students of the destruction of the 10 tribes by Assyria (2 Kings 17:23) and the captivity of Judah under Babylon (2 Chronicles 36:20), both of which scattered the Jewish people around the world.

2. What does this crowd indicate about God's planning? Why was it important to have Jews from "every nation" become followers of Jesus?

c. The Pentecost Events

We can learn many lessons from the giving of the Holy Spirit on Pentecost. This study explores the specific context of the Jewish feast of Pentecost and its implications for the fulfillment of Pentecost. This focus is not to diminish the other meanings of that great event, including the other gifts of the Spirit and the beginning of the new church.

1. **The Jews believed that Pentecost celebrated Moses' receiving of the Torah from the Lord on Mount Sinai.**

   - Acts 2:1–3—God's presence was accompanied by the sound of wind, tongues of fire, and the gift of language (tongues).

     Exodus 19:16–19—God's presence was accompanied by the sound of thunder, fire, and smoke. (Note that the Hebrew word for *thunder* is literally translated "voices.")

   - Exodus 32:1–4,19–20,27–28—When the Torah was given, the people were worshiping the calf. As a result of God's anger, *about* 3,000 people died.

     Acts 2:38–41—When the Spirit was given, the people repented, and *about* 3,000 people believed (came to spiritual life). Paul pointed out that the letter of the law kills, but the Spirit gives life (2 Corinthians 3:6).

   - Exodus 31:18—At Mount Sinai, the law was written on stone tablets.

     2 Corinthians 3:3—At Pentecost, the law was written on the hearts of the people (Jeremiah 31:33).

   - Exodus 24:13—Sinai was called "the mountain of God." This is where the Torah was given.

     Isaiah 2:3—The mountain on which Jerusalem was built was called "the mountain of the Lord."

     Ask your students to answer the following questions:

     a. How does it help you understand Pentecost to recognize that it was a celebration of the giving of the Torah on Mount Sinai?

     b. Why would God plan so precisely and carefully to make sure fulfillment of His promise occurred on this day?

     c. If the Torah became the teacher for the Old Testament community of people, what became the teacher for the new community of Jesus' followers? (Answer: *Torah* means "teaching," and the Spirit is to be our Teacher. See John 14:26.)

2. **God's presence was in the Holy of Holies in the Temple. On the fulfillment of Pentecost, it moved out of "the house" into a new "temple"—the people of God. This is the key to Pentecost: It gave God's power to His people!**

- Exodus 25:17–22—God met Israel on the cover of the ark between the cherubim.

- 2 Chronicles 5:7–8,13–14—The ark and the presence of God moved into the Temple.

- Ezekiel 10:4–5,18–19, 43:1–5—In Ezekiel's vision, God's glory left Solomon's Temple before it was destroyed. In his later vision, it returned to the new Temple. (Some scholars believe this refers to the second coming of Jesus; others think it refers to the Spirit returning to the restored Temple of Jesus' time. It is likely that both beliefs are true. Certainly, the Temple symbolized the presence of God to the Jews of New Testament times.)

- Acts 2:1–4—"The house" (probably the Temple) was filled with the sound of a roaring wind, and fire rested on the disciples. Note the following points:

  The Hebrew term for "Holy Spirit" (*Ruach HaKodesh*) means "Holy Wind." (See Isaiah 63:10–11, where *Ruach HaKodesh* is translated as "Holy Spirit"). Throughout the Old Testament, *Ruach*, or "wind," is the word for "Spirit" when applied to God (Genesis 1:2). So, clearly, the sound of the wind was supposed to remind the audience of the presence of God (Ezekiel 37:9,14; John 3:8).

  The Temple readings that day (Exodus 19:1–20:26; Ezekiel 1–2) refer to the sound of wind (Ezekiel 1:4; see also verse 24) and the presence of fire (Exodus 19:18) as evidence of God's presence.

- Romans 8:9; 1 Corinthians 3:16–17, 6:19—The church as a community, and the believer as an individual, became the new Temple (3:16).

The symbolism of this fulfillment can be summarized as follows: God's presence had been recognized in the Temple. God's presence moved (with the wind and the fire as evidence) into a new "temple"—the community of Jesus and the individual disciples.

Ask your students to answer the following questions:

a. Where is God's presence today?

b. How does God's presence there affect how God's people should live? How is God's presence made known in our world?

c. Where do you look to find the presence of God? NOTE: Point out that in addition to His presence in believers, God's presence can be found in experiences. It is clear, though, that one dimension of the life of a follower of Jesus is to become His presence, His love, and His truth to the world (1 Peter 2:12; Matthew 13–16).

- Acts 1:8, 4:1–4, 19:20; 2 Corinthians 4:7

a. What does it mean to you that there is no greater power than the presence of God?

b. Why did God give His power to His followers?

c. How can you become a more powerful witness for God?

3. **The Jewish feast of Shavuot (Pentecost) was a feast celebrating the harvest God provided.**

- Leviticus 23:16–17—An offering of new grain and the firstfruits of the wheat harvest was brought to express thanks that the harvest had begun.

- Matthew 9:37–38; Luke 10:1–3; John 4:34–38—Jesus used the image of the harvest to describe those who would come to believe in Him. In a real sense, Pentecost was a fulfillment of Shavuot because it produced the "firstfruits" of the harvest of people, just as Shavuot celebrated the firstfruits of the grain harvest.

Ask your students to answer the following questions:

a. On this basis, why did God send His Spirit on Pentecost?

b. Read Acts 2:37–41. What is the result of proclaiming God's Word when it is blessed with His Spirit?

c. Read Acts 4:4, 5:14, 6:7. What was the rate of growth in the young community? What kind of people were added to the church? NOTE: Most, if not all, of them were Jewish.

d. What must God's community do today if we are to change our world with His message? How can we seek out God's Spirit more intentionally?

e. What can you learn about God's love, knowing that He was willing to "dwell" in an earthly temple of stone, the soul of a sinful human being?

4. **The Jewish feast of Shavuot is an expression of thanks to God for the gift of the harvest. One expression of being thankful is sharing with those who are in need.**

- Leviticus 23:22—The evidence of true thankfulness (true celebration of Shavuot) was not only bringing gifts to God, but also caring for the less fortunate.

- Acts 2:44–45—One might say that the evidence of true *fulfillment* of Pentecost is also care for the poor. (That is not to say that this is the only, or even the most important, part of Pentecost. Yet there is a sense in which being filled with the Spirit means showing concern for others.) The fact that these events took place on Pentecost highlights that connection. (See Galatians 5:22–26. The fruit of being filled with the Spirit affects the way we treat others.)

  One Jewish believer has said, "A Jew could not truly celebrate Shavuot without concern for the poor." In the same way, a follower of Jesus cannot experience the fulfillment of Pentecost without concern for those in need.

Ask your students to answer the following questions:

a. What does this teach the follower of Jesus who would be filled with the Spirit today? (How can Shavuot be fulfilled in our lives?)

b. Think of an example of a Spirit-filled Christian you know. What evidence of the Spirit's presence do you see in this person's life? What is his or her attitude toward people in need?

c. Jews read the book of Ruth on Pentecost. Why? How does this help highlight the meaning of Pentecost? NOTE: Ruth, a Gentile, was brought into the faith. She was poor, and she gleaned from Boaz's crop.

d. How did the help Ruth received from Boaz change the world? (See Ruth 4:17; Matthew 1:1,5–6.)

e. How might your helping someone make a difference in the world?

f. Who is an example of someone who was helped by a follower of Jesus and as a result went on to make a difference in the world?

g. Caring for those in need is not limited to helping those with physical needs. What other needs are we called to address? How do you demonstrate this dimension of being filled with the Spirit?

h. Think of someone who has a need that you could help meet but aren't. What is the need? How could you help meet it? If you feel comfortable doing so, relate your answer to the rest of the class.

i.   What can you plan to do to show God's presence, His Spirit, to this person through your actions?

After your students have given their answers, have them spend a few moments in prayer, asking God's Spirit to motivate and enable them to see the needs of others and find ways to meet them.

Conclusion

It is amazing how precisely Jesus fulfilled the feasts that had been celebrated for more than 1,200 years. He died on Passover (as God's Lamb), He was buried on the Feast of Unleavened Bread (as the Bread of Life), He arose on the Feast of Firstfruits (as the firstfruits of those who will be raised to life), and He sent His Spirit on Pentecost so His followers could begin "harvesting" those who would believe. Pentecost can be a powerful reminder to Christians that they have become the dwelling place for God's Spirit—His Temple. As Christians, we must become the presence of Jesus in our world. We must speak His words, demonstrate His love, and always try to bring His presence to our culture. As the Torah was the teacher through the Old Testament, the Spirit became the Teacher for the community of Jesus.

THE FEAST OF SHAVUOT

Leviticus 23:15–22; Deuteronomy 16:9–12; Numbers 28:26–31;
Exodus 23:16

Three times a year, all God's people were to appear before Him at the place He chose. The Jewish people determined that place to be the Temple in Jerusalem, where God's presence lived among the cherubim in the Holy of Holies. At *Pesach* (Passover), *Shavuot* (Pentecost), and *Sukkot* (Tabernacles), the Jews from around the world who were faithful to Yahweh went to the holy city on pilgrimage. The joyful crowd, speaking the languages of the countries from which they had come, crowded into the city—throngs of people singing, celebrating, making arrangements for their religious obligations, and finding places for their families. The city was alive with the passion and joy that only a religious festival could provide. The modern celebrations of Christmas and Easter pale in comparison to the magnitude of those great religious festivals. Their meaning and ceremony were deeply rooted in the past, but they also provided hope for the future as people were assured of God's continued care for them. It was no accident that those feast days were the times God selected for the great redemptive acts of Jesus, the Jewish Messiah. On the festival of Shavuot, He revealed His presence in a whole new way.

THE NAME OF THE FESTIVAL

This feast had several designations in the Bible. In Hebrew it was called *Shavuot,* meaning "weeks" (Exodus 34:22; Deuteronomy 16:9–10), from which the English "Feast of Weeks" was derived. This designation was taken from God's command to celebrate "seven full weeks" after the Sabbath of Passover week (Leviticus 23:15), placing the festival in the third month of the religious year, the month Sivan. Greek-speaking Jews referred to the feast as *Pentecoste,* meaning "50 days" (Acts 2:1), from which the English "Pentecost" was derived. This name was based on God's command that a special offering of new grain was to be made on the fiftieth day after the Passover Sabbath (Leviticus 23:16). It was also called "the day of firstfruits" (Numbers 28:26). (This is to be distinguished from the Feast of Firstfruits, which celebrated the beginning of the barley harvest—Leviticus 23:9–14.) This name was based on the offering of new grain and two loaves of bread baked from new grain as thanks for the wheat harvest. The name Feast of Harvest (Exodus 23:16) was based on the same harvest season.

CELEBRATION IN THE TEMPLE

The people observed Shavuot by bringing gifts to the Temple in Jerusalem and presenting them to the priests. An offering of new grain was presented as a gift of thanksgiving, along with two loaves of bread, baked from the finest flour made from new wheat grown in the land of Israel. According to tradition, each loaf was about 10 inches wide and about 16 inches long.[1] In addition, a basket of the seven species of the fruit of the land was brought to the Lord by each family (Deuteronomy 8:8).

Special sacrifices were made on the fiftieth day after Passover Sabbath. These included seven male lambs, one young bull, and two rams (Leviticus 23:18) as burnt offerings. One male goat was offered for a sin offering and two lambs for a fellowship offering. Even the best thank offerings (the grain, the two loaves, and the baskets of the seven species) were affected by sin and required a sin offering seeking atonement and a fellowship offering seeking renewed relationship with God. These symbols and their meaning form the background to the events of the Pentecost on which God sent His Spirit.

Following the ceremony of offerings, the Jewish people spent the afternoon and evening in a great festive meal, to which they were to invite the poor. This was both to rejoice in the renewed fellowship with God and to keep God's commandment to provide for the poor. Since true thanksgiving was demonstrated by a generous spirit toward those in need, God commanded the Israelites, "When you reap the harvest of your land, do not reap to the very edges of your field or gather the gleanings of your harvest. Leave them for the poor and the alien" (Leviticus 23:22; see also 19:9–10).

These special ceremonies took place after the normal morning sacrifice and worship service in the Temple, which began at dawn and ended in midmorning. A great crowd of pilgrims would gather in the Temple courts, filling the massive courtyard, during the morning prayers. As the offerings were presented and the sacrifices were made, portions of the Bible were read. According to Jewish history, those portions were Exodus 19–20 (the story of God's presentation of the Torah—including the Ten Commandments—to Moses on Mount Sinai) and Ezekiel 1–2 (Ezekiel's vision of God appearing in fire and wind). The fact that these activities occurred around 9:00 in the morning had great significance for the celebration the year Jesus died and was raised. As God had met the Israelites on the "mountain of God" (Exodus 24:13), on Shavuot He met them on the Temple Mount, "the mountain of the Lord" (Isaiah 2:3, 66:20).

SHAVUOT AND MOUNT SINAI

Sometime before Jesus' birth, a new emphasis was added to the harvest festival of Shavuot. The rabbis determined that this feast was the time when the Law (the Torah, including the Ten Commandments [2] had been given to Moses on Mount Sinai. Though the Bible does not specify the time of God's appearance to Moses, there are biblical reasons that indicate the rabbis' decision was probably right.

- Shavuot, celebrated 50 days after Passover, is in the month Sivan, the third month. The children of Israel reached Mount Sinai "in the third month" (Exodus 19:1). Since Passover and Sukkot were linked to the Exodus experience of Israel, it seemed right that the third pilgrim festival must be as well. At the very least, the giving of the Torah occurred in the third month, the month of Shavuot.[3]

- Torah taught that "man does not live on bread alone" (Deuteronomy 8:3), so it was appropriate to celebrate Torah on Shavuot, which emphasized God's gift of bread (the grain harvest symbolized by the two loaves).
- King Asa and the people of Judah assembled for a covenant (Torah) renewal in Jerusalem in the *third month,* which was the season of Shavuot, making another connection with Torah and the feast of the harvest.

The Essenes of Qumran, though they celebrated Shavuot on a different day than did the Temple authorities in Jerusalem, apparently had a covenant renewal celebration that day. The book of Jubilees, written well before Jesus' time, referred specifically to the Torah being given on Shavuot. It is clear that the people of the first century celebrated this feast to thank God for the harvest and to praise Him for the gift of Torah, which had been given in that same season. Though it is impossible to know whether the giving of the Law happened on the same day as Shavuot, the Bible clearly puts them in the same season at least. The Jewish people remembered them on the same day—a fact that had startling ramifications for the events of a certain Shavuot in New Testament times.

A CHRISTIAN SHAVUOT

Jesus returned to heaven 40 days after His resurrection (Acts 1:3). He told His disciples to return to Jerusalem to wait for the Holy Spirit and the power it would bring. The belief in the Spirit of God was not new for the disciples, for the Old Testament spoke of the *Ruach HaKodesh* (literally the "Holy Wind"), which empowered God's people (Isaiah 63:10–11; Psalm 51:11). The disciples remained faithful as Jews, meeting continually in the courts of the Temple (Luke 24:50–53). They must have had great expectations for the upcoming Shavuot. After all, Jesus had made this an unusual feast season—He had died on Passover, had been buried on the Feast of Unleavened Bread, and had been raised on the Feast of Firstfruits.

When the day of Pentecost (Shavuot) came, the disciples were together in "one place."[4] Many Christians assume that the place was the Upper Room, where the disciples had been staying. Instead, the evidence indicates that the place was in or near the Temple, possibly on the Temple Mount itself. Some scholars believe they were on the great staircase south of the Temple, where the pilgrims entered the Temple Mount (probably more than 1 million pilgrims during a feast). Though it is impossible to pinpoint an exact location for these events, there is significant support for placing this Pentecost event in an area of the Temple.

- It was Shavuot. All pilgrims gathered in the Temple for the service on this festive and holy day. Certainly, the disciples, who were "continually" in the Temple courts (Luke 24:53), would have been in the Temple on that day also.
- Great crowds from everywhere gathered to listen to Peter and the other disciples. Where would great crowds have gathered on a holy

feast day at the time of Temple service? Clearly, they would have been in the Temple somewhere (Acts 2:6–12).

- The disciples were all in one place. The sound of a great wind filled "the whole house" (Acts 2:2) where they were. The Temple is still called "the house" by Jewish people, referring to God's house. Even in Acts, it is called "the house" (Acts 7:47).[5]

- Peter declared that it was 9:00 in the morning, the time of the Pentecost service in the Temple. Certainly, the crowds, to say nothing of the disciples, would have been in the Temple at the time Shavuot ceremonies were conducted. Some believe that 9:00 was the time during which the selected passages were read, describing the appearance of God on Mount Sinai (in thunder, lightning, fire, and smoke) and Ezekiel's vision of His appearance (with the sound of wind and with fire).

- Peter spoke of the tomb of David as being there (Acts 2:29). The Bible recorded that David was buried in the "City of David" (1 Kings 2:10), the part of Jerusalem located near the Temple Mount.

- Three thousand people were baptized in response to the teaching of the disciples (Acts 2:41). Near the Southern Stairs, the pilgrim entrance to the Temple Mount, were *mikvoth*, ritual baths used by the worshipers before they entered the Temple grounds. There were not many places in Jerusalem with enough water for that many baptisms. The proximity of these many pools, already believed to symbolize the removal of the uncleanness of sin, is evidence that this location was near the Temple.

The events that occurred that Shavuot morning must have exceeded all the disciples' expectations. God's Spirit filled them with power and gave them abilities and gifts they could not have imagined possible. That same Spirit opened the hearts and minds of thousands so the community of Jesus grew from around 100 to more than 3,000 within a few hours. And the 3,000 came from every nation in the world. When they returned to their own cultures, they were eager missionaries who had to spend no time getting to know new cultures or languages. God's plan for the descendants of the survivors of the destruction of Israel (2 Kings 17) and the captivity of Judah (2 Chronicles 36) had been made thousands of years before. Now here they were, free under the government of Rome to return to Jerusalem and their Temple for Shavuot. When they arrived, God acted, and they became the first members of a great community of people. All Jews knew their Scriptures and the ways of God. At Pentecost they could add the final chapter—the coming of His Messiah.

THE MEANING OF SHAVUOT FOR CHRISTIANS

No event has been more significant for the ministry of the church than what happened on Shavuot that year. So much has been written over the centuries seeking to explain the meaning and significance of being "filled with the Spirit." We as Christians can learn from the Jewish setting of Shavuot in which these events took place.

There are remarkable parallels between the fulfillment of Pentecost and the events that occurred on Mount Sinai more than 1,200 years earlier. Since the Jews of Jesus' day believed that Pentecost celebrated the gift of Torah to Moses, these parallels would have been powerful to those Jewish believers. Note the following:

- Both events occurred on mountains known as "the mountain of God" (Exodus 24:13; Isaiah 2:3).

- Both involved similar sounds and symbols, such as wind, fire, and voices (Exodus 19:16–19; Acts 2:1–3). Note that the Hebrew for "thunder" (kolot) means "voices" (Acts 2:4). Jewish tradition said that the Israelites heard God speak in 70 languages.

- Both events involved the presence of God (Exodus 19:18,20; Acts 2:4).

- *About* 3,000 people died because of their sin when Moses received the Torah (Exodus 32:28). *About* 3,000 people believed (were born again into new life) when the Spirit came (Acts 2:41).[6]

- At Mount Sinai, God wrote His revelation on stone tablets (Exodus 31:18). On the fulfillment of Pentecost, God wrote His law on people's hearts as He had promised He would (2 Corinthians 3:3; Jeremiah 31:33).

- *Torah* means "teaching." The Spirit, given on Shavuot, also became the "Teacher" of the new community of Jesus' followers (John 14:26).[7]

These parallels are amazing evidence of God's careful planning, ensuring that the coming of the Spirit occurred in a context in which it was understood. The followers of Jesus were to be God's community. Their teacher, applying Torah in light of Jesus' work, was to be the Spirit of God. When the Spirit applies God's teaching to the hearts of people, there will always be life. Shavuot for the believers was as foundational and formative as Sinai had been for God's congregation, Israel. As Christians, we are in the tradition of Sinai, but Shavuot declares that God's Spirit brings us life.

The fulfillment of Pentecost provided another image that explains the Spirit's work. As noted above, Shavuot was the feast that celebrated the end of the wheat harvest. Jesus had frequently talked of the "harvest" of people who were to join His community (Matthew 9:37–38, 13:24–29,36–43; Luke 10:1–2; John 4:34–38). On Shavuot, the day of celebrating the harvest, His promise came true. Thousands believed and were brought to God (probably in the Temple).

There is another image of Shavuot that can help us understand the meaning of the events that year. God's presence had always been symbolized in the Temple since Solomon had built the First Temple. That was God's way of living among His people.

- Exodus 25:17–22, 40:34–38. God had agreed to meet His people on the cover of the ark. The ark was placed in the Tabernacle, where God's presence was symbolized by cloud and fire.

- 2 Chronicles 5:1–14, 7:1–3. The ark and God's presence, symbolized by fire, moved into the Temple.

- Ezekiel 1:4–28. Ezekiel's vision of God's presence in the Temple included fire and wind.

- Acts 2:1–3. The Spirit of God came to "the house" where the disciples were. God's presence was symbolized by wind and fire.

The symbolism seems clear. God's presence was in the Temple. It had been accessible to the people only through the high priest once a year (Hebrews 9:25). When Jesus died, the veil that blocked the people's access to God was ripped (Matthew 27:51), showing that through Jesus' blood, God can be approached at any time, by anyone.

On Pentecost, God moved out of "the house" (Temple) where He had revealed Himself and moved into a new temple—the community of the followers of Jesus (1 Corinthians 3:16–17, 6:19). They became God's new dwelling, His Temple.

The implications of this change are staggering. As the Temple had demonstrated God's presence to the world, the Christian community must demonstrate God's presence to our hurting world. We must bring His love, His truth, and His redemption to our culture, our communities, and our families. If the people around us are to see and know God, they will see Him through us. We have received the power to be His witnesses (Acts 1:8).

It is hard to comprehend why God would choose flawed human beings to be His temple, representing His presence. Of course, it is not easy to understand why God would dwell in a temple made with human hands, either (2 Chronicles 2:6). It is the infinite wisdom of God that led Him to choose to be present in our world through His people.

The question we must face is simple: How well do we represent God's presence? His love? His healing touch? If we believe in His Son, we have been empowered. Now we must be faithful as the Spirit writes His Torah (Law) on our hearts so that the world may know that He is God.

CONCLUSION

A final connection to the Jewish festival of Shavuot concerns the care for the poor. The feast provided opportunity for the people to give thanks to God and to bring gifts, expressing this gratitude. But true thankfulness involves not only thanking God the provider, but also sharing with others. In God's original instruction for this feast, He concluded by commanding the farmers to leave some of their crops in the field so the poor could harvest with dignity and also experience God's provision (Leviticus 23:22; see also Leviticus 19:9–10). In a sense, God was saying, "Don't come to say thanks to Me if you have no concern for those in need."

If the New Testament Pentecost is to be understood on the basis of the Old Testament feast of Shavuot, fulfillment must include concern for those in need. Many of the gifts of the Spirit described by Paul (Galatians 5:16–26) involve concern for others. But the clearest sign that the Spirit's coming was a fulfillment of the spirit of Shavuot is found in the event itself. The early believers, who were filled with the Spirit, held everything in common and shared with everyone who had need. This was a true Pentecost. As the new temple of God's presence, these people could not help but be concerned for others, who learned of God and His love through their acts of generosity.

Christians today are called to the same mission. Jesus' community and its members are His temple, His presence in our world. The Spirit teaches us (and others through us) that God is alive and real. We can share His love and His ways with others so they can know Him, too. People in need become the litmus test of the presence of the Holy Spirit in our lives. If we claim to have experienced Shavuot but have no concern for others, we are wrong. The Spirit leads His people to bring the presence and power of God to bear on all who need His healing, caring, correcting touch.

NOTES

1. The Mishnah (Menahoth 11.4) indicates that the loaves were seven handbreadths long and four wide. These loaves had protrusions of dough in each corner to represent the horns, or protrusions, on the corners of the altar.

2. *Torah* means "teaching," not "law" in the sense that Christians might think. This designation stressed a vibrant message for life, for it was to be continually taught and applied to all situations. Though it did provide "laws," or rules for life, it was not simply an organized collection of rules. It was much more—it was life itself.

3. *Passover* commemorated the deliverance the Israelites experienced when they became a nation. *Sukkot* celebrated the end of the 40 years of wandering, which resulted in the possession of the land God had promised. *Shavuot* celebrated the covenant God had made with Israel, which provided the life His people were to live.

4. The story is told in Acts 2.

5. The Old Testament frequently used this designation for the Temple. See Ezekiel 40:5, 42:15, 43:10; 2 Chronicles 3:4, 5:7, 6:9, 7:1, 7:3. See the King James Version, which translated the Hebrew as "house" rather than "Temple," the structure referred to as "the house" or "the house of the Lord."

6. Paul spoke of the comparison between the Torah for Israel and the Spirit for the church. He pointed out that the letter kills, but the Spirit (which did not negate Torah) brings life as the Torah is written on the heart (2 Corinthians 3:3–6).

7. I am indebted to David Stern for this point. His work *Jewish New Testament Commentary* is an excellent study of the Jewish context of the New Testament. His treatment of Acts 2 is exceptional in providing understanding of Shavuot as it was described in the New Testament.

TOTAL COMMITMENT

For the Teacher

Throughout this curriculum series, we have learned that God makes Himself known through His people. God expects His people to live in such a way that the world may see God through their lives. The faithful people of the Bible—like David, Ruth, Hezekiah, and Esther—lived out their commitments to God and were blessed for doing so. Others lived for themselves—Ahab and Jezebel, for example—and were successful for a while. When they died, though, they left behind nothing of value because of their failure to recognize God as the focus of their lives.

We complete our study of the land and the people of Israel by looking at one of the greatest, most powerful people who ever lived in the land of Israel. There has never been another king like Herod, but unfortunately, he lived only for himself. He left a legacy in the scattered remains of his glorious building projects, including the incredible harbor city of Caesarea, where the video for this lesson was filmed. Yet despite Herod's self-serving perspective, God had a purpose for him. His accomplishments helped the early believers bring the message of an even greater King to the world. Herod even helped bring the gospel to non-Jews—the Gentiles. Your students will be blessed to discover that God can use people like Herod. They will be challenged to live in a way that Herod never did—living to bring honor to God by showing others what He is like and how to find Him.

To begin this study, ask your students to name the greatest kings and queens the land of Israel has known. Let them give several names and briefly state why each individual was great. Tell your students that this study will focus on the greatest of the kings, helping us discover true greatness before God.

Your Objectives for This Lesson

At the completion of this section, you will want your students:

To Know/Understand

1. Why Herod built Caesarea.
2. The various buildings and features of Caesarea.
3. The Bible events that happened at Caesarea.
4. The contrast in worldviews between Jerusalem and Caesarea.
5. The way the early missionaries faced the cultures of their day.
6. How God used Caesarea.
7. The story of the two stones.
8. How God uses evil for good.

To Do

1. Commit to being witnesses for God in their culture.
2. Learn to build and live for God and not for themselves.

3. Recognize the need to speak out against cultural evils rather than try to escape them.

4. Make a total commitment to live for God as His witnesses.

How to Plan for This Lesson

Because of the volume of material in this lesson, you may need to divide it into several class sessions. To help you determine how to do that, the lesson has been broken into segments. Note that the time needed may vary significantly, depending on elements such as the leader, the size of the class, and the interest level of the class.

If you wish to cover the entire lesson in one session, you should complete Unit One. This unit provides a guided discussion covering the major points in the video. It does not go into great depth. If you wish to go into greater depth on any of the points in Unit One, they are covered more thoroughly in the remainder of the material.

How to Prepare for This Lesson

Materials Needed

Student copies of the maps:	"The Roman World"
	"Land of Jesus' Ministry"
Overhead transparencies:	"The Roman World"
	"Land of Jesus' Ministry"
	"New Testament Chronology"
	"Caesarea"
Student copies of the handouts:	"Herod the Great" (Lesson 22)
	"In Herod's Footsteps: The Dynasty Continues"

Video: **Total Commitment**

Overhead projector, screen, TV, VCR

1. Make copies of the maps listed above for your students.

2. Prepare the overhead transparencies listed above. (You'll find them at the back of the book.)

3. Make copies of the handouts listed above for your students. (If possible, students should receive and read these handouts before the lesson.)

4. Review the geography of the lands of the Bible from the "Introduction."

5. Determine which **unit** and which **Digging Deeper** sections, if any, you want to use in your class session(s). NOTE: You can use these sections in any order you wish (e.g., you might want to use **Digging Deeper III,** but not **Digging Deeper I** or **Digging Deeper II**).

6. Prepare your classroom ahead of time, setting up and testing an overhead projector and screen (for the overhead transparencies) and a TV and VCR. If you plan to hand out biblical references for your students to look up and read aloud, prepare 3x5 cards (one reference per card) to distribute before class.

Lesson Plan
UNIT ONE: Video Review

1. Introductory Comments

The city of Caesarea represented several things. It was the crowning accomplishment of Herod the Great. It was the gate to Rome and the entryway for the Roman worldview into the land of Israel. It was a very pagan city where people held the humanistic values of Hellenism. But it was also the place where several early believers went to challenge this pagan lifestyle with the message of Jesus—not only among the common people, but also among those who shaped the culture. It was the place where the gospel first reached the Gentiles in large numbers. Its port, which Herod built to win fame and fortune for himself, was the place from which the early missionaries left on their travels. A study of these contrasts in the city of Caesarea can provide an opportunity for you to discover whether you have made a total commitment to God and His message, and how you can address the pagan values and practices in our own culture.

2. Show the Video *Total Commitment* (18 minutes)

3. Map Study: Caesarea

HINT: *Begin this map study session by reviewing the geography of the overall region and working down to the city the lesson is dealing with—Caesarea.*

Using the overhead transparency "The Roman World," point out the following areas, and have your students locate them on their maps.

> Rome
> Mediterranean Sea
> Egypt
> Judea
> Caesarea
> Asia Minor

Using the overhead transparency "Land of Jesus' Ministry," point out the following areas, and have your students locate them on their maps.

> Bethlehem
> Jerusalem
> Capernaum
> Galilee
> Sea of Galilee
> Idumaea
> Caesarea
> Joppa
> Via Maris
> Masada
> Herodion
> Jericho

4. Guided Discussion: Herod's Caesarea

a. Caesarea

Caesarea was one of Herod's greatest accomplishments. One of the wonders of the ancient world, it was a magnificent city with modern stadiums, a theater, and running water. Its construction took place from 22 to 9 B.C. Herod spared no expense in making it the greatest seaport in his world.

Using the overhead transparency "Caesarea," explore the features of this demonstration of Herod's magnificence. Note the relationship of the city to the Mediterranean Sea. There was no natural harbor, so Herod had to create one. The city was built around this harbor.

Point out the major features of Caesarea:

> harbor (Sebastos)
> palace
> theater
> amphitheater
> hippodrome
> temple of Augustus
> aqueduct

b. Caesarea and the Gospel

Ask your students to read the following passages and answer the questions.

- Matthew 27:11–26; John 18:28–40—Pontius Pilate, the Roman governor of Judea, lived in Caesarea. A stone found in 1961 was a dedication plaque for a temple Pilate built.

1. How close did Pilate get to the truth?

2. Do you think Jesus hid His message from the powerful secular world?

3. What can you learn from Jesus' interaction with Pilate?

- Acts 10:1–46

1. Who was Cornelius? Where was he from? Where did he live?

2. What was Peter's message? How did Peter present the message to his powerful audience?

3. How did this audience react to what Peter said?

4. What can you learn from this story? (NOTE: Caesarea could be compared to Hollywood, and Cornelius was one of the culture shapers of his day.) How can you apply Peter's example to our culture?

5. How did Peter's vision affect your life? NOTE: People who are not Jewish would not have received the gospel unless God had opened the way, as He did here with Peter. Caesarea was the place where the gospel first formally went to Gentiles.

- Acts 12:1–5,18–24—Herod Agrippa was the grandson of the king who built Caesarea. The entire family was committed to bringing secular values to the nation. History recorded that this event took place in the theater of Caesarea (where the video *Total Commitment* was filmed).

1. What was Herod's reaction to the Christian message?

2. What was Herod living for? How was he like his grandfather? (See Matthew 2:13–18.)

3. How do the values of parents affect their children?

4. What kind of people today are like Herod?

5. What can you learn from Peter's reaction to Herod's resistance?

- Acts 9:28–30, 11:25–26, 27:1—Paul started at least two missionary trips at Caesarea. Herod's port, built to bring Roman support and culture to the area and to bring Herod wealth and fame, was used by God to spread the gospel.

1. What does this teach you about God and His control over circumstances?

2. Can you think of another example in which God used evil people or events to accomplish His purpose? NOTE: Genesis 50:19–20 provides one example.

3. What elements of our culture are used for sinful purposes but also can enhance the spread of God's message? How could Christians make better use of these things?

- Acts 23:31–35, 24:24–26, 25:23, 26:9–32—Agrippa II was Herod the Great's great-grandson, and Bernice was Agrippa's sister; Felix was the Roman governor married to Drusilla, grand-daughter of Herod the Great; Festus was Felix's replacement; Paul was kept in Herod's palace in Caesarea (Acts 23:35).

1. What was Paul's message to these powerful, pagan people?

2. Why do you think he didn't compromise his message to make it more acceptable or to preserve his own safety?

3. What can you learn from these stories?

c. **Application**

Ask your students to answer the following questions:

1. What in our culture is comparable to Caesarea (the source of pagan values)? How can Christians boldly confront these values?

2. What can you do to more effectively challenge the pagan world around you?

3. How important is a person's lifestyle to his or her message? Does your lifestyle give you opportunities to speak your message? How?

4. Why do you think Jesus has demanded total commitment from His followers?

5. How does total commitment show itself in the Christian's life?

5. **Conclusion**

Two types of stone are shown in the video *Total Commitment*. From these stones, we can learn a key lesson in being God's witnesses and pointing others to Him. One of these stones is marble; the other is limestone. Remember their stories.

Marble—The great king Herod imported marble from Italy to build his glorious city of Caesarea. Many of Herod's cities and buildings were covered with this stone. He built these magnificent structures so people would remember him and honor him as a great king. Herod lived for himself.

Today these magnificent creations are in ruins. Pieces of marble litter the land and are buried under the sea. At Caesarea, much of Herod's beautiful marble washes up on the shore of the Mediterranean, where it was thrown by conquering armies. People walk along the shore and pick up broken pieces of Herod's monuments to himself. Because he built only for himself, nothing is left but ruins. Most people remember nothing of Herod except his slaughter of babies in Bethlehem at Christmastime.

Limestone—When he was a boy, King David picked up limestone in a small brook in the Valley of Elah. Because he was a shepherd, he was familiar with slings and stones. When his God was challenged, David did the only thing he knew how to do in defense—he threw a stone.

Before David killed Goliath, he told his giant enemy why he was going to throw the stone: "The whole world will know that there is a God in Israel" (1 Samuel 17:46). David saved God's people, Jesus' earthly ancestors, and he has never been forgotten. His is one of the first stories children learn. The effects of what he did will endure forever because what he did, he did for God and not for himself.

Herod and David were both great kings. Both loved stones. Herod built for himself, and people today pick up the ruins of what he left behind. David acted for God, and we will never forget his great legacy.

We, too, have been given stones. Our stones are talents, opportunities, resources, and training. Some of us have marble—many talents and great opportunities and resources. Others have limestone—ordinary talents and responsibilities. It doesn't matter what stones we have; we are building with our lives. The question is, Whom do we build for? If we are building for ourselves, whether marble or limestone, someday others will pick up the broken pieces of our dreams—because that's all that will be left. If we are building for God, whether marble or limestone, what we build will stand forever.

Spend a few moments in prayer, asking our Lord to help us commit totally to Him as His witnesses so that the world may know that He is the one true God.

UNIT TWO
"Caesarea: Herod's Glorious Seaport"

1. Introductory Comments

We have one last theme to learn in this study: God did not limit His message to the land of Israel or to the Jews. His command was that His followers "go and make disciples of all nations" (Matthew 28:19). In an ironic way, God used the accomplishments of Herod—the self-centered genius who came so close to the true King, Jesus—to fulfill part of this great commission. Christians must hear God challenge them to be His witnesses everywhere. But we must learn from Herod's failure as well. Herod lived so that the world would know about Herod. We must live so that the world may know about God.

2. Map Study: Caesarea

HINT: *Begin this map study session by reviewing the geography of the overall region and working down to the city the lesson is dealing with—Caesarea.*

Using the overhead transparency "The Roman World," point out the following areas, and have your students locate them on their maps.

> Rome
> Mediterranean Sea
> Egypt
> Judea
> Caesarea
> Asia Minor

Using the overhead transparency "Land of Jesus' Ministry," point out the following areas, and have your students locate them on their maps.

> Bethlehem
> Jerusalem
> Nazareth
> Capernaum

Galilee
Sea of Galilee
Idumaea
Caesarea
Joppa
Via Maris
Masada
Herodion
Jericho

3. Review the Overhead Transparency "New Testament Chronology"

Using the overhead transparency "New Testament Chronology," highlight the following dates for your students:

63 B.C.	Roman conquest of Judea
37 B.C.	Herod's reign begins
4 B.C.	Herod's death
ca. 6 B.C.	Jesus' birth
ca. A.D. 30	Jesus is crucified
ca. A.D. 35	Paul's conversion
A.D. 44	Herod Agrippa's death
A.D. 46–61	Paul's missionary trips
A.D. 57–59	Paul's imprisonment in Caesarea
A.D. 66–73	First Jewish Revolt against Rome
A.D. 70	Destruction of Jerusalem and the Temple

4. Show the Video *Total Commitment* (18 minutes)

5. Guided Discussion: Herod and Rome

Students should read the handout "Herod the Great" before beginning this study.

a. The Idumaean King

The contrast between Jesus and Herod is much more significant to the writers of the Bible than one might expect. We have established that there is a geographical link. Jesus was born five miles from Herod's main palace in Jerusalem and less than that from his greatest palace at the Herodion. Bible readers have always known that Herod enters the Christmas story as the evil tool of Satan, who would end God's planned redemption by slaughtering the baby boys of Bethlehem.

But there is an even greater link between these two kings, a spiritual connection that clarifies the historical and the geographical. God planned for Herod to be in place so the person and work of Jesus would be seen in exactly the way He wanted. To understand this connection, we must explore the person of Herod more fully in contrast to the person of Jesus.

It was difficult for those who heard of Jesus' birth to accept that He was Messiah. He entered our world poor and weak—a baby born in a stable to a young peasant girl. By contrast, Herod was incredibly strong. It was even more difficult to comprehend because of *who* each man was. Read the following passages and discover the dilemma.

1. Genesis 25:21–26. Who would be the dominant person or nation? Contrary to cultural expectations, the older would serve the younger. Esau ultimately would serve Jacob.

2. Genesis 25:30, 36:1. Who were the descendants of Esau? The Edomites, which means "red," were the family line of Esau. They lived in the reddish mountains to the east and south of the Dead Sea.

3. Numbers 24:15–19. What prediction was made about the nation of Israel? About its relationship with Edom? The prophet Balaam, by God's revelation, predicted a star and scepter from Jacob—both cultural symbols of royalty. The result was that Edom would be conquered.

4. Numbers 20:20; 1 Kings 11:15; 2 Kings 8:20; Ezekiel 25:12–14; Obadiah 8–12. What characterized the history of relationships between these two nations? How was it like the relationship between Jacob and Esau? Note that the history of these two nations involved conflict and hatred.

5. Isaiah 34:8–15; Jeremiah 49:7–11; Ezekiel 35:15; Amos 1:11, 9:12; Obadiah (the entire book deals with this relationship). What did God predict would ultimately happen to Edom and Esau's descendants? Note that the complete destruction of Edom would occur in the "day of the Lord," synonymous with the coming of the Messiah.

   Conclusion: Stress that though there was constant conflict between the descendants of Esau and Jacob, ultimately Jacob's line would conquer Esau's and be enthroned forever in the person of the Messiah.

6. Point out to the class that (1) Herod was a powerful king who destroyed all opposition and (2) Herod's father was Idumaean (New Testament pronunciation of *Edom*, though referring to a territory greater than Edom), and his mother was a Nabatean (capital at the rose-red city of Petra, the actual territory of Edom). Ask your students to give their description of Herod as the people of the time would have known him. Then ask them to recognize the dilemma that Matthew 2:1 posed for the people of Jesus' time:

   • How could such a weak, insignificant baby be God's Messiah when compared with Herod? What do you know that Jesus' original audience didn't know to help you see through the dilemma?

   • Could you have bowed to Jesus when Herod seemed so powerful? Why or why not? Why was it such a great act of faith to believe in Jesus?

b. Caesarea: The Link to Rome

Herod was motivated by three things. (1) He was obsessed with maintaining his security from the real or perceived threats of his own subjects and other countries in the region. (2) He wanted to be linked to Rome because it provided a commercial market for the products of his land, it provided the imperial troops that kept him in power, and it provided Hellenism, the worldview Herod sought to establish in his kingdom. And (3) he wanted to go down in history as Israel's greatest king. Herod lived for his own glory.

Herod decided to build his own seaport and harbor because the other ports on the eastern coast of the Mediterranean were either outside his kingdom (e.g., Ptolemais) or hostile to him (e.g., Joppa). A seaport would also provide a contact point between the great trade route that passed through Israel from the east (Persia, Babylonia, and the Orient, as well as the Arabian peninsula) and from Rome across the sea. Herod wanted to curry favor with Rome because he needed its support to remain in power. Thus, through this planned seaport would travel spices, perfumes, incense, gold, silk, and the local olive oil—all on their way to Rome.

The location Herod chose to build his seaport was a small town on the Mediterranean with no natural harbor of its own. The new population—comprising Gentiles and soldiers from his army, to whom he gave land to settle there—was largely loyal to Herod (though there was also a large Jewish community whose resistance to Rome would spark the First Jewish Revolt).

Caesarea, which had the largest man-made harbor in the world, made Herod's realm a great commercial center. It brought in vast wealth, which he used to fund his other building projects: the Temple Mount in Jerusalem, Masada, Sebaste (Samaria), Jericho, the Herodion, and many others.

Herod named his city in honor of his patron, Caesar Augustus. The harbor was named Sebastos, the Greek translation of "Augustus."

Ironically, God used Herod's city for His own, and not Herod's, glory. There thousands of Gentiles first believed in Jesus; Philip spent nearly his entire ministry; and Paul either left or returned from all four of his missionary trips. These events will be highlighted later in this lesson.

c. Thoughts for Discussion

Ask your students to answer the following questions:

1. Can you think of other examples of unbelieving people or evil things that God used for good? (Possible answers: Jesus was crucified and raised from the dead; the Persian king Cyrus allowed the exiled Jews to return home—2 Chronicles 36:22–23; Joseph's brothers sold him, and God made him ruler of Egypt.)

2. Read Genesis 50:19–20. How does this apply to Herod's construction of a city designed to glorify pagan culture and Herod himself?

3. How does Genesis 50:19–20 apply to our world today? Can you think of a modern example of God using evil to accomplish His own good purposes? Discuss your example with the class.

OPTIONAL — Digging Deeper I: Herod the Builder *(40–60 minutes)*

(This section requires the use of the optional full-color overhead-transparency packets from Sets 3 and 4. For information on ordering them, see page 307.)

A. Lecture

Herod was one of the greatest builders Israel has ever known. Everything he built was on a massive scale, unheard of in his world. He used the most beautiful materials, including marble, granite, mosaics, frescoes, and gold. Everything he built seemed to defy nature. Masada's palace hung on the end of an 1,800-foot mountain. Jericho's palace was an oasis in the Judean desert. The Herodion was a huge, man-made mountain. The Temple Mount in Jerusalem was the largest in the world and included stones that weighed more than 500 tons each. Caesarea included a freshwater swimming pool in the Mediterranean.

It is important to recognize the greatness of Herod in order to fully understand the choice of faith people were called to make by accepting Jesus, the poor Galilean rabbi, as Messiah. God often uses the unexpected and the weak.

This exercise provides a review of Herod's building projects. Help your students see the genius Herod was from a *human perspective.* Then lead them to understand that God works from a very different point of view.

B. Visual Insights

If you have the optional full-color overhead-transparency packet and leader's guide for Set 3 (Lessons 11–18), this would be an appropriate place to view Overhead Transparencies 20 ("The Herodion: A Mountaintop Fortress"), 21 ("Inside the Herodion"), 22 ("The Herodion's Pool), and 23 ("The Herodion: Lower Palace"), along with their descriptions on pages 19–21 in Lesson 11; Overhead Transparencies 25 ("The Fortress Masada"), 26 ("Cistern of Masada"), 27 ("Storehouses of Masada"), and 28 ("The Opulence of Masada"), along with their descriptions on pages 43–45 in Lesson 12; Overhead Transparencies 18 ("Sepphoris Theater"), 41 ("Sepphoris: Bird on a Hill"), and 42 ("The Theater at Caesarea"), along with their descriptions on pages 144–145, in Lesson 16.

C. The Glory of Caesarea

Caesarea was one of the wonders of the ancient world. It was a magnificent city with modern stadiums, a theater, and running water. Its construction took place from 22 to 9 B.C. Herod spared no expense in making it the greatest seaport in his world.

Using the overhead transparency "Caesarea," note the relationship of the city to the Mediterranean Sea. There is no natural harbor, so Herod had to create one. Caesarea was built around this harbor. Point out the major features of this city to your students.

> harbor (Sebastos)
> palace
> theater
> amphitheater
> hippodrome
> temple of Augustus
> aqueduct

1. The Harbor

- The harbor was constructed on the coast, where there was no natural bay. Herod's workers created this harbor by building two breakwaters. The south breakwater was 600 yards long, and the north one was 300 yards long.

- The base for these breakwaters was made of concrete blocks, poured under water (sometimes over 100 feet deep). These concrete blocks measured 40 by 50 feet in size and were more than five feet thick. Archaeologists have discovered some of them with the wood forms still in place. Hydraulic concrete was a new invention in Herod's time. The concrete was made of volcanic sand that had to be imported from Italy.

- The entrance to the harbor was in the northwest corner. Two towers, topped with huge statues of Herod's family, stood on each side of the entrance. A lighthouse guided ships to port. It could be seen from miles away. It was named after Drusion, one of Augustus's sons.

- Lining the breakwaters and the harbor were vaulted storage rooms for the huge amounts of goods that passed that way.

- A smaller inner harbor was located near the temple of Augustus.

- The early missionaries found this harbor convenient as they came and went, bringing the gospel to the world. God had a different purpose for the harbor than Herod did.

2. The Palace

- Josephus described the splendor of Herod's palace. The consensus of scholars is that the palace was located on the peninsula.

- The palace's central feature was a large pool cut into the soft rock of the peninsula. It was 115 feet long, 60 feet wide, and eight feet deep. It is likely that a statue stood on a square base in the center of the pool. The pool is believed to have held fresh water. It would have been typical of Herod to defy nature by building a freshwater pool out in the saltwater of the Mediterranean.

- Colonnaded rooms surrounded the pool. On the west, a semicircular colonnade extended out to sea for the enjoyment of Herod's guests.

- On the east were various rooms, many with mosaic floors, including service rooms for the palace, hot and cold baths, and a large dining hall.

- It is likely that the apostle Paul spent two years of his life there as he was "kept under guard in Herod's palace" (Acts 23:35).

- While in Herod's palace, Paul had an opportunity to share the gospel with the most powerful people in the land of Israel (Acts 24–26).

Ask your students the following questions:

How did God use the glory of Herod's palace to spread the message about Jesus?

What are some examples of how God still uses the "magnificent" and the "powerful" to proclaim Jesus?

3. **Theater**

- Herod was determined to bring the Roman worldview, Hellenism, to his God-fearing subjects. Hellinism is similar to humanism; it is a people-centered lifestyle that glorifies human knowledge, accomplishment, and experience—a remarkably modern perspective. Herod introduced the theater, one of the leading culture-shaping institutions, to the Jewish people.

- The theater apparently was placed outside the city because its obscene and bawdy performances may have offended the Jews of the city.

- In Herod's day, the theater at Caesarea seated approximately 4,000 spectators, who sat on stone benches. The floor of the orchestra (the semicircular space in front of the stage where important people sat) was made of colorfully painted stone in Herod's time and later was paved with marble. The front of the stage (orchestra wall) was made of painted stone, imitating marble. There were six wedge-shaped sections of seats. The Bible recorded the death of Herod Agrippa I (Acts 12:19–23), which, according to Josephus, took place in the theater. It is also possible that Paul was interrogated there by Felix (who was married to Drusilla, Herod the Great's granddaughter) and Festus, as well as Agrippa II and Bernice, his sister (Acts 24–26).

- Caesarea's theater was seductive and overwhelming to the Jewish people, and it was resisted by the religious community. The values represented by Caesarea (and its theater) were antithetical to those of Jerusalem (and the Temple). Followers of Jesus today would do well to remember His words as they struggle in the conflict between Jesus' values and those of modern-day Hellenism, human secularism.

Ask your students the following questions:

What institutions in our culture would compare with Herod's theater? What kind of effect do these institutions have on our culture? How?

What are some examples of ways in which Christians compromise their values with the secular values of the culture? How do the culture-shaping institutions of our time affect the Christian community?

How can we affect our culture by participating in it but resisting its effect on us?

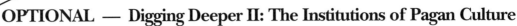

OPTIONAL — Digging Deeper II: The Institutions of Pagan Culture
(30–45 minutes)

HINT: *If you have Set 3 of this series, you may want to refer to Lesson 16, Unit 2, Step 2, Guided Discussion 3, section c ("Jesus and the Theater"), pages 142–143, and* **Digging Deeper V** *("The Theaters of Jesus' Day"), pages 144–146, for more information on this topic.*

A. The Hippodrome and Amphitheater

Point out the following information to your students.

- The hippodrome has only recently been discovered. Archaeologists have not published information concerning whether it dates to the time of Herod. Another hippodrome lay east of the city.

- The amphitheater has not been excavated, though its location is known.

- Herod promoted Hellenism through the sports festivals he sponsored in Caesarea and Jerusalem. The games would have been similar to the Olympics. Athletes came from all over the world, seeking glory and the prizes awarded by Herod himself.

- The games were often dedicated to pagan gods. They were performed in the nude. At some time, they involved bloodshed in human and animal gladiatorial contests. The religious Jews thought them immoral.

- During the First Jewish Revolt (A.D. 66–73), 2,500 Jewish prisoners were slaughtered in these arenas as gladiators or in combat with animals.

Ask your students to answer the following questions:

1. How are the values of our culture influenced by the world of sports?

2. Are athletics appropriate for Christians? What non-Christian values does our sports world promote?

3. How can Christians participate in sports without being affected by the non-Christian values they include?

4. How can Christians use athletics to honor God?

B. The Temple of Augustus

Point out the following information to your students.

- Herod built a great platform on arches. On the platform he built one of the largest temples in the world at that time. He dedicated it to the goddess Roma and the "divine" emperor Augustus. The foundations were larger than 125 feet by 175 feet, and the temple is believed to have towered nearly 100 feet above the raised platform.

- Archaeologists believe the walls were coated with plaster made from marble dust, which made the temple gleam white in the sun. It could be seen for miles around. The temple housed colossal statues of Roma and Augustus. Sacrifices to these gods were made by the people in front of the building.

Ask your students the following questions:

1. Why do pagan cultures create pagan gods? Are the two related? How?

2. What are the "gods" of our culture? Does our culture create pagan worldviews, or does the worship of these gods produce the views? Why do you answer as you do?

3. Read Acts 15:20,29; 1 Corinthians 8:1, 12:2; 1 Thessalonians 5:21; Revelation 9:20. Why were idols attractive in that world? Why would someone leave God to serve an idol?

4. Why are "idols" (false gods) attractive to people today? Why would people in our world choose to leave God for such idols?

C. The Aqueduct

Point out the following information to your students.

- There were no natural sources of fresh water in Caesarea.

- The aqueduct was nearly nine miles long. It collected water from springs on the slopes of Mount Carmel. The water was carried in a plastered channel that crossed a river on a bridge. It was then carried over lower areas on a series of arches and through a channel cut in the sandstone hills of the area.

- It provided fresh running water for the city and for Herod's palace.

D. Conclusion

Spend a few moments in prayer. Ask God to teach us how to use the institutions of our culture for His glory.

OPTIONAL — Digging Deeper III: The City of Caesarea *(40–60 minutes)*

(This section requires the use of the optional full-color overhead-transparency packet. For information on ordering it, see page 307.)

HINT: *The information in this section corresponds to some of the material given in **Digging Deeper II** above. It would be helpful to have the overhead transparency "Caesarea" available to compare with the ruins shown in the overhead transparencies below.)*

Overhead Transparency 49. Ruins of the Harbor. These ruins are of harbors built after the time of Herod. His harbor, which was built on concrete foundations in the sea, is no longer visible, although the base of the breakwater still exists beneath the water. This spectacular accomplishment brought Herod great wealth, which he used to fund his many other building projects, including the Temple Mount in Jerusalem. The harbor brought Roman culture and military support for Herod's rule to Israel. It is ironic that little remains of Herod's greatness besides a bad reputation and spectacular ruins. Despite the purposes Herod had in constructing the harbor, God used it as the starting or ending point of several of the missionary expeditions of the early Christians. Unlike Herod's kingdom, the kingdom Jesus established continues to grow.

Imagine standing with Paul as he looked out at the Mediterranean. God asked him to sail across that sea to bring Jesus to that world. Paul had the courage and dedication to go—not once, but several times. God gives a mission to each of us. We can all learn from the willingness of Paul.

Overhead Transparency 50. Scenes from Caesarea. Top: Herod's Arena. The remains of a great arena (or hippodrome—meaning "horse track") are emerging from the sand dunes of the Mediterranean shore. The stone seats in the foreground show the beginning of the curve of the southern end of the stadium. The Mediterranean Sea has eaten away the other side of the arena. The length of the stadium is apparent as the benches continue in the distance. In several places, walls were built by later civilizations who no longer used the arena. The northern end is near the buildings in the distance, showing how large the stadium is. The buildings on the left in the distance stand on the base of the breakwater of Herod's harbor. Since no results have as yet been published of these excavations, it is not clear who built this arena. Herod built a stadium in Caesarea, but it may not have been this one. The magnitude and style of this arena, however, do reflect those he constructed at places like Jericho and Jerusalem.

Herod brought the "games" into the Jewish culture as part of his attempt to Hellenize his kingdom. The events included Olympic contests of running, wrestling, and throwing the javelin. Chariot races were quite popular, as were gladiatorial contests involving men and animals. The games were often dedicated to pagan gods. The religious Jewish community found these arenas and their contests at odds with their belief in God, but the arenas were present in most large Hellenistic cities. They certainly had an influence on the local population, religious or not. Paul's use of athletic imagery (1 Corinthians 9:24–27; 1 Timothy 4:7) indicates his ability to communicate in the language and pictures that were familiar to his audience. As in our society, it would have been difficult to participate in activities like the games without accepting the pagan cultural values they encouraged.

Bottom: The Aqueduct. Herod's aqueduct was several miles long, bringing water to Caesarea from springs at the foot of Mount Carmel. For much of the distance, the water channel rests on a seemingly endless procession of arches. The plastered structure on the arches contains channels about 16 inches wide and 30 inches deep, in which the water flowed. It took amazing skill to build this long channel, beginning at the proper height so the water was still flowing when it reached the end. It took enormous wealth to pay the labor force needed to accomplish projects like this one. Caesarea was a key to Herod's prosperity.

Overhead Transparency 51. Herod's Palace. Only recently have these scattered remains been identified as Herod's palace. In the center was a freshwater pool now largely filled with silt and stones from the building itself. In the center is the podium believed to be the base for a large statue, probably of the emperor. The pool was 115 feet long, 60 feet wide, and eight feet deep. A freshwater pool out in the saltwater of the Mediterranean Sea was typical of Herod's projects, many of which seemed like attempts to defy nature.

Around the outside of the pool were the colonnaded buildings of the palace. Little remains of them except the marks on the seal rock seen to the right of the pool. The stone remains on the left date to a later period. In the distance, the curved western end of the palace is visible. Originally, it probably had a marble floor and a curved row of columns. People would have been on that marble "deck," enjoying the waves of the sea breaking against the palace. In the foreground, the colored sandbags cover a mosaic floor that was probably in the large dining room of the palace. The remains give some indication of the glory of Herod's construction. That the palace is in ruins highlights the fact that his work did not last because he built only for himself. Paul, who was imprisoned in this palace (Acts 23:35), spoke of a greater King for whom he was building. The kingdom of his King is still being built and will stand forever.

Overhead Transparency 52. The Ruins of Herod's Dream. These photographs show some of the remains of Caesarea. They hint at its original glory and the genius of the man who created this great port city. These ruins help us face the real question in life: For whom do we build? Ultimately, the answer to that question is far more important than what we build or how we build it. Jesus' building (1 Peter 2:5) still stands, is still being expanded, and will last forever. The rabbi from Galilee, who grew up learning how to build (probably with stone as much as wood), built a far greater house than did the Edomite king who used marble to construct the most glorious structures of his day.

Upper Left: **Mosaic Floor.** The remains of a mosaic floor in Herod's palace at Caesarea give hints of its former glory, although it has been nearly destroyed over time. Herod used mosaic floors frequently in his construction. Typically, his floors had designs like those shown here, using varying colors and geometric shapes.

Upper Right: **Marble Frieze.** This large piece of marble frieze (trim along the top edge of a building) was pulled from the Mediterranean by archaeologists. The beauty of the design is still evident after nearly two millennia. Since Israel has no natural marble, it had to be shipped from elsewhere, often from Italian quarries across the Mediterranean. Herod's love of extravagance and the finest building materials brought marble into his country in quantities unheard of before his time.

Lower Left: **Roman Statue.** The second commandment forbade making images. Hellenistic culture glorified the human form. These two worldviews clashed in the days of Herod as he tried (and largely succeeded) to mold his kingdom into a Hellenistic one. He imported great numbers of marble statues like this one to grace his palaces and fortresses. The religious Jews resisted this deliberate attempt to introduce what they viewed as paganism into their world.

Lower Right: **The Pilate Stone.** While excavating the theater in 1961, archaeologists discovered this stone, which was being used as a step in a small stairway. When they had uncovered it, they found that it was in secondary use. Originally, it had been the dedication stone for a temple that had stood nearby. The first line of writing on the stone ends with the name of the temple: *Tiberieum,* named after the emperor Tiberius. Line two gives the name of the one who dedicated the temple: *Pontius Pilatus*—Pontius Pilate. The third line gives his title: prefect of Judea. The fourth line is unreadable but probably indicated that he dedicated the temple. Since Pilate was in office from approximately A.D. 26–36, and Jesus was crucified by Pilate around A.D. 30, the stone was placed around the time of, if not during, the ministry of Jesus. In this temple, people offered their allegiance to the "divine" Tiberius. Ironically, Pilate met the real King of the universe but did not realize it.

OPTIONAL — Digging Deeper IV: Caesarea and Jerusalem *(20–30 minutes)*

Jewish tradition described Caesarea as the daughter of Edom. This is probably a reference to Rome. Edom, Israel's implacable enemy of the Old Testament, had become an "insiders' code" reference to Rome. As Edom had been a cruel enemy, so was Rome. As Edom was quite pagan, so was Rome. God's judgments against Edom were applied to Rome (Amos 1:11; Ezekiel 25:12, 35:12–14; Psalm 137:7; Obadiah). It is also likely that Caesarea was called the daughter of Edom because it was built by Herod, an Idumaean (Greek for "Edomite"). Whatever the reason for the identification, it clearly indicates that the Jews thought of Caesarea and its culture as a pagan enemy.

Make the following points to your students:

- Rome intentionally tried to shape world culture to make it Roman (Hellenistic). This happened in much the same way that the United States has helped shape the culture of the rest of the modern world.

- Herod was determined to speed up that process in Israel. Caesarea was a truly Roman city in every way. It was also the entryway of Hellenistic culture into the land. It became the Roman capital of the country.

- A first-century rabbi said: "If you hear that Caesarea and Jerusalem are both in ruins or both are flourishing peacefully, it cannot be true. Believe only a report that Caesarea is destroyed and Jerusalem is flourishing or that Jerusalem is destroyed and Caesarea is flourishing." The rabbi's statement indicates that the religious Jews understood that the secular values and practices so common in Caesarea were in complete opposition to those in Jerusalem, where Jews went to worship God in the Temple. The hedonistic spirit of Caesarea cannot exist peacefully with the God-seeking spirit of Jerusalem. The self-serving pleasure of the theaters and the arenas of Caesarea could not be accepted by people who lived to honor Yahweh, Creator of the world.

- Caesarea was a city designed totally for self-indulgence, glorifying human pleasure (and sin!).

Ask your students to answer the following questions:

1. What are some examples of activities in our culture that are like those in Caesarea? Discuss them with the class. (Possible answers: mindless television programs, seeking pleasure for its own sake [e.g., alcohol, gambling, etc.].)

2. Jerusalem represents the search for meaning and purpose in life by honoring God. Jerusalem existed to show the world what God is like. Jerusalem represents living up to commitments and being responsible for those whom God has trusted to our care. What are some aspects of our culture that are like that of ancient Jerusalem? (Possible answers: church, family, Christian business.) Who do you know whose life is similar to the values of ancient Jerusalem?

It is important to recognize that Israel was in the midst of a war for the souls of the people during New Testament times. Would they seek God, live for Him, and show the world what He was like by their lifestyle, or would they adopt Hellenism with its self-centered, pleasure-seeking, immoral lifestyle? As the Jews would have said, would Caesarea or Jerusalem prevail? Is there a similar war for the soul of our culture? How can you recognize it? Who is winning? What can you do about it?

Spend a few moments in prayer, asking God to give you a renewed dedication to resisting the pagan values around you. Ask Him to give you opportunities to spread God's message in our culture, as many people did at Caesarea.

6. Guided Discussion: It Happened at Caesarea

Caesarea was a fully Roman city whose culture was Hellenistic. Its lifestyle was one of pursuit of pleasure, self-centered glorification of human accomplishment, and hedonistic participation in the latest entertainment. The spirit of Caesarea was permissiveness—as long as no one's right to gratification was affected.

Caesarea was the entryway of Hellenism into Israel. It is true that not all Romans and Greeks came by way of Herod's port, but many did. The centurion of Capernaum (Matthew 8:5–13), the soldiers who crucified Jesus (Mark 15:39,44–45; Luke 23:47), and Cornelius the centurion (Acts 10) probably came through Caesarea. Pilate, another important figure in Jesus' ministry, also lived here.

God's purpose for Caesarea was much greater than Herod's desire to spread Hellenism. Not only was Caesarea the beginning or ending point for many of the missionary expeditions described in the Bible, but it was also the place where many of God's people spoke His message boldly to the pagans of their day.

The spirit of Caesarea (remarkably modern) was in direct conflict with the God-centered culture described in the Bible. The religious Jews resisted it passionately, sometimes violently. They avoided it when they could. Yet several of those dedicated to making God the center of their lives had an opportunity (sometimes in Caesarea) to share that message with those most responsible for introducing Roman culture to their world.

This section will highlight some of those confrontations and the people who dared bring God's Word to their modern culture. It will also consider how God chose to use the most modern city of that day for a very different purpose from what its creator (Herod) had envisioned. Each of the following people and events is somehow related to Caesarea. Explore that relationship, then note how boldly God's message was declared to the pagans. Think about what you can learn from the godly people who stood up to the culture of their time. In a very real way, you live in "Caesarea," too. How will you respond? What is God going to do through you?

a. Pilate and Jesus

Read Matthew 27:11–26; John 18:28–39. If possible, ask one or more of your students to read the preceding passages aloud. Then point out the following information to your students.

- Pilate was the Roman governor of Judea.
- Caesarea was the Roman capital of Judea.
- Pilate probably came to Israel from Rome via Caesarea and lived in Caesarea. A stone plaque was recently found, indicating that Pilate dedicated a temple in Caesarea to the Roman emperor Tiberius.

Ask your students to answer the following questions:

1. What do Pilate's questions of Jesus tell you about Pilate?

2. Hellenism makes truth dependent on human reason. How does this help explain the question in John 18:38?

3. What do Jesus' answers reveal about His desire to tailor His message to fit Pilate's pagan worldview?

4. How is our culture similar to Hellenism? What is truth in our culture? How is God's value system different from Hellenism? What is your view of truth? (See Psalm 31:5; John 17:7.)

5. What are some examples of people in our world who are similar to Pilate (i.e., the culture shapers)? How would you proclaim your view of God and the world to them?

6. Do you "hide" from the secular world around you, or do you challenge it with Jesus' message? What are some ways you can challenge it?

7. How can Jesus' followers today be more effective in presenting God's worldview and values to contrast the secular humanism of our time? Give specific examples of how this could be done.

8. What could you do to present God's worldview to those around you? Are Christians afraid of the secular world? Why or why not?

b. Peter and Cornelius

Read Acts 10:1–48. If possible, have several students read sections of the preceding passage aloud. Then ask them to answer the following questions:

1. Who was Cornelius?

2. What were Cornelius' religious beliefs? How did he live?

3. Whom did he invite to hear Peter's message?

4. How did this Gentile arrive at a belief in God? (Give this question serious thought.)

5. Who was Peter? What kind of person was he? Where was he?

6. Why did he need a vision before he was ready to go to the Romans? (See Acts 10:14,28–29.)

7. What was Peter's message? (See Acts 10:34–43.)

8. Why did Peter make such a bold proclamation? (See Acts 10:42.)

9. How would you have predicted that these non-Jewish, Roman soldiers would react? (NOTE: Remember—they were under Pilate's command.) Why?

10. How did they react? What caused this reaction? (See Acts 10:44.)

11. What are some lessons we can learn from this story, which happened in Caesarea? (Possible answers: No one is too unclean for God's forgiveness or for the gospel; God can open anyone's heart; we must be willing to proclaim boldly, even to those who we suspect have a different set of values.)

Again, Caesarea became the setting where God's kingdom message was spoken boldly in a very pagan, human-centered culture. The result, by God's blessing, was spectacular.

Ask your students to answer the following questions:

1. Why does the Christian community sometimes "hide" from secular culture and values (even in churches that do not reach out and speak out)?

2. How could you speak to the very heart of the culture around you? Do you have to be in that culture to speak to it? Why or why not?

3. How can the church develop a more "relevant" method or message without compromising the message's content? (NOTE: Peter walked 30 miles to bring Jesus' message to a very secular setting. He didn't just sit back and say, "If they want what I have, they must come to me.") Do you ever pursue non-Christians the way Peter did? Does your church?

4. How do you think God could transform the non-Christian elements of your world the way He did Cornelius and his family and friends? When have you seen Him do so?

5. Choose one way you might bring Jesus' message to the culture around you. Then spend a few moments in prayer, asking God for the strength you need to follow through on your intentions.

c. **Herod Family Pride**

Students should read the handout "In Herod's Footsteps: The Dynasty Continues" before beginning this section.

Read Acts 12:1–24. If possible, have your students read the story aloud, taking turns reading a verse or section. Tell your class that Josephus, a Jewish historian of that time, included this story in his writings. He added some more details:

- Agrippa I was Herod the Great's grandson.

- Agrippa I had been educated in Rome and had become a close friend of Caligula and Claudius, emperors of Rome. Claudius gave him Herod the Great's entire kingdom.

- The festival noted in Acts was in honor of the emperor Claudius.

- Herod's royal robe that day was made of silver, dazzling in the sun.

- The audience took place in the theater (where the video for this lesson was filmed). (See **Digging Deeper I,** "Herod the Builder," study C, section 3, in this lesson.)

- Josephus said Herod died of extreme pain in the stomach.

Ask your students to answer the following questions:

1. How was Agrippa I like Herod the Great, who built Caesarea? NOTE: Let students think about this for a while and then discuss their answers with the class. (Possible answers: Herod the Great tried to kill Jesus [Matthew 2:13–18]; Agrippa I killed James and planned to kill Peter [Acts 12:1–3]; both were driven by a desire for power and glory [Matthew 2:13–18; Acts 21–23].)

2. Read Acts 12:23. Whom did Herod live for? What was the result of his attitude?

3. What do we do that is similar to the way Herod lived? Discuss your ideas with the rest of the class.

4. Why is it so difficult to direct attention to God instead of ourselves? Is it fair to say that many societal and family problems are caused by people living for themselves? How can you avoid that problem?

d. Caesarea and Paul: Paul's Missionary Journeys

Paul, the great early missionary, spent a significant amount of time in Caesarea. It was for him a gate to and from the mission fields to which God had called him. Ironically, the great port Herod had built to bring in Roman culture and arms, to make himself wealthy through trade, and to establish his reputation as the greatest builder in the history of Israel was used by God to enhance the spread of the gospel.

Since God is working to bring redemption and restoration to His world, it is logical that He uses obedient people and good things to serve His purposes. But He also uses ungodly people and evil situations to accomplish His plan of salvation.

- Acts 9:30, 11:25–26. On Paul's (Saul's) first missionary journey, he went from Damascus to Caesarea (on the trade route) and then to Tarsus and Antioch. There the believers were first called Christians. The seaport of Caesarea was the place from which Paul sailed to Tarsus.

- Acts 18:22. Paul returned to Caesarea from his second mission trip. From there, he probably went to Jerusalem ("went up and greeted the Church"—verse 22—probably referred to Jerusalem) and then to Antioch—probably by ship, though the text does not say how he traveled.

- Acts 21:7. Paul returned to Caesarea from his third journey; then he went to Jerusalem, where he was arrested (Acts 21:17–35).

- Acts 23:23–35. Because Paul appealed to Caesar, he was sent to Caesarea and kept under guard in Herod's palace.

- Acts 24–26. Paul was examined by two prefects (Roman governors), Felix and Festus, and by Herod Agrippa II, the great-grandson of Herod the Great.

- Acts 27:1. From Caesarea's port, Paul sailed on his final journey, stopping in Rome and several other places before he was executed.

Ask your students to answer the following questions:

1. What can you learn from the fact that God allowed Herod to build a seaport that would be so important in the early spread of the faith, even though it was intended for other purposes? NOTE: The gospel first went to the Gentiles here—Acts 10. Philip spent 25 years in ministry in this city as well—Acts 8:40, 21:8.

2. Can you think of other great accomplishments God has used or is using for His kingdom? Discuss them with the class. (Possible answers: printing presses, radio, television, computers.)

3. Why is it important to use the best means our culture can provide to spread the gospel? Why would it have been unwise for Paul to walk rather than use the port of pagan Caesarea and the

wicked Herod? How is that example similar to Christians using tools of the culture to bring God to our world, even if others have used them for sinful purposes?

4. What would happen if Christians refused to use tools like television to spread God's message because others have used them for evil? Why?

5. Given that God will use human accomplishments for His purposes, why was it so foolish for Herod to build only for himself? How does that help you?

e. Caesarea and Paul: Paul's Appeal to Caesar

Paul went to Caesarea, the ultimate in pagan cities in ancient Israel. He met with the most powerful people of his day—people who were completely committed to the worldview that supported the Roman lifestyle of Caesarea. How did he react? Did he compromise his message? Did he say what was politically acceptable? The following passages hold the answers to these questions and can teach us some powerful lessons. The events described in these verses all took place in Caesarea.

- Acts 21:27–36—Paul was arrested.

- Acts 23:23–35—Paul was sent to Caesarea and held in Herod's palace.

- Acts 24—Paul was tried by Felix, the Roman governor.

- Acts 24:24–25 (Drusilla was the daughter of Herod Agrippa I)—How did Paul's knowledge of his audience affect his message?

- Acts 25–26—Paul was tried before Festus, the new Roman governor, and Herod Agrippa II, the Jewish king.

- Acts 26:1–23—What was Paul's message in this passage? Did the powerful people of the culture affect his message here?

- Acts 26:24—How did the Roman commander respond to what Paul said?

- Acts 26:28—How did Agrippa respond?

Ask your students to answer the following questions:

1. What lessons can you learn from Paul's confrontation with the sinful culture of his day (and those who shaped it)?

2. Read Matthew 28:19; Acts 1:8; Luke 21:12. To whom are Jesus' followers called to be witnesses? How can you witness to the powerful people of the world?

3. How can the Christian community become more effective in being God's witnesses in a culture that does not recognize Him? How can you?

4. Have you ever "watered down" your witness? If you're comfortable doing so, give an example to the rest of the class. Why is it so easy for us to change our message when we're presenting it to others?

5. How can you be more effective in pointing others to God at work? at school? in your family?

OPTIONAL — Digging Deeper V: So Close *(15–30 minutes)*

Few people were as close to salvation as the Herod family was. Few had so many opportunities to meet the Messiah and to hear His teaching. Look up the following verses, and notice the encounters the Herod family had with Jesus and His message:

Herod the Great	Matthew 2:1–8,13–18
Antipas (son of Herod the Great)	Mark 6:14–29; Luke 23:8–12
Agrippa I (grandson of Herod the Great)	Acts 12:1–5,18–24
Drusilla (wife of the governor Felix and daughter of Agrippa I)	Acts 24:24–26
Agrippa II (great-grandson of Herod the Great)	Acts 25:13,23, 26:1–29
Bernice (great-granddaughter of Herod the Great)	Acts 25:13,23, 26:1–29

Ask your students to answer the following questions:

1. Why do you think no one in this family believed Jesus' message?

2. Read Acts 26:28. What is ironic about this conversation between Paul and Agrippa II?

3. Why is it so important for people to respond to Jesus' message immediately when they hear it?

4. If someone is close to believing in Jesus, what can we do to help move him or her closer to saving faith?

7. Guided Discussion: Back Where We Started

In the first lesson of this series, "Standing at the Crossroads," we learned that God places His people on the crossroads of the world as standing stones. We went to Gezer, an ancient ruin, because it is at the crossroads of the ancient trade route sometimes called the Via Maris, where the whole world could see God's people as standing stones—people whose very lives pointed to God like the stones ancient peoples erected to testify that God had acted in that place.

Jesus went to live and teach in Galilee by the Via Maris, which is translated "the way of the sea" (Matthew 4:15). He, too, taught at a location where the world could see Him, for it needed His message and saving work.

The first Christians were also brought to the crossroads. Caesarea, on the Via Maris, linked Israel with the rest of the world. These Christians had an opportunity to speak to the world. The powerful people who shaped the culture were in their audience. These first Christians were standing stones. They spoke and acted boldly and obediently. They did not compromise their message, and they did not hide in churches and synagogues. They lived among those who needed Jesus, and they spoke and lived their faith. They were sometimes ridiculed and persecuted, but God was honored. And through them, many people (including modern-day non-Jewish Christians) around the world came to know Israel's God and His Messiah.

Now it is our turn. We, too, live on the crossroads—especially those of us who have access to modern technology. We are engaged in shaping our world; the world is watching us. God's call for us is to be standing stones and teachers, bold proclaimers of God's message to a world that is in dire need of it. If we are living as anything less, we do not have the total commitment that Peter, Paul, and so many others showed.

Ask your students to answer the following questions:

a. How are you God's witness?

b. Have you committed yourself totally to God? If so, how does it show in your life?

c. What are some examples of ways God changed the world through the witness of His people?

d. How can He use the witness of His people to change it today?

e. Who is your favorite Bible character? How was that person God's witness? Make a commitment to God to try to be more like that person as you witness in your world.

Conclusion

Two types of stone are shown in the video *Total Commitment*. From these stones, we can learn a key lesson in being God's witnesses and pointing others to Him. One of these stones is marble; the other is limestone. Remember their stories.

Marble—The great king Herod imported marble from Italy to build his glorious city of Caesarea. Many of Herod's cities and buildings were covered with this stone. He built these magnificent structures so people would remember him and honor him as a great king. Herod lived for himself.

Today these magnificent creations are in ruins. Pieces of marble litter the land and are buried under the sea. At Caesarea, much of Herod's beautiful marble washes up on the shore of the Mediterranean, where it was thrown by conquering armies. People walk along the shore and pick up broken pieces of Herod's monuments to himself. Because he built only for himself, nothing is left but ruins. Most people remember nothing of Herod except his slaughter of babies in Bethlehem at Christmastime.

Limestone—When he was a boy, King David picked up limestone in a small brook in the Valley of Elah. Because he was a shepherd, he was familiar with slings and stones. When his God was challenged, David did the only thing he knew how to do in defense—he threw a stone.

Before David killed Goliath, he told his giant enemy why he was going to throw the stone: "The whole world will know that there is a God in Israel" (1 Samuel 17:46). David saved God's people, Jesus' earthly ancestors, and he has never been forgotten. His is one of the first stories children learn. The effects of what he did will endure forever because what he did, he did for God and not for himself.

Herod and David were both great kings. Both loved stones. Herod built for himself, and people today pick up the ruins of what he left behind. David acted for God, and we will never forget his great legacy.

We, too, have been given stones. Our stones are talents, opportunities, resources, and training. Some of us have marble—many talents and great opportunities and resources. Others have limestone—ordinary talents and responsibilities. It doesn't matter what stones we have; we are building with our lives. The question is, Whom do we build for? If we are building for ourselves, whether marble or limestone, someday others will pick up the broken pieces of our dreams—because that's all that will be left. If we are building for God, whether marble or limestone, what we build will stand forever.

Spend a few moments in prayer, asking our Lord to help us commit totally to Him as His witnesses so that the world may know that He is the one true God.

IN HEROD'S FOOTSTEPS: THE DYNASTY CONTINUES

Herod lay dying in his opulent palace in Jericho. He had been seriously ill for a long time. From the description in Josephus's writings, Herod had gangrene, severe itching, convulsions, and ulcers. His feet were covered with tumors, and he had constant fevers. The stadium of Jericho was filled with loved and important people from around his land who were to be killed at the moment of his death, lest no one mourn when he died. It didn't seem to matter that they would not be mourning for him.

As he lay on his deathbed, Herod's thoughts may have turned to the rabbis and their students whom he recently had executed for tearing down the Roman eagle from the Temple gate because it violated God's law against images. Perhaps he reflected on his beloved wife Miriamne's two sons whom he had drowned in the palace swimming pool next door. He could have remembered the execution of his favorite son, Antipater, only days ago for plotting against him—Antipater, the one who was to take his father's place. Or maybe he thought about the 45 members of the Sanhedrin whom he had murdered, the hundreds of family and staff whom he had suspected of plotting against him, or the thousands of subjects who died in his brutal campaign to claim a country they believed he had no right to rule. It is possible Herod also recalled—though only briefly—the massacre of a few boy babies in a town near his massive fortress Herodion, soon to be his tomb.

HEROD'S WILL

As he lay dying in Jericho, Herod revised his will to reflect the execution of his son Antipater. Archelaus—his son by Malthace, his Samaritan wife— was given the best territory: Judea, Samaria, and Idumaea. Herod Philip— son of Cleopatra, his fifth wife—was to rule the area northeast of the Sea of Galilee: Gaulanitis, Batanea, Trachonitis, and Auranitis. Herod Antipas, another son of Malthace, was given Galilee and Perea. Shortly after completing this will, Herod died and was buried with pomp and circumstance in the Herodion, overlooking the fields of Bethlehem.

Greedy for more territory, Herod's sons went to Rome to ask for additional lands. A delegation from Judea and Jerusalem, fed up with the Herod dynasty, also went to Rome to request that the emperor, Augustus, appoint someone else to govern them. While they were gone, the country was in turmoil. Still upset over Herod's assassination of the rabbis and their students, Jews rioted in Jerusalem on Pentecost. The Roman governor from Syria came with soldiers, and fighting flared around the country. Judah, a Zealot from Gamla, seized Sepphoris and plundered the armory and palace.

Roman troops brutally put down the revolt. Jerusalem was reclaimed from the rebels, and more than 2,000 of them were crucified. Sepphoris also was retaken, and the inhabitants—those who survived, at least—were sold into slavery.

Finally, Augustus made his decision. To the great disappointment of nearly everyone, he honored Herod's will. The land would belong to Herod's three sons, though none of the brothers was made king. Archelaus was made an ethnarch, a position slightly higher than tetrarch, which his brothers received.

It was 4 B.C., and Joseph and Mary learned this news in a dream (Matthew 2:19–23).

HEROD ARCHELAUS

Archelaus ruled in Jerusalem for 10 years. He hunted down the delegation that had gone to Rome, and as a true son of his father, he executed them and their families and confiscated their property. Archelaus had all of Herod's evil qualities, and his reign was as bloody as his father's had been. In A.D. 6, another delegation of Judeans risked their lives and went to Rome to accuse Herod of breaking the emperor's command to govern peacefully. Archelaus was summoned to Rome and exiled to Gaul—at which point he promptly disappeared from history. Judea, Samaria, and Idumaea were named the Roman Province of Judea, to be subject directly to Rome under a military prefect ominously given full power to inflict the death penalty. Coponius was appointed the first prefect; Pontius Pilate came later. Judea no longer gave allegiance to the Herod family.

During Archelaus's short, bloody reign, Joseph and Mary, who had fled to Egypt during Herod the Great's reign because he had tried to kill their baby, were told by God that Herod was dead (Matthew 2:1–23). It was safe for them to return home. When they came to Judea, where they apparently planned to settle (maybe in Bethlehem?), they heard about Archelaus and decided they would not risk facing another bloodthirsty Herod's fear of losing his throne (Matthew 2:22). They skirted his territory and settled in Nazareth, under Herod Antipas's rule, thereby fulfilling prophecy (Matthew 2:23).

People did not soon forget the cruel Archelaus. Years later, the bloody beginning of his reign would provide the basis for a clever though probably dangerous parable (Luke 19:11–27). Jesus, however, would conduct His ministry under the watchful eye of Archelaus's younger brother.

HEROD PHILIP

Herod Philip received the territory north and east of the Sea of Galilee. This area was large but fairly poor. Philip was a peace-loving tetrarch, an excellent administrator, and a just ruler. The majority of his subjects were Gentiles, which may have spared him the burden of having to deal with the internal struggles of the Jewish people and the constant appearance of one self-proclaimed messiah after another.

Philip established his capital at Caesarea Philippi, expanding a largely pagan town and building a temple to its gods. Jesus later brought His disciples here to impress upon them the reality that His church would become the dominant community in the world (Matthew 16:13–20). It was in this pagan setting that Peter professed Jesus as *the* Messiah.

Philip also built a city—named Julias—near or on the site of Bethsaida, close to where the Jordan River enters the Sea of Galilee. Jesus' disciples Peter, Andrew, and Philip came from this town (John 1:43–44).

Herod Philip married his niece Salome, daughter of Herodias and a noted dancer, according to his brother (Matthew 14:1–12). After a reign of 37 peaceful years, Philip died and was buried at Julius.

The rule of his half brother, Herod Antipas, wasn't as peaceful. Antipas was the only Herod to meet the Messiah.

HEROD ANTIPAS

History's View

Antipas is remembered as an outstanding ruler who brought peace and prosperity to his land for more than 40 years. His territories of Galilee and Perea were among the most religious in Israel. Antipas tried to avoid offending his Jewish subjects and their commitment to the Torah—for example, by refusing to mint coins with images on them. Both the Pharisees and the Herodians (a largely upper-class, secular group that probably formed during his reign) supported him.

Just three miles from Nazareth, Antipas built the magnificent city of Sepphoris, which functioned as his capital. The boy Jesus certainly must have watched Sepphoris being built on a hill north of His hometown. Perhaps He even worked there, since many of the builders (carpenters) in the area contributed to Sepphoris's construction.

Herod Antipas's greatest project was the city of Tiberias on the shore of the Sea of Galilee. Constructed near hot springs, it was one of the most beautiful cities in Galilee. It had the best of everything, including a stadium, hot baths, and a great palace. The religious Jews of the area (where Jesus ministered) were unwilling to enter Tiberias because it was supposedly built over a cemetery and was therefore defiled according to Old Testament law (Numbers 5:2). The city was probably completed shortly before Jesus moved to Capernaum a few miles away. Tiberias was clearly visible to the citizens of Capernaum (as well as to the Zealots at Gamla, who hated Herod with a passion that only religious commitment can create).

Throughout most of his life, Antipas had the support of Tiberius, the Roman emperor for whom his capital was named. When Tiberius died, Antipas's rival and relative Herod Agrippa (Agrippa was Antipas's father's grandson) accused him of plotting against Rome. Caligula, the new emperor, exiled Antipas and claimed his property. At this point, Herod Antipas passed quietly from history.

The Bible's View

The Bible presents a very different picture of this son of Herod the Great. According to New Testament writers, Antipas was a scheming weakling who was the archenemy of Jesus of Nazareth. Antipas had married the daughter of the Nabatean king Aretas. During a visit to his brother Philip (not the Herod Philip who was king in the north), Antipas fell in love with Herodias, Philip's wife. Antipas divorced his wife and married his brother's wife while Philip was still alive. Because this was forbidden by law (Leviticus 18:16), Herod Antipas incurred the bitter opposition of the religious Jews he ruled, including a desert preacher named John whose mission, to prepare a way for the Lord in the wilderness, had no room for such blatant disobedience—and by the king, no less (Matthew 14:1–12; Mark 6:14–29). John's call for turning from sin, symbolized by baptism, was popular with religious Jews, who expected the Messiah at any time. If the way (i.e., everyone living by God's law) was prepared, Messiah would certainly arrive.

John's harsh criticism of Antipas struck a nerve. He was arrested and imprisoned. On the occasion of Herod Antipas's birthday, Herodias's daughter Salome (who would later marry Herod Philip) danced provocatively and obtained Antipas's favor. Her mother encouraged Salome to ask for John's execution, for she, too, was tired of being publicly criticized by this popular figure. Trapped, and probably not entirely sober, Herod Antipas concurred, and John was beheaded. (Some scholars place the execution at Tiberias, barely five miles from Jesus' town of Capernaum.) The event was to haunt Herod. The Jewish people loved John and hated Antipas. The king, believing John was a genuine prophet, feared the consequences until nearly the end of his life (Luke 23:6–12).

To make matters worse, his divorced wife fled to her father, King Aretas, who declared war on his unfaithful son-in-law. Herod was defeated, an event his subjects attributed to his breaking God's law. Caligula sent an army to rescue him and protect his kingdom. But this was the beginning of the loss of Roman support. Herod Antipas's ungodly marriage eventually led to his downfall despite the execution of his critic. John's execution also brought opposition from another, greater Jewish Rabbi.

ANTIPAS AND JESUS

Herod Antipas was the only member of his family to come face-to-face with Jesus. His father, Herod the Great, had lived close to Jesus' birthplace in Bethlehem and had even searched for the baby (Matthew 2:1–18). But apparently Herod had never met Jesus. Philip lived only a few miles from the area where most of Jesus' miracles were performed (Matthew 11:20–21), but there is no record of the two men meeting. Antipas, on the other hand, spent years trying to meet Jesus and finally had an opportunity.

After John's murder, Herod and Jesus were in constant opposition. Jesus criticized Antipas by name (Mark 8:15; Luke 13:31–33), calling him "that fox"—the cultural equivalent of "wimp." When the two men finally did meet in the courtroom where Jesus was on trial for His life, Jesus refused to speak to Herod (Luke 23:9). Herod mocked and abused Him (Luke 23:11; Acts 4:27), thereby missing his opportunity for salvation. In the end, Antipas was no better off than his father or brothers.

Antipas's life was haunted by his execution of John and the appearance of Jesus. He feared that Jesus was John raised from the dead (Mark 6:14–16; Matthew 14:1–2; Luke 9:7–9). Nevertheless, he plotted Jesus' death (Luke 13:31–33), of which the Pharisees warned Jesus.

Jesus' execution proved to be far more earth-shattering than John's, but Antipas didn't live long enough to learn that reality.

THE OTHERS

Herod Agrippa I

Herod the Great loved his wife Miriamne more than anything. When he had her executed for a supposed affair, his grief knew no bounds. Yet he executed her son without a second thought. Ironically, her grandson, Herod Agrippa I, continued the Herod dynasty: He governed territory formerly belonging to Philip (the area north and east of the Sea of Galilee) from A.D. 37–41 and was king of Judea from A.D. 41–44. While in Rome for his education, Agrippa became friends with Caligula, who as emperor was Agrippa's supporter. When Caligula died, the new emperor, Claudius, continued to support him, and for a short time, Agrippa's territory was nearly equal to that of his grandfather.

Agrippa also knew about Jesus. He determined that the followers of Jesus, his uncle Antipas's nemesis, must be stopped. Agrippa killed the disciple James and imprisoned Peter and others (Acts 12:1–19). Agrippa's frustration must have been as great as Antipas's, because Peter disappeared. Proving he was a full-blooded Herod, Agrippa had the guards executed.

Later, Agrippa went to Caesarea to celebrate a festival in honor of the emperor Claudius. Receiving the adulation of the admiring crowds, Agrippa was struck down—a victim of family pride (Acts 12:19–23).

Herod Agrippa met Jesus' disciples and heard the gospel. His son, Agrippa II, refused to go even that far.

Herod Agrippa II

Herod Agrippa II was 17 years old when his father fell down dead in Caesarea. Like his father, Agrippa II was educated in Rome. In A.D. 50, Caesar appointed him king over a small fraction of his father's territories. He had some authority over Jerusalem and was allowed to appoint the high priest.

Agrippa II did much to advance the Hellenistic culture in his kingdom. When the Jewish revolt against Rome began in A.D. 66, he tried to persuade his subjects not to fight the Romans. At that point, he fully supported Rome and was even wounded in the battle for Gamla, near Jesus' town of Capernaum. When the Romans finally defeated the Jewish rebels, Agrippa II invited the legions to Caesarea Philippi to rest and celebrate.

In Acts 21, the Roman commander of Jerusalem arrested a "rabbi," Paul, who had created a riot on the Temple Mount. To make sure that Paul, a Roman citizen, received a fair trial and was not lynched by an angry mob, the officer sent him to Caesarea (Acts 24). Governor Felix, who was married to Agrippa's sister Drusilla (granddaughter of Herod the Great, daughter of Agrippa I), left office before a sentence was passed. He was succeeded by a man named Festus. When Agrippa II and his sister Bernice (granddaughter of Herod the Great, daughter of Agrippa I) came to Caesarea, Festus invited them to Paul's arraignment (Acts 25). Agrippa asked to hear Paul's defense (Acts 25:22). Both Bernice and Agrippa heard a ringing proclamation of the good news of Messiah, Jesus of Nazareth, had been born near Herod the Great (who tried to kill Him), had preached near Herod Antipas (who tried to kill Him), who had been tried by Antipas (who sentenced Him to die), and who had founded a new movement of Jews and Gentiles (whom Agrippa I tried to kill). Festus thought Paul was mad (Acts 26:24), and Agrippa II, though fascinated, was not persuaded (Acts 26:28). He and Bernice determined that Paul was not guilty but allowed him to be sent to Caesar in Rome (where Paul, too, would be killed).

SO CLOSE

There have been few families in history who came so close to the greatest message the world has ever heard. One after another, the Herods met or knew of Jesus and His followers. One after another, they killed or tried to kill anyone connected to Him. How anyone could be so close and yet so far is hard to understand. Maybe the Herod family, who were descended from Esau and Edom, simply fulfilled the prophecies (Genesis 25:23; Numbers 24:17; Obadiah 8–21).

The most powerful family of kings Israel had known for many years had the opportunity to meet and serve the King of the universe. Instead, they exemplify the ultimate fate of those who do not recognize the Messiah. They lived only for themselves and not so that the world may know "that there is a God in Israel" (1 Samuel 17:46).

GLOSSARY

Antonia: Herod the Great rebuilt the Hasmonaean fortress in Jerusalem next to the Temple Mount and renamed it the Antonia after Mark Antony. Roman troops were stationed here.

Babylon, Babylonians: Hebrew, *Babel*. Capital city of Mesopotamia, located on the Euphrates River and neighbor to Assyria. Considered at the time of the prophet Jeremiah to be the greatest and most beautiful city of the Near East. An enormous political and economic power that held great influence over the Israelites. In 586 B.C., the Babylonians took the children of Israel into an exile that would last 70 years. The return from this exile established a people to whom Jesus would be born and a kingdom in the land of Israel.

Bar Kochba Revolt: Another name for the Second Jewish Revolt against Rome (A.D. 132–135). The leader of the revolt was a man named Bar Kochba.

Belial: Hebrew meaning "useless." Came to be applied to the devil by the Essenes and the early Christians (2 Corinthians 6).

Bethsaida: One of the three main towns of Jesus' ministry in Galilee. This small, prosperous fishing village on the north shore of the Sea of Galilee was renamed Julias and rebuilt by Herod Philip. Home of apostles Peter, Philip, and Andrew. Near this village, Jesus performed the miracle of feeding 5,000 people. Its location was uncertain until recently, when archaeologists excavated the ruins.

Beth Shean: City at the eastern entrance to the Jezreel Valley. The Philistines hung Saul's and Jonathan's bodies from its walls.

Caesarea: Port city and provincial capital of the Roman province of Judea. Herod built a spectacular man-made harbor with two breakwaters to link the country with world commerce.

Caesarea Philippi: Large Hellenistic city rebuilt and renamed by Herod Philip. Located on Mount Hermon in the upper Jordan Valley near the Spring of Panias, one of three headwaters of the Jordan River and site of a great pagan temple dedicated to Pan, the Roman fertility god.

Canaan, Canaanite: Old Testament name for the Promised Land, meaning "land of purple," probably referring to the color of dye produced by shellfish along Canaan's coast. *Canaanite* refers to one who lived in Canaan; a synonym for merchant or trader; the people in Israel before the Israelites arrived.

Chorazin (Korazin): City just north of the Sea of Galilee where Jesus performed many miracles. Jesus condemned the city for its unbelief.

colonnades: Rows of columns spaced evenly apart that support arches or a roof. First-century Roman streets often had colonnades on both sides.

Dead Sea: An inland lake in the Great Rift Valley known as the Salt Sea; 50 miles long and 10 miles wide, the salt content is five times more concentrated than the ocean and is uninhabitable by marine life. The Essene community lived in the wilderness along the Dead Sea.

Dead Sea Scrolls: Commentaries or instruction manuals for the Essene community; discovered in 1947 by the Dead Sea in caves near the ruins of Khirbet Qumran. They provide valuable insights into the beliefs of one religious community from the time of Jesus; they contain many references showing common themes, language, and beliefs with the teachings of Jesus, John the Baptist, and the early church. They also help verify the most accurate texts of the Old Testament. Though these scrolls are 1,000 years older than other Hebrew manuscripts, there are few differences, and they indicate the miracle of God's protection of His Word throughout history.

Decapolis: Ten Hellenistic cities established at the time of Alexander the Great east of the Sea of Galilee and north of Perea. Later, the Roman emperor Pompey organized the cities into a league named the Decapolis, largely populated by Roman army troops. In one ancient Jewish belief, the area was populated by pagans Joshua had driven out of the Promised Land (Joshua 3) and became "off-limits" to Jews who followed God's law. In the New Testament, the name refers to some cities where Jesus ministered to Gentiles and demonstrated His willingness to bring His message to everyone who needed to hear His words.

Egypt, Egyptian(s): Land and civilization south and west of Israel that flourished along the banks of the Nile River. During the time of Moses, home to enslaved Jews. Part of the Roman Empire during the first century. Throughout the Bible, Egypt was economically dependent on the eastern civilizations of Mesopotamia (Babylon, Assyria, and Persia). Trade routes connecting Egypt to these empires ran through mountain passes of Israel. By placing His people between the Egyptians and the eastern empires, God guaranteed that the whole known world would hear His message.

En Gedi: Means "spring of the wild goat." A canyon and surrounding hills filled with springs that enabled a lush oasis to flourish on the Dead Sea's barren, western shore. Here David hid from Saul and possibly wrote several psalms.

Essene(s): A highly organized religious group that renounced the priestly establishment and saw themselves as God's soldiers. They strengthened their bodies, minds, and spirits for the battle they believed would usher in the new age. The Dead Sea Scrolls found at Qumran may have been their library. Some believe that John the Baptist belonged to this group, because his message was similar to that contained in the Dead Sea Scrolls. Some of the beliefs and practices of the Essenes resembled those of Jesus and the early church.

fresco: Design created by painting water colors onto wet plaster.

frieze: A design or series of low-relief sculptures forming an ornamental, horizontal band around a room or between the architrave and cornice of a building.

Gamla: Aramaic meaning "camel," because from a distance this ridge in the Golan Heights (Gaulanitis) looks like a camel's hump. Located north and east of the Sea of Galilee. Home to nationalistic Pharisees (Zealots) who sought deliverance from Roman oppression and probably were responsible for the frequent questions to Jesus regarding the nature of His kingship and an ongoing desire to appoint Him king. After a brutal battle, the city fell to Vespasian in A.D. 67. Josephus recorded that 9,000 people died rather than surrender to the Romans.

Gennesaret. *See Sea of Galilee.*

Great Rift Valley: Valley east of Israel where the Sea of Galilee and the Dead Sea are located. Also known as the Jordan Valley.

Hallel: A selection of Psalms comprising Psalms 113–118 and 135–136 and chanted during Jewish feasts.

Hasmonaean: Dynasty of Jewish kings belonging to the family also known as the Maccabees.

Hebron: Ancient city of Judah at the southern edge of the Hebron Mountains, north of the Negev and approximately 19 miles south of Jerusalem. Abraham lived here and purchased a tomb in this area where he, his wife Sarah, Isaac, Rebecca, Jacob, and Leah were buried. David's capital for the first seven years of his reign. Herod built a large enclosure around the cave of Machpelah, where Abraham was buried.

Hellenism: Name for the culture and worldview of the Greeks. It was antithetically opposed to the God-centered worldview of the Jews. Hellenism makes the human being the ultimate in reality. The human mind is the basis for truth, the human body is the ultimate in wisdom, and human pleasure is the ultimate goal in life. It is the ancestor of modern humanism.

Herod the Great: Decreed king of Judea by the Romans in 40 B.C. Poorly accepted by the Jews because of his questionable heritage as a descendent of Esau and a native of Idumaea (Edom). Most infamous for trying to kill the infant Jesus by ordering the slaughter of all male babies under two years old in Bethlehem. Remembered for the brutality of his reign.

Herodian: Anything pertaining to Herod the Great and the Herodian period; or the political party that dominated Herod Antipas's territory and politically and economically supported Roman overlords.

Herodion: Fortress built by Herod the Great (ca. 20 B.C.) near Bethlehem. It was a fortified palace and is reported to be the place of Herod's burial.

hippodrome: From the Greek *hippus* ("horse") and *dramas* ("course"). Referred to a horse-racing course, or circus.

Herod built hippodromes in Caesarea, Jericho, and Jerusalem, where horse races, chariot races, and Olympic-style games were held as part of his attempt to Hellenize Israel.

Idumaea: Another name for the city of Edom, meaning "red." Located south of the Dead Sea and west of Arabah; home of Herod the Great. Some early followers of Jesus came from Idumaea (Mark 3:8).

Jericho: Oasis next to a spring in the Great Rift Valley north of the Dead Sea. First city captured by the Israelites after wandering in the desert for 40 years.

Jerusalem: Located in the Judea Mountains west of the Dead Sea, on the rim of the Great Rift Valley at the edge of the Judea Wilderness. King David captured the mountain spur, and the existing town, Jebus, which became "David's City," the Israelites' religious and political center. David purchased a threshing floor, the traditional site where Abraham prepared to sacrifice his son Isaac to God, as the future site of God's Temple that Solomon eventually built (2 Chronicles 3:1). God the Father sent Jesus to Jerusalem to complete His messianic work by being executed, buried, and raised on the same mountain of Abraham's attempted sacrifice and where sacrifices in the Temple were made. This created a physical link between events of Jewish history and followers of Jesus. In the Bible, "heavenly Jerusalem" symbolized God's heavenly kingdom that will come at the end of time.

Jezreel Valley: Means "valley of Megiddo." A fertile, agricultural valley whose strategic location led to frequent battles for control over the world trade route between the west and Mesopotamia. Used by biblical writers as the symbolic setting of the final triumph of God's power over evil, Armageddon. Nazareth is nearby.

Jordan River: Hebrew *Yarden*, meaning "the descender." Headwaters are fed by snow melt on Mount Hermon and underground springs; flows into the Dead Sea; where John the Baptist baptized Jesus.

Judea: Region of Israel, named for the tribe of Judah, where Jerusalem was located. Ruled by Herod the Great and later given to his son Archelaus; then directly under Roman authority. The Judean Temple leadership resisted Jesus' message and ministry.

Judea Wilderness: The eastern slopes of the Judea Mountains form a 10-mile-wide, 30-mile-long hot, dry wilderness frequently used as a refuge for those in hiding or seeking a spiritual retreat, including the Essenes at Qumran, John the Baptist, David, and Jesus. Site of Masada, the last battle in the First Jewish Revolt.

legion: A military designation. Composed of spear men, archers, tacticians/strategists, calvary, and reserves. Some of the best Roman legions, including the tenth, were stationed in Israel during the first century. *Legion* also was used to describe a host of demons or an army of angels.

Maccabee: Family of high priest Mattathias and his son Judah, who revolted against oppressive Antiochus, king of Syria, a Seleucid Greek; Judah cleansed the Temple after defilement by the Syrians. The Jews remained free, ruled by the Maccabees (family name: Hasmonaean) until 63 B.C. The Maccabee symbol of a palm branch became a national symbol of freedom. Hanukkah (or the Feast of Dedication) celebrated Judah Maccabee's cleansing of the Temple.

Masada: A fortress expanded by Herod the Great to include a palace; on a mountain plateau on the Dead Sea's shore near Idumaea. David wrote, "The Lord is my rock and my fortress" (Psalm 18:2), a possible reference to this flat mountain plateau. Along the 1,000-foot mountaintop, Herod built a wall with 37 towers to defend against attackers and carved a three-level palace into the mountain face. Fearing Mark Antony would give his kingdom to Cleopatra of Egypt, Herod fortified Masada as an escape. Last place held by rebels in the First Jewish Revolt; they committed suicide rather than surrender. A symbol for the Jewish people of their determination to remain free.

mikveh (pl. mikvoth): A ceremonial bath where a person immerses to become ritually clean according to Jewish law. A mikveh must be at least four and one-half feet deep and hold no less than 195 gallons of water. Most water was piped in from cisterns filled by aqueducts that were connected to rivers or streams, necessary to provide "living water" (clean, cold, running water) to ensure purity. Water often was stored next to the mikveh in a special reservoir (otzar). Worshipers immersed before entering the Temple Mount. Background to Christian baptism; probable that a mikveh was used for baptisms on the Christian fulfillment of Pentecost.

Mount Arbel: Mountain ridge 1,000 feet above the Sea of Galilee. Site of a brutal battle in 38 B.C. between Galilean Jews and Herod the Great for control of Galilee.

Nabatean: Arabs who lived south and east of Israel and who significantly affected New Testament events. A highly advanced civilization that developed the ability to farm wilderness areas. Controlled the spice trade and trade routes that crossed Israel from Arabia.

Negev: Means "dry" or "parched." Desert on the southern edge of Israel, south of the Judea Mountains. The Israelites wandered here during their 40 years in the wilderness. Home of Jacob, father of the 12 tribes, and many desert nomads and spice traders.

Palestine: Name given to the Promised Land after the Second Jewish Revolt (A.D. 132–135). It derives from the word *Philistia* and was used by the Romans to denigrate the Jews.

peristyle garden: Cultivated garden inside a colonnaded area. Herod the Great built several peristyle gardens, including at Jericho and the Herodion.

Pharisees: Means "separated ones." Descended from the Hasidim ("pious ones"); considered obedience to Torah to be the heart of a godly life. Separated from sinful ways and people in their desire to be faithful. Believed strongly in God's judgment and a resurrection where men would be rewarded or punished according to their deeds. Constituted the largest Jewish sect during Jesus' lifetime; exerted great control over society through synagogues.

Pool of Siloam: Located near where the Tyropoeon Valley joins the Kidron; supplied drinking water for a large portion of Jerusalem. Water for the pool came from the Spring of Gihon through Hezekiah's Tunnel. Jesus sent a blind man He had healed here to wash the mud off his eyes.

procurator: Roman military governor. Pontius Pilate was procurator of Judea.

Ptolemies: Descendants of Ptolemy I (one of the generals of Alexander the Great), who ruled over Egypt from 323 B.C.

to 198 B.C. Israel was under their control during this time. Generally, they were benevolent rulers, though they sought to spread the influence of Hellenism among the Jews.

Qumran: A small community near the northern end of the Dead Sea, inhabited from 130 B.C. to A.D. 70, probably by the Essenes. The Dead Sea Scrolls were found near this settlement.

rabbinic Judaism: Jewish religious practice after the Temple was destroyed (A.D. 70) that centered on the Torah and its interpretation by the rabbis.

Sadducees: Wealthy Jewish aristocracy, claiming descent and authority from the high priest Zadok. Oversaw Temple; theology based on the first five books of the Bible; did not believe in an afterlife or that God interfered in human lives. Notoriously corrupt; disliked by the common people; helped to preserve their own political power and wealth by collaborating with the Romans. As the majority of the 70-man religious council (Sanhedrin), they wielded great authority over the nation's everyday affairs. Had the most to lose by Jesus' ministry, as He challenged Temple authority. Many scholars believe the Sadducees were responsible for plotting to kill Jesus—having Him arrested, interrogated, and then released to the Romans.

Sanhedrin: Means "council." Jewish supreme court; highest religious council, composed of 70 members and the high priest. The number 70 traditionally was based on Moses' appointment of 70 elders (Numbers 11:16) to administer Israel's affairs. Used by the Romans to administer daily affairs. Predominantly Sadducees, the religious faction most threatened by Jesus' ministry, who plotted against, interrogated, and released Him to the Romans.

Scythopolis (Beth Shean): One of the oldest Decapolis cities. Originally, Beth Shean, renamed Scythopolis, or "City of Scythians," following Alexander the Great's conquest. Reputation for abundant water and fertile land. Located on the road Galileans walked in the Great Rift Valley to Jerusalem.

Sea of Galilee: Freshwater lake filled by the Jordan River; located in the Great Rift Valley and site of first-century commercial fishing industry; significant for a trade route on its northern shore. Jesus spent the majority of His ministry around here, including the miracle of walking on water.

Sepphoris: Greek for Hebrew *zippor*, meaning "bird," because the town perched like a bird on a mountaintop in Lower Galilee. Hellenistic city built as Herod Antipas's regional capital; a major urban center of Hellenistic culture and power, with 20,000 inhabitants. Built three and one-half miles from Nazareth during Jesus' childhood and youth; possible that He and His earthly father, Joseph, worked here as a builder.

Shavuot: Means "weeks"; also known as Pentecost or the Feast of Weeks. It's celebrated 50 days after the Sabbath following Passover.

sicarri: An extremist sect of the Zealots heavily involved in the First Jewish Revolt. They were named after their short, curved dagger *(sica)*, which they used to assassinate Romans and Jewish collaborators.

sons of light: Name the Essenes (writers of the Dead Sea Scrolls) gave themselves as followers of God. Their enemies (Romans and the apostate priesthood in Jerusalem), in their opinion, were the sons of darkness. The New Testament uses this language also (1 Thessalonians 5:5).

Syria: Nation or area north and east of Israel. Old Testament: a bitter enemy of Israel. New Testament: large province (including Israel) under Roman control. At the time of Jesus, a large Jewish community lived in its capital, Damascus.

Tabernacles (Festival, sanctuary, Sukkot): The seventh yearly feast (Leviticus 23) when all males were required to come to Jerusalem. The people celebrated Israel's wandering in the desert by living in temporary shelters. Included a water ceremony as part of prayer for rain.

Temple Mount: The ridge on which Jerusalem's Temple was built, and/or the platform on which the Temple and its courts stood. King Herod's platform was supported by massive walls, the tallest standing 160 feet, and measured more than 1,500 feet long, north to south, and more than 900 feet wide, east to west. It accommodated 200,000 pilgrims.

Tiberias: Capital built by Herod Antipas on the Sea of Galilee's western shore; named for the emperor Tiberius. Believed to be built over a cemetery and so considered unclean by religious Jews. After A.D. 70, it became a center of Jewish religious thought.

Torah: Hebrew for "teaching"; the first five books of the Bible, God's covenant with Israel, given to Moses. Primarily a teaching about God and His people; a guide to live by rather than a collection of laws. When Jesus said He came to fulfill Torah, He meant how to live by the teachings and demonstrate the meaning of Torah.

Via Maris: Latin for "way of the sea." Possibly the name of the international trade route between the Mesopotamian empire (east) and Egypt (west), or a small portion of one near the Sea of Galilee. Matthew wrote that Jesus settled near Capernaum by "the way of the sea," meaning the Via Maris, and as such He conducted His ministry in an area that was public because of the main road that ran through it.

wadi: Mountain canyon that carries water only when it rains; dry riverbed with occasional flash floods.

Yahweh: Israel's God; means "I am" or "I am what I am," indicating that God is completely self-determined, dependent on no one for His being or power. The most sacred and holy name of God; other references to the divine as "God," "Lord," or "Almighty" are titles. Jewish people of Jesus' time avoided saying this name for fear of using it in vain. To refer to God, they used *Adonai* (Greek for "Lord" or "Master").

APPENDIX

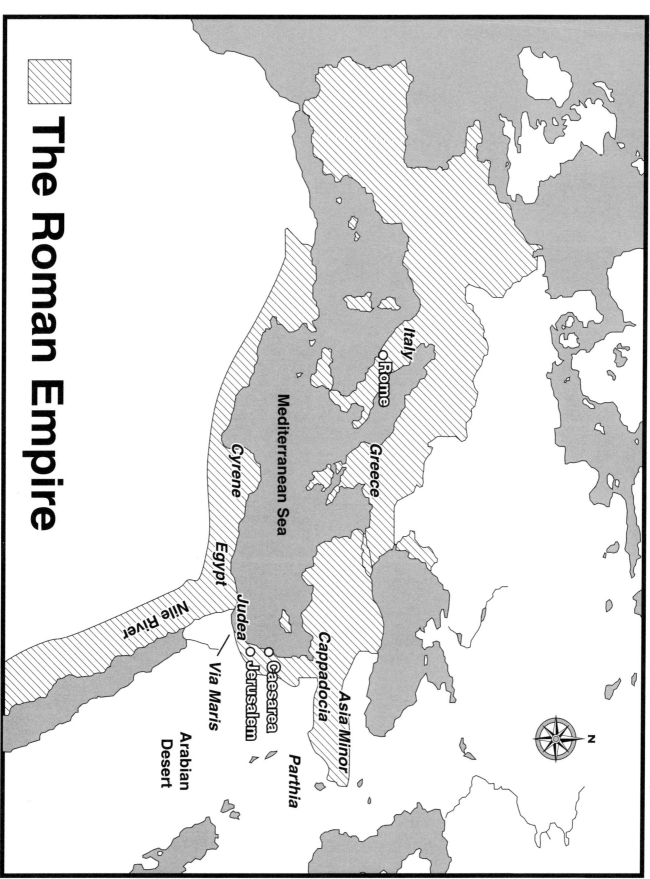

The Roman Empire

Italy
Rome
Greece
Mediterranean Sea
Cyrene
Egypt
Nile River
Judea
Via Maris
Caesarea
Jerusalem
Arabian Desert
Parthia
Cappadocia
Asia Minor

N

Topography of Israel: New Testament

Mediterranean Sea

Sea of Galilee

Via Maris: Way of the Sea

Dead Sea

Coastal Plain

Shephelah

Central Mountain Range

Negev

Judea Wilderness

○ Jerusalem

Bethlehem

Qumran

○ Jericho

GREAT RIFT VALLEY

○ **En Gedi**

Moab Mountains

Capernaum ○

Decapolis

N

Galilee

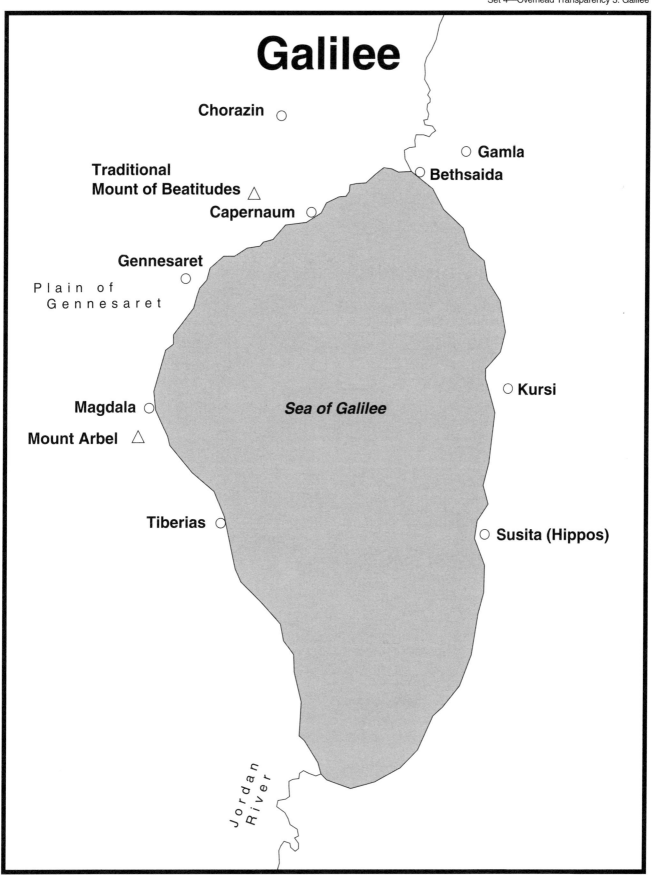

Chorazin ○

Gamla ○

Bethsaida ○

Traditional
Mount of Beatitudes △

Capernaum ○

Gennesaret ○

Plain of
Gennesaret

Sea of Galilee

Kursi ○

Magdala ○

Mount Arbel △

Tiberias ○

Susita (Hippos) ○

Jordan River

Land of Jesus' Ministry

Mediterranean Sea

Mount Hermon

○ Dan ○ Caesarea Philippi ○ Gamla

G A L I L E E

Capernaum ○

Sea of Galilee

○ Kursi

○ Susita

Joppa

○ Nazareth

○ Caesarea

Decapolis

Jordan River

Perea

Jericho ○

Jerusalem ○

Bethlehem ○

Judea Wilderness

Herodion

Dead Sea

Masada

Judea Mountains

Idumaea

○ Joppa

Dan ●

● Caesarea-Philippi   ▲ Mount Hermon

Chorazin ●

Plain of
Gennesaret

Capernaum ●

Bethsaida ●

Tiberias ●

Gamla ●

Sea of
Galilee

Kursi ●

Jordan River

Susita (Hippos) ●

● Beth Shean

Decapolis

Set 4—Overhead Transparency 5. Galilee of Jesus' Ministry

CHRONOLOGY
OF BIBLE TIMES

BC

586 BC	Babylonian Captivity of Judah	
ca 500 BC	Return to Israel	
332 BC	Alexander the Great conquers Palestine	
330–198 BC	Rule of Hellenistic Ptolemies over Jews	
198–167 BC	Oppression under Hellenistic Seleucids	
167 BC	Maccabee revolt	
167–63 BC	Hasmonaean (Maccabee) kingdom	
63 BC	Roman conquest of Judea	
37 BC	Herod's reign begins	
ca 6 BC	Jesus' birth	
4 BC	Herod's death	
4 BC–AD 6	Archelaus rules Samaria, Judea, and Idumaea	
4 BC–AD 39	Herod Antipas rules Galilee and Perea	
ca AD 27–30	Jesus' ministry	
ca AD 30	Jesus is crucified	
ca AD 35	Paul's conversion	
AD 44	Herod Agrippa's death	
AD 46–61	Paul's missionary trips	
AD 57–59	Paul's imprisonment in Caesarea	
AD 66–73	First Jewish Revolt against Rome	
AD 70	Roman destruction of Jerusalem during First Jewish Revolt; the Temple is destroyed	
AD 73	Masada falls	
AD 131–135	Bar Kochba Revolt (Second Jewish Revolt)	

AD

Gethsemane

Mount of Olives

Temple Mount

KIDRON VALLEY

Spring of Gihon

DAVID'S CITY

WESTERN HILL

Tyropoeon Valley

Hezekiah's Tunnel

Hinnom Valley

Pool of Siloam

A David's City
B New City
C Upper City
D Business District
E Temple Mount
F Lower City

1 Eastern Gate
2 Southern Stairs
3 Royal Stoa
4 Robinson's Arch
5 Wilson's Arch
6 Tyropoeon Street

8 Antonia
9 Tadi Gate
10 Pool of Bethesda
11 First Wall
12 Second Wall
13 Garden Gate

15 Golgotha (?)
16 Garden Tomb
17 Spring of Gihon
18 Hinnom Valley
19 Theater
20 Citadel and Herod's

21 Essene Quarter
22 Mansions
23 Mount of Olives
24 Kidron Valley
25 Huldah Gates

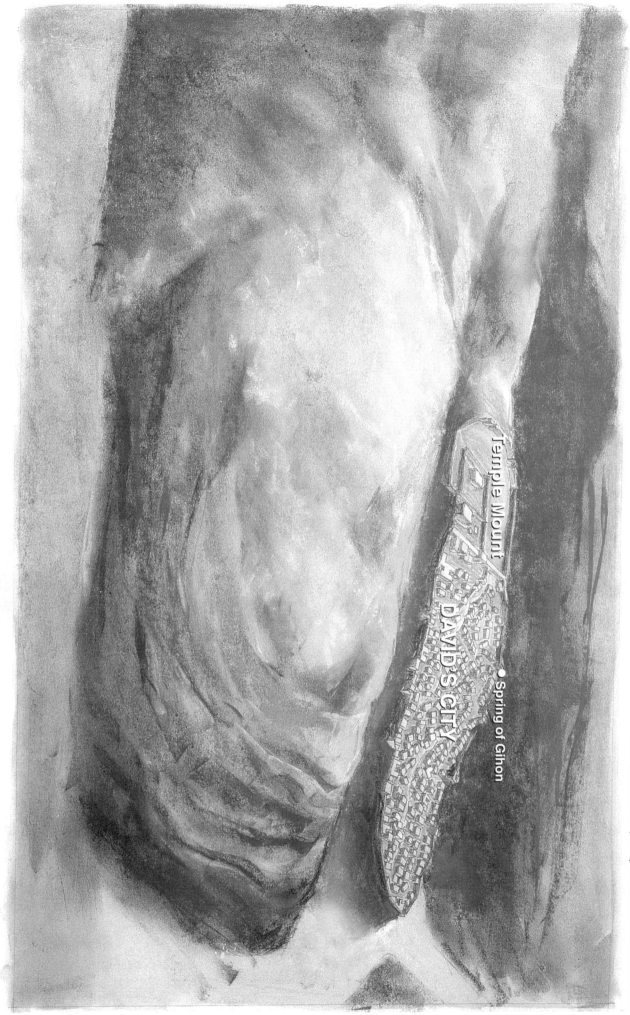

Temple Mount

DAVID'S CITY

● Spring of Gihon

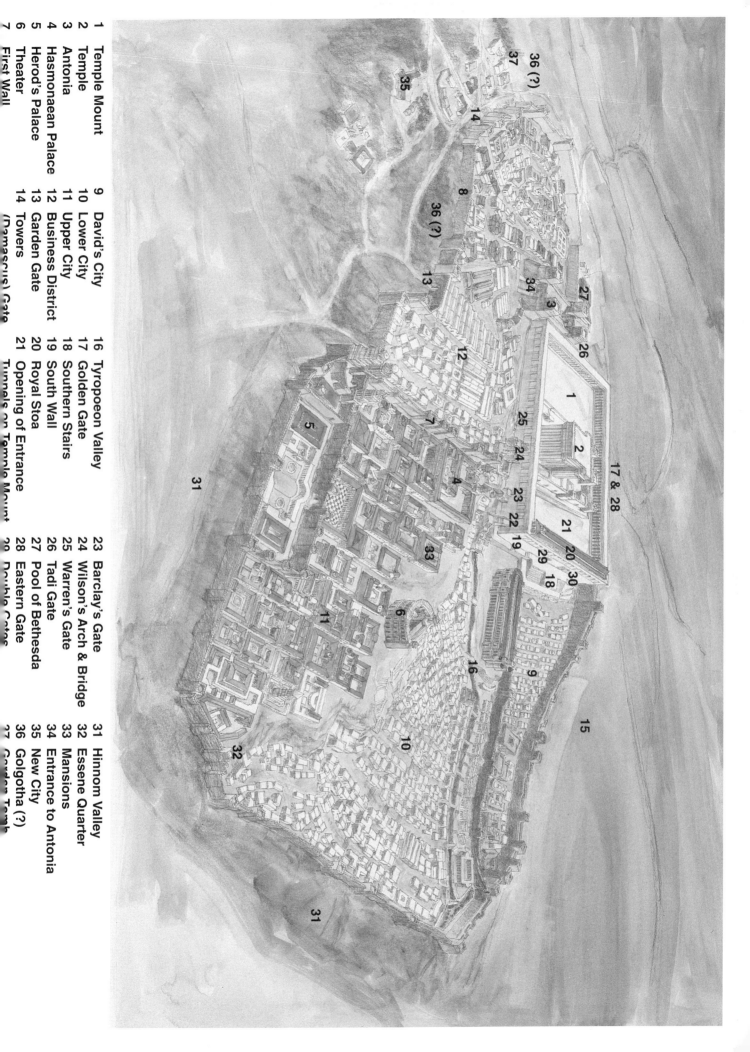

1 Temple Mount
2 Temple
3 Antonia
4 Hasmonaean Palace
5 Herod's Palace
6 Theater
7 First Wall

9 David's City
10 Lower City
11 Upper City
12 Business District
13 Garden Gate
14 Towers
   (Damascus) Gate

16 Tyropoeon Valley
17 Golden Gate
18 Southern Stairs
19 South Wall
20 Royal Stoa
21 Opening of Entrance
   Tunnels on Temple Mount

23 Barclay's Gate
24 Wilson's Arch & Bridge
25 Warren's Gate
26 Tadi Gate
27 Pool of Bethesda
28 Eastern Gate
29 Double Gate

31 Hinnom Valley
32 Essene Quarter
33 Mansions
34 Entrance to Antonia
35 New City
36 Golgotha (?)
37 Garden Tomb

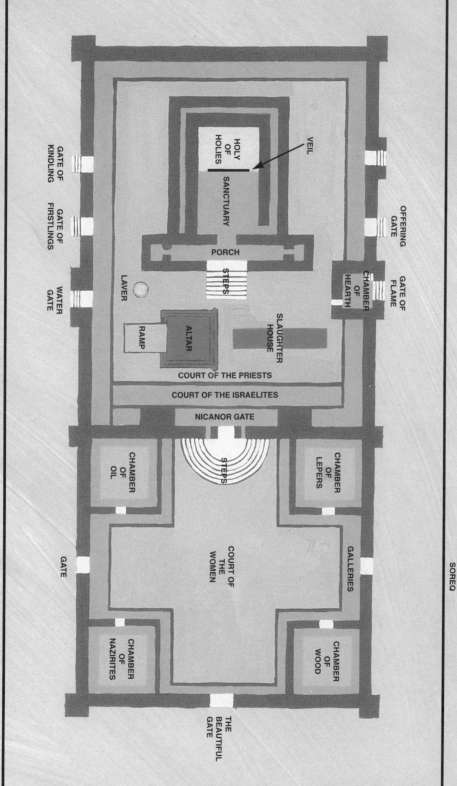

GENTILE COURT

GENTILE COURT

GENTILE COURT

GENTILE COURT

SOREQ

GATE OF KINDLING

GATE OF FIRSTLINGS

WATER GATE

GATE

OFFERING GATE

GATE OF FLAME

CHAMBER OF HEARTH

HOLY OF HOLIES

VEIL

SANCTUARY

PORCH

STEPS

LAVER

RAMP

ALTAR

SLAUGHTER HOUSE

COURT OF THE PRIESTS

COURT OF THE ISRAELITES

NICANOR GATE

STEPS

CHAMBER OF OIL

CHAMBER OF LEPERS

COURT OF THE WOMEN

GALLERIES

CHAMBER OF NAZIRITES

CHAMBER OF WOOD

THE BEAUTIFUL GATE

1 Temple
2 Royal Stoa
3 Solomon's Colonnade
4 Southern Stairs
5 South Wall

7 Triple Gates
8 Ritual Baths
9 Plaza
10 Robinson's Arch
11 Barclay's Gate

13 Warren's Gate
14 Place of Trumpeting
15 Tyropoeon Street

Herod's Expansion

Hasmonaean Expansion

0   50m

1   Holy of Holies
2   Altar of Incense
3   Table of Showbread
4   Altar
5   Porch
6   Bronze Sea
7   Holy Place
8   Veil
9   Menorah

OLIVE
PRESS

A Theater
B Palace
C Temple of Augustus
D Harbor (Sebastos)
E Lighthouse
F Aqueduct
G Amphitheater
H Hippodrome

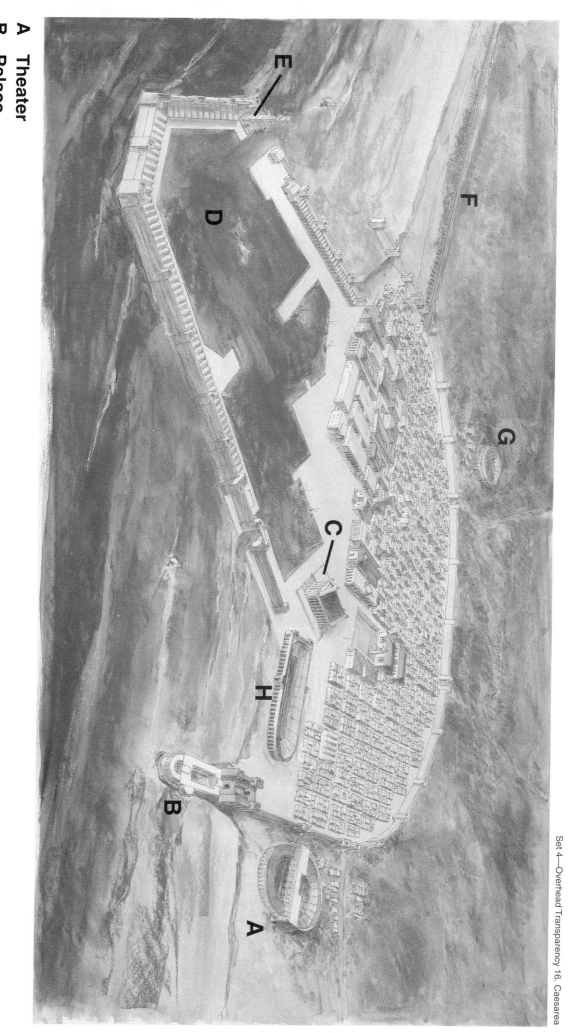

Ray Vander Laan is an ordained minister in the Christian Reformed Church and has taught religion in Christian schools for over 18 years. He has degrees from Dordt College and Westminster Seminary and is completing doctoral work at Trinity College. Ray Vander Laan has immersed himself in the cultural context of the Bible throughout his career. Deeply committed to the inspiration of the Scriptures, he applies God's Word specifically to modern culture and life situations. The series **That the World May Know**™ is based on study tours that Ray Vander Laan leads regularly in Israel.

To order the optional full-color overhead-transparency packet for Set 4, Faith Lessons 19–27, write to Focus on the Family, Educational Resources Department, P.O. Box 15379, Colorado Springs, CO 80935-5379, or call 1-800-932-9123.

That the World May Know ™ would make a great gift for family and friends. Sets 1, 2, 3, and 4 are available at a Christian bookstore near you.

ENCOUNTER THE SAVIOR AS NEVER BEFORE!

Wander the Galilean hillsides . . . tarry along the dusty Jericho Road . . . hear wind rustle through the olive trees, and smell the sea's salty air. . . . Journey back to the world of Jesus' day and behold a historically sound, culturally accurate look at the Man, His ministry, and His message.

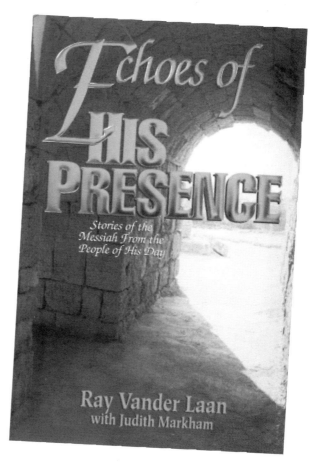

Through page after page of insightful glimpses into the lives of a rabbi, a shepherd, a bridegroom, a disciple, a mason, and an ailing woman, the undeniable significance of Jesus Christ, the Messiah, unfolds. You'll come to appreciate how He lived, what He did, the words He used—and what He meant—*and* be fascinated at how truly relevant the Scriptures were then and still are today! You'll be awed by the extent to which God goes to prove His love. And . . . if you listen closely . . . you'll begin to hear the *Echoes of His Presence* in your own life.

Available in hardcover and on audiocassette.

DON'T MISS THE OTHER VIDEOS AND LESSONS IN THE SERIES!

Discover the life-changing relevance in God's Word with **"That the World May Know,"** Focus on the Family's intriguing faith discovery series. Hosted by Ray Vander Laan, these insightful videos transport viewers to the land of the Old and New Testaments to reveal the Scriptures' "hidden" meaning and bring the Bible to life for today's believer. Each VHS set contains two closed-captioned videos and is available with either a personal devotion guide or a comprehensive leader's guide for small-group discussion. Full-color overhead transparencies are also available.

Set 1, Faith Lessons 1-5

The key to understanding today's culture is recognizing God's involvement with ancient Israel.

Set 2, Faith Lessons 6-10

The key to confronting evil in today's culture is dependence on God.

Set 3, Faith Lessons 11-18

The key to impacting our culture is understanding how Jesus impacted His.

Set 4, Faith Lessons 19-27

The key to godly living within today's culture is empowerment through the Holy Spirit.

Available at Christian bookstores everywhere.